Death, Desire and Loss
in Western Culture

*Radical Tragedy: Religion, Ideology and Power in the
Drama of Shakespeare and His Contemporaries*

Political Shakespeare
(editor, with Alan Sinfield)

Sexual Dissidence: Augustine to Wilde, Freud to Foucault

JONATHAN DOLLIMORE

Death, Desire and Loss
in Western Culture

ALLEN LANE
THE PENGUIN PRESS

ALLEN LANE
THE PENGUIN PRESS

Published by the Penguin Group
Penguin Books Ltd, 27 Wrights Lane, London w8 5tz, England
Penguin Putnam Inc., 375 Hudson Street, New York, New York 10014, USA
Penguin Books Australia Ltd, Ringwood, Victoria, Australia
Penguin Books Canada Ltd, 10 Alcorn Avenue, Toronto, Ontario, Canada m4v 3b2
Penguin Books (NZ) Ltd, 182–190 Wairau Road, Auckland 10, New Zealand

Penguin Books Ltd, Registered Offices: Harmondsworth, Middlesex, England

First published 1998
Published in Great Britain by Allen Lane The Penguin Press 1998
1 3 5 7 9 10 8 6 4 2

Set in 11/14pt PostScript Monotype Sabon
Typeset by Rowland Phototypesetting Ltd, Bury St Edmunds, Suffolk
Printed and bound in Great Britain by The Bath Press, Bath

A CIP catalogue record for this book is available from the British Library

ISBN 0-713-99125-9

Contents

V THE DESIRE NOT TO BE: LATE METAPHYSICS AND PSYCHOANALYSIS

VI RENOUNCING DEATH

VII THE AESTHETICS OF ENERGY

VIII DEATH AND THE HOMOEROTIC

Acknowledgements

Special thanks to Percival Mars, who changed me, to Alan Sinfield and Rachel Bowlby for changing me some more. And to Helena Dollimore for her wit and for keeping me half honest.

Others deserving of thanks include Leo Bersani, Elizabeth Clark, Laura Chrisman, Bob Davenport, Margretta de Grazia, Rodney Hillman, Tony Inglis, Richard King, Penny McCarthy, Charles Martindale, Peter Osborne, William Outhwaite, Peter Stallybrass, Kate Soper, Ted Timms, Cedric Watts. I am very grateful to the Humanities Research Board of the British Academy for the grant which made the time to write some of this book.

For permission to reprint copyright material, the author and publishers gratefully acknowledge as follows:

For *The Complete Letters of Sigmund Freud to Wilhelm Fliess, 1887–1904*, translated by J M Masson, copyright 1985 to J M Masson and Sigmund Freud Copyright Ltd, reprinted by permission of Harvard University Press; for *Collected Poems*, C P Cavafy, (1990) to Chatto & Windus on behalf of C P Cavafy; for *Thomas Mann: Diaries 1918–1939*, Ed R & C Winston, (1983) to Andre Deutsch Ltd; for 'Our Shadows' by Alan Brayne in *Take Any Train* ed. Peter Daniels (1991) to Peter Daniels, The Oscars Press; for 'The Second Coming' and 'Supernatural Songs, VIII' from *The Collected Poems of W. B. Yeats* (1971) to A P Watt Ltd on behalf of Michael Yeats; for 'Death in Venice' from *Selected Stories* by Thomas Mann (1988) to Martin Secker & Warburg; for *Letters 1889–1955* by Thomas Mann (1970) to Martin Secker & Warburg; for extracts from "On Sexuality" from

ACKNOWLEDGEMENTS

"On the Universal Tendency", "On Metapsychology", "Beyond the Pleasure Principle", "Why War?", "Civilisation and its Discontents", and "Civilisation, Society and Religion" from *The Standard Edition of the Complete Works of Sigmund Freud* translated and edited by James Strachey to Sigmund Freud Copyrights, The Institute of Psychoanalysis and The Hogarth Press; for 'Burnt Norton', in 'Four Quartets', *Collected Poems 1909–1962* by T. S. Eliot (1944) to Faber and Faber; for 'Lullaby' in *Collected Poems* by W. H. Auden (1944) to Faber and Faber.

Every effort has been made to contact or trace copyright holders. The publishers would be grateful to be notified of any additions that should be incorporated in the next edition of this volume.

Introduction

Hugo, the protagonist of Oscar Moore's 1991 novel *A Matter of Life and Sex*, initially promises to be the horny adolescent so desirable in modern culture: knowing and streetwise, yet innocently narcissistic too – the 'sassy street urchin who knew what he wanted and wanted it now'; the 'flouting, flaunting rudeboy' who doesn't come into tissues, preferring instead 'to see his sperm fly'. Full of life, and the more so for being wildly dissident. But in this narrative he is also the boy who courts death through sex and who dies of AIDS. Eventually, in the midst of anarchic sexual yearning in a Paris bathhouse, death is entertained with a strange calm amid the desperate urgency of it all. 'With sex choking his throat and thumping against his chest', Hugo throws himself

into the clinch of sex with the smile of one preparing his last fix. There, in the stream of sweat and hallucination of amyl . . . as the man's penis swelled and loomed . . . and Hugo's mouth and eyes drooled in one gasping hunger, a quiet voice whispered – this could be the boy that kills you. And a quiet voice answered back – so then, this is the way to die. (pp. 29, 39, 116, 49, 146)[1]

Compare that with a reviewer of James Miller's controversial 1993 biography of Michel Foucault, whom some regard as the most significant philosopher of the late twentieth century:

In the autumn of 1983, after he had already collapsed and less than a year before his own death, [Foucault] could still be found in the baths and bars. He laughed at talk of 'safe-sex' and reportedly said [to D. A. Miller] 'to die for the love of boys: what could be more beautiful?' (Lilla, p. 4)

Miller takes this as evidence of Foucault's attraction to death – suicide especially – and reminds us that, in Foucault's immensely influential *History of Sexuality*, the philosopher speaks of 'the individual driven, in spite of himself, by the sombre madness of sex' (*History*, I.39). For his part, the reviewer remarks solemnly that Foucault 'remained a glutton for sexual danger and excess' (p. 4).

To die for the love of boys is one thing. But what about killing them? In 1983 a rumour was circulating alleging that Foucault, in James Miller's words, 'knowing he was dying of AIDS . . . deliberately tried to infect other people with the disease' (p. 375). The supposed link between homosexuality and death is often imagined to include both impulses: the suicidal and the murderous. This too has a parallel in Moore's novel,[2] where, some one hundred pages on, we read of the same or another Parisian bathhouse in which Hugo 'fucked a man in the backroom . . . and released jets of poisoned spunk into his bowels' (p. 255).

Moore's is a novel in which sex and death, desire and disease, weld together in lurid deathbed dreams which have significant cultural precedents; they invoke, for instance, the medieval or Jacobean obsession with death as somehow the motor of life:

In this light people changed all the time. One moment they were pristine youth, the next a skull peered through the dark and cavities replaced the eyes. (p. 137)

Jacobean too is the way in which age is read back into youth; future death, and the decline that leads ineluctably to it, is vividly imaged as the truth of the here and now:

The dark was never dark enough in the bathhouse. Light played tricks, switching the pretty boy of one minute into a skeleton the next, the lissom youth suddenly chomping toothlessly on his dick, a body muscled and rippling in the spotlight that sagged and collapsed in the harsher light of the showers . . . He didn't know anymore whether he was standing or lying, whether this was sex or death. (p. 304)[3]

A Matter of Life and Sex is emphatically not a text from the punitive moral right in which AIDS is a punishment for promiscuity, the wages of sin. Hugo lives and dies according to the creed of a guiltless and even blameless fatalism; even at his most compulsive and driven he seems to refuse all the old moralizing mystifications. Simply, 'sex has been his making and his undoing', something he regarded as at once addictive and absurd and which, indulged, kills him as surely as would abstinence (p. 145).

But if Hugo remains mostly free of guilt, remorse, reproach, or the desire for redemption – all attitudes of earlier times, and returning in our own – it is the more significant that much of the past is echoed in this fatalistic binding together of sex and death. From the outset, Hugo's fate (death) seems to be latent in his desire. AIDS is not so much a punishment for promiscuity – the wages of sin – as a brutal material proof of something known but never quite comprehended, namely that death inhabits sexuality: perversely, lethally, ecstatically. And this has led some to regard the vision of this novel as almost as offensive as the homophobia of the moral right, just as others have denounced Miller's biography of Foucault.[4] Yet Oscar Moore remained unrepentant; in one of the last pieces he wrote before he died of AIDS-related illnesses at the age of thirty-six in September 1996, he reiterated the view which seems to have inspired his novel: 'sex and sexual knowledge have always been inextricably bound in an embrace with death' ('Rites', p. 16).[5]

Moore draws on a death/desire connection which perhaps found its most extreme statement in the Renaissance, but which is endemic to Western culture more generally and, in recent times, has been revived in relation to male homosexuality. In certain hostile representations of AIDS, homosexuality and death have been made to imply each other: homosexuality is seen as death-driven, death-desiring and thereby death-dealing.[6] As Moore's novel makes clear, contesting these negative representatives (homosexuality = pathology = death) could never be just a question of substituting positive ones (homosexuality = health = life). Male homosexual desire has been regarded in diverse ways by gay people themselves – as death-driven, as revolutionary, as benign, as redemptive, as self-shattering, as impossible of fulfilment, to name but some. Several of these ways of thinking about it clearly disturb those striving to establish an affirmative gay identity politics. And not surprisingly: on the one hand, this connection of homosexual desire and death has been made by those who want homosexuals literally to die; on the other, it is also part of homosexual history, as it is part of a more general cultural history. But with a difference: the sexually dissident have sometimes known more about this connection, confronting and exploring what the sexually conventional may share yet disavow. In particular, the sexually dissident have known that the strange dynamic which, in Western culture, binds death into desire is not the product of a marginal pathological imagination, but crucial in the formation of that culture. That is one argument of this book.

Loss and desire

That there are connections between death and desire is a commonplace, but a perplexing one; after all, desire is on the side of life, life is opposed to death, therefore desire also must be opposed to death. Thom Gunn writes:

> My thoughts are crowded with death
> and it draws so oddly on the sexual
> that I am confused
> confused to be attracted
> by, in effect, my own annihilation.
>
> ('In Time of Plague')

Gunn is right: although manifest and pervasive in Western culture, especially its art, this age-old connection of death and sexuality does become confusing when we stop to think about it. Mostly we don't think about it – especially when we think we know about it. What this suggests is that here the commonplace works as a kind of disavowal, allowing us to see and not see at the same time.[7] We recognize and register the sex/death connection, but in a way which precisely allows us not to 'see' it. By acknowledging an 'obvious' connection between desire and death, the commonplace encourages us to forgo thought about it. Some things remain unknown not because they are occluded or unspoken, but because they circulate constantly and visibly as commonplaces. As I write, a radio arts programme previews a new production of John Webster's *The White Devil* (1612). We are told that the commonplace theme of this and other Jacobean tragedies, namely the connection of sex and death, has renewed relevance in our own AIDS-inflicted age. The urbane chatter of the culture journalist quietly keeps at bay the questions that form: *Why* were the Jacobeans obsessed with this connection? *Does* AIDS really make it a renewed obsession for us, and if so how?

For the Jacobeans, as for us, what connects death with desire is mutability – the sense that all being is governed by a ceaseless process of change inseparable from *an inconsolable sense of loss somehow always in excess of the loss of anything in particular*. W. B. Yeats put it succinctly enough: 'Man is in love and loves what vanishes, / What more is there to say?' ('Nineteen Hundred and Nineteen'). The experience of change and loss exerts an incalculable influence on the development of our culture. Western metaphysics and Western religion derive from that experience, especially as it led to repeated attempts to distinguish between appearance and reality. Broadly speaking, the world we experience was said to be the world of appearances, the domain of unreality, deception, loss, transience and death – to be contrasted with an ultimate, changeless reality which was either deeper within or entirely beyond the world of appearance. This immanent or transcendent reality was also said to be the source of absolute, as distinct from relative, truth, and even of eternal life. Some of the greatest literature in the West derives from the tension between the desire for that ultimate reality to exist, and thereby redeem loss, and the conviction that, in reality, it does not.

Typically, the process of change and decline *in time* is more disturbing than the idea of not being at all; as Sir Walter Ralegh put it some 400 years ago, under the sway of time 'all is dissolved, our labours come to nought'; mutability destroys not only living things, but all human endeavour:

> all droops, all dies, all trodden under dust;
> the person, place, and passages forgotten;
> the hardest steel eaten with softest rust,
> the firm and solid tree both rent and rotten . . .
> ('The Ocean to Scinthia', ll. 235, 253–6)

Ralegh here takes the omniscient overview, the long, solitary perspective across time and loss. Others realize the effects of mutability in the fleeting, transient moment; future loss, change and ultimately death are felt as somehow always discernible in the here and now – in the silence of a room recently inhabited, or the sound of the wind in one not yet occupied:

> Now first, as I shut the door,
>   I was alone
> In the new house; and the wind
>   Began to moan.
>
> Old at once was the house,
>   And I was old;
> My ears were teased with the dread
>   Of what was foretold,
>
> Nights of storm, days of mist, without end;
>   Sad days when the sun
> Shone in vain; old griefs and griefs
>   Not yet begun . . .
>
>   .   .   .   .   .   .
>
> . . . I learned how the wind would sound
>   After these things should be.
>   (Edward Thomas, 'The New House')

In his poem 'Logs on the Hearth' (1915) Thomas Hardy writes not of future loss, but of loss already incurred. He recalls a childhood moment when he and his sister were climbing a tree. She is now dead, the tree has been felled, and the poet is watching a log from it burning in the grate:

> The fire advances along the log
>   Of the tree we felled,
> Which bloomed and bore striped apples by the peck
>   Till its last hour of bearing knelled.
>
> The fork that first my hand would reach
>   And then my foot
> In climbing upward inch by inch, lies now
>   Sawn, sapless, darkening with soot.

Where the bark chars is where, one year,
    It was pruned, and bled –
Then overgrew the wound. But now, at last,
    Its growings all have stagnated.

My fellow-climber rises dim
    From her chilly grave –
Just as she was, her foot near mine on the bending limb,
    Laughing, her young brown hand awave.

Being unselfconsciously alive is conveyed in a precise image of something ordinary: the movement of 'climbing upward inch by inch'. The fork 'that first my hand would reach / And then my foot' (and this was a tree climbed many times) is really seen only now; or rather, seeing it again in the grate – 'Sawn, sapless, darkening with soot' – is to remember the familiar feel of it, while seeing it for the first time in the fuller, but never complete, perspective *of* time. The sense of loss is most intense in the visual detail ('Where the bark chars'), and in the longer history which the detail evokes: the bark was pruned, bled, recovered, became the stronger for it, only *then* to die. Hardy's sister is recalled in a moment of unselfconscious happiness now frozen for ever in the haunting immobility of the photographic image: 'Just as she was, her foot near mine on the bending limb, / Laughing, her young brown hand awave.' We grieve because someone loved is lost for ever. But there is another aspect to the experiencing of a loss which is inconsolable and somehow in excess of any specific grief: images like those in Hardy's poem register a happiness somehow only known in retrospect, when it is irretrievable. Happiness is somehow never fully knowable in the flux of time: *then* it was experienced as inconsequential, *now* as irrevocably gone. Happiness is always in a past where it never quite existed at the time.

If, in the tradition of *carpe diem* ('seize the day'), knowledge of mutability and loss tends to intensify rather than diminish the existential value of the transient moment, it is also true that an easy, unqualified celebration of that moment is rare; many poems in the *carpe diem* tradition register not just the desire to capture the moment, but the existential difficulty of doing so. We need to stop, and yet we cannot. In one of the most famous of all *carpe diem* poems, 'To His Coy

Mistress', Andrew Marvell (1621–78) describes being chased by time towards oblivion:

> But at my back I always hear
> Time's wingèd chariot hurrying near;
> And yonder all before us lie
> Deserts of vast eternity.

The very passing of time, which makes us so keen to seize the day, is also what somehow prevents us doing so; the day slips ineluctably through our hands.

Such verse is rarely if ever about simply seizing the day; it is also about how time and change, driving us towards a horizon of oblivion, make it hard to seize anything, let alone the day, which, after all, is itself a measure of time.[8] And if we do manage to halt time imaginatively, isolating the moment, it is often then only to encounter within it the haunting stillness of non-being. The so-called spots of time in Wordsworth's *Prelude* come to mind, or this, from T. S. Eliot's *Four Quartets*:

> Sudden in a shaft of sunlight
> Even while the dust moves
> There rises the hidden laughter
> Of children in the foliage
> Quick now, here, now, always –
> Ridiculous the waste sad time
> Stretching before and after. (p. 20)

This inability to seize the day is more fundamentally an inability to realize our desires in a world governed and destroyed by time, and it points to a further, even more disturbing and paradoxical, dimension of desire itself. Mutability is the stuff of life; without it, life literally would not be possible. If, with regard to the natural world, this truth is accepted with a wise–sad equanimity, in relation to human life it is more usually regarded as traumatic, and in relation to human desire as an intolerable contradiction.

Here is one of the most significant factors of all in the connection of desire and death. On the one hand, mutability is the ineluctable enemy of desire because it ceaselessly thwarts it: 'Man is in love and loves what vanishes.' In another poem, 'The Definition of Love', Marvell describes a love subjected to time and change as 'begotten by Despair / Upon Impossibility'. On the other hand, movement, motion, change, inconstancy are the very stuff not just of life but also of desire; that is to say, *mutability is also the inner dynamic of desire*. As T. S. Eliot put it, 'Desire itself is movement / Not in itself desirable' (p. 20); or, in the words of Shelley, desire is 'that unrest which men miscall delight' (*Adonais*, XL). In other words, mutability animates desire even as it thwarts it. Put slightly differently, the very nature of desire is what prevents its fulfilment, what makes it 'impossible'.

I shall argue that this contradiction becomes profoundly important in the formation of identity and gender in Western culture, not least in the way it renders desire seemingly impossible, or at least futile and self-defeating. It is an overriding reason why the lack which *is* desire comes to be regarded as inherently incapable of satisfaction and linked to death. Thus apparently always defeating itself, desire comes to seem destructively insatiable, a permanent lack whose attempted fulfilment is at once the destiny of the self and what destroys it, leading the poet to cry, in Shakespeare's Sonnet 147, 'I desperate now approve / Desire is death'.[9]

Those lines of Eliot's just quoted perfectly conjoin the ambivalent attitudes in Western culture towards both desire and movement: desire as undesirable movement. Illicit desire is especially prone to being conceptualized as aberrant movement. For example, the idea of deviation – itself the conceptual heart of the idea of perversion – is about a movement which is dangerous or subversive: to deviate = to go astray. Conversely, the good, the safe and the true are about not deviating (sticking to the straight and narrow), while related virtues like order, stability and harmony presuppose restricted, limited or controlled movement, often echoing the ultimate metaphysical ideal of fixity, predetermination or stasis: the fixed origin, fixed destiny, fixed identity, and so on. And yet, as we shall see, even as it idealizes the predetermined and the static, no culture has a more significant history of obsessive, expansive, restless movement.

The death of man?

I explore the history of this movement in a way which leads to a questioning of some of the emerging orthodoxies of contemporary thought, especially in relation to the so-called 'death' of man. Briefly, this is the argument that there has occurred, relatively recently and somewhat momentously, the collapse of a Western humanist ideology of individualism. Whereas once the Western expansionist project (for example in the spheres of religious domination, cultural imperialism, colonization or the formation of empire) was underpinned by a powerful and confident sense of individual selfhood, in our own time – and corresponding to the crisis if not the collapse of that expansionist era – we have witnessed the death of this individual and 'his' universal counterpart, 'man'.

For several decades now, if not longer, the humanities have been dominated by this claim. But, as we shall see, in the Western tradition the individual has always been in crisis, energized and driven forward by the same forces of mutability and death which destabilize and fragment. That passage from Marvell's poem cited earlier is interesting in this context too, describing as it does being driven from behind by time into a future of non-being, the deserts of a vast eternity. And those like John Donne (below, Chapter 5) find it easy to make the perverse imaginative leap whereby the real material energies of the universe seemingly reside not in the generative life-force but in the disintegrative potency of death. Even more perversely, the disintegrative power of death is found at the heart of generation. And time and again this most pessimistic of visions, even as it renounced the world, remained an indispensable component of a culture of ceaseless activity whose 'agent' was, precisely, the individual in crisis.

Much of this is half-sanctioned in the most revered of all Western aesthetic genres, tragedy, as it rehearses one of the more enduring paradoxes animating the energies which have 'made' Western culture: even as we are driven forward by a secular fear of failure, we resort to the metaphysical reassurance that such failure is ultimately inevitable. And if that reassurance sometimes invites renunciation and withdrawal, it rather more often redoubles the secular effort by imparting to it a fatalistic 'lift'. After all, Enoch Powell's famous observation that 'All political lives . . . end in failure because that is the nature of politics and of human affairs' (p. 151) may well have become a truism, but it does not deter politicians, whose actions often imply sympathy with Macbeth's reflection on his own increasingly murderous and self-defeating attempt to hang on to power: 'I am in blood / Stepp'd in so far, that, should I wade no more, / Returning were as tedious as go o'er' (III.iv.135–7). A truism of the modern world it may be, but it took a classical scholar to come up with it.

The 'crisis' of the individual is less a crisis than a recurring instability deriving from the theological obsession with death, loss and failure. And it does not set in only at the point when the expansionist tendencies of Western culture falter; on the contrary, it has always been an integral, facilitating aspect of those tendencies. Like the expansionist project, if less obviously, that crisis and the theology from which it derives both have a history and have made history, especially at the point where they intersect as the conviction that death and loss simultaneously drive and frustrate desire. While it would be wrong to regard this conviction as unique to Western culture – Buddhism, after all, regards desire or craving as the source of all suffering – the forms it has taken in the West have been distinctive. I have in mind especially those intellectual and aesthetic developments across the last two millennia which have driven death ever further into desire – from the Christian belief that man, through transgressive desire, brought death into the world, with the consequence that henceforth it would haunt desire as the source of all suffering (e.g. Romans 5:12, 6:23), to the psychoanalytic theory of the death drive, whereby, as Freud put it, ' "*the aim of all life is death*" ' (*Beyond the Pleasure Principle*, p. 311).[10]

Developing the Christian narrative into one of its more agonized and radical theological formulations, Augustine contended that a death-infected mutability pervades desire, and is transmitted from one generation to the next via semen and the 'unclean motion' of the sexual act (below, Chapter 3). This means that mutability is also experientially ever-present as the anarchy of a desire always potentially out of control (even down to the unruly 'motions' of erection) and always threatening to undo the self. And when, much later, Donne or any one of a number of his contemporaries describes man as a fragile *being* all the time *being* disintegrated by aberrant desire ('I find myself scattered, melted', *Selected Prose*, p. 114) he is making mutability even more central to both individual identity and desire.

Such earlier accounts of desire as the radical undoing of the virtuous self may seem of little interest today, especially if we assume them to be no less obsolete than they are objectionable. On the other hand, we might listen closely when our psychoanalyst tells us that unconscious desire, permanently at odds with the demands of civilization, is what will always wreck the ego's attempt to forge a coherent sense of self. In certain respects only the terminology is different, and Freud, in founding psychoanalysis, certainly drew on a theological past.

Further, the considerable intellectual and political influence of Augustine focuses a paradox which came to fascinate Freud: even as it preaches the inherent instability, futility and misery of mortal existence, this theology of death keeps its adherents reluctantly future-directed – savaged internally by death and change, they are also driven forward by them. Religiously, the desire for eternity would be expressed in life as a conflict between the need to struggle forward and the yearning to return, both paths leading to a divine death – that peace that passes all understanding. If theology intensifies, thwarts, deflects and exploits a desire for death, Freud's theory of the death drive (below, Chapter 14) is at once a brilliant reworking of that theology and a devastating challenge to it.

Eroticizing death

Well before Freud, there were those who entertained the attraction of death almost as scandalously as he did. They did not need a theory of the death drive to know that if death both drives and frustrates desire it is also what desire may seek in order to be free of itself. As Hamlet famously meditated, to die is a consummation devoutly to be wished. From the earliest times, death has held out the promise of a release not just from desire but from something inseparable from it, namely the pain of being individuated (separate, differentiated, alone) and the form of self-consciousness which goes with that – what philosophers like Schopenhauer call the principle of individuation (*principium individuationis*). In other words, death holds out the promise of a release from the very individuality whose formation would have been unthinkable without it.

Identity is experienced ambivalently, and the urge to consolidate it is complicated by the wish to relinquish it. The seductiveness of the idea of this death of the self has always been a part of Western individualism. And, with that energetic, perverse hubris so characteristic of this individualism, there will be those who seek death not only as the release from desire, but also as its object; from the earliest times, but later increasingly, death becomes eroticized; already for Hamlet it was a 'consummation'. In context (*Hamlet* III.i.63) the word is precisely significant, meaning both satisfying climax and being consumed or vanishing into nothing. (It is sometimes said that Hamlet's problem is that he cannot or will not act, suffering as he does from an inertia of the will. Actually, Hamlet is the epitome of the individual 'in crisis' racked with desire, obsessed with death, and thereby driven to act.)

If death is most famously eroticized by Wagner in *Tristan and Isolde*, many others have done it no less memorably, including Keats in 'Ode to a Nightingale':

3
Fade far away, dissolve, and quite forget
  What thou amongst the leaves hast never known,
  The weariness, the fever, and the fret
. . . .

  Where youth grows pale, and spectre-thin, and dies,
  Where but to think is to be full of sorrow
  And leaden-eyed despairs
. . . .

6
. . . for many a time
I have been half in love with easeful Death
. . . .

Now more than ever seems it rich to die,
  To cease upon the midnight with no pain,
  While thou art pouring forth thy soul abroad
  In such an ecstasy!

Keats's letter to Fanny Brawne of 25 June 1819, written just weeks after this ode, says something similar, and rather directly:

I have two luxuries to brood over in my walks, your Loveliness and the hour of my death. O that I could have possession of them both in the same minute. I hate the world: it batters too much the wings of my self-will, and would I could take a sweet poison from your lips to send me out of it. From no others would I take it. (*Letters*, p. 271)

Desire, the source of so much pain, also holds out the promise of the pleasurable death of the self – or at the very least of what I call 'self-disidentification'. And here we confront just some of the various ways in which the distinction between literal and metaphoric death is so obvious, yet always being confused: why does the weave of Western aesthetic culture owe as much to the confusion, endlessly rehearsed in 'fantasy', as to the distinction itself, equally insistently rehearsed in 'reality'?

If God always held out the promise of death – the peace that passes all understanding – then, as we see in later chapters, when humanists like Feuerbach took God back into man they took back death too. Influential developments in modern thought internalize death as never before. This is true of writers as diverse as Hegel, Schopenhauer, Heidegger, Freud, Bataille and Kojève, all of whom contribute to one of the most fascinating paradoxes of modern philosophies of human identity: death is taken into consciousness in a way which is at once an expansion and a nullification of consciousness (below, Parts IV–V). Perhaps it has always been the case that the radical elements in humanism have included a strain of anti-humanism whereby consciousness identifies with what threatens it, and especially with what it submits to, thereby empowering and destabilizing itself both at once.

It is certainly the case that in the West submission to death is never quite what it seems. Alongside or inside an abject submission to death there is often an arrogant identification with it. Similarly, while the instabilities, anxieties and contradictions to be found in subjectivity can be truly self-destructive, they are also the precondition, and the incentive, for such an identification. As we shall see, from Christian theology to post-modernism, a desiring identification with death is one of the most remarkable aspects of our culture. Some post-modernists seek empowerment in a quest for perpetual instability – hence in part their preoccupation with the death of man, the death of the author, the death of the subject. (By replacing 'individual' with the more technical term 'subject', cultural theorists are conveying the idea that our subjectivity, far from being autonomous, is 'subjected' to the historical and social structures which determine it.) Far from being radically innovative, as their adherents claim, such recent ideas are mutations of older ones. Devotees of post-modern theory, often ignorant of intellectual history, remain unaware of the extent to which earlier ways of thinking which it claims to have entirely superseded remain obscurely active within it.

Sexual/gender differences

It has been said that the 'man' who has recently died was indeed exclusively male, and the ideologies he served quintessentially mascul-inist. It will be clear in what follows that the Western preoccupation with death, desire and loss is also significantly gendered. In one respect it could hardly be otherwise, given that the vast majority of the writers who appear here are male (and quite a few conspicuously misogynist as well – Schopenhauer and Nietzsche included). Even when (like Schopenhauer and Nietzsche) they are hostile to Christianity, it is that religion which remains the most significant precedent for their misogyny – especially the narrative of the Fall, which resonates power-fully in our culture to this day. It was or is a narrative in which woman is held responsible for bringing death and mutability into the world. As might be expected, there is no dearth of psychoanalytic explanations for this association of women with death, ranging from chronic unconscious male fear of engulfment or even castration in sexual intercourse, to the difficulty of the boy child leaving the mother for another woman. It has also been suggested that there might be a deep envy of women's procreative ability (womb envy).

Recently Camille Paglia had gone rather further, arguing that men's fear of women is natural, even rational, and biologically (anatomically) grounded. And she does so in the context of a larger argument which also associates women with death and which revives the idea that nature is most fundamentally a force of degeneration. For Paglia human history is a struggle between the Apollonian and the Dionysian. By the latter she means not a tame, humanized liveliness, but an instinctual and amoral life-force rooted in competition: 'we are only *for* something by being *against* something else'. More fundamentally still, the life-force is also a force of death, dissolution and destruction; nature itself operates according to the principle of the 'chthonian', which means 'of the earth' – 'but earth's bowels, not its surface . . . the blind grinding of subterranean force, the long slow suck, the murk and ooze' (pp. 5–6). And if we have an evolutionary revulsion from slime, it is precisely because it is the site of our origin.

All culture, says Paglia in an argument which resembles that of Georges Bataille (below, Chapter 17), including aesthetics and science, is built on the repression or evasion of the chthonian, and of the fact that there are no stable objects in nature, only the erosion of natural force, reducing everything to fluid, the primal soup from which new life struggles into being:

Everything is melting in nature . . . An apple tree laden with fruit: how peaceful, how picturesque. But remove the rosy filter of humanism from our gaze and look again. See nature spurning and frothing, its mad spermatic bubbles endlessly spilling out and smashing in that inhuman round of waste, rot, and carnage . . . Nature is the seething excess of being. (pp. 1–6, 41–2)

Men create culture as a defence against nature, and, since women are identified with nature, culture is also a defence against female nature, which is, Paglia insists, essentially chthonian – nature is a 'miasmic swamp whose prototype is the still pond of the womb'. Furthermore, 'Feminism has been simplistic in arguing that female archetypes were politically motivated falsehoods by men. The historical repugnance to woman has a rational basis: disgust is reason's proper response to the grossness of procreative nature' (p. 12).[11]

It follows, for Paglia, that all relationships are necessarily exploitative, and there is a radical disjunction between the sexes which begins and ends in the body. Sex is unfree, inhumane, compulsive and aggressive, characterized by a 'daemonic instability' (p. 13). It is also regressive, a ritualistic acting out of past histories – biological and social – with the result that 'every orgasm is shaped by psychic shadows' (p. 4). More elementally still, in sex we are caught up in a 'backward movement towards primeval dissolution'; sex threatens annihilation. This, says Paglia, is why so many men turn away or flee after sex: 'they have sensed the annihilation of the daemonic' (pp. 4–5). Male sexuality is especially and inherently insecure, always haunted by the prospect of failure and humiliation ('a flop is a flop'), and even when apparently successful it is inherently mutable, going from erection through orgasm to detumescence: 'Men enter in triumph but withdraw in decrepitude. The sex act cruelly mimics history's decline and fall' (p. 20). Which also means that male sexuality is inherently manic-depressive and always driven beyond and haunted by its own impossibility of fulfilment: 'Men know they are sexual exiles. They wander the earth seeking satisfaction, craving and despising, never content. There is nothing in that anguished motion for women to envy' (p. 19). For everyone, she says, the only perfect freedom is death (p. 3).

Unsurprisingly, it is in the feminism which Paglia repeatedly attacks that we find an opposing perspective to hers. Most feminists would reject the way in which Paglia associates female sexuality with death, seeing death as much more a concern of male sexuality, but even then making the connection historically contingent rather than naturally necessary.

Simone de Beauvoir was the author of *The Second Sex*, crucially formative for modern feminism. It was a book which not only changed the lives of thousands of women, but, according to Toril Moi, 'posed every one of the problems feminists today are working to solve' (p. 3).[12] So it is instructive to learn that Beauvoir's intellectual and cultural achievements were inextricably bound up with death. She wrote tirelessly; Moi observes that her autobiographies and letters alone run to well over a million words (p. 4). In this writing, ageing and death are recurring themes, even obsessions. At the end of *The Prime of Life* she writes, 'One night in June 1944, I tried to exorcize death with words. I excerpt some of my notes here . . .'; to write at all becomes 'my last and greatest recourse against death' (pp. 475–6). In *Simone de Beauvoir: Encounters with Death*, Elaine Marks contends that all Beauvoir's writings may be seen as desperate efforts to exorcize death with words (p. 11). Put another way, it was death which drove her to write. Death was both a violation of her being and what imparted to it an anguished energy (Marks, *passim*; Moi, pp. 236–52).

For Beauvoir death is ever-present as mutability – a profound sense of loss arising from but always exceeding the realization of one's own physical decline: 'The ephemeral was my lot. And down the stream of Time, history bore its vast jumble of incurable ills, its brief moments of glory' (p. 473). And yet for Beauvoir death is about terror rather than the seduction of non-being: 'I could not bear to think of myself as finite and ephemeral, a drop of water in the ocean; at times all my endeavours seemed vanity, happiness became a false lure, and the world wore the mocking, illusory mask of Nothingness' (p. 475). Men have, of course, written about the terror of non-being. But, from the history which I explore in this book, I hazard the generalization that it is men more than women who experience the seduction of non-being.

Feminist writers who draw on philosophy and psychoanalysis are inclined to regard the gendering of death as complex. Although, as we've seen, psychoanalysis provides many models for explaining a male fear of female sexuality – and especially a male association of female sexuality and death – it is also the case that women psychoanalysts like Melanie Klein, Julia Kristeva and Juliet Mitchell do not locate the convergence of sexuality and death within the male psyche alone.

In her predominantly psychoanalytic study *Over Her Dead Body*, Elisabeth Bronfen argues that gender constructions are 'supplementary to the division between life and death' (p. 266). Bronfen's theme is the pervasive aesthetic connection between death and femininity, themselves the two central enigmas of Western discourse. She shows how the image of the dead or dying woman is so pervasive in our culture that we often fail to see it. Edgar Allan Poe once said, 'The death of a beautiful woman is, unquestionably, the most poetical topic in the world' (Bronfen, pp. 59–60). For some feminists, such a remark epitomizes the hatefulness of patriarchal society in aesthetic disguise – a kind of necrophilic misogyny. For Bronfen, such a response to Poe's remark involves the erroneous assumption of a straightforward connection between cultural image and experienced reality – an assumption 'which defuses both the real violence of political domination and the power of representations' (p. 59). It also ignores the multiplicity of themes which are condensed and displaced in the image, and its ambivalent fusion of subversive as well as conservative drives, all of which lead Bronfen not simply to reject Poe's remark, but to question it psychoanalytically. Why a *dead* woman? Equally important, why a *beautiful* woman? And, above all, 'why the unconditioned "unquestionably", why the superlative "*most* poetical"'? What emerges from Poe's remark are some enduring paradoxes and contradictions in our culture. For instance, beauty is found to be not the life-affirming opposite of death, but its mask – a mask allowing for an insecure translation of anxiety into desire. Further, Bronfen argues that aesthetics and femininity stand in an analogous relation to death, in that both, by giving the illusion of intactness and unity, cover the insupportable extent of lack, deficiency and transiency in life itself.[13]

If writers as different as Paglia and Bronfen confirm the sense that the Western preoccupation with desire's relations to death is undoubtedly gendered, as are the forms this preoccupation takes, they also suggest the inadequacy of simplistic or reductive accounts as to how or why. We do not have to accept their own perspectives to share with them the conviction that this is something that crucially involves, but goes beyond, gender. My own response to the claim that this preoccupation is essentially and only the preserve of men is simply to recall that we have been here before: feminists have contended that certain kinds of reprehensible behaviour are confined to men, just as lesbians and gays have contended that other kinds of behaviour are confined to heterosexuals, only to then have other feminists, lesbians and gays lay claim to precisely the behaviours denied to them, and, in the process, revalue those behaviours as more than simply reprehensible.

Social death

In the last century fears of failure have intensified in proportion to the conviction that the social order can or should be engineered. These fears have been expressed as a heightened concern about the threat of social death – the fear that society is endangered, even to the point of possible extinction, by forces intrinsic to it, as distinct from external agents. This fear has included the conviction that contemporary society, and probably the entire civilization, is being threatened by degenerating life-forms – the racial other, the sexual deviant, the urban poor, to name but some. The most elaborated account of this idea was provided by degeneration theory (below, Part III).

Degeneration theorists did not invent the idea of social death, but they refined and evolved it enormously, and the murdering, annihilat- ing strains of Stalinism, Nazism and fascism borrowed from them. What we discover (Part VI) is that revolutionary movements also find the rhetoric of social death useful as a way of conceptualizing those elements within the social which prove recalcitrant. Fears of social death are partly a consequence of enormous cultural changes from the Enlightenment onwards, but they also incorporate modern mutations of older anxieties about (uncontrollable) change and death. In some ways the conviction that the social can or should be controlled intensifies these older anxieties but changes them too: now the mutable social deviant – shifting and degenerating and full of aberrant desire – becomes both a justification of social engineering and a scapegoat for its failures.

Social historians speak of an increasing denial of death in modern times (Part III). But in the writing which this book examines there is, rather, a continuing and intensifying preoccupation with death in this period. Philosophically, aesthetically and erotically, modernity now intensifies and refines, now struggles against, now seeks to nullify that merciless immanence of death discerned by a formative earlier tradition. But there is at least one profoundly influential area of modern thought where something like a denial of death does seem to occur. It derives from the belief that change – or at least social change – can be controlled through praxis (Part VI). The seminal figure here is Marx, and the crucial idea (by no means his alone) is that we can master change and not merely be helplessly subject to it. As Marx would put it in the third of his *Theses on Feuerbach*:

The coincidence of the changing of circumstances and of human activity or self-changing can only be grasped and rationally understood as revolutionary *practice*. (Bottomore and Rubel, p. 83)

This represented a momentous shift in thinking, for reasons which are well-known. Once the vehicle of death, change is now harnessed into the service of life, becoming both the route to a different and better existence – via revolution, or at very least social transformation – and the essence of what it is to be human. In other words, we realize our potential to change the world by simultaneously recognizing that change and potentiality (rather than metaphysical fixity) are the grounds of what it is to be human; as Marx puts it in the passage just cited, in revolutionary praxis the changing of society and of the self coincide. This is why revolutionary fervour either ignores the question of death (Marx hardly mentions it) or scorns what it regards as the mystifying quietism of the traditional preoccupation with change as the grounds of death. But when revolution fails, even when more moderate aspirations for social improvement are frustrated, the preoccupation with death returns. In retrospect we can see that it was never far away – not least in the way that for intellectuals like Herbert Marcuse (Part VI) political radicalism is at some level an attempt to sublimate the melancholy that haunts them.

It was sometimes claimed that praxis abolished the philosophical need for renunciation, and even abolished if not death itself then at least what Marcuse derides as 'the ideology of death'. But this overlooked the fact that for Stoics like Seneca and Marcus Aurelius (Part I), and in a different way later Christian writers like Sir Walter Ralegh (Part II), the metaphysics of death was never dissociated from, or intended to pre-empt, worldly engagement; nor did it derive only from the direct experience of the failure of such engagement – on the contrary, the obsession with death was involved in the effort of engagement from the start, and it strangely intensified human endeavour. But for the philosophical advocates of a *social* praxis it seems necessary to ignore, reduce and even repress the significance of death. The case of Jean-Paul Sartre, perhaps the most politically involved philosopher of the postwar era, is especially significant (Part IV).

The aesthetics of energy

Another movement in modern thought involves a conception of change which is different again. Now it is the belief that Western decadence can be overcome only through a non-rational, self-risking immersion in change (Part VII). Represented most brilliantly by Friedrich Nietzsche, the concern is less to control change than to identify with it – ecstatically, sacrificially and even masochistically.

Nietzsche (below, Chapter 16) reacted violently against a meta-physics of death which he believed had been undermining Western culture at least since Socrates and was manifested as world-weariness, an incapacity for struggle and resistance, '*a yearning for extinction, cessation of all effort*' (*Birth*, p. 11): in brief, a wish to die. Nietzsche came to believe that this decadence found its most refined expression in Schopenhauer and Wagner, both of whom he had earlier revered but now vehemently repudiated. Wagner had himself been profoundly influenced by Schopenhauer – most especially by his philosophical vindication of death. This is Wagner writing about what he had found in Schopenhauer:

the genuine ardent longing for death, for absolute unconsciousness, total non-existence. Freedom from all dreams is our only final salvation. (*Wagner on Music and Drama*, p. 270)

This is exactly the world-weariness Nietzsche came to despise. He insisted that, rather than escaping the world of change by succumbing to the death-wish, or by seeking to transcend it metaphysically (in practice much the same thing), one had to enter into a Dionysiac identification with it, thereby serving and exemplifying the will to power, even to the point of welcoming destruction and the shattering of self. So in his identification with change there remains an embrace of death – an urgent need simultaneously to energize and to annihilate selfhood.

This further shift in the conception of mutability resonates through modernity, and if anything becomes even more significant for the post-modern, albeit in an attenuated form. Compared to it, the famous pronouncement of Nietzsche's madman ('God is dead') seems derivative. But, like many radical breaks, it both disguises and facilitates equally 'radical' continuities – not least because, as I argue, what Nietzsche calls the decadent tradition represents not a faltering of the Western expansionist enterprise (of, in his terms, its will to power), but a significant strand of it. So this tradition is not the antithesis of the will to power but its precursor, and the Nietzschean embrace of change is in certain respects a mutation of its way of thinking, not a breaking with it. This is one reason why Nietzsche remains intensely concerned with the necessity of combating the tendency towards social death consequent upon the perceived decline of Western culture.

Bataille (Chapter 17) is different again, and is particularly influential in taking the idea of the self-annihilating excess of desire to its limits, such that in ecstasy the distinction between death and desire almost ceases to signify. And D. H. Lawrence (Chapter 18) exemplifies a fascinating and recurring contradiction in modernity – now seduced by death as release, now obsessed with a radical individualism as an escape from the social death which is destroying Western culture. What makes Lawrence of the utmost significance still is that he exemplifies the extreme crisis of a modern philosophy of individualism that professes to be life-affirming yet is beleaguered by virtually every death-obsession in the Western tradition.

It is also via Lawrence that I return in Part VIII to the importance of homosexuality, now invested with extraordinary redemptive potential, even as it is also the focus of intense cultural, psychic and political anxieties about degeneration and death.

In this book I have wanted to reach non-specialist readers without making the patronizing assumption that they will be alienated by all but the superficial. I have not just summarized texts from afar, but have preferred instead to explore them close-up in the hope of getting inside a writer's mood, language, sensibility and philosophy. But I have only included material which I regard as potentially interesting and accessible to any thoughtful reader.

To say I've ranged widely is only another way of saying I've left out a great deal. I hope my subject exonerates me from the task of trying to be exhaustive. Certainly as I wrote it this book became a daily *memento mori*. I even came to see books themselves differently, especially in the remoter parts of libraries and second-hand bookshops. The title of a forgotten book and the dust it collects have a stillness which conveys that sense of past activity and present absence for which death is another word. Without death there would be no philosophy. So said Schopenhauer, Montaigne and many others. In fact without death there would be nothing – least of all books.

I

THE ANCIENT WORLD

I

Eros and Thanatos, Change and
Loss in the Ancient World

Fragments

Because the full texts for all Greek prose authors before Herodotus
(*c.* 485–*c.* 425 BC), and all philosophical writing before Plato (*c.* 428–
c. 348 BC), are lost, we know their writings only through quotations,
reports and paraphrases in later literature which survived the collapse
of ancient civilization. Traces, mutability, the obscurity that comes
in time: of these the Greeks often wrote, and these now characterize
the Greeks' history, despite the best efforts of scholars. Even the act
of historical recovery – most especially archaeological recovery –
hauntingly confirms the mutability of culture. Every success in getting
closer – particularly the most spectacular – only confirms the remote-
ness, the inaccessibility of that which is gone for ever.

Some of the earliest surviving texts speak poignantly of transience
and mutability and the suffering they bring. This is Mimnermus
(*fl. c.* 630 BC), of whose work little survives – 'nothing but fragments
of a passionate philosophy of life' (Levi, p. 71):

like the leaves that the many-blossomed season of spring brings forth when
they grow swiftly in the light of the sun . . . we enjoy the flowers of our
youth for a short span of time . . .[1]

He goes on to say that, because time brings old age 'full of suffering',
death is to be preferred to longevity (Trypanis, p. 135).

Of the work of Anaximander, who was probably born in 610 BC
and died in 545, only one quotation survives, and translations of that
vary significantly; there the difficulties of translation are compounded
by the elusiveness, the changeableness of a distant fragment which

3

Cornford in 1912) called 'strange and paradoxical', adding, 'the more we think about it the more preposterous it seems' (p. 11). Here are three differing translations:

Things perish into those things out of which they have their birth, according to that which is ordained; for they give reparation to one another and pay the penalty of their injustice according to the disposition of time. (Cornford, p. 8)

All the heavens and all the worlds in them come to be from the one limitless element: and the source out of which all existing things come to be is the same into which they are also resolved, by necessity, as they pay penalty and retribution to one another for their injustice according to the assessment of time. (Levi, p. 97)

Out of those things from which their generation comes [namely, the opposing powers], into these again does the destruction of things take place, in accordance with what is right and necessary; for they make amends and pay the penalty to one another for their aggression [adikia, injustice] according to the ordinance of Time. (Kahn, p. 18)

What is the 'limitless element' from which everything comes? It certainly isn't God. Others translate it as something 'undefined' or 'indefinite'; perhaps the origin of all things is a state we can best understand as 'undifferentiation'. In Kahn's translation it is different again: 'opposing powers'.

Cornford construes from Anaximander's fragment a threefold level of existence. First there is the multiplicity of individuated things; this is the world we know. Then there are the elements out of which these things emerge: earth, air, water and fire. Certainly there was a belief at the time that life is born of a conflict between these elements. A conflict, not a benign mixing: the point was that these elements were in perpetual war with each other. These are the 'opposing powers' of Kahn's translation. Individuated forms of life eventually dissolve back into the elements. But the elements are not permanent; they too eventually dissolve back into the primary, formless, indefinite state of things. What is most puzzling to us, perhaps, is that the destruction of life is described morally. The implication seems to be that birth, the individuation of things from the formless via the conflict of the

4

elements, is a crime, and that death and dissolution of these things are a reparation for this injustice: 'The manifold world, in Anaximander's view, can arise only by robbery and misappropriation' (Cornford, p. 10). One modern view of the universe is that life-forms are intricate, complex, organized, sometimes symmetrical unities which miraculously emerge from the formlessless of the primordial. As Cornford remarks (pp. 10–11), it is as if Anaximander has the opposite view: the emergence of life is a state of increasing instability, a move through conflict of elements into the disorder and instability and injustice of individuated life-forms. (And, strange as this seems, perhaps this view is not unfamiliar: as we will see in Chapter 4, Freud's theory of the death drive will echo it.)

In the fragments of Heraclitus (533–473 BC) we find an even more acute sense of the universe as being in a state of permanent change and ceaseless conflict:

One must understand that war [*polemos*] is shared and Conflict [*eris*] is Justice, and that all things come to pass (and are ordained?) in accordance with conflict. (lxxxii)[2]

In the most beautiful order Heraclitus discerned a random heap of dust:

The fairest order in the universe is a heap of random sweepings. (cxxv)

The perception of mutability, transience and change leads to a profound sense of an equivalence between life and death:

immortals are mortal, mortals immortal, living the others' death, dead in the others' life. (xcii)

The name of the bow is life; its work is death. (lxxix)

For souls it is death to become water, for water it is death to become earth; out of earth water arises, out of water soul. (cii)

There is even an equivalence between eros and death: Hades, the god of death; Dionysus, the god of eros – these are one and the same (cxvi). Consequently there is no stable identity either of things or of persons:

One cannot step twice into the same river, nor can one grasp any mortal substance in a stable condition, but it scatters and again gathers; it forms and dissolves, and approaches and departs. (li)

We step and do not step into the same rivers; we are and are not.[3]

I went in search of myself. (xxviii)

For Heraclitus there is no sense of personal immortality – the universe in flux involves the complete annihilation of the individual. Such annihilation is the condition of remaining part of the whole. Heraclitus' insistence on conveying his thought through paradox, inversion and the collapsing of binary oppositions has been regarded with suspicion. Lucretius for one mocked 'the darkness of his speech', regarding it as the affectation of a charlatan (p. 46). But, as we shall see, paradoxical expression is inseparable from a profound sense of change, mutability and loss.[4]

Parmenides (c. 515–c. 450 BC) develops a very different philosophy. He elevates reason, logic and deduction over the world of sense, perception and induction; the former give truth, the latter only decep-tive opinion and delusion. This is to be a crucial distinction. Parmen-ides argues that change is not the essence of things; rather, there is permanence within apparent change. This is the 'It is' – that which, says Parmenides, is 'uncreated and indestructible . . . complete, immovable and without end . . . all at once, a continuous one'. It cannot have come from what is not, because 'it can neither be thought nor uttered that anything is not . . . Thus is becoming extinguished and passing away not to be heard of' (Burnet, pp. 174–5). It is this unchanging world of which we have true knowledge (as distinct from unreliable opinion). With Heraclitus the ultimate reality is inseparable from change; for Parmenides it is essentially distinct from it. Parmenides also privileges stasis over motion. Cornford argues that, in the process, he 'expurgates' the Dionysiac view that life and death are inseparable and form a perpetual process of change (p. 220). Implicit here is that fundamental duality of the mutable and the immutable which will so profoundly influence Western philosophy. It does not appear for the first time with Parmenides, being already present in the older conceptions of the universe, but with him it becomes influential. But

Parmenides could not explain the relationship between the unchanging world and the world of change and mutability; in fact they seemed unconnected. Not so for Socrates (*c.* 470–399 BC) and Plato.

The death of Socrates ('the sun is still upon the mountains')

One view of the Greeks, influential to this day, is that, because they lived at its dawn, the pessimism, neurosis, guilt and alienation which later come to define Western civilization, and which are said to derive mainly from Christianity, were unknown to them. They were imagined to combine the health and vitality of the pagan (without its barbarism) with the intelligence and culture of the civilized (without its neurosis). The result – at least in the Hellenic ideal – was that 'man is at unity with himself' (Pater, p. 222).

Nietzsche's view of the Greeks was not that simple, but it was comparable. In the 1886 preface to *The Birth of Tragedy* (originally published in 1872) he regards Greek tragedy during its greatest period as deriving from 'a *strong* pessimism' rooted in a Dionysiac 'plethora of health [and] plenitude of being' and 'the youthful condition of the race'; this is to be contrasted with a modern European decadent pessimism marked by 'weakened instincts' and, of course, the death-wish – that 'yearning for extinction, cessation of all effort'. This decadent pessimism, according to Nietzsche, also characterized the ancient Hindus. Its principal modern manifestation is Christianity. But what is especially interesting about Nietzsche's version of this view is that he believed that the problem mainly began with the Greeks: in his opinion Socrates was already decadent (*Birth*, pp. 4–15). So far as Nietzsche is concerned, decadent forces were already at work in Greek culture, notwithstanding its general vitality. In this Nietzsche is expressing an obsession characteristic of his time which we will encounter later, namely the idea that the more vital the life-force is, the more vulnerable it is to the forces of degeneration. In one sense Nietzsche is right: in Platonism, and then in Epicurean and Stoic philosophy, there is a preoccupation with some of the ideas about desire and death subsequently influential in Western culture, including the sense of desire as being characterized by lack, absence, loss and, increasingly, futility.

In 399 BC Socrates was charged with heresy and corrupting the minds of the young (one of his most intimate pupils had been the infamous Alcibiades, remembered now only as a traitor whose actions had helped destroy his country). He was found guilty and condemned to death. In his final address to the court, he declared that death is not to be feared, because it entails one of two things: immortality or annihilation. Immortality would be reassuring for obvious reasons, although Socrates presents these somewhat facetiously, but so too would be that state of annihilation in which we have no consciousness of anything ever again. This, says Socrates, would be a profound gain, akin to dreamless sleep, which is the best sleep of all, preferable even to waking life, not least because 'the whole of time . . . can be regarded as no more than one single night' (Plato, *Apology*, p. 75).

Can we detect here a death-wish? Certainly Socrates in his final address welcomes his own death, and even seems to engineer it. In effect he chose the death penalty, refusing to go into exile, bribe himself free or be smuggled out of prison. Schopenhauer, the greatest advocate of the death drive before Freud, paraphrases thus the words of Socrates just cited: 'even if death deprived us of consciousness for ever, it would be a wonderful gain, for a deep, dreamless sleep is to be preferred to any day, even of the happiest life' (*World*, II.586). Nietzsche is unequivocal:[5]

Socrates *wanted* to die – it was not Athens, it was *he* who handed himself the poison cup, who compelled Athens to hand him the poison cup . . . 'Socrates is no physician,' he said softly to himself: 'death alone is a physician here . . . Socrates had only been a long time sick . . .' (*Twilight*, p. 34)

Certainly Socrates' philosophy involves a turning away from the world – something one cannot help recalling when reading in the *Phaedo* about his last moments. Crito, Socrates' intimate friend, urges him to delay taking the poison which is to kill him: 'the sun is still upon the mountains'. Socrates replies, 'I should only make myself ridiculous in my own eyes if I clung to life and hugged it when it has no more to offer' (Plato, *Phaedo*, p. 182).

In the *Phaedo* Socrates attempts to demonstrate the immortality of the soul by means of a manifestly inadequate logic which need not detain us here. But in the process he makes the famous assertion that philosophers are always 'directly and of their own accord preparing themselves for dying and death'. This is because they are forever struggling to attain the state of wisdom which only death affords. In life, says Socrates, we are constantly subject to the deceptions of sense, and the delusions of bodily desire; the soul, which is the agent and vehicle of truth, is 'contaminated' by the 'imperfection' of the body. The truth which it and the philosopher seek is possible only when the soul is liberated from the body in death. Hence the true philosopher desires death throughout his life, and even in life endeavours to become 'half-dead'; in all these respects 'true philosophers make dying their profession' (pp. 107–8, 113). This is not the later 'romantic' merging of desire and death, but it lays down a precondition for it: the connection of death and truth. For Socrates the only way to acquire 'pure knowledge' is to 'get rid of the body and contemplate things by themselves with the soul by itself' (p. 111).

Here is the basis of Western metaphysics, and a crucial influence on Christianity; it is the most influential attempt to escape from the mortal world of flux and change and decay. Nothing lasts; everything is transient: but for Socrates – and later for Plato – 'pure knowledge' is possible. It is achieved by the soul's recognition that every mutable thing derives its identity from an original 'form'. Such forms constitute a changeless realm of ultimate truth which is also the ultimate reality; by contrast with this transcendent realm, the mutable world of sense, body, change and alteration is always somehow unreal and untrue. And the soul itself fundamentally, essentially, belongs to this realm of ultimate, unchanging truth. If the body and its desires are lost in the unreal world of change, the soul desires and seeks out that which is essentially permanent, this being its own true nature as well.

The (Platonic) forms are uncreated, indestructible, eternally beyond corruption; it is just because they do not exist in space and time that they are the perfect origin and absolute justification of everything that does so exist. We desire forms like Beauty, but they are not accessible to our senses, only to pure thought – the immortal, thinking soul. Which means that the true object of desire is always elsewhere and always reached rationally/spiritually. Thus for Socrates in the *Phaedo* ultimate reality and true knowledge (themselves inseparable) are associated with the soul, and error and desire with the body. Christianity and an entire subsequent tradition of idealism find inspiration here – not least in the way that, in the shadow of death, Socrates offers immortality and annihilation as imagined alternatives. Except that they also cease to be – in fact never were – clear alternatives. Time and again the representation of immortality is realized in the language of oblivion; transcendence and eternity promise the dissolution of identity, the cessation of desire, the still point of the turning world.

Shelley

It is difficult to exaggerate, and impossible to summarize briefly, the extent of the influence of Platonism. Rather than trying, I glance forward to one powerful instance of that influence. Shelley's poetic expression of (Neo)Platonism conveys more than most books on the subject. But there is another and overriding reason for choosing Shelley, and it anticipates one of the main subsequent themes of this book. The most politically radical of all the romantic poets, his considerable interest in Platonic idealism was, as Jennifer Wallace observes, undoubtedly deployed for political ends, as in *Prometheus Unbound* and the *Defence of Poetry*.[6] That is to say, he wanted to use Plato on the side of praxis: the committed endeavour to social transformation and human emancipation. Yet the stronger pull of Platonic idealism for Shelley was towards the opposite of praxis: renunciation, escape, transcendence as annihilation. The seduction of death haunts even political radicalism, at least in its romantic forms.

His poem *Adonais* is a lament for the death of John Keats, and a highly wrought pastoral elegy.[7] When, some way into the poem, and with due modesty, Shelley himself arrives on the scene ('Midst others of less note, came one frail Form', l. 271) he comes to sing the praises not of Adonais/Keats, but of radical death, expressing a desire to die in and through a desire for, and an identification with, the beautiful youth who is already dead. The poem ends, famously, with a Neoplatonic vision in which the loss, suffering, mutability and lack which characterize existence in this world are transcended through an embracing of 'the Eternal, which must glow / Through time and change' (ll. 340–41):

> The One remains, the many change and pass;
> Heaven's light forever shines, Earth's shadows fly;
> Life, like a dome of many-coloured glass,
> Stains the white radiance of Eternity,
> Until Death tramples it to fragments. – Die,
> If thou wouldst be with that which thou dost seek!
> Follow where all is fled!   (ll. 460–66)

The poem moves through different conceptions of death. Initially death is personified as evil monster: parasitic, vampiric, sexually sadistic, full of predatory desire. Finally the oblivion of a more radical death easily kills off this personification (' 'tis Death is dead, not he'), which was, after all, only a vindictive manifestation of life, not death. Another conception of death is more arresting: death as the essence of life, in the sense of an internal, natural process of expenditure, dissolution and unbinding. 'Quickening life' has at its heart a 'sacred thirst' which impels it to consume itself in 'change and motion'. 'Baser things' do not resist this; lacking consciousness, they 'Diffuse themselves; and spend in love's delight, / The beauty and the joy of their renewèd might' (ll. 164–71). As with most other philosophers (including Plato) and poets, Shelley is deeply ambivalent towards this sense of life and death as inseparable – hence the embracing of redemption in the Platonic One.

Shelley's Neoplatonism offers transcendence indistinguishable from regression, unity indistinguishable from dissolution. So transcendence functions less to redeem or even explain life's lack than as an 'affirmation' which enables the poet to endorse death, to finally cry the louder, 'Die, / If thou wouldst be with that which thou dost seek!' (ll. 464–5). Or perhaps it is the case that what is yearned for – the stasis of radical undifferentiation – dissolves also the differences between transcendence and regression, unity and dissolution: 'No more let Life divide what Death can join together' (l. 477). And if I want to add a pause, even an exclamation, after 'more', it is only because that is just what is being pleaded: *No more.* By contrast, human desire, 'that alone which knows' – which uniquely knows, and so knows in a state of aloneness – is an 'unrest which men miscall delight' and is always in the shadow of what makes it unrealizable: 'fear and grief / Convulse us and consume us day by day' (ll. 354, 349–50).

Desire as lack: Plato's Symposium

The scenario in which desire seeks in the undifferentiation of the One release from the anguished impossibility of its own fulfilment recurs time and again in the Western tradition. And in Plato's *Symposium* can be found one of its most influential dramatizations. It is an account of how sexual desire, originating in a traumatic division of perfect wholes, became an experience of incompleteness, loss and lack which ruined identity – and so severely that desire henceforth becomes an experience haunted by death.

The myth is related by Aristophanes, and he is speaking specifically of 'the lover of boys', but he adds that his account is applicable to all those lovers whose 'soul . . . has some other longing which it cannot express, but can only surmise and obscurely hint at' (p. 63). Originally, he says, there were three sexes: male, female, and hermaphrodite. The last of these had the characteristics of both male and female. It has since become extinct, though its name survives 'and that solely as a term of abuse' (p. 59). Each type of human was a whole, with four legs, four arms, two faces on the one head, two organs of generation, and everything else to correspond. They were formidable and hubristic creatures who even dared to attack the gods. To weaken them, Zeus cut each of them in two:

Man's original body having been thus cut in two, each half yearned for the half from which it had been severed. When they met they threw their arms round one another and embraced, in their longing to grow together again, and they perished of hunger and general neglect of their concerns, because they would not do anything apart. (p. 61)

When one member of the pair died, the remaining one 'sought after and embraced another partner, which might be the half either of a female whole (what is now called a woman) or a male'. They went on perishing in this way until Zeus took pity on them and moved their reproductive organs to the front, making intercourse as we now know it possible. If heterosexual intercourse occurred, the race would be continued; if homosexual, then desire would be satisfied 'and men set free from it to turn to other activities'. It is from this distant epoch, then, that human love as we know it derives – 'the love which restores us to our ancient state by attempting to weld two beings into one and to heal the wounds which humanity suffered' (p. 62).

For Aristophanes, each person remains incomplete. Those deriving from the original hermaphrodite sex seek halves of the opposite sex, those deriving from the female search for other women, while those who are halves of males pursue males: 'they always cleave to what is akin to themselves' (p. 63). 'Such boys and lads are the best of their generation, because they are the most manly. Some people say they are shameless, but they are wrong. It is ... high spirit and manliness and virility' which lead them to love their own kind (p. 62). Though for different reasons, Socrates later concurs with Aristophanes: love exists only in relation to some missing object, therefore 'one desires what one lacks' (pp. 77, 76). Here then, splitting or dividing is the founding principle of desire. Originating in a division which is a kind of death, desire becomes an experience of lack rooted in loss; caught up somewhere between past loss and future lack, it will remain unrealizable and always come to consciousness as the seemingly inescapable condition of restlessness, dislocation, lack – and anxiety.

Although the Greeks did not regard sexual acts as sinful, and did not classify and discriminate between them in the modern sense, they were the cause of anxiety. In Volume 2 of *The History of Sexuality* Michel Foucault identifies three related aspects of this anxiety, all of which, but especially the last two, connect sexuality with death and 'disturbed and threatened the individual's relationship with himself and his integrity as an ethical subject in the making'. The first was the violence of the act – a violence which 'confounded the will' and disorganized the emotions. The second concerned the self-expenditure of copulation: ejaculation meant the loss of vital, life-sustaining fluids – even a wasting of the body's resources. The third was about the way procreation was linked to the future death of the individual:

For Aristotle and Plato alike, the sexual act was at the point of junction of an individual life that was bound to perish – and from which, moreover, it drew off a portion of its most precious resources – and . . . [in the words of Plato] a partaking 'of immortality by means of coming-into-being'. (pp. 135–6)[8]

Eros and thanatos, and the unbinding of the self

A poem by Meleager (c. 140–70 BC) evokes the experience of being profoundly disturbed by a wonderful youth:

> At 12 o'clock in the afternoon
>   in the middle of the street –
>   Alexis.
>
> Summer had all but brought the fruit
>   to its perilous end:
>   & the summer sun & that boy's look
>
> did their work on me.
>   Night hid the sun.
>   Your face consumes my dreams.
>
> Others feel sleep as feathered rest;
>   mine but in flame refigures
>   your image lit in me.
>
>   (Jay, p. 142)

This was a recurring topic for Greek lyric poetry, and for comedy and tragedy: intense desire unbinds the unity of the self or dissolves its resolve, reduces it to obsession, illness, madness or even death; or splits it into self-division, or contradictory moral evaluation, or wrecks it with the ambivalence of love and hate fused in the same desire.[9]

Undoubtedly there is much in this view of extreme desire which resonates with the modern reader. Yet in important respects it is also strange – most especially, perhaps, in the way that desire, for all its destructive effects on the human subject, is conceptualized as something invading from without rather than, say, working intimately from within. This is Pindar describing his desire for a beautiful boy: 'I melt like wax as the heat bites into it' (Carson, p. 15). It is not advisable to generalize about such a wide body of writing across such a long period, but, while many poems surviving from ancient Greece are indeed about being wrecked by desire, they are rarely about the futility or impossibility of fulfilment of desire as we will encounter it later. And yet for the Greeks 'eros' implies lack, the want of what is absent: 'lack is [Eros's] animating, fundamental constituent' (p. 63). This is not just a lack of the desired object, but a profound state of loss – potentially the loss of self. We should remember too that 'Change of self is loss of self, according to the traditional Greek attitude' (p. 154): the Greeks were obsessively aware of manifold ways in which desire would unbind the defended self, and specifically of the way it would promise to complete a self tormented by lack, only to undermine it the more.

In *Love in Ancient Greece* Robert Flacelière claims there were three legends which proved that

the Greeks had meditated on the mysterious bonds between love and death long before the chivalrous society of the Middle Ages and such tales as that of Tristram and Yseult, which in fact contains a good many reminiscences of ancient writers. The Greek myths in question are those of Orpheus and Eurydice, Admetus and Alcestis, Protesilaus and Laodamia. (p. 44)

But in his discussion of these myths what Flacelière discerns is something much more conventional: namely the 'triumph' of love over death, as for example in the story of how Alcestis gives up her own life to save her husband's. As for Orpheus, he finds himself in the underworld only because he has gone there to search for his dead wife, Eurydice. And, as Phaedrus points out in *The Symposium*, he does not die in order to follow her there but prefers to enter the underworld alive. Protesilaus dies suddenly, shortly after his marriage to Laodamia; they implore the gods to allow them to be reunited, and Hades permits this – but only for a few hours. What Flacelière admires in these myths is 'lovers who know in their hearts that their love is stronger than death' (pp. 47–8). These are myths which register the gulf between human love and death.

More recently the archaeologist Emily Vermeule has revealed in some detail how in early Greek myth and art eros and thanatos are indeed closely associated – for example in the idea of the Gods taking through death a mortal they love,[10] or in the way that Homer mockingly treats enemies as lovers, with 'love and death as the two sides of the same instant', and more generally in myth and literature, where eros and thanatos become 'two aspects of the same power' (pp. 157–9). Vermeule's chapter on this topic, subtitled 'The Pornography of Death', begins with a revealing fragment from the early (seventh century BC) poet Alcman: 'in limb-relaxing longing (*pothos*) she [a woman] looks more meltingly than sleep (*hypnos*) and death (*thanatos*)' (p. 145).[11] Here sleep and death connect with desire – but not any desire: Plato tells us that, whereas *himeros* refers to a desire whose fulfilment is possible and anticipated, *pothos* refers to a suffering desire for what cannot be fulfilled, for what is absent (*Cratylus*, p. 455). As such it is also an expression of mourning whose intensity could be sufficient to kill (Vermeule, p. 154). So, it is an unfulfilled desire which suggests death; as Jean-Pierre Vernant says of the same Alcman passage, 'The figure of the beloved woman whose image haunts and escapes the lover intersects with that of death' (pp. 101–2).

From Vernant and other scholars we learnt that the Greeks of the archaic period conceptualized the body – by which was usually meant the adult male body – as radically mutable, because permeable to the diverse and conflicting forces which animate it. Death was not only a horizon, an ending, but intrinsic to life itself. In this period being and the privation of being are inextricably intertwined, and 'the other side of a luminous youthful body is an ugly faded one'; the experience of human beauty is inseparable from the sense of human transience, exhaustion and decay. These Greeks lived 'between the shadows of death where they finally must lose themselves and the pure luminosity of the divine which remains inaccessible to them' (pp. 32–3, 44). We know clearly enough that the Greeks revered youthful beauty; what Vernant stresses is how this reverence occurred in the shadow of death – this is a beauty whose apprehension was inseparable from an equally acute sense of its loss and decline. Thus Menander's famous remark 'He whom the god loves dies young', and the attraction for the Greeks of the idea of a beautiful death.

To die young in battle was not only to be immortalized as a hero, it was also to escape the decline and decay of old age. Far from being tragically cut short, youthful beauty, virility and strength were profoundly confirmed in heroic death – not least because they were thus released from the attrition of time and destruction. Through heroic death, human (i.e. mortal) excellence 'no longer has to be measured indefinitely against others and keep proving itself in confrontation; it is realized at one stroke and forever'. The heroic youthful death in battle is in a sense a pre-empting of the decrepitude of old age: 'The way to escape old age is by dying in the flower of one's youth, at the acme of one's virile strength. Through death the hero is now fixed forever in the brilliance of an unchanging youth' (pp. 85–6). Conversely, when the old die in battle they become ugly, even obscene. Thus Priam in Homer's *Iliad*:

it looks well enough for a young man killed in battle to lie there with his wounds upon him: death can find nothing to expose in him that is not beautiful. But when an old man is killed and dogs defile his grey head, his grey beard and his privy parts, we plumb the depths of human degradation. (p. 399)

After Hector had been killed by Achilles, other warriors gathered round looking at the dead body, admiring its beauty – and mutilating it: 'They gazed in wonder at the size and marvellous good looks of Hector. And not a man of all who had collected there left him without a wound' (p. 407). Then Achilles subjected the body to 'shameful outrage', dragging it in the dust. Before combat Hector had tried to make a bargain with Achilles, suggesting they agree that the victor refrain from this defilement of the other's corpse. Achilles had refused. The mutilation and defilement of the body was an attempt to rob the corpse of its beauty in death.

The song of the Sirens

In Greek culture not only is death feminized, but, according to Vernant, 'Death and woman arose in concert together' (p. 98).[12] In Hesiod, for example, the seductiveness of women is in complicity with the nocturnal powers of death; in relation to Medusa, Vernant finds that 'the strange beauty of the feminine countenance, brilliant with seduction, and the horrible fascination of death, meet and cross' (p. 150). But it is through close attention to the language and imagery of *The Iliad* that Vernant illustrates how combat to the death is associated with the (heterosexual?) erotic embrace.

Inside this association is the fear of being weakened, unbound and undone. Such weakening results from desire for a woman. It also results from fear. But, in the military combat, fear seems to bear the traces of this desire displaced on to the male combatant under the threat or enticement of death. The poet Tyrtaeus (*fl.* 685–668 BC) imitates the passage from the *The Iliad* cited earlier, accentuating even more the association of youth, beauty and violent death in battle:

Nothing is improper for the young, nothing as long as a man has the bright flower of lovely youth. While he is alive the men who see him admire him and the women desire him; and he is beautiful when killed in the first line of battle. (Trypanis, pp. 127–8)

Although Vernant, who discusses this passage, does not make this point, it surely seems that an admiring identification *with* the young warrior is complicated by a (sublimated?) desire *for* him which includes an imagining of his 'beautiful' death. Death and woman may have arisen together, but their association was surely inflected by homo-eroticism.

Book XII of Homer's *Odyssey* recounts the famous story of Odysseus' encounter with the seductive song of the Sirens. Circe warns him beforehand of the danger: 'The thrilling song of the Sirens will steal his life away.' They charm and seduce men irresistibly. All who succumb never return home but die right there. The Sirens are surrounded by the corpses of such men – 'high banks of mouldering skeletons which flutter with the rags of skin rotting upon the bones' (trans. Shaw, pp. 170–71). The Sirens are said to sing from within a flowering meadow; Vernant points out that meadow, or *leimon*, was a word used to designate female genitalia (p. 104). So, even before Odysseus actually encounters the Sirens, a connection is made between sexual desire and death, and the fatally seductive object is feminine. Moreover the desire is overwhelming – literally irresistible. Circe tells Odysseus that to survive the encounter his companions must stop their ears with wax, to be deaf to the Sirens' charm. Circe then says to Odysseus:

For your own part, perhaps you wish to hear their singing? Then have yourself lashed hand and foot into your ship against the housing of the mast, with other bights of rope secured to the mast itself. Ensure also that if you order or implore your men to cast you loose, their sole response shall be to bind you tighter with cord upon cord. (Homer, *Odyssey*, trans. Shaw, p. 170)

This is done. When the encounter takes place we learn something more about why the Sirens are so seductive. They implore Odysseus to come to them; they treat him as a hero and promise him that they will send him on his way the possessor of divine knowledge: 'we know all things which shall be hereafter upon the fecund earth' (p. 174). As Vernant points out, the Sirens 'celebrate in his presence that very Odysseus whom the song of the *Iliad* immortalizes: the virile male warrior'; in their song Odysseus sees himself not as he is, 'struggling precariously amid the dangers of the world, unsure of the future, but as already immortalized in legend' (p. 105). That is a crucial aspect of what is so seductive about the encounter. As predicted, Odysseus finds the Sirens irresistible and commands his men to free him. They refuse, binding him even tighter.

This episode challenges interpretation even as it demands it; and in a way which reminds us that it originates from a culture which in certain respects is as strange as in other respects it is antecedent and familiar. And, if it is appropriate to talk of the unconscious in relation to this episode, it also reminds us that the unconscious is subject to cultural difference and is stranger and more alien than we would like to believe. What is being seduced is mortal, sexual desire for beauty, strangeness and otherness, and the mortal (sexual?) desire for a legendary immortality. But those mouldering remains tell us that this over-whelming desire leads not to an exalted, immortalizing death, perhaps not even to an ecstatic one, but precisely to a death of the kind which the Greeks most feared: without funeral, without tomb, and rotting anonymously on the shore, indistinguishable from the other corpses in the pile. The lure of death – to be free of finitude, contingency, danger; to be immortalized in legend – is confounded by the anonymity of actual death. In a sense, then, the act of self-overcoming involves a refusal not of mortality but of immortality.

Destructive desires: Epicureanism

Epicurus (341–271 BC) was born less than a decade after the death of Plato. Also a citizen of Athens, he lived during a period of unprecedented political conflict; cultural, economic and democratic decline within the cities was accompanied by warfare between them. He regarded man as tormented and obsessive, full of boundless 'empty desires' or 'empty striving' (*kenospoudon*) which afford no enduring satisfaction but cause a yearning which 'goes off into infinity' (Nussbaum, p. 112).[13]

Crucially, Epicurus believed that such impossible desires stem from false beliefs about the world, and especially about the objects of desire. These beliefs sometimes generate an intense and destructive anxiety in the individual. To correct rationally those beliefs is to be free of destructive desire and to be returned to a condition of natural desire, the essence of which is that it has a limit, can be satisfied, and does not make impossible demands upon the individual. A remark attributed to Epicurus' disciple the Roman poet Lucretius (*c.* 99–55 BC) makes this commitment to reason, and thereby to philosophy, especially clear: 'By a passion for true philosophy every disturbing and burdensome desire is undone.' This is in fact the main purpose of philosophy – an activity which, for Epicurus, was vain and pointless if it did not alleviate 'the suffering of the mind' (Nussbaum, p. 154; Epicurus, p. 133).

Epicurus said 'sexual intercourse has never done a man good, and he is lucky if it has not harmed him' (p. 123), but it is in Lucretius' *On the Nature of the Universe*, written some two centuries after Epicurus' death, that this view of sexual desire is articulated more severely than ever before. Lucretius, following Epicurus, describes a universe made up of two things: atoms and the void in which they ceaselessly move.[14] If the atoms are unrestricted by each other they remain discrete and in perpetual movement in the void. The universe as we know it, the existence of animate and inanimate things, arises from the fact that these atoms do restrict each other's movement; the materiality of things and life itself arises from arrested movement. But the arresting of movement can only be temporary. It is not exactly a harmonious coexistence but a clashing, restrictive intermingling: literally everything which exists derives from the conflict, collision and conjunction of atoms. Lucretius describes a world in which the motions which bind atoms into being are in ceaseless conflict with other motions which unbind and disintegrate those same atoms:

The destructive motions can never permanently get the upper hand and entomb vitality for evermore. Neither can the generative and augmentative motions permanently safeguard what they have created. So the war of the elements that has raged throughout eternity continues on equal terms.

There is a kind of balance then, but one inseparable from the potentially tragic sense of death's proximity to life; the foregoing passage continues:

Now here, now there, the forces of life are victorious and in turn vanquished. With the voice of mourning mingles the cry that infants raise when their eyes open on the sunlit world. Never has day given place to night or night to dawn that has not heard, blent with these infant wailings, the lamentation that attends on death. (pp. 76–7)

It is an amoral universe in which the new is built from the wreckage of the old, and the birth of some things is inseparable from the death of others (pp. 35, 125). This is a philosophy resolutely materialist in outlook, and which repudiates belief in providence, immortality and Platonic idealism. While Lucretius' universe is astonishingly fecund, it is also 'blind' in the sense of being without spiritual essence and *telos*, and with a destructiveness at the very heart of creation.

This is especially true with respect to desire. What Lucretius calls 'this deplorable lust for life' results in 'no one knowing what he really wants and everyone forever trying to get away from where he is'. In this condition satisfaction remains beyond our grasp:

So long as the object of our craving is unattained, it seems more precious than anything besides. Once it is ours we crave for something else. So an unquenchable thirst for life keeps us always on the gasp. (pp. 128–9)

For Lucretius this is supremely true of sexual desire, which in its acute unrequited form is described as a 'festering sore [which] quickens and strengthens'. Sexual desire in the male is compared to dying, or at least injury, and warfare. Be the object of his desire a boy or a woman, the male is drawn towards them with the purpose of ejaculation, just as 'the wounded normally fall in the direction of their wound: the blood spurts out towards the source of the blow; and the enemy who delivered it, if he is fighting at close quarters, is bespattered by the crimson stream' (p. 163). Lovers anticipate that their 'speechless yearning is a presentiment of bliss', but they are wrong: vain is the hope that the flame and pain of love will be quenched by the possession of the beloved; on the contrary, 'this is the one thing of which the more we have, the more our breast burns with the evil lust of having'. It's like a man trying to drink in a nightmare – 'while he laps up a rushing stream he remains thirsty in the midst'. Lovers yearn to become one but remain separate; orgasm gives only temporary relief, and lovers (echoing Aristophanes' myth in Plato's *Symposium*) 'in aimless bewilderment . . . waste away, stricken by an unseen wound'. Wealth, patrimony and reputation diminish or are lost entirely. For Lucretius desire is impossible, in the sense that it is self-defeating – i.e. the frustration which it experiences is an internal, necessary condition of itself (rather than being, for instance, the consequences of the contingent unattainability of the object of desire); 'Lovers' passion is storm tossed, *even in the moment of fruition*, by waves of delusion and incertitude', for '*from the very heart* of the fountain of delight there rises a jet of bitterness that poisons the fragrance of the flowers'. All this attends on desire which is requited; the ills of unrequited love are immeasurably worse (pp. 163–5; my emphasis). Desire should be reduced, controlled and to a great extent eliminated. One of Epicurus' fragments reads, 'If you wish to make Pythocles rich, do not give him more money, but diminish his desire' (p. 127).

Unremarkably then, death is not to be feared. From his materialist position Epicurus had argued for the mortality of the soul; in death it dissolves back into nature, like the body. Death is the inevitable dispersion of the atoms whose temporary arrangement constituted us. In that sense death is not an external agent but the innate condition of life itself. To fear death is irrational, because while we are alive death is not, and when death comes we are not:

So death . . . is nothing to us, since so long as we exist, death is not with us; but when death comes, then we do not exist. It does not then concern either the living or the dead . . . (Epicurus, p. 85)

Jacques Choron says that this argument 'has limitations, for it applies only to *one* aspect of this fear, namely the fear of what happens after death' (*Death and Western Thought*, p. 62). But surely it is more inclusive than that: death as complete annihilation guarantees the end of the fear we now feel about death. Knowing that this fear is itself of finite duration, we are in a better position to extricate ourselves from it now. In other words, if I fear death in the sense of fearing not being alive, not being here, etc., I can be reassured that the oblivion which is death will obliterate that fear too. Quite simply I will not be here to have the fears I now have about not being here. And if Epicurus has been regarded as having considered the problem – the mortality of the soul – as the solution, it can be replied that this criticism presupposes the desirability of the immortality of the soul.

Lucretius stresses the pain and inevitable disappointments of life as another reason for not fearing its loss. And now, additionally, there is a strong sense that 'the care-free calm of death' is desired; in redeeming us from suffering, death grants us peace and rest more profound than any known in life, even in the deepest sleep:

One who no longer is cannot suffer, or differ in any way from one who has never been born, when once this mortal life has been usurped by death the immortal. (pp. 102, 122–5)

Above all we must remember that 'eternal death . . . the time of not being' is 'no less for him who made an end of life with yesterday's daylight than for him who perished many a moon and many a year before' (p. 129). In the attitude of reflective detachment from life which Epicurus and Lucretius sought is a paradoxical, valued insight: sometimes it is fear of death rather than the desire not to live which drives one to suicide; or rather the fear of death comes to be manifested as the desire not to live.

Stoicism

Seneca (*c.* 4 BC–AD 65) writes at length of how difficult it is to be happy, and of the inevitable failure of those who seek fulfilment through involvement in worldly affairs. For him the human condition is essentially one of restless dissatisfaction. He is another philosopher for whom desire or passion[15] is the great evil: to desire is to be unfree, conflicted, miserable, futile. The things we most desire are what most disappoint – especially power. And Seneca should know, being for a period of his life one of the most powerful men in the world.

He draws sketch after sketch of types of dissatisfied human being, all recognizable to this day. They are those who are restless with themselves, wretched because caught up in diverse efforts to realize their desires, all of which are ultimately futile. This man is possessed by insatiable avarice, that by trivial enterprises; another is exhausted by an ambition for power ever thwarted by its depending upon the votes of others; yet another is driven restlessly across land and sea in pursuit of profit. Some are worn out by unrequited attendance upon the great, others are precipitated into one pointless thing after another, driven by a 'fickleness which is rambling and unstable and dissatisfied with itself'; yet others 'acquire with toil what requires greater toil to hold', or spend their life working for a position which, when eventually achieved, they are too old to sustain: 'the object of the toil was their epitaph' ('On the Shortness of Life', pp. 48, 69, 72–3). The problem is that

> Most men ebb and flow in wretchedness between the fear of death and the hardships of life; they are unwilling to live, and yet they do not know how to die. (*Epistulae Morales*, I.17)

Our desires are cheated by the mutability which characterizes our existence; nothing lasts, and most things are succeeded by their opposite. The more successful we are, the more we fear failure – and our fears usually turn out to be well founded:

> There is a terror in our very pleasures, and this vexatious thought in the very height of them, that they will not last always, which is a canker in the delights even of the greatest and the most fortunate of men. (*Morals*, p. 126)

Overpreoccupied with objectives and 'unaware of our ceaseless and rapid journey through life', our own life 'vanishes into an abyss'. There is a fundamental incompatibility between the mutability of the world and human desire. That is why, if the science of life requires a whole lifetime to master, so too does the science of dying ('On the Shortness of Life', pp. 58–9, 55). In a sense they are the same thing.

As he anatomizes human dissatisfaction with life, Seneca occasionally describes conditions which in our own time we have pathologized. What Seneca, following Lucretius, regards as a failing experienced by all to a greater or lesser degree, the psychoanalyst might discern as repression, neurosis, depression or a split personality:

As Lucretius says: 'Each man always flees himself.' But what is the good if he cannot get away from himself? He follows close and is his own most burdensome companion ... We are too unstable to put up with anything, and cannot bear hardship or pleasure or ourselves or anything else for long. Some men have been driven to death by this failing ... ('On Tranquility', p. 82)

Nothing epitomizes Seneca's philosophy more than the following remark about possession and loss: 'No good thing renders its possessor happy, unless his mind is reconciled to the possibility of loss' (*Epistulae Morales*, I.17). For Seneca this is true of material possessions and, if anything, even more true of life itself. We cannot live if we are not prepared – literally – to die: 'I shall never be frightened when the last hour comes; I am already prepared and do not plan a whole day ahead' (I.363).[16] But it transpires that there are different senses of loss entailed by what he says. Most dramatically there is the loss of one's own life. But that, in a sense, is the easiest loss of all, since 'nothing ... is lost with less discomfort than that which, when lost, cannot be missed' (I.365). This fact is supposed to help fortify us against the mutability of our fortunes: unexpected disaster can come at any time, often when it is least expected, at the height of our success. Seneca infers from this inevitability of loss that we should not worry about it – first, precisely *because* it is inevitable, and the wise man not only accepts the inevitable but wills it, thereby escaping necessity by willing it (I.365); second, because if we assume the worst it turns out to be less terrifying than we thought, containing 'nothing fearful except the actual fear' (I.173); and third, and most radically, because he proposes we disconnect the present from the future: 'It is indeed foolish to be unhappy now because you may be unhappy at some future time' (I.167).

Another kind of loss becomes apparent when Seneca elsewhere describes how revisiting old haunts can 'stir up a sense of loss that has been stored away in the soul, not bringing back dead memories, but rousing them from their dormant state'. He compares this with coming across some possession of a dead friend 'which renews the mourner's grief, even though it has been softened by time'. The experience of loss returns as if the loss happened but a moment ago – 'for what is not "but a moment ago" when one begins to use the memory?' This comes from an essay on the brevity of life. 'Infinitely swift', says Seneca, 'is the flight of time, as those see more clearly who are looking backwards. For when we are intent on the present, we do not notice it, so gentle is the passage of time's headlong flight.' This is no less true for being a commonplace. But Seneca gives a disquieting reason for why it is so:

All past time is in the same place; it all presents the same aspect to us, it lies together. Everything slips into the same abyss. (I.323)

This idea of all past time as equally present in the same dark absence ('Omnia in idem profundum cadunt') is hardly ours, in the late twentieth century. Don't we rather think of time, even past time, as linear – at least to the extent that the more remote the time/experience, the more tenuous our memory of it? Yet on reflection this patently is not true: a memory of a traumatic event in the distant past can wreck our equanimity at any time in the present. Moreover, we know that the significance of an event, even the way it is recalled in memory, is not constant; notoriously, it can be the subsequent memory of the event, rather than the initial experience of the event, which disturbs.

From realpolitik to renunciation

Seneca discerns the futility of worldly affairs not from a position of ascetic withdrawal, but from the centre of power and worldly ambition which he knew at first hand. He belonged to the élite who ruled the

Roman empire yet whose power to dispense death could never defend them from it – not natural death, obviously, but not violent death either. The briefest account of Seneca's life reminds us of the extraordinary violence of his times. He himself was three times sentenced to death. On the first occasion the sentence was revoked. The second occasion arose after he was unjustly accused of an illicit intrigue with a princess called Julia. The charge was brought by Messalina, the wife of the then emperor, Claudius, in AD 41. Julia was exiled and put to death. Seneca was condemned to death but had the sentence commuted to banishment. He was exiled to Corsica. At the same time he lost his son and two nephews.

He spent some seven years in exile, returning to Rome only after a fundamental change in power relations made it possible. During Seneca's exile Messalina took a lover, Silius, and between them they tried to seize power from Claudius. The plot failed, and both Messalina and Silius were put to death. Claudius remarried, to his niece, Agrippina, who recalled Seneca from exile to have him tutor her son, Nero. It was at this point that Seneca joined the ruling élite of the Roman empire. Only a few years later Agrippina murdered Claudius, and Nero succeeded to power at the age of seventeen. Five years after that Nero murdered Agrippina. Seneca tried to retire from court affairs, offering to return to Nero all his wealth, but Nero refused to let him. Nevertheless Seneca managed to go into semi-retirement.

In AD 65 there was a conspiracy against Nero in which Seneca was dubiously implicated. The conspiracy failed, and Seneca was condemned to death. Like most men of his rank, he was allowed to take his own life in what is one of the most famous, most theatrical performances of death ever recorded, in which Seneca was almost certainly identifying with, if not actually imitating, Socrates. There was the same resignation, but not so unworldly or disinterested as to forgo the opportunity of counter-condemnation: What did you expect, Seneca asked his friends, of an emperor who had already murdered his mother and destroyed his brother? It was predictable that such a man would also murder his guardian and tutor. Seneca's death was slow: severing an artery in the arm failed to bring death, as did severing others in the legs, and then poison. Tacitus records that he suffered excruciating pain, but that his eloquence still continued to flow with its usual purity. He called for his secretaries, and dictated, while life was ebbing away, that farewell discourse, which has been published, and is in everybody's hands. (I.501)

In fact there is no surviving record of that farewell discourse. Seneca was then placed in a hot bath, and eventually died. His wife insisted on dying with him, but she survived her own attempted suicide.

Seneca gives a great deal of advice on how to live – some of it contradicted by what he says elsewhere. He insists, for example, that we must plan every day as if it is our last, and live for the day. But, on Seneca's own admission, even the day eludes us. The poet tells us to grasp the day, lest it fly away, but 'It will fly anyhow, even if you do grasp it, and so your speed in using time must compete with time's own rapid pace' ('On the Shortness of Life', pp. 56, 58). Only the philosopher really lives. He has access to the knowledge of the sages, who occupy a realm not unlike eternity itself – 'a boundless and timeless region', to be contrasted with the 'petty and ephemeral span' of the here and now (p. 66). This too is unpersuasive, at least when we consider the extent to which, in Western culture, knowledge itself is a source of misery. And, judging from his own continued need for political influence and power, Seneca himself did not find it persuasive either.

A key principle of Seneca's philosophy is that we should withdraw into, know and become dependent upon only ourselves. The aim of life is stability of mind, well-being of soul, a state of serenity 'without excitement or depression' – what Seneca calls tranquillity ('On Tranquility', p. 80). One should remain detached, uninvolved:

It is important to withdraw into one's self. Association with a different sort of people unsettles ideas made orderly, reawakens passions, and aggravates mental cankers not yet thoroughly healed. (p. 104)

But Seneca goes on to tell us that in fact we need society as much as we need solitude. And in the same essay we are told that we should sometimes deliberately destabilize the equilibrium of the self through intoxication. Again, this is still the cautious Seneca – such destabilization should not be indulged in too often or to excess – but the way he describes the value of this suggests a wish to undermine the very self upon which his philosophy depends:

only a mind that is excited is capable of great and transcendent utterance. When it has spurned the trite and the commonplace and has been impelled aloft by the demonic urge, then and only then can it sing a strain too grand for mortal lips. So long as it is under its own sway the mind cannot attain the sublime ... It must tear itself from the trodden path, palpitate with frenzy, take the bit in its teeth and run away with its rider to reach the height it would fear to climb in its own strength. (p. 106)

Not surprisingly, then, Seneca has often been accused of inconsistency. Quintilian (*c.* AD 35–95) remarked that this inconsistency was because he took too little trouble with philosophy (Sandbach, p. 159). Perhaps it was rather because he mixed philosophy with politics. It is sometimes assumed that philosophers speak more truly from a position of independence – a principled withdrawal from worldly affairs, or just the security of the academy. But this same independence also isolates them from the reality they profess to know. Seneca arguably demonstrates that inevitable, insightful failure of philosophy when it engages with the reality it seeks to know.

More difficult than the question of inconsistency is the related question of Seneca's alleged hypocrisy.[17] Dio Cassius (AD 155–235) observed that, 'while denouncing tyranny, Seneca was making himself the teacher of a tyrant', and, while having nothing good to say of flatterers, Seneca himself constantly fawned upon the powerful – especially when he was in exile. Further, he denounced the rich but amassed a huge fortune of his own; while censuring the extravagance of others, he possessed, among many other things, '500 tables of citrus wood with legs of ivory, all identically alike', upon which he served banquets. Dio Cassius also accuses Seneca of licentiousness, including taking delight 'in boys past their prime, a practice he also taught Nero to follow' (Introduction to 'On the Shortness of Life', p. 8). Writing some 1900 years later (1975), F. H. Sandbach declares, 'It is hard for the Englishman of today to approach Seneca with sympathy.' Perhaps more important for 'the Englishman of today' than liking boys who were too old – after all, he is more likely to be upset by those who like boys too young – is the fact that Seneca acquiesced in crimes that culminated in matricide, and that his sudden calling in of loans which he had made to the powerful in Britain helped precipitate the revolt of Boudicca.

The evidence against Seneca is not entirely reliable, but undoubtedly he was much more ambivalent towards worldly success and wealth than his philosophy suggests. Certainly he was miserable in exile. And this has caused a real problem for his readers, from contemporaries of his, right through to the present. It strikes me that both the hypocrisy and the inconsistency that critics find in Seneca, rather than discrediting the philosophy, are one of the most engaging things about it. There is a memorable passage in Tacitus describing the exchange between Nero and Seneca when the latter asked to be allowed to retire. Life at court had become too dangerous, and Seneca was becoming too compromised. His enemies were gaining power. It is an exchange imbued with the indirection of *realpolitik*. Seneca flatters Nero and expresses himself full of gratitude for the wealth bestowed upon him by the Emperor, but he feels that now it is time to resign that wealth because it is becoming the object of censure; whereas Nero can

tower above the passions of ill-designing men; I am open to their attacks; I stand in need of protection . . . Life is a state of warfare; it is a long campaign, in which a man of years, sinking under a load of cares, and even by his riches made obnoxious, may crave leave to retire.

Nero will have none of it. Though equally flattering, he tells Seneca, in effect: You helped make me what I am, and if you leave me now I will be vulnerable to censure, even disgrace and ruin; so I still need you. Tacitus adds:

To this flattering speech Nero added fond embraces, and all the external marks of affection. Inclined by nature to disguise his sentiments, and by habit exercised in the arts of dissimulation, he knew how to hide under the surface of friendship the malice of his heart.

The subtext of Nero's reply to Seneca is surely this: You the philosopher give me the tyrant respectability; that was the deal, and there's no going back on it now. He is also telling Seneca that he (Seneca) is too steeped in the machinations of power to back out now. With a vicious irony, Nero refuses Seneca's request to retire with a dissimulating eloquence born, he says, of Seneca's own 'care and instruction' (Tacitus, I.446−8).

If Seneca's description of the malaise of the human condition is unrivalled, his advice on how to survive it has more often than not been found unpersuasive,[18] probably because he was never as convinced as he pretends. His advice about the need to withdraw into the self, and his claim that philosophy is the true way of happiness, may have stemmed as much from the need to sustain his role as sage as from his beliefs. But there is another aspect to all this, namely Seneca's realism, the more chilling for being uncynical. He sometimes promises a transcendence of suffering, desire and loss, but he only ever really gives a strategy for their partial diminution through reason, to be supplemented by sustained repression of that part of them – the major part – which remains. Freedom lies not in the possibility of radical renunciation, but in the rational effort of partial control. He exalts the role of reason and philosophy, but in the end his own philosophy suffers from the limitation which he attributes to those who would proceed by that specious 'verbal' kind of philosophy which he vehemently opposed: 'they do not abolish the passions in this way; they only moderate them' (*Epistulae Morales*, II.287). In practice, for Seneca, reason is far more the instrument of repression than of freedom.

This is apparent in the letter where he reproves a correspondent, Lucilius, for his restless travelling. It reveals, says Seneca, an unsteady spirit, 'and the spirit cannot through retirement grow into unity unless it has ceased from its inquisitiveness and its wanderings. To be able to hold your spirit in check, you must first stop the runaway flight of the body' and 'lay aside . . . desire'. The past must be consigned to oblivion; one's eyes must 'unlearn' what they have seen. Travelling awakens desire and will 'bring back your old cravings'. This, for Seneca, is disastrous, since even a whole lifetime properly dedicated to the suppression of desire and the welcoming of death is insufficient to accomplish the task (II.53–5).

Seneca never accomplished it. He exchanged one social position for another, to the end remaining in thrall to his reputation and his audiences. His theatrical death says as much. But what kept him a victim of desire and of the social was an uncynical realism which knew the attraction of death. Seneca's preoccupation with death, his insistence that we should at all times be ready to die, is offered as a philosophy of life, of how to live well. Yet, when he tells us that without the will to die no one can have the will to live, and that to avoid fear of death one must think of it constantly, we sense a desire for, or at least a fascination with, death. His readiness to condone suicide is a case in point. He welcomes the fact that death is so easy. Suicide is not only a way of escaping a life which is intolerable, but more importantly a way to escape the hold that others have over you; it is an assertion of human freedom: 'the best thing which eternal law ever ordained was that it allowed to us one entrance into life, but many exits' (Epistles LXX, 'On the Proper Time to Slip the Cable', II.57–73, and LXXVII, 'On Taking One's Own Life', II.169–81). Seneca describes a 'lovely dream' in which 'I was already weary of myself, beginning already to despise the fragments of my shattered existence, and feeling that I was destined to pass over into that infinity of time and the heritage of eternity' (III.169). According to J. M. Rist, Seneca abandons the older Stoic view that life and death are equally matters of indifference: 'Fundamentally Seneca's wise man is in love with death. He is looking for a tolerable pretext to die' (p. 249).

Marcus Aurelius: the seduction of oblivion

Increasingly in the Western philosophical tradition, mutability comes to involve a profound experience of loss which inflects everything, including our very identity – our essence or lack of it. Freud wrote of an encounter with a famous poet afflicted with an 'aching despondency' at life's mutability: everything seemed beyond enjoyment because always on the edge of oblivion. That the beauty around him, 'like all human beauty, and all the beauty and splendour that men have created or may create', was 'fated to extinction' meant that it became 'shorn of its worth by the transience which was its doom' (below, Chapter 14).

Whereas for this poet mutability and transience were the problem, for ancient philosophers like the Stoic Marcus Aurelius (AD 121–80) they were, in a sense, the solution. Marcus Aurelius, who has been described as the last Stoic, builds a whole philosophy of life upon the perception and the acceptance of, even the yearning for, oblivion. He seemingly regards mutability and loss with complete equanimity. It's true that this is in part because of a belief in the ultimate unity of nature (*Meditations*, IV.40ff; VII.9, 19), the sustaining power of 'inwardness', and the importance of living virtuously – that is, in accord with 'truth and justice' (VI.47). But these beliefs are hardly the comforting ones of Christianity – there is no anthropomorphic projection, no insistence on immortality or an afterlife of any kind. The real consolation seems to be oblivion itself. We live for an instant, only to be swallowed in 'complete forgetfulness and the void of infinite time on this side of us and on that' (IV.3).

Marcus Aurelius repeatedly invites contemplation of the lives of those now dead, not with the aim of historical empathy, but to meditate on their insignificance in order to gain a historical and existential indication of one's own. He sees transience in the struggle of daily life – 'think how many ere now, after passing their life in implacable enmity, suspicion, hatred . . . are now dead and burnt to ashes' (IV.3). No matter how powerful they were, nothing, but nothing, of these people now remains, and even the memory of them will soon evaporate. Not even legend is immortal; it too sinks into 'absolute oblivion' (IV.32, 33; VI.37). The life of each of us is always almost over, and our name will survive not at all or only for a while, and even then as 'a far off echo' (II.6; V.33). In a little while we will have forgotten all the world, and the world us (VII.21). Nowhere before this is the ephemeral, transient nature of life so extensively discerned:

Of the life of man the duration is but a point, its substance streaming away, its perception dim, the fabric of the entire body prone to decay, and the soul a vortex, and fortune incalculable, and fame uncertain. In a word all things of the body are as a river, and the things of the soul as a dream and a vapour; and life is a warfare and a pilgrim's sojourn, and fame after death is only forgetfulness. (II.17)

The essence of the universe is mutability: everything existing 'is already disintegrating and changing . . . everything is by nature made but to die' (X.18). This means that we too are in perpetual transformation and decay, and that each change is a kind of death (IX.19, 21), and everything that now exists is, in its dissolution, the seed of that which will eventually exist (IV.36). Crucially, there is no evil in change (II.17; IV.42), but the fact of perpetual change requires us to scorn everything that is mortal (IX.28), and its study is 'conducive to greatness of mind', including the commitment to 'justice in all present acts and contentment with [our] present lot' (X.11). The length of one's life is irrelevant: 'For look at the yawning gulf of Time behind thee, and before thee at another Infinity to come. In this Eternity the life of a baby of three days and the life of a Nestor of three centuries are as one' (IV.50). To desire is to be permanently disappointed and disturbed, since everything we desire in this world is 'empty and corrupt and paltry' (XI.11; V.33).

Death is the release from, among other things, 'the swayings of desire' (VI.28). Further, 'The act of dying too is one of the acts of life', and 'The fate of all things' is to be 'either etherealized into the Universal Substance, if that indeed be one, or dispersed abroad' (VI.2, 4). Death is a dissolution, a return to a state of undifferentiation so complete that those who 'gaze upon the ruins of time will be buried under them'; it is also a release, and a good (IX.33; VI.28, XII.23, 35), and 'it is no more a hardship for the coffer to be broken up than it was for it to be fitted together' (VII.23). Whereas birth is a combination of the elements, death is a dispersal of them; even the soul does not outlast the body, but lasts only for a while before being changed and diffused (IV.5, 21). Repeatedly Marcus Aurelius remarks that either the universe is controlled by a providence, in which case 'you can suffer nothing', or it is not, in which case you might as well be rid of it:

Either a medley and a tangled web, and a dispersion abroad, or a unity and a plan and a Providence. If the former, why should I even wish to abide in such a randon welter and chaos? Why care for anything else than to turn again to the dust at last? Why be disquieted? For, do what I will, the dispersion must overtake me. But, if the latter, I bow in reverence, my feet are on the rock, and I put my trust in the Power that rules. (VI.10; cf. II.11, IX.39)

Virtually everything else that Marcus Aurelius says supports the first of these possibilities: the rock of trust – even trust itself – is as transient as everything else.

Yet from all this Marcus Aurelius derives a philosophy of inner detachment and virtue. To a modern reader this can seem strange: nothing endures, yet there is a principle of reason governing the universe. And the rational virtue that man is urged to seek has no support beyond the very self which is fleeting and unreal and inadequate to the task. Even more perplexing is that with Marcus Aurelius we again confront the remarkable fact that this is a philosophy of renunciation written from the centre of events. Seneca was an emperor's right-hand man; Marcus Aurelius was an emperor whose *Meditations* were probably written during the last years of his life, when he was confronted with a series of disasters, including plague and insurrection, and engaged in constant military struggles and the persecution of Christians. The *Meditations* were possibly not even intended to be read by anyone else. This philosophy of detachment and virtue, this insistence on the insignificance of worldly affairs, did not diminish the apparent need for the military action and the persecution. To the extent that the inner detachment generates a different and superior perspective on the world – a kind of indifference – it could be regarded as an attitude not only compatible with the brutalities occurring in the world, but also sanctioning them. We find this increasingly in later centuries: an attitude which prima facie entails renunciation actually coexists with and reinforces a culture of quest and domination.

2

'All Words Fail through Weariness': Ecclesiastes

Perhaps the most hauntingly lyrical of all meditations on the interweaving of death, desire and mutability is Ecclesiastes. Its main theme is the transience and futility of human endeavour: 'I have seen all the works that are done under the sun; and behold, all *is* vanity and vexation of spirit' (1:14, AV).[1] In the Ecclesiastes of the Authorized Version of the Bible, the word 'vanity' recurs around forty times. It has become *the* word to express that welding together in one experience of transience and futility. The Hebrew word is *hébel*, which means vapour – that which is unsubstantial, momentary and profitless, fleeting as a breath, and amounting to nothing:

The traditional translation 'Vanity of vanities, all is vanity', can be freely expanded to read: 'Everything in life is hollow and utterly futile; it is the thinnest of vapors, fleeting as a breath, and amounts to nothing.' (Scott, p. 202)

Often *hébel* is conjoined with the phrase 'grasping at the wind': again inanimate nature, even as it becomes the breath of life, epitomizes futility.

Human life passes 'like a shadow' (6:12, Scott).[2] Not only human life, but all animate things dissolve into an oblivion which is confirmed in the larger natural order, not only in its long-term effects but in its ever-present moment; it is as if the writer can hear oblivion in the wind and see it in the rivers:

Blowing toward the south and veering toward the north, ever circling goes the wind, returning upon its tracks. All the rivers flow continually to the sea, but the sea does not become full; whither the rivers flow, they continue to flow. All words fail through weariness, a man becomes speechless; the eye cannot see it all, nor the ear hear the end of it. (1:6–8, Scott)

For us, more than two millennia later, our horizons of oblivion have extended; now they are thought of in terms of the truly incomprehensible: cosmic distance and cosmic time, the silent spaces between the stars. Yet we still hear oblivion in the monotony of the wind, and without ever hearing the end of it. This is not a romantic view of inanimate nature (that is, a view of nature as that with which mind or spirit might correspond or merge); nor is it about finding in natural continuity the quasi-religious reassurance of an eternity in mutability. The romantic sensibility will at times try to tame this sense of nature as oblivion, only to find it re-emerging inside itself. This sense also remains significant in formative (and very different) modernist texts. At the risk of another jarring juxtaposition, I again want to glance forward, briefly.

Hearing the wind

Shelley in 'On Love' remarks that when feeling alienated from human kind we turn to inanimate nature for solace; then the sound of the wind and of rivers is profoundly inspiriting: 'in the motion of the very leaves of spring in the blue air there is then found a secret correspondence with our heart. There is eloquence in the tongueless wind and a melody in the flowing of brooks.' These things, by some 'inconceivable relation to something within the soul, awaken the spirits to a dance of breathless rapture, and bring tears of mysterious tenderness to the eyes' (p. 861). But often mysticism finds, at the heart of the transcendence it craves, not the life source so much as stasis, unity and oblivion. And some of the greatest romantic – and modernist – literature is about the failure or absence of this desired correspondence with nature, and a feeling of alienation not dissimilar to that found in Ecclesiastes. Shelley's own *Adonais* is an invitation to death, as in a very different way are the 'rioting invasion of soundless life' that Conrad's Marlow encounters in Africa (below, Chapter 10) and the mutability which Virginia Woolf evokes in *To the Lighthouse*:

In spring the garden urns, casually filled with wind-blown plants, were gay as ever. Violets came and daffodils. But the stillness and the brightness of the day were as strange as the chaos and tumult of night, with the trees standing there, and the flowers standing there, looking before them, looking up, yet beholding nothing, eyeless, and so terrible. (p. 147)

The section of the novel in which these lines occur, 'Time Passes', is one of the most powerful evocations of inanimate nature – the blindness behind the beauty, the silence inside the movement, 'the fertility, the insensibility of nature' (p. 150). This is not a godless nature; it is far beyond that. Darkness descends, and the sea cannot be distinguished from the land. The lights are extinguished, and with 'a thin rain drumming on the roof a down-pouring of immense darkness began', unhurriedly but exhaustively dissolving all material forms and human identities. On the beach in this darkness the sleepless will find no harmony with nature; *contra* Shelley, there is nothing here to make 'the world reflect the compass of the soul' (p. 140). The noise of the rain and the surf speak only silence. Residual human activity is insignificant: Mr Carmichael stays up longer than the others, reading Virgil. Finally he too puts out the light; nearby, Mrs Ramsay dies. The house is closed up, the weeks turn to months and 'the silence . . . week after week, in the empty room, wove into itself the falling cries of birds, ships hooting, the drone and hum of the fields, a dog's bark, a man's shout': 'Only the Lighthouse beam entered the rooms for a moment, sent its sudden stare over bed and wall in the darkness of winter' (pp. 141–2, 150). Years later the house is opened up again; those who have survived return, but still they are surrounded by the silence of inanimate nature which seems the louder inside the human habitat, inside the walls that would keep it out (p. 155).

From its own time onwards Ecclesiastes has been regarded as one of the most heretical books in the Bible. Certainly it diverges quite radically from, and even repudiates, some of the fundamental tenets of other biblical writers, most notable the idea of a divine purpose revealed to man. In Ecclesiastes God is unknowable, and the insistence that 'there is nothing new under the sun' (1:9, Scott) would seem to preclude the idea of divine providence, or at least providential intervention. It is as if an inscrutable God has deliberately created a universe devoid of himself; one in which there is no discernible moral law, and where eternity is ultimately the darkness of death and, more immediately, the permanent, restless yet monotonous movement of inanimate nature, whose immense scale only emphasizes the brevity and insubstantiality of human life. For these reasons alone the inclusion of Ecclesiastes in the canons of Judaism and of Christianity has long been regarded as inexplicable.

It was probably written around 250 BC, and possibly by more than one writer, although it is generally agreed that the main part of the text was written by someone called Qoheleth (about whom little is known). Some inconsistency in the text may be due to later editorial interventions by others, intended to counter Qoheleth's more extreme statements. Some scholars have detected the influence of Greek philosophy, but even if this is so, it would only have been indirect. Its more obvious sources include the so-called wisdom movement of the Near East, whose literature has fascinating similarities to yet much older Egyptian and Mesopotamian thought.

One strand of this movement broods on the meaning of life, especially as revealed in the fact of undeserved suffering, and inclines towards a radical, pessimistic questioning of cultural and religious orthodoxy – such as is found in Ecclesiastes and Job. We discern in this movement something like the death-wish, if by that is meant a desire not to be alive. Ecclesiastes declares that the dead are more fortunate than the living, and he who has not yet been born is still more fortunate (4:2–3). A stillborn child is better off than one who lives in misery:

Though its coming is futile and it departs in darkness, though its name is hidden in darkness and it has no burial place; though it never saw the sun nor knew anything – it rests more peacefully than he. (6:4–5, Scott)

This compares with Job's cry:

Why died I not from the womb? . . . For now I should have lain still and been quiet. I should have slept: then had I been at rest, With kings and counsellers of the earth, which built desolate places for themselves . . . there the weary be at rest . . . *There* the prisoners rest together; they hear not the voice of the oppressor. The small and great are there; and the servant *is* free from his master. (3:11–19)

And both Ecclesiastes and Job echo a much earlier text in the wisdom tradition, called 'A Dispute over Suicide'. This is thought to date from the end of the third millennium BC (Pritchard), which means that the death-wish perhaps found cultural expression at least four thousand years ago.

Another point worth nothing is that the period to which 'A Dispute over Suicide' is attributed, between the Old and Middle Kingdoms, was an especially disturbed one, when established values had broken down. The work, part of which is missing, laments the collapse of all social values and the alienating isolation of the individual which results; a recurring refrain is 'To whom can I speak today?' The speaker is weary of his life and debates with his soul whether he should end it:

> Death is in my sight today
>> Like the odour of myrrh
>> Like sitting under an awning on a breezy day.
> Death is in my sight today
>> Like the odour of lotus blossoms,
>> Like sitting on the bank of drunkenness.
> Death is in my sight today
>> Like the *passing away* of rain,
>> Like the return of men to their houses from an expedition.
> Death is in my sight today
>> Like the clearing of the sky,
>> Like a man *fowling thereby* for what he knew not.
> Death is in my sight today
>> Like the longing of a man to see his house (again),
>> After he has spent many years held in captivity.
>
>> (Pritchard, p. 407)[3]

Returning to Ecclesiastes, we also find something anticipating the impossibility or futility of desire – that sense that our wants are intrinsically incapable of satisfaction – epitomized in the descriptions of men who labour endlessly but who cannot be satisfied with their riches, or who have everything but can enjoy nothing (4:8; 6:2). Qoheleth tells us that he too has amassed silver and gold, built houses, gardens and parks, possessed more cattle than anyone else, and purchased slaves. He became greater than anyone else, even to being able to have anything he desired. But all this was 'futility and a grasping at the wind' (2:11, Scott). In short, 'He that loveth silver shall not be satisfied with silver; nor he that loveth abundance with increase'; man's wants 'are never satisfied' (5:10, AV; 6:7, Scott). Death is the great leveller (2:16).

The positive notes in Ecclesiastes add up to a resigned, undefiant, form of *carpe diem* which will be echoed by non-religious or agnostic writers through the centuries: true wisdom recognizes that 'For with more wisdom comes more worry, and he who adds to his knowledge adds to his pain' (1:18, Scott); true wisdom leads one back to the simple things in life, which one then ceases to take for granted and understands properly for the first time. Be grateful for being alive, no matter how briefly; enjoy the pleasures of life, even though they are outnumbered by sorrow (11:7–10). In short: 'eat and drink and be happy' for tomorrow we will die (8:15, Scott).

Ecclesiastes accepts life without understanding it. And work too: satisfaction can be found in it, not from the profit it brings, but simply in the doing of it (3:13). But this commitment to work is definitely not praxis: that is, optimistic, energetic engagement in order to change things fundamentally. Qoheleth is fatalistic, both metaphysically and socially. Nothing can be changed, not even – especially not – social injustice. In this respect it is important to note that Qoheleth does not, like some other biblical writers (e.g. Isaiah), identify with the oppressed. His social fatalism may be a corollary of his general philosophy, but we can legitimately speculate with Scott that it is also a consequence of the fact that Qoheleth 'was one of the leisured beneficiaries of the social system' (p. 200), who, as we saw, once sought happiness in wealth and excess (2:1–11). Again we are led to reflect on the fact that the philosophical meditation on death frequently occurs not only in times of acute crisis, but also among those who are privileged educationally, economically and in other respects. Time and again the benefits of privilege – wealth, property, power, pleasure – will be attacked as *especially* worthless; less often will they be given up. Seneca, as we saw earlier, is only one of the most notorious cases in point, and a reminder that it is in the nature of privilege that it takes itself for granted, even when under attack from itself.

At the end of Ecclesiastes is the familiar paradox of *carpe diem* literature: on the one hand, we must live spontaneously in the here and now, forgetful of future oblivion; on the other, to live fully in the here and now we must remember impending oblivion. Yet for some, including the poet and the philosopher, to remember oblivion is to be tormented by it – even to the point of being unable to live. Hence the attraction of those who live spontaneously. Youth and spontaneity are attractive to those who lack both; they come to be revered from the position of irrevocable loss. In Ecclesiastes we are told to be happy 'remembering that the days of darkness will be many, and what lies ahead is oblivion', and a young man is invoked and urged to revel spontaneously in his youth: 'Banish care from your mind . . . for dark-haired youth is fleeting.' But then, immediately, 'In the days of your youth, remember your grave.' This line marks the beginning of the remarkable poem which ends Ecclesiastes, which can see the present only in relation to its passing, which looks into the bustle of the living moment only to see future death and loss: 'The pitcher shattered at the spring, / And the water wheel broken at the cistern' (12:6, Scott).

3

Escaping Desire: Christianity, Gnosticism and Buddhism

By the time of the early Christian ascetics, mutability has become savage; now, inextricably bound up with sin, it is the active agent of death, which is now located firmly *inside* desire.

A secular repudiation of the Christian idea of sin has resulted in a secular misunderstanding of it, and a failure to realize the extent to which the psychology of sin, far from being cast off with the religion which invented it, still informs contemporary culture. The underlying significance of sin in Western culture is a paradoxical one: the concept of sin becomes culturally prominent as human beings begin to take responsibility for what they cannot, as well as what they can, control; there is a sense in which the idea of sin, even at its most abject, is hubristic. When the innocent submit to guilt and remorse, they can strangely empower and energize themselves through the very abjection which is also the expression of their impotence.

In recent times the Christian association of sex, sin and death has been most visible in the fundamentalist claim that AIDS is God's or nature's way of taking revenge upon the supposed sinfulness and unnaturalness of homosexuality. But it would be wrong to assume this is Christianity's only legacy. There is another – one which is more theological and searching, which addresses the experience of desire's impossibility, and which remains the more active in 'secular' culture for being largely unrecognized. In fact, whereas the strident fundamentalist belief in death and illness as punishment for sin is irrelevant if not meaningless to most people living today, this other, more obscure, Christian sense of desire's impossibility speaks strangely, disturbingly, to many.

For the early Christian Fathers there are three interrelated aspects

43

of the impossibility of desire: the vicious intimacy of desire with death, its experience as loss and lack, and the fact that it is beyond fulfilment. These are woven together in a vision which drives death into the heart of desire, and intensifies the perverse and paradoxical dynamic binding the two. The crucial idea behind all this is that death enters life with the Fall. More exactly, it enters the world with sin and transgression (Genesis 3:16–19; Romans 5:12); as Aquinas puts it in *Summa Theologiae*, not only is death the punishment for sin, but sin is the cause of death and of the disunity of human nature. Sin removed the 'original justice' which integrated the human subject, physically and spiritually. Without that justice 'not only did human nature suffer in the soul by disorder among [its] powers, but because of the body's disorder, it became subject likewise to corruption' (Aquinas, p. 452). Desire – and especially sexual desire – is at the heart of this disorder. Sexuality comes with, or as a consequence of, death, as does the conflicted divide between the sexes (sexual difference), and even marriage, in the sense that marriage is necessitated by death and even perpetuates it; in the words of John Chrysostom (*c.* 347–407): 'marriage . . . springs from disobedience, from a curse, from death. For where death is, there is marriage' (p. 22).

'Marriage', writes Ton H. C. Van Eijk, is 'the farthest degree of alienation from paradisiac life' (p. 230). Van Eijk has summarized texts originating in a gnosticizing milieu in which marriage and desire 'are nearly exclusively linked with death'. In The Gospel of the Egyptians, for example, is the same idea that to procreate is to nourish death. To abstain from procreation is to hasten the end of the world and so defeat death. Typically it is woman who is held responsible for perpetuating death, directly so by giving birth to that which must die, but also symbolically in that the world and desire might be described as female (pp. 209, 216–17). The more orthodox Christian view is that marriage, the institution of procreation, is connected with death mainly in that it is necessitated by it; death enters life at the Fall, and procreation compensates for it, both in the sense that the dead are replaced, but also in that procreation becomes a more than functional consolation for mortality.

For Gregory of Nyssa (*c.* 335–*c.* 394) nature deceives us as to the tragedy of life. We all know and experience the evils of life, yet we allow nature to delude us into underestimating their significance. Most especially a 'smouldering grief' haunts even – especially – the supreme advantages of life – wealth, youth, affection, glory, power, renown and more (p. 13). This grief is not merely what we feel when these joys end, as of course they must; rather, joy actually produces and intensifies this grief. There is the treachery and hatred which one person's happiness arouses in others. But that's not the point; in fact, Gregory is prepared to assume for the sake of his argument that such treachery and hatred do not arise, since they are irrelevant to the fact that, for the happy,

the very sweetness of their life is the fomenting of their grief. For as long as men, these mortal and perishable creatures, exist and look upon the tombs of those from whom they came into being, they have grief inseparably joined to their lives even if they take little notice of it. (p. 14)

Death eternally 'dissipates our present joy'. And if we could foresee the future, 'how frequent would be the race of deserters from marriage to virginity!' We would see beauty, wealth, power persist for a short time only.

And nor do these joys merely fade; more tormenting is the way they unstably mutate into their own opposites. This occurs because, through mutability, death is at work in life, 'everywhere fastening itself upon each of our pleasures' (pp. 14, 27). The bridegroom beholds his beloved only to shudder at the realization of her mortality and to realize that her beauty must come to nothing. And this realization is ever-present – a vivid, tormenting sense of the skull beneath the skin: 'in place of what he now beholds there will be bones, disgusting and ugly, with no trace, no reminder, no remains of this present blossoming'. In childbirth, what dominates is not the birth of the child but the fear of either the child's or the mother's death. And, if both mother and child are fortunate enough to live, there is the special heartache caused by a child's own vulnerability in life – a heartache which the mother feels more than anyone. And then there is the grief of the bride who loses her husband – a grief which includes 'a longing for death, which often increases to the point of death itself'. The only way to escape the evil of death 'is not to attach oneself to anything changeable' (pp. 14–17, 27).

John Chrysostom also dwells on the misery of the mother who suffers herself the misfortunes which befall her family – 'her husband, her children . . . her children's wives and children. The more the root spreads out into more shoots, the more its cares abound' (p. 90). More generally, 'the fear for the living that always unsettles the soul is no less than the grief for the dead'. In fact it is more severe, since time soothes one's grief for the dead, but anxiety for the living 'must either exist constantly or end in death alone' (p. 90).

It is therefore without hesitation or apology that Gregory declares:

the bodily procreation of children . . . is more an embarking upon death than upon life . . . Corruption has its beginning in birth and those who refrain from procreation through virginity themselves bring about a cancellation of death by preventing it from advancing further because of them . . . they keep death from going forward . . . Virginity is stronger than death . . . The unceasing succession of destruction and dying . . . is interrupted. Death, you see, was never able to be idle while human birth was going on in marriage. (pp. 48–9)

In life, desire, sexuality and even sexual difference are, for Gregory, what permit death to thrive. Therefore, to renounce them, especially through virginity, is to achieve a state in which 'the power of death is somehow shattered and destroyed'. The goal of true virginity is a freedom from death and mutability in order to be able to see God (pp. 42, 49). Again, the grief of which Gregory speaks is not merely the consequence of joy eluding us or coming to an end; rather it is the experience of joy itself which has actually produced and intensifies this grief: 'the very sweetness of their life is the fomenting of their grief'. Again, death is seen not simply as eventual demise, but as a devastating, living mutability which overdetermines life with a terrible sense of loss, and does so even or especially before anything has actually *been* lost.

Modern readers may recoil in dismay, even anger, from this kind of pessimism. But it is too easy to dismiss Christian sexual renunciation as a squeamish, pathological or neurotic attitude to the body long since overcome in our own enlightened and secular times. It was not a fastidious puritanism on the question of sex that motivated Gregory and his like, and they sought not the repression of the sexual drive *as such*, but rather to be released from the ravaging effects of death, mutability and time both *on* desire and *as* desire: these things at once engender desire and render it impossible. As Peter Brown reminds us in *The Body and Society*, death and mutability were starkly present at that time: this was a society 'more helplessly exposed to death than is even the most afflicted underdeveloped country in the modern world'; for the population of the Roman empire to remain even stationary it appears that each woman would have had to bear an average of five children. And nor were the early Christians concerned solely with the attempt to maximize control over the body (something also apparent in our own time, though pursued by different and more varied means). On the contrary, sexual renunciation promised resurrection, the abundance of peace which only the freedom from desire can afford, and the prospect that 'even the rigid boundaries between the sexes might trickle away in the liquid gold of a "spiritual" body'. In short it constituted 'a heroic and sustained attempt . . . to map out the horizons of human freedom. The light of a great hope of future transformation glowed behind even the most austere statements of the ascetic position.' And ascetic preaching threatened to overturn the traditional structures of urban society; it was perceived as endangering the institutions of slavery and of private wealth, denying the subjection of women, and obliterating social distinctions: 'women and slaves would appear dressed alike, their social status and their sex obliterated by a common dress'. Further, 'for young males . . . to meditate sexual renunciation was to meditate social extinction' (Brown, pp. 286–8, 298, 442). To dismiss these aspects of early Christian history as entirely due to a squeamish attitude to the body is just ignorant. Without doubt, these early Christians were, in their own way, sexually as well as socially dissident[1] – something lost in the bland apologetics of modern Christianity.

Drawing death from our origin: Augustine

In Augustine (354–430) we encounter an account of desire and death which is as severe as it is paradoxical. The human subject is somehow made responsible for a contradictory injunction from God:

Then it was said to man: 'Thou shalt die if thou sin'; now it is said to the martyr: 'Die to avoid sin.' Then: 'If you break My laws, you shall die'; now: 'If you refuse to die, you break My laws.' That which we feared then if we offended, we must now choose, not to offend ... Then did sin purchase death, and now death purchases righteousness ... (*City of God*, trans. Healey, 13.4)

Chapter 11 of Book 13 of *The City of God* is entitled 'Whether One may be Living and Dead both Together' – a consideration introduced by the previous chapter's contention that mortal life might rather be called death than life, since 'Our whole life is nothing but a course unto death.' This is not death as culminating event: we are just as close to death now as we are tomorrow or next year, because 'every man [is] *in* death as soon as ever he is conceived' (my emphasis). Death is in process every day, every hour, every minute, pervading life as the principle of mutability, and it 'is so grievous unto us, as neither tongue can tell nor reason avoid' (13.11).

Death infects desire because it was born in the transgressive passion of our first parents. God warned Adam that if he ate of the forbidden fruit 'thou shalt surely die' (Genesis 2:17). Adam did eat, of course, and this 'concupiscential disobedience' henceforth bound man 'to death by necessity' (*City of God*, 13.3); he became the slave to death. Augustine is relentless in driving the point home: death, he says, is 'propagated' by man. Death and sexual desire are inseparable, and they ravage mankind because of the sins of our first parents. For the rest of history, for all subsequent generations, this first transgression leads the flesh to contend forever against the spirit, 'and with this contention are we all born, *drawing death from our origin*', and we experience both that conflict and the pain of death *as* desire. Augustine leaves no room for doubt: death, mortality and desire infected the human semen which then existed, and they remain in it from generation to generation (13.13–14; my emphasis).

Furthermore, transgressive desire is a state of anarchy which generates the perpetual undoing of the self: Adam's first transgression meant that the soul forsakes God, this being the first death; but the soul also enters into a struggle with the flesh, a revolt through sexual lust which is experienced as a self-undoing which is another kind of death. Sexual pleasure 'assumes power not only over the whole body, and not only from outside, but also internally; it disturbs the whole man ... So intense is the pleasure that when it reaches its climax there is an almost total extinction of mental alertness; the intellectual sentries, as it were, are overwhelmed' (14.16).

Such is the radical, fallen mutability of desire, epitomized in the 'unclean motion of the generative parts', in disorderly and ugly movements – especially the unruly male erection:

The motion will be sometimes importunate against his will, and sometimes immovable when it is desired, and being fervent in the mind, yet will be frozen in the body. Thus wondrously does this lust fail man ... sometimes resisting the restraint of the whole mind, and sometimes opposing itself by being wholly in the mind and in no way in the body at the same time. (14.16)

Desire is not only 'totally opposed to the mind's control, [but] quite often divided against itself' (14.16, trans. Bettenson). This was paramount for Augustine; sexual desire is a form of helplessness, a terrible, impossible craving that consumes and reduces the subject to misery. The modern reader who finds Augustine's theology alien or reprehensible may yet recognize the experience of mutability which impelled him to it:

wretched is every soul bound by the love of perishable things; he is torn asunder when he loses them, *and then he feels the wretchedness, which was there even before he lost them.* (4.6; my emphasis)

For the last twelve years of his life Augustine engaged in a bitter dispute with Julian of Eclanum, defending his own severe interpretation of the Fall against the latter's more benign views. Augustine reiterated the fundamental point: death and sexual desire are forms of punishment which man brought upon himself. Neither is 'natural'. Original sin changed the nature of nature itself. All are affected, all guilty. The human condition is helpless and miserable, ravaged by death and desire, yet we remain quintessentially responsible. We cannot choose but to suffer in our desires, and die, but it is our fault. Julian of Eclanum felt that this account undermined the belief that the world which God created is essentially good, and that man, even in his fallen condition, remains a part of a positive and innocent natural order – albeit one which includes death and sexual desire – and also that man retains free will.

Augustine won the argument and, as Elaine Pagels points out in her account of this dispute, his views not only became the dominant influence on Western Christianity, both Catholic and Protestant, but deeply influenced Western culture, Christian or not, and most particularly in its attitudes to suffering, death and desire (pp. xxvi–xxvii; Chapter 6 *passim*). In effect Augustine was arguing that human beings are incapable of self-government; the ravages of death, desire and sin generally are too great. The growing acceptance of his view coincided with Christianity ceasing to be a persecuted movement and becoming the official religion of authorities governing vast and diffuse populations. And yet, as Pagels also remarks, the requirements of an authoritarian state for ideological means of social control cannot explain the subsequent survival and influence of these views: 'were it not that people often *would rather feel guilty than helpless* ... I suspect the idea of original sin would not have survived the fifth century' (p. 146). Of course it did, along with the acute sense of life itself as a form of death. Calvin, one of the most influential figures in the Protestant reformation which so profoundly shaped modern European culture, is, if anything, even more emphatic than the early Church Fathers. Because human desire is a permanent source of misery, he says in his *Institutes* (1536), and because residence in the world is 'but immersion in death', we must 'ardently long for death, and constantly meditate upon it' (III.ix.4).

The cause of death is love: Gnosticism

Existing alongside the official Christian Church, but also infiltrating, influencing and challenging it, was Gnosticism. Its adherents believed that the material world was created by an evil demiurge and must be rejected; the body itself was regarded as a kind of grave, a corpse endowed with sense; a precondition for uniting with a divine source of knowledge or *gnosis* is that we escape from this fabric of ignorance, this support of wickedness, this bondage of corruption, this cloak of darkness, this living death, this sensate corpse, this tomb you carry around with you . . . (*Hermetica*, Tractate VII; in Grant, p. 224)

Such a view of the body and mortal existence generally meant that redemption in this world was impossible. This led to unorthodoxy, especially in morality, where freedom from conventional behaviour was claimed, and deliberate transgression was sometimes advanced.

The treatise called *Poimandres* (probably dating from the second century) offers a version of the death/desire connection rather different from anything encountered so far. It presents primal man as dual in nature, both mortal and immortal. This is because a divine creation was followed by a fall into nature. Mind, 'which is God, being both male and female . . . gave birth to a man like himself'. But man broke free of the realm of mind and reason, inclining towards the lower world of nature, and revealing to that world, in the form of himself, the beauty of God. Having beheld 'the never satiating beauty of [man]', seeing his 'wonderfully beautiful form reflected in the water, and his shadow on the earth', Nature fell in love. Man, having seen in Nature 'this form like himself, reflected in the water', reciprocated. Thereafter man, unlike all other creatures of earth, is of a dual nature – immortal because of his origins, mortal because of his descent into nature: 'though he is superior to the framework, he has become a slave in it'. He is immortal because of his control over all things, mortal because subject to destiny (*Poimandres*, in Grant, pp. 213–14). Here, apparently, is a precursor of the Narcissus myth. Hans Jonas comments:

the revealing of [man's] divine form from on high to terrestrial Nature is at the same time its mirroring in the lower elements, and by his own beauty thus appearing to him from below he is drawn downward. (p. 161)

Also apparent in this idea of a fall into nature through image-reflection is the Gnostic dialectic between Light and Darkness, itself very suggestive for the death/desire dialectic. Jonas finds three characteristic ideas here: first, the Darkness becomes enamoured of the Light and gets possession of a part of it; second, the Light becomes enamoured of the Darkness and voluntarily sinks into it; third, and most intriguingly, a ray of the Light is projected into the Darkness and is there held fast – the Light becomes trapped by the Darkness it illuminates.

Poimandres declares that man was also 'created male and female because of his derivation from the bisexual Father' (Grant, p. 214). Eventually, however, this bisexual unity, and indeed 'the bond uniting all things', was broken by God. The text continues:

For all living creatures, previously bisexual, were parted, as was man; they became on the one hand male, on the other female. At once God spoke by a holy word [*Logos*], 'Increase and multiply, all creatures and creations, and let him who has a mind recognize himself as immortal, *and know that the cause of death is love*, and know all the things that exist.' (p. 215; my emphasis)

'And know that the cause of death is love' – originally the love which drew man into his affair with Nature. Eros, which is not only sexual love, but worldly desire more generally, ensnares man in the world while not itself being exclusively of the world, also belonging to the sphere of darkness and death. Here is a Gnostic, largely non-Christian version of the inflection of desire by death, and of the former's impossibility: 'he who has loved the body, which comes from the deceit of love, remains wandering in the darkness, suffering in his senses the things of death'. The body also derives from 'that abhorrent darkness . . . by which death is nourished'. To the man who submits to it, desire proves self-destructive; such a man 'does not cease having a desire for his limitless appetites, insatiably fighting in the dark, and this torments him and increases the fire upon him' (pp. 216–17).

There are similarities here with Aristophanes' myth in *The Symposium* and the Christian narrative of the Fall. First, there is the transition from unity to division; second, in relation to that division, the experience of desire as loss and absence and the compulsion to reunite; third, desire as the perpetuation of loss, and even (or especially) of death. Having said that, no account of such remote philosophies should underestimate their strangeness for the modern Western reader. Reading them now is sometimes to experience the uncanny in an almost Freudian sense – that is, to encounter something more or less strange yet somehow also obscurely familiar. This is especially so with Gnosticism and Buddhism, but also with some of the Greeks, and the early Christian writers. It is also the case that what we encounter here are not origins or direct influences in the sense of ideas which can be confidently identified as embryonic for later forms; nor is it a matter of confidently retracing a process of development. Philosophies like Gnosticism exist in the region of a past horizon, which is to say a horizon we cannot get back to and which becomes ever more distant.

Such horizons mark a limit of what we can see and know. The only thing we can say for certain about them is that there is something beyond them which we can never reach. So when I talk of 'Western culture' I do not mean a bounded entity culturally distinct from other cultural entities adjacent or prior to it, but something with shifting horizons, shifting limits perceived hesitantly and distantly from inside rather than confidently from without. Often we know that there were once routes across to what is now perceived as different and alien. Maybe they just ceased to be used, or they may have been violently closed. Whatever, let us not sentimentalize the past by assuming peaceful and harmonious coexistence; human wars have done the work of time in advance, and cultural interaction has always involved cultural struggle. Somewhat similarly, ideas are not the sole invention of individuals. Even the most seemingly original and important writers are often rearticulating ideas already circulating within their culture, responding, but also contributing, to cultural changes which bring those ideas into renewed prominence. Individual writers are the focus for something that existed before them but which they rearticulate in ways which have profound, inestimable effects upon the subsequent history of thought. Again, the process has often been violent, or at the very least has involved appropriation, suppression and distortion.

The illusion of the self: Buddhism

If, as recent research suggests, Gnosticism was more influential in the ancient world that was once thought,[2] it is also possible that Gnosticism may itself have been influenced by Buddhism. Certainly there are similarities – especially in the conviction that desire or craving is the fundamental cause of suffering in a radically mutable world. At the same time, Buddhism's differences from Western Christianity are equally, if not more, significant – not least concerning the self, sin and striving.

Siddhartha Gautama (560–477 BC) was a prince who, because of his high privilege, encountered suffering and death relatively late in life. Legend tells us that when he did eventually encounter them the trauma was the greater, and changed his life: he became Buddha, the Enlightened One. In the religion he founded, life is experienced as a permanent intrinsic unsatisfactoriness manifested as suffering (*dukkha*) and pain:

birth is painful, old age is painful, sickness is painful, death is painful, sorrow, lamentation, dejection, and despair are painful. Contact with unpleasant things is painful, not getting what one wishes is painful. In short the five groups of grasping [the elements, *skandhas*, which make up a person] are painful. ('Sermon at Benares', in Burtt, p. 30)

Everything about life involves suffering and dissatisfaction, a sense of lack. If we strive to overcome that lack we fail, and suffering becomes marked by a renewed craving, now intensified by an acute sense of loss. Suffering derives directly from the fact that *everything* that exists is radically mutable. In particular, happiness, if it is achieved, cannot last. Suffering haunts happiness from the outside and the inside. Where Buddhism differs from Western religions is in the full acceptance of mutability; happiness lies in achieving that acceptance.

Suffering is perpetuated by, and inseparable from, ignorance, and mitigated by wisdom. The deepest ignorance is to fail to see, or to disavow, the fact that everything that exists is mutable and transient. The force of this position may be seen, again, in contrast with Christianity; for the Buddhist the source of suffering is ignorance rather than sin. And the real source of suffering is desire (*kama*) or craving (*tanha*, literally 'thirst'), both of which are intrinsic to, constitutive of, humankind.

There is a Buddhist doctrine of 'conditioned arising' or 'dependent origination' which asserts that everything that exists is dependent on certain prevailing conditions; nothing is intrinsically self-sufficient, independent or stable. This is especially true of selfhood. Buddhism completely denies the idea of a transcendent or autonomous self so powerful in Western religion and philosophy. To believe that there is some essential inner self or consciousness which is the real me, ultimately identifiable apart from everything that happens to me, is an illusion:

What we call a personality is just an individual stream of becoming; a cross-section of it at any given moment in an aggregate of the five *skandhas* which (as long as it continues) are in unstable and unceasing interaction with each other. (p. 86)

There is no 'I'. Even to believe in an 'I' which possesses emotions (albeit helplessly) is mistaken. One of the problems with desire, and why it cannot make us happy, is that it presupposes a self which does not exist; at the core of our being we are empty. Everything that constitutes the individual is marked by the unsatisfactoriness and suffering which is *dukkha*. Nor is there such a thing as the soul. The person is only a fleeting series of discontinuous states held together by desire, by craving. When desire is extinguished the person is dissolved. Since life and suffering are synonymous, the extinction of desire is the goal of human endeavour. Until that happens we continue to exist through a series of rebirths. It is not death as such which is deplored, but rebirth; it is not death but rebirth which we must escape. So much so that in some early texts rebirth is described as 'redeath'. Desire perpetuates life, which is synonymous with suffering, and which leads to death. Desire perpetuates death; it keeps one dying.

The self is merged with ultimate reality not by identifying the core of the self (soul/essence) with ultimate reality (God/the universal) but by extinguishing self into non-being (nirvana). This is the aspect of Buddhism which has fascinated Western philosophers like Schopenhauer and artists like Wagner; with whatever degree of misinterpretation, they have been drawn by the ideas of empowerment through renunciation, nullification and quiescence; of the apparent ability to move freely with the mutability and change which are the apparent cause of suffering; of choosing freely not to pursue the illusion of freedom, in a sense to eliminate the illusion of self; of becoming discontinuous, mindless. Not to escape mutability but to become it; not to just go with the flow of endless change, but to become it. To achieve the state of nirvana – that is, a state of being which is essentially empty of desire and striving. The wisdom of Buddhism does not desire to transcend change or to affirm an essential ultimate relationship of self to the absolute and unchanging (Platonic forms, the Christian God); nor does the Buddhist desire to die or to cease to be (the death drive): he or she does not desire annihilation but rather learns how to cease desiring. Nirvana is the utter cessation of desire or craving; it means extinction.

II

MUTABILITY,
MELANCHOLY AND QUEST:
THE RENAISSANCE

4

Fatal Confusions: Sex and Death in Early Modern Culture

To know how to live one must first know how to die. This, one of the recurring existential themes of the Western philosophical tradition, is already, by the early modern period, an inherited idea. But it is also most memorably expressed at that time.

Now one learns how to live by a profound meditation upon death, and even a renunciation of the very desire to live. But in that resignation there may be a kind of affirmation deriving from the acceptance of insignificance; death is understood as a material reality which levels social distinction by dissolving and obliterating all traces of human culture, or rather by reducing them to the most enduringly insignificant trace of all: dust. In this sense death is *the* reality principle, and meditation upon it reduces the individual to that silence which is our destiny, which signifies our insignificance while alive, and which is always materialized in the very immobility of the death's head itself. Provisional silence is the precondition of the meditative act, and a deeper silence is also its objective. And the death's head remains there still: reminding of life's brevity, but perhaps for that same reason being also the focus of a melancholy wonder at being alive at all.

Meditation, however, is both about getting things clear and about losing the distracted, obsessive self which, increasingly in Western culture, was the presupposition of getting anything clear. Which is one reason why we could never remain silent for long: we had to speak, or write, the meditation. Nevertheless, this still occurred with respect to the silence, just as lone individuals praying urgently whispered their message to God in the silence of the church, or the preacher declaims his message above that silence. Only the silence remains, in the transcendent stasis of stained-glass figures irradiated by light; most supremely in the divinely immobile, ecstatic image of Christ on the cross, whose pain promised eventual peace in redemption, the peace that passes all understanding, the peace of zero tension, the ultimate silence. But the speaking about death (epitomized, as we shall see, in John Donne declaiming in St Paul's against the dying life even as he is literally dying himself) moves increasingly centre stage.

All this contrasts greatly with attitudes prevalent in our own times – although some of these can be traced back to this period. The philosopher Francis Bacon (1561–1626), who was also Lord Chancellor under James I, wrote an essay 'Of Death' which treats its subject casually, even perfunctorily. He considers that philosophers have tended to make too much of death – especially the Stoics, who 'by their great preparations made it appear more fearful' (p. 41). To a great extent, says Bacon, death is man's creation. In tone the essay is rationalist, even proto-Enlightenment; Bacon wants to demystify death. Perhaps we can also detect here that attitude which, according to some, leads to a 'denial' of death in modern life (below, Chapter 8). Whatever, Bacon was a significant exception. For other writers, death could never be considered too much.

Sir Thomas More, in 'The Four Last Things', dwells on death with the aim of renouncing desire. He gives voice to that early modern concern to try to feel death 'on the pulse'. Nothing, says More, more effectively withdraws the soul from the 'wretched affections of the body than may the remembrance of death' – providing, that is, we 'remember it not hoverly [inattentively], as one heareth a word and let it pass by his ear, without any receiving of the sentence [meaning] into his heart'. Language deceives even, or especially, as it means. We must not only 'hear this word "death" but also let sink into our hearts the very fantasy and deep imagination thereof'. And nor are visual representations of death adequate (More had in mind the graphic 'Dance of Death'). The task is to introspect death, to discover that 'deep conceived fantasy of death in [one's] nature, by the lively imagination graven in thine own heart'. Only then do we realize that life is a kind of death, or rather 'one continual dying' (pp. 467–8).

Montaigne

The essays of Montaigne (1533–92) freely confess an obsession with death. In his memorably entitled essay 'That to Philosophize is to Learn how to Die' (*c.* 1572) he announces, perhaps proudly and certainly without apology, 'Since my earliest days, there is nothing with which I have occupied my mind more than with images of death'; if anything this preoccupation was greatest in 'the most licentious season of my life'.[1] This essay is indebted not just to Seneca but also to other classical sources, especially Cicero and Lucretius, and shifts between different registers. In one place Montaigne asks, after Lucretius, 'Why should we fear to lose a thing which once lost cannot be regretted?'; yet a page later he is preoccupied with a severe sense of death-in-life. Thus, citing Manilius ('Even in birth we die; the end is there from the start'), he adds, again after Lucretius, 'Death is the condition of your creation . . . The constant work of your life is to build death. You are in death while you are in life . . . during life you are dying' (*Complete Essays*, pp. 60, 64, 65).[2]

In a later essay, 'Of Physiognomy', the emphasis is modified. Whereas Montaigne had previously paraphrased Cicero approvingly ('to philosophize is nothing else but to prepare for death'), in the later essay (*c.* 1585) the paraphrase is different ('*The whole life of a philosopher is a meditation on death*'), as is Montaigne's gloss on it: now, to anticipate death too obsessively is to detract from life (pp. 56, 805). Even more significant is that the severest formulation of all in the earlier essay – 'the goal of our career is death. It is the necessary object of our aim' (p. 57) – is repudiated in the later essay: 'death is indeed the end, but not therefore the goal, of life; it is its finish, its extremity, but not therefore its object. Life should be an aim unto itself . . .' (p. 805). Correspondingly, whereas the earlier essay's contention that death is the aim of life might be seen as an uncanny anticipation of Freud's death drive, encapsulated in 1919 in his proposition that 'The aim of all life is death' (below, Chapter 14), Montaigne's later repudiation of that proposition could also be read as a repudiation of that drive ('Life should be an aim unto itself').

The difference would appear to be decisive. Jacques Choron, for example, detects here a shift from a stoical attitude to 'the new Renaissance spirit', something 'distinctively modern in its vigorous affirmation of life and resolute turning away from the preoccupation with and preparation for death' (*Death and Western Thought*, p. 98). In fact my invocation of Freud is misleading, and there is less difference between the earlier and later essays than those like Choron would have us believe; in certain respects the tendency of the earlier essay is the same as the later: it is all about how to come to terms with death in order to be able to live. This is not just a question of learning to live *with* death, or of embracing the Senecan proposition that those who do not have the will to die do not have the will to live; it is also a question of regarding death in a way which rehabilitates not *life* so much as living, the process of quotidian existence. Montaigne put this most memorably when he wrote, 'I want death to find me planting my cabbages, but careless of death, and still more of my unfinished garden' (p. 62). In resignation there is a kind of affirmation which it takes a lifetime to discover. Montaigne's attitude of a wise, moderately enabling resignation remains significant in subsequent centuries, but, as we shall see in later chapters, other, more pessimistic, views have been and continue to be more culturally formative.

Eros and thanatos: Ariès and de Rougemont

> But thy delight is death, and blood thou only desirest,
> Therefore bring me to death, take living blood from Amintas,
> For my delight is death; death only desireth Amintas.
> (Abraham Fraunce, *Lamentations*, 11.108–10)

Choron identifies the new Renaissance spirit in terms of a vigorous affirmation of life and the turning away from an older preoccupation with death. Notoriously, though, the Renaissance was also when eros and thanatos began to be associated in new and disturbing ways, from Nicolas Deutsch's *Death and the Young Woman* (1517), which depicts a decaying corpse having sex with a young woman, to Shakespeare's apparently more restrained (yet, as we'll see, no less disturbing, albeit in subtler ways) story of the erotic death of Romeo and Juliet.

Philippe Ariès, the most significant recent historian of death, dates the disturbing association of thanatos and eros from the sixteenth century. From then until the eighteenth century they are associated with increasing degrees of intensity. He describes it as a major phenomenon, but with little explanation as to why it occurred. Indeed, he proposes not to analyse it in detail since it occurred less in 'the world of real, acted-out events' than 'in the obscure and extravagant world of phantasms' and 'the depths of the unconscious'; consequently, 'the historian studying it ought to transform himself into a psychoanalyst' (*Western Attitudes*, p. 56; *Hour*, pp. 369, 393). Elsewhere he finds that, from the beginning of the sixteenth century onwards, not only sexuality but violence and fear invade a domain in which life and death have become inseparable:

Until the seventeenth century, the two concepts of death and life with all their respective associations were kept separate. Subsequently, they destroyed and encroached upon each other. Life was now impregnated with death. Today we refer to taboos when we might more correctly speak of saturation. (*Images*, pp. 176, 211; cf. *Hour*, pp. 369–74)

Eroticism and violence are also inseparable, the first being an aspect of the second, as in the torments of the martyrs (*Images*, pp. 180, 210; *Hour*, pp. 372–3). Ariès finds here an unconscious manifestation of 'that blend of love and death, pleasure and pain, that will later be called sadism'; it gives rise to macabre eroticism (*Hour*, pp. 370, 373). A preoccupation with necrophilia emerges at the end of the eighteenth century and the start of the nineteenth: 'the beautiful young corpse now acquired in the aesthetic sensibility a place reminiscent of that of the young ephebe in Hellenistic culture' (*Images*, p. 210).

Ariès is more descriptive than analytic; often he does not explain the changes he charts. Which means that the increasing connection of sex and death remains perplexing and mainly significant as a manifestation of the psychic and spiritual unhealth of modern man. Ariès's preference is for the attitudes to death allegedly found in the earlier ages (below, Chapter 8).

A more suggestive account of the death/desire convergence is Denis de Rougemont's 1940 study *Love in the Western World*. For de Rougemont, passionate love in the Western tradition is a perversion and/or displacement of religion, even a hubristic surrogate religion seeking spiritual transcendence where it cannot be found, namely in human sexual desire. What it finds instead is an inversion of such transcendence – i.e. death. This, essentially, is the impossibility at the heart of desire. And one does not have to accept his own intransigent and often reductive analysis, nor indeed his own religious investment (agape over eros), to see truth in this.

He regards the medieval *Tristan and Iseult* story as a founding representation of the inherent perversity of a certain kind of desire or 'archetypal anguish'. This story is at once a legend, a romance and a myth – 'a kind of archetype of our most complex feelings of unrest'. De Rougemont also finds here the greatest European myth of adultery (pp. 301, 18). Tristan and Iseult are in an ecstatically contradictory position because they

do not love one another. They say they don't and everything goes to prove it. *What they love is love and being in love* ... What they need is not one another's presence, but one another's absence. *Thus the partings of the lovers are dictated by their passion itself.*

Parting is an obstruction, and the passion of the two lovers creates such obstructions because these are what it really wants. And behind this desire for obstruction is nothing less than the desire for death, which passion ultimately serves:

The love of love itself has concealed a far more awful passion, a desire altogether unavowable, something that could only be 'betrayed' by means of symbols such as that of the drawn sword and that of perilous chastity. Unawares and in spite of themselves, the lovers have never had but one desire, the desire for death! . . . In the innermost recesses of their hearts they have been obeying the fatal dictates of a wish for death; they have been in the throes of *the active passion of Darkness.* (pp. 40, 43, 44, 47, 48; de Rougemont's emphasis)

De Rougemont traces the origins of this desire for death to heretical religious movements of Eastern origin, notably the Cathars in the twelfth century. Whereas orthodox mysticism of that time was an especially effective discipline for transcending passionate love, heretical mysticism enabled a fatal crossing and confusion between the divinizing eros and sexual passion (pp. 145, 178–9).

For de Rougemont, the history of passionate love in all great literature from the thirteenth century to the present is the history of the secularization of this crossing and confusion, of the tragic and more and more desperate attempts of eros 'to take the place of mystical transcendence by means of emotional intensity'.[3] Crucially, the modern cult of passion is a secularized, obsessive repetition of 'a spiritual heresy *the key to which we have lost*' (p. 145; my emphasis). De Rougemont suggests yet another originating and reinforcing factor in the myth: both passion and the longing for death which it involves connect with the Western idea that the individual reaches self-awareness in suffering, and on the verge of death; in Western culture, suffering and understanding are inextricably connected; in romanticism, suffering – especially the suffering of love – operates as a privileged mode of understanding (pp. 53–4).

He attributes to the passionate-love myth an interesting social structure and function, especially in its original form. Culture at once expresses and conceals the fact that the secret objective of this love is death or self-annihilation; it conceals it by expressing it. Indeed it is the function of myth to do just this: to provide a disguised or obscure expression of what can no longer be said openly. Typically the expression will conform to socially acceptable conventions – here, in the romance, chivalry is the convention – in order to explore an antisocial content. Passionate love is also shrouded in contradiction: emotionally we desire it, yet ethically and rationally we deplore it. The myth, and not least its obscurity, allows us to live the contradiction without actually confronting it (pp. 21–4). Extending his argument to culture more generally, de Rougemont suggests that today we desire passion and its paradoxically annihilating consequences, but only on condition that we do not have to admit it. This paradoxical interanimation of passion and death is the secret which Europe has at once repressed and preserved (pp. 16, 52–3).[4] What all this means is that the Tristan myth, which has been agitating us for eight hundred years, is inextricably cultural and libidinal, at one and the same time 'a passion sprung from dark nature, an energy excited by the mind, and a pre-established potentiality in search of the coercion that shall intensify it' (p. 24).[5] In de Rougemont's account, mysticism is not, as others (especially psychoanalysts) contend, a sublimated expression of sexuality, but vice versa (p. 149).

Even as he is sensitive to the dynamics of desire, de Rougemont wants to save it and the world (or myth and culture, at least) from its degenerate forms.[6] As in a different way is Ariès's history of death, de Rougemont's account of the death/desire dynamic is also a theory of history, and a narrative of historical decline and the errors of modernity.

The courtly-love myth, he argues, was formed when the ruling caste was striving to establish social and moral order; the myth precisely contained 'the surges of the destructive instinct' (p. 23) – that is, it allowed it expression, but within a structure which limited its damaging effects. The '*social function* of the sacred myth of courtly love . . . was to order and purify the lawless forces of passion. Its transcendental mysticism secretly directed the yearnings of distressed mankind to the next world, and concentrated them there' (p. 251). But as the social bonds subsequently slackened, or the social group disintegrated, so the myth degenerated: the passion it once contained now spread out into everyday life and invaded the subconscious, where it 'invoked, or if necessary invented, new compulsions' (pp. 23–4). It found its apotheosis in Wagner's *Tristan and Isolde* – a work which restored the mislaid significance of the legend in all its virulence, and which, contrary to popular opinion, does not glorify sensual desire. On the contrary, its 'melodies in their distressing morbidity disclose a world in which carnal desire has become no more than an ultimate and impure apathy of souls in process of curing themselves of life' (p. 243).

Subsequently the myth ceases to be a form of social cohesion and becomes an instrument of lawless violence, a fallen myth, and the more dangerous for being so; antisocial and 'anti-vital forces long dammed up by the myth' are unleashed, and there occurs a severance of the bonds holding society together. In its austere original form, the myth of passionate love expresses desire controlled, more or less; in its subsequent profane forms, desire is out of control, and increasingly so since '*it has been our dramatic luck to have opposed passion with weapons foredoomed to foster it*' (p. 333).[7] All this is potentially catastrophic: de Rougemont claims that the gradual profanation of the myth can be traced not only in literature but also in European warfare and its methods: 'Like passion, the taste for war follows on a notion that life should be ardent, a notion which is the mask of a wish for death' (p. 331). As he revised the book (1956) it seemed possible that the world was on the brink of total atomic war (pp. vi, 253, 286 and Book V, 'Love and War', *passim*). As the myth of passionate love permeates downwards, a crisis of cultural order ensues, most acutely in the institution of marriage upon which the social order rests. The myth is especially 'vulgarized and popularized' in poetry and the middle-class novel (pp. 245–7).

De Rougemont recognizes something profoundly important about the death/desire convergence, only to foreclose on its analysis with a moralizing and reductive critique of modernity. As we shall see, he is not alone in this. His account of the Tristan myth in earlier periods has also been questioned. Irving Singer argues persuasively that de Rougemont not only misrepresents the nature of courtly love, but misleadingly confuses it with romantic love; also, that he erroneously conflates the medieval and the modern versions of the Tristan legend. Singer claims too that de Rougemont overestimates the death/desire connection in Western culture. For Singer this connection, expressed as *Liebestod*, is really only developed in the last two hundred years, although occasionally foreshadowed in earlier times. Thus de Rougemont 'has arbitrarily forced the vast complexity of Western ideas about love into constraining categories drawn from the last two centuries. He has interpreted humanistic thinking about passion as if it all derived from a single type of romanticism' (*The Nature of Love*, Vol. 2, esp. pp. x–xi, 28, 77, 114, 298–9). However, Singer himself is so committed to an affirmative humanistic attitude which sees love as an 'ideal completion of life rather than a search or secret hungering for death' (p. xi) that he in turn disregards the extent, as well as the different forms, of the pre-romantic preoccupation with the death/desire dynamic.

Mutability as death in life

Crucial to the death/desire convergence, and something largely ignored by de Rougemont, was an intensified preoccupation with the oldest of themes: mutability. Increasingly in the early modern period it is regarded as an instability which simultaneously disintegrates and drives both the world and the self. This is partly, as John Kerrigan suggests, because of the invention of mechanical time, of the clock.[8] And yet the preoccupation was already there. If we think of the surrealist's stopped clock, at once explicable, melancholy and utterly mysterious, it seems modern; and so it is. But it is also evoking the mesmerizing stillness of its antecedent, the sundial, which, precisely because it had no moving parts to stop, conveyed all the more powerfully the same sense of death *in* time; as Shakespeare put it, 'Thou by thy dial's shady stealth mayst know / Time's thievish progress to eternity' (Sonnet 77). Regarded metaphysically, the clock, with moving hands, and which ticks, is different only in that its stillness and silence are the louder, the more relentless. This image of stillness within movement – elsewhere, of course, a metaphor for eternity – is here, in the sundial and the clock, an image of death as immanent within life.[9]

This immanence of death preoccupied many early modern writers, and in a way which rendered equanimity such as Montaigne's difficult if not impossible. At heart the problem is mutability. Of the rose, so persistently invoked in the mutability tradition, George Herbert says, with fine economy, 'Thy root is ever in its grave, / And thou must die' ('Virtue'). The source of life is always already the place of death. Others write eloquently of the temptation to turn to pleasure as a way of drowning this apprehension of death. But, because it is itself subject to mutability, pleasure becomes a kind of death in itself:

Punish not thyself with pleasure . . . the race of delight is short, and pleasures have mutable faces. The pleasures of one age are not pleasures in another, and their lives fall short of our own. Even in our sensual days, the strength of delight is in its seldomness or rarity, and sting in its satiety: mediocrity is its life, and immoderacy its confusion. (Sir Thomas Browne, 'Christian Morals', pp. 221–2)

Perhaps happiness rather than pleasure is the way. But the problem here is twofold. Happiness too is mutable; because it is an event within life itself, it inevitably leads to adversity – it might even be said that happiness produces adversity – since *'fortune lays the plot of our adversities in the foundation of our felicities'*. Adversity is to felicity as death is to life: latent within it. Further, 'since in the highest felicities there lieth a capacity of the lowest miseries, she hath this advantage from our happiness to make us truly miserable: for to become acutely miserable we are to be first happy' (p. 231; my emphasis). For Browne all this is tolerable because there is still design in adversity: 'All things began in order, so shall they end, and so shall they begin again; according to the ordainer of order and mystical mathematics of the city of heaven' ('Garden of Cyrus', in Craik, p. 328). So here the voice of melancholy is also a voice of moderation. For Browne the contemplation of death is ideally an obedient praxis, a practical wisdom. Again, learning how to die is learning how to live.

For other writers desire is so wracked by mutability it becomes the agent of death. Sexual ecstasy might itself be a kind of death – an obliteration of identity, of self. For Shakespeare's Troilus, even to anticipate sexual ecstasy is to expect death; this is a pleasure which is so 'subtle-potent' it obliterates sense and 'distinction', a 'swooning destruction', which enacts death:

> What will it be
> When that the wat'ry palates taste indeed
> Love's thrice repurèd nectar? Death, I fear me,
> Swooning destruction, or some joy too fine,
> Too subtle-potent, tuned too sharp in sweetness
> For the capacity of my ruder powers.
> I fear it much, and I do fear besides
> That I shall lose distinction in my joys . . .
> (*Troilus and Cressida*, III.ii.18ff.)

As Edmund Spenser warns in 'Two Cantos of Mutabilitie', 'thy decay thou seekst by thy desire' (VII.vii.59.3). Philip Sidney declares

'Leave me, O Love, which reachest but to dust' ('Leave me, O Love', l. 1; Williams, p. 174). Consider how, in this extraordinary line, 'Love' is both the beloved object *and* the poet-lover's desire: the beloved turns to dust, even or especially as she (or he) reaches for the poet, who in turn turns to dust in the self-same process. That's to say, not only do we decay, but desire hastens the process of decay: desire itself (re)turns us to dust; life, desire, are self-defeating aberrations: '*reachest but to dust*': *the embrace of love is itself a dynamic of self-dissolution.*

5

'Death's Incessant Motion'

John Donne's sense of tormenting contradictions at the heart of existence – 'to vex me contraries meet in one' (Holy Sonnets, XIX.1) – and his obsessive, energetic expression of this torment are at once idiosyncratic and representative. His preoccupation with the metaphysics of death, and his behaviour around his own anticipated death, has always fascinated his readers. He preached his most famous sermon, 'Death's Duell or, a Consolation to the Soule, against the Dying Life, and Living Death of the Body', when he was visibly dying. According to Izaak Walton's account, written in 1640, his congregation inferred that he was preaching his own funeral sermon and was, in a sense, dying for them, appearing as he did with 'a decayed body and a dying face' (p. 75). Two weeks before his death he covered himself in his winding-sheet and in that posture had his portrait painted and then hung by his bed. Finally, he adopted the position in which he would be buried – requiring, Walton tells us, 'not the least alteration' (p. 82).

Some twenty-three years earlier, when he was around thirty-seven, Donne had written *Biathanatos* (*c.* 1608), the first English defence of suicide or what he calls 'self-homicide'.[1] Equally remarkable, for the time, was that in the preface to that work he explicitly attributed its writing to his own susceptibility to a death-wish. This desire to die, and the consequent contemplation of suicide, he would experience 'whensoever any affliction assails me'. *Any* affliction:[2] here is a symptom of what was then called melancholia, now depression – a degree of distress disproportionate to the occasion, further instanced by the example which Donne gives in *Biathanatos* of Beza, a man 'eminent and illustrious, in the full glory and noon of learning', who wanted

71

to kill himself for no other reason than that he had scurf. It was, adds Donne, his own attraction to death which led him to empathize with those who succeed in taking their own lives, and to write in their defence (p. 39). Donne argues that suicide is universal among human kind: 'in all ages, in all places, upon all occasions, men of all conditions have affected it, and inclined to it'. His argument is that the desire to die is bred in us by nature, and confirmed by 'custom' (p. 78). In fact this desire is so natural that it actually flourishes where custom permits it. It is also widespread across cultures, and especially in Christian culture.

It has been remarked before that this anticipates Freud's theory of the death drive, but with the crucial proviso that Donne emphasizes not the desire for non-being suggested by Freud, but rather the opportunity which death affords of achieving the transcendence of self in the afterlife (p. liii – Introduction by Rudick and Battin). This is well said, but, as we shall shortly see in relation to Castiglione and William Drummond, the two things (annihilation of self/transcendence of self) are rarely distinct; the 'desire of supreme happiness in the next life by the loss of this' (p. 193) is inseparable from ceasing to desire, ceasing to be; the eternity promised by death is the eternal absence of desire, loss, division; it is the stasis of non-consciousness, 'that *one death*, the *final dissolution* of body and soul, the end of all' that Donne looks forward to in his final sermon (*Selected Prose*, p. 315).

Donne's attraction to death had different aspects. There was clearly a death-wish in the modern sense: 'If man knew the *gain of death*, the *ease of death*, he would solicit, he would provoke *death* to assist him, by any hand, which he might use.' Again: 'O who, if before he had a being, he could have sense of this misery, would buy a being here upon these conditions?' This could evolve into the aspiration to a religiously erotic annihilation and resurrection – 'that death of rapture, and of ecstasy [in which] . . . I shall find my self, and all my sins interred, and entombed in [Christ's] wounds . . .' (pp. 117, 125, 150). The image of Christ on the cross is crucial in Donne: Christ's Passion becomes a kind of paradigm of suicide (pp. 169–73); in the words of Donne's recent editors, it 'reveals the very incarnation of God to be in fact a suicide Himself' (*Biathanatos*, p. lxxx). According to Jorge Luis Borges, whereas Donne's avowed purpose in *Biathanatos* is to palliate suicide, his underlying aim is to indicate that Christ committed suicide. If this is so, Donne's indirection is understandable, since he would be saying in effect that, for Christianity, world history is organized around an act of self-destruction; Christ on the cross, supposedly the redemption of the world, becomes the death drive incarnate. Borges ends his essay with a reflection on the idea of Philipp Batz that 'we are fragments of a God who destroyed Himself at the beginning of time because he did not wish to exist. Universal history is the obscure agony of those fragments' (pp. 91–2).

In his own perverse way Donne theorized something like the death drive in the first of his *Paradoxes*, which is entitled 'That All Things Kill Themselves' and which begins:

To affect yea to effect their own deaths, all living things are importun'd. Not by Nature only which perfects them, but by Art and education which perfects her . . .

'Perfection': from the latin *perficere* – to accomplish, bring to an end; for Donne the perfection which living things aspire to is literally their end; death is even encoded in life's drive for perfection. This is a natural process, but, under the influence of art and education, 'so much the more early they climb to *this perfection, this Death*'. Further, 'if then the best things kill themselves soonest (for no perfection endures) and all things labour to this perfection, all travail to their own Death' (pp. 1–2; my emphasis).

There is another, equally paradoxical, aspect to this: when Donne, like so many other of his contemporaries, dwells on the ways things die and disappear – on how death literally *decomposes* in a way which is so incessant and systematic as to be almost purposeful – it is as if it is here, in the forces of disintegration rather than generation, that the real energies of the universe are at work.

'The everlasting flux of time'

In his last sermon Donne tells his congregation that the womb is not a place of life but a place of death from which we are delivered unto 'the manifold deaths of this *world*': we come from the mother's womb 'to *seek a grave*', and 'We celebrate our own funerals with cries, even at our birth; as though our *threescore and ten years of life* were spent in our mother's labour, and our circle made up in the first point thereof' (*Selected Prose*, pp. 312–13). Life is synonymous with dissatisfaction, the futility of desire, youth being spent in anticipation, old age in regret.

When Donne speaks of the 'Variable, and therefore miserable condition of Man', he is making the common assumption that mutability and misery imply each other. More urgently, life is conceived as a process of disintegration towards non-being. In a sermon of commemoration for Lady Danvers he imagines her in the grave, 'mouldering, and crumbling into less, and less dust, and so [with] some *motion*, though no *life*'. As he puts it elsewhere, even in the grave we have to endure still another death, that of '*corruption* and *putrefaction* and *vermiculation* [i.e. being infested or eaten by worms]'. And even as dust we remain in motion, 'such are the *revolutions* of the *graves*'; our dust will be mingled with that of the highway, of every dunghill, every puddle and pond, and this is 'the most deadly and peremptory *nullification* of man, that we can consider'. There can be no happiness inside the inverted eternity which is 'the everlasting flux of Time'. Time is 'but the *Measure of Motion*' and the condition of absence. Past and future are not – 'one is not, now, and the other is not yet' – while the present 'is not *now* the same that it was, when you began to call it so in the *Line*'. If then this '*Imaginary half-nothing, Time* be of the *Essence* of our *Happinesses*, how can they be thought *durable?*' Only with death will time be no more; in this sense death is a deliverance from death, since life is itself a series of movements '*from death* to *death*' (pp. 99, 285, 319, 131, 167, 311–12).

Hence the pervasive yearning for stasis – the more acute because the only fixity man knows, the only essence he possesses, is this misery of permanent mutability: 'Man hath no *centre* but *misery*; *there* and only *there*, he is *fixed*, and sure to find himself' (p. 133). And to be conscious of that misery is a kind of death, an agonized awareness of absence and deprivation. In one of his most famous poems, 'A nocturnall upon *S. Lucies* day, Being the shortest day', Donne expresses vividly the Renaissance sense of desire's impossibility, of being 'ruin'd' by love:

74

> I am re-begot
> Of absence, darkness, death; things which are not.
>
> . . . .
>
> I, by love's limbeck, am the grave
> Of all that's nothing.

The absence of a fixed centre – or rather the experience of the centre as metaphysical absence and disintegration – preoccupies Donne:

This is *Nature's nest of Boxes*; The Heavens contain the *Earth*, the *Earth*, *Cities*, *Cities*, *Men*. And all these are *Concentric*; the common *centre* to them all is *decay, ruine . . . Annihilation.*

Man is a fragile being, all the while disintegrating, decaying and melting. 'I find myself scattered, melted,' he declares in one sermon. He also invokes images, familiar at the time, which anticipate later notions of entropy:

the dust of dead kings is blown into the street, and the dust of the street blown into the River, and the muddy River tumbled into the Sea, and the sea remaundered [returned] into all the veins and channels of the earth . . .

In the *Devotions Upon Emergent Occasions* (1624) disease and fever become the images for this condition of 'everlasting dissolution, dispersion, dissipation' (*Selected Prose*, pp. 114, 102, 172).

The reason why this ruin is centrifugal, disintegrating outward from the centre of things, is because we were originally made of nothing: 'that which is not made of *Nothing* is not threatened with this annihilation' (p. 114). Man conspires with this inner tendency to dissolution in terms which again anticipate the Freudian death drive:

> We seem ambitious, God's whole work to undo;
> Of nothing he made us and we strive too,
> To bring ourselves to nothing back . . .
>   (*An Anatomie of the World*, ll. 155–7)

Human consciousness is not what enables one to transcend misery, but that which intensifies it. In the *Devotions* this is vividly expressed as hypochondria and melancholy, both of which exacerbate the sickness by anticipating it: 'we are not only *passive*, but *active*, in our own *ruin*'. Melancholy is especially self-destructive. Donne finds here an analogy with the state: 'as the *vapours* most pernicious to us, arise in our own bodies, so do the most dishonourable *rumours*, and those that wound a *State* most, arise at home' (*Selected Prose*, pp. 136, 118–19). Donne writes about mortality, disease and death from his sickbed, which, for a while at least, seemed to him as if it would be his deathbed too. It is here that his most celebrated lines occur. If they do indeed express that deep humanistic empathy which has been attributed to them, it is an empathy rooted in an obsessive preoccupation with one's own mortality and lack of self-sufficiency ('*Now, this Bell tolling softly for another, says to me, Thou must die*'):

No man is an *Island*, entire of itself; every man is a piece of the *Continent*, a part of the *main* . . . Any Man's death diminishes *me*, because I am involved in *Mankind*. (pp. 125–6)

What recurs in early modern writing is the sense of death not simply as the end of desire, nor simply its punishment; shockingly, perversely, death is itself the impossible dynamic of desire. And not just desire; life more generally is animated by the dynamic of death, as in another of George Herbert's brilliant images. He perhaps has in mind the way that dust or leaves collect in a corner, blown there by the eddying of the wind: 'this heap of dust; / To which the blast[3] of death's incessant motion, / . . . / Drives all at last' ('Church-monuments'). Here, energy and movement – ostensibly the essence of life – are more truly the dynamic of its dissolution, the incessant motion, the *driving* force of death.

For these writers, death does not merely end life but disorders and decays it from within; its force is indistinguishable from the life-force. Death is not merely an ending but an internal undoing. The most cosmic, most culturally necessary of all binary oppositions, life versus death, is thus subjected to collapse; the absolutely different is inseparable from what it is not, cannot be. The absolutely other is found to inhere within the self-same as nothing less than the dynamic of its dissolution. *Media in vita in morte.* That is why life is experienced as a living death; as Donne puts it, 'How much worse a death than death, is this life . . . !' (*Selected Prose*, p. 315). And all of this was already in a sense popular, in that the sense of death as paradoxically

vital, of evil somehow being more alive than good – wickedly alive –
had been reflected in the antics of the vice figure of medieval drama,
and of course in the 'Dance of Death'.

Cosmic decay

The early modern obsession with mutability found an extreme and
fascinating expression in the conviction that the universe was in a state
of chronic and irreversible decline. This idea was vividly expressed in
literature, philosophy and theology, which constitute a revealing
record of a melancholic obsession with impending disintegration.[4]
The most famous literary expression of decay is Donne's *An Anatomie
of the World*, where the symptoms of ineradicable decline include
failing energy and a desperate lack of harmony and symmetry:

> what form soe'er we see,
> Is discord, and rude incongruity.

This is accompanied by an acute sense of dislocation: 'as mankind,
so is the world's whole frame / Quite out of joint'. There is also a
conviction that we are suffering from an *inherent* corruption such
that the world has become 'rotten at the heart', and we who yet
survive in it suffer from 'Corruptions in our brains, in our hearts, /
Poisoning the fountains, whence our actions spring'. Above all is the
sense of social decline and disorder:

> 'Tis all in pieces, all coherence gone;
> All just supply, and all relation:
> Prince, subject, father, son, are things forgot . . .
> (ll. 323–4; 191–2; 243; 330–31; 213–15)

Likewise with Sir Walter Ralegh's expression of the idea in his
History of the World:

And as all things under the Sun have one time of strength, and another of
weakness, a youth and beauty, and then age and deformity: so Time itself
(under the deathful shade of whose wings all things decay and wither) hath
wasted and worn out that lively virtue of Nature in Man, and Beasts, and

Plants; yea, the Heavens themselves being of a most pure and cleansed matter shall wax old as a garment; and then much more the power generative in inferior Creatures . . . (p. 144)

As in Donne, the cosmic and the social are inseparable; Ralegh makes this observation in the context of a discussion about *social* degeneration of the present age, something which is a reflection of the larger cosmic decline, but also self-engendered: in education, child-rearing, early marriage, and 'above all things the exceeding luxuriousness of this gluttonous age' man is contributing to his own irreversible decline.

The entire debate about cosmic decay makes sense only in the context of the Fall, the human transgression that introduced death and mutability into the world. Unsurprisingly, biblical precedents were cited (Ralegh's reference above to the heavens waxing old like garments echoes Psalm 102, where it is said that the heavens 'shall perish . . . yea, all of them shall wax old like a garment'); but so too were very different versions of the idea, for example Book II of Lucretius' *The Nature of the Universe*. But from around the mid sixteenth century the idea takes greater hold in relation to the observations of those like Copernicus, Kepler and Galileo which suggested that the earth was not at rest at the centre of the universe, but in motion around the sun, and that the heavens, hitherto regarded as perfectly beyond the mutability and corruption of earthly things, were in fact also subject to the same forces. Mutability traumatically extended its domain – and in a way which seemed to threaten the very basis of theology and metaphysics.[5]

Mutability gives rise to the idea that life is a process of disordered, aberrant movement, and once again the cosmic and the social connect analogically: the problems of social mobility – especially masterless, vagrant men and errant women – epitomized the instability of the earth itself; all deviated from the metaphysical ideal of fixity.[6] In Spenser's *The Faerie Queene* we read of a world which is 'run quite out of square' and now grows 'daily worse and worse'; a world in which we find 'creatures from their course astray / Till they arrive at their last ruinous decay'. In the final unfinished ('unperfite') fragment of this vast poem the poet dreams of regaining perfect stasis, fixity and integration in

that same time when no more *Change* shall be,
But steadfast rest of all things firmly stayed
Upon the pillars of Eternity,
That is contrair to *Mutability*:
For, all that moveth, doth in *Change* delight:
But thence-forth all shall rest eternally

(V.proem, 1, 6; VIII.2)

Lovers who covet death: Castiglione's The Courtier

I have remarked before how mutability comes increasingly to be internalized – that is, experienced not just as the enemy of desire but also as its inner dynamic. This is a complex but crucial development which, as we shall see, affects the formation of identity and gender. Furthermore, in the religious writing of Donne, Wyatt and others, masochism can be seen to have its origins in this internalization of mutability.

In Book IV of Castiglione's *The Book of the Courtier* love is regarded as a form of blind longing. In the experience of physical desire – 'a very rebel against reason' – the soul is deceived by the senses into error and false opinion, especially in thinking that fulfilment lies in consummation (pp. 303–4). Not so: to think so is to be moved with 'false opinion by the longing of sense. Whereupon the pleasure that followeth it, is also false and of necessity full of errors.' In short, physical desire is impossible of fulfilment; it leads to loathing, and even hatred of the beloved; those who pursue this desire are inevitably obsessive; they are like the fevered who 'dream they drink of some clear spring' yet are never satisfied. This suggests why, despite the loathing and hatred, they are doomed to repeat the experience of desire's impossibility, 'and with the very same trouble which they felt at the first, they fall again into the raging and most burning thirst of the thing, that they hope in vain to possess perfectly'. Added to this, we are tempted to desire that which is deceptively beautiful – 'a certain lavish wantoness painted with dishonest flickerings' (pp. 304–5, 311).

Eventually, says Castiglione, to covet the beauty of another is only to covet one's own death:

These kind of lovers therefore love most unluckily, for either they never come by their covetings ... or else if they do ... they come by their hurt, and end their miseries with other greater miseries: for ... there is never other thing felt, but afflictions, torments, griefs, pining, travail ... [Their lot is] to be wan, vexed with continual tears and sighs, to live with a discontented mind, to be always dumb, or *to lament, to covet death* ... (p. 305; my emphasis)

The young are especially susceptible; some are led into such great error that they not only hurt the woman they love, 'But rid themselves out of their life' (p. 317).

None of this is the fault of beauty; all beauty is perfectly good; it derives from God and is like a circle, 'the goodness whereof is the Centre. And therefore, as there can be no circle without a centre, no more can beauty be without goodness' (pp. 308–9). But note how goodness is here associated with stasis; it is the (lifeless?) still centre of beauty. To the charge that some women and men who are beautiful are the more deceitful, proud and cruel for being so, and 'many times [the] cause of infinite evils in the world, hatred, war, mortality, and destruction, whereof the razing of Troye can be a good witness' (p. 308), Castiglione's narrator replies that it is not their beauty which makes them thus:

Neither yet ought beautiful women to bear the blame of that hatred, mortality, and destruction, which the unbridled appetites of men are the causes of ... Provocations of lovers, tokens, poverty, hope, deceits, fear, and a thousand other matters overcome [them]: and for these and like causes may also beautiful men become wicked. (p. 311)

By contrast (and here he is following Plato), the *rational* apprehension of beauty possesses it perfectly and leads eventually to a release from sensual desire's 'long wandering in vanity', taking us instead to the divine origin and end of all beauty, the 'innermost secrets of God', and a heavenly release from desire itself. In fact this transcendent desire entails a kind of death-wish, namely the wish for the death of desire itself, which is also, inevitably, a wish for the death of the self as currently known: 'there shall we find a most happy end for our desires, true rest for our travels, certain remedy for miseries'; there we shall 'hear the heavenly harmony so tunable, that no discord of passion take place any more in us' (pp. 306, 313, 321–2). The fantasy of desire absolutely realized is also the fantasy of oblivion: a release from, the complete annulment of, desire. And the impossibility of desire is now metaphysically inverted: in this heaven we will drink from the bottomless fountain of contentment 'that always doth delight, and never giveth fill'. Temporal death promises the ultimate release from – the eternal death of – desire. One at least in the narrator's audience is sceptical: such beauty, 'without the body, is a dream' (p. 307); another declares that love and reason are simply incompatible (pp. 307, 312).

For William Drummond, writing in 1619, death as complete oblivion is devoutly to be wished; it is 'the Thaw of all these vanities which the Frost of Life bindeth together' (p. 156). The inversion is apposite: life is a frost which binds; death the thaw. George Herbert uses the thaw/frost–life/death metaphor the other way around, and in the expression of a sentiment far removed from Drummond's:

> Grief melts away
> Like snow in May
> As if there were no such cold thing ...
> ('The Flower')

Herbert is re-experiencing life with the intense appreciation that comes when moving from the shadow of grief; Drummond wants to move from grief to the oblivion of death. Here is the death-wish in early modern form – that desire for a state in which humankind, in Drummond's words, 'nothing knows, and is of all unknown' (p. 160).

Death is a release of the soul into a heaven where there shall be 'an end without an end, Time shall finish ... Motion yielding unto Rest', this being 'the last of things wishable, the term and centre of all our Desires' (pp. 171, 165). Crucially, this is a fantasy of desire as *absolutely* realized in relation to the metaphysical concept of the absolute: that is, a God who does not desire. Desire implies lack, hence imperfection. To be eternal and hence non-mutable is also to be free of desire. Conversely, to be human is to be mutable and to desire. So the absolute object of desire is, experientially, a fantasy of the *absolute release from desire*, i.e. death of desire/death of self.[7] For Drummond, the yearning for undifferentiation is a desire both for non-being and for transcendence in metaphysical unity. Theologically there is here every difference in the world between non-being and God. Experientially there is not; we struggle towards eternal life from mundane life – the life of death – only to find this transcendence conceptualized in terms close to death: eternity, stasis, oblivion. For those like Drummond, the pain of death is allayed in and through an identification with death. Which is one reason why in Christianity the desire for death has to be regulated, sublimated and, in the form of suicide, demonized.

The futility of endeavour

If ignorance of the future is hardly bliss, but rather the source of intense anxiety, life may nevertheless depend on it. In the second part of Shakespeare's *Henry IV* the insomniac, beleaguered King asks sleep why it will not 'steep my senses in forgetfulness'. Lamenting the mutable world, he too discerns the way its destructive effects somehow seemingly tap an innate tendency to dissolution:

> O God, that one might read the book of fate,
> And see the revolution of the times
> Make mountains level, and the continent,
> Weary of solid firmness, melt itself
> Into the sea . . .

So corrosive is the process of time that to foresee it would rob even the most ardent youth of the desire to live:

> . . . how chance's mock,
> And changes fill the cup of alteration
> With divers liquors! O, if this were seen,
> The happiest youth, viewing his progress through,
> What perils past, what crosses to ensue,
> Would shut the book, and sit him down and die.

> (III.i.45–56)

Death inside life melts it into the sea or reduces it to dust. This is not only, perhaps not even mainly, a question of physical dissolution so much as the annihilation of significance and meaning consequent upon this manifestation of death being also the manifestation of life, or rather of *desire*; mutability saturates desire even as it facilitates death. The death-wish derives from such perceptions; often, as in Drummond and Castiglione, it is half submerged as the aspiration to transcendence; at other times it is more explicitly the seduction of oblivion, and the release from effort.

Typically the oblivion of death is compared to a deep sleep wherein we find freedom 'from those Vexations, Disasters, Contempts, Indignities, and many many Anguishes, unto which this Life is envassalled and made thrall' (Drummond, p. 153). But death is also a more perfect kind of sleep. It is exactly this idea that Despaire uses to tempt the Red Cross Knight in Spenser's *The Faerie Queene*. Here death also restores us to an *original* (innocent?) condition of 'eternal rest' which the living 'want and crave' but 'further from it daily wanderest'. The 'little pain' of dying 'brings long ease, / And lays the soul to sleep in quiet grave', just as 'Sleep after toil, port after stormy seas, / Ease after war, death after life does greatly please' (I.ix.40). Here, again, is the idea that somewhere inside consciousness is a regressive desire not just for death *per se* – the escape from consciousness – but for the oblivion of that more perfect state of non-being which preceded consciousness.

However, sleep also throws us into a condition which is the complete opposite of this deep forgetting: conscious and unconscious fears return in exaggerated, nightmarish form. Drummond's meditation on death from which I've been quoting was initially called 'A Midnight's Trance', because the writing of it was prompted by terrible dreams full of a strange mixture of apprehension, sorrow and horror (p. 147).[8]

Drummond's anxious dream, like Donne's impassioned denunciation of life, reveals something of the greatest significance, which is the subject of the next chapter: that when we continue the struggle for existence we do so because of being fragmented, unstable and death-ridden. Somehow the same condition which motivates the deeply regressive desire for oblivion is also the source of a restless dissatisfaction which keeps us moving forward, albeit reluctantly.

6

Death and Identity

Our nature consists in movement. Absolute stillness is death. (Pascal, *Pensées*, p. 126)

The preoccupation with death probably always involved problems of identity, but in the early modern period they became more acute. In the context of secure faith and a belief in an underlying order in Creation, the meditation on death might well arrive at a view of human identity as being essentially or ultimately coherent and unified, though not of course immediately so – not, that is, in the existential experience of self. Thomas Browne speaks of the importance of knowing oneself but also of the difficulty of doing so. Modern psycho-analysis might concur with his contention that 'the greatest imperfec-tion is in our inward sight . . . and while we are so sharp sighted as to look through others, to be invisible unto ourselves; for the inward eyes are more fallacious than the outward' (*Christian Morals*, p. 249).[1] There is also something proto-psychoanalytic about Browne's belief that our dreams may 'intimately tell us ourselves' in ways which conscious introspection cannot (*On Dreams*, p. 176; cf. *Letter to a Friend*, pp. 190–92). The revealing difference is, of course, that for Browne dreams tell us about our selves, rather than our unconscious. Freud's sense of the unconscious as being the place of our repressions, of our other selves (plural) and of forbidden desires which can wreck the socially organized ego, is not Browne's: 'Persons of radical integrity will not easily be perverted in their dreams' (*On Dreams*, p. 176). And, although he concedes that man is a conflicted being, living in 'divided and distinguished worlds', Browne nevertheless has faith in the possibilities of integrating the conflicting demands of, for example, faith and reason with those of passion and desire (*Religio Medici*, pp. 53, 34). He also believes that, in spite of bad dreams, inner division and the corruption of the world, one really can become who one truly is:

Though the world be histrionical, and most men live ironically, yet be thou what thou singly art, and personate only thyself. Swim smoothly in the stream of thy nature, and live but one man. To single hearts doubling is discruciating . . . He who counterfeiteth, acts a part; and is, as it were, out of himself . . . (*Christian Morals*, pp. 252–3)

Browne contains mutability within an ethical-religious perspective. Even so, he retains an acute sense of death in life, and of the potential instabilities in identity which this entails. Those who experienced these things in ways which could not be contained or resolved in Browne's terms were much more troubled. It is in Elizabethan and Jacobean drama that we find an exploration of identity in terms of what Browne calls its histrionical/ironic mode – that is, identity as necessitating the duplicitous opposite of an authentic, honest subjectivity. Time and again in such drama Browne's belief in the ultimate accessibility of true identity is repudiated.[2]

Mutable identities, or the heart 'ravel'd out in discontents'

Ideally, the integrity of the individual self derived from the unchangeable soul; it was that which protected one from the confusion of the social. In philosophical terms the soul was a substance – that which possessed properties without itself being a property. But repeatedly in the literature of this period the soul proved insubstantial, and mutability then became the shifting ground of identity.

The extent to which this was a topic of widespread cultural concern can be inferred from the satirical and facetious treatment it gets in John Marston's little-known yet interesting play *What You Will* (1601). A character called Lampatho sets out to discover the truth about the soul of man; he wants to know if it exists, and, if so, of what it consists. Most urgently, he needs to know if it is independent or dependent. He finds only the 'cross'd opinions' of diverse intellectuals, the reading of whom 'Did eat my youth' (l. 881). Even after intensive study, these conflicting intellectual opinions cancel each other out and leave him disillusioned: 'The more I learnt the more I learnt to doubt: / Knowledge and wit, faith's foes, turn faith about' (ll. 847–8). And if knowledge is sinfully hubristic – 'strive not to be over-wise: / It drew destruction into Paradise' (ll. 204–5) – this is not because it replaces faith with an alternative, liberated secular identity and purpose. On the contrary, it destroys faith and leaves the individual in a state of socially vulnerable disorientation: 'My heart is ravel'd out in discontents' (l. 814).

Quadratus tells Lampatho to abandon his search for the truth of the self and instead throw himself into social life: 'row with the tide; / Pursue the cut, the fashion of the age'. But to do so requires 'sly dissemblance'; in pursuing worldly affairs one must be deceptive: 'Those that their state would swell / Must bear a counter-face' (ll. 886–7, 913, 923–4). The 'counter-face' is less a matter of evil duplicity than a condition of the social itself. This play is a comedy about dress-disguise and the opportunities it affords for confused and refused identities. The 'counter-face' can be achieved with little more than a change of dress: 'give him but fair rich clothes, / He can be ta'en, reputed anything' (ll. 937–8). If the inner self so easily evaporates into the persona appropriated, this is because ' "Custom is a second nature" ' (l. 1021), and because identity is disturbingly a question of recognition: 'All that exists / Takes valuation from opinion' (ll. 159–60).[3]

The truth of desire is also sought in terms of the deep self, yet it too is shown to be radically social, an effect of social being. For Albano this is the consequence of living in a fallen age. Ideally love should be

> eternal, always one,
> As is th'instiller of divinest love:
> Unchang'd by time . . .

But in fact

> The soul of man is rotten
> Even to the core: no sound affection.
> Our love is hollow-vaulted, stands on props
> Or circumstance, profit or ambitious hopes
>
> (ll. 1031–8)

The obsessed lovers in this play are social in another sense: they would never have fallen in love had they not previously learned of love. Lampatho is transformed from reclusive ascetic scholar into besotted lover by the rhetoric of love – a language which dissolves his 'spirit' into the 'fashion of the age'.

Even the death meditation was becoming a social practice, analogous to the self-conscious performance of the melancholic.[4] The genre of the meditation, like that of melancholy, implies a state of introspection regardless of who might be watching or listening – something inward, private and personal. In fact the written meditation is a mode of writing with its own rules, and usually presupposes at least a reader if not an audience. And by now it often proceeded by reference as much to past texts on the subject as to the individual writer's personal experience.

Briefly, the death meditation – this most private of meditations on a universal theme – gains its meaning in relation to an existing cultural history, and is a form of cultural self-presentation. This is one reason why those who meditate on death often present themselves as such; like the melancholic, which they often are, they *perform* the meditation. When Montaigne tells us that nothing has more occupied his mind than images of death, he glosses this with a description of himself thus occupied:

Amid ladies and games, someone would think me involved in digesting some jealousy by myself, or the uncertainty of some hope, while I was thinking about *I don't remember whom*, who had been overtaken a few days before . . . by death, on leaving a similar feast, his head full of idleness, love, and a good time, like myself; and thinking that the same chance was hanging from my ear . . . (*Complete Essays*, pp. 60–61; my emphasis)

Compare this with a passage from Lucretius which Montaigne refers to in his own text:

men often talk from the bottom of their hearts when they recline at a banquet, goblet in hand and brows decked with garlands: 'How all too short are those good times that come to us poor creatures! Soon they will be past and gone, and there will be no recalling them.' (pp. 123–4)

Even if the similarity between the scenarios is not conscious on Montaigne's part, it is still not coincidental. This scenario recurs in the traditions of both melancholy and the meditation on death. Perhaps when Montaigne prefaces his own self-description by saying that he is 'by nature not melancholy, but dreamy' he is wanting to distinguish his thoughtful meditation from a maudlin melancholy. But see too how effectively Montaigne frames himself by way of being true to the detail of the genre: he tells us in passing that he has already forgotten the man he was thinking about. Yet Montaigne's text survives, as does that image of Donne wrapped in his winding-sheet, waiting to die.

In 1614 Sir Walter Ralegh, imprisoned in the Tower of London, and himself expecting to die, meditated on death and the way it defeats our projects and disintegrates our identities:

[Death] tells the proud and insolent that they are but abjects, and humbles them at the instant; makes them cry, complain, and repent, yea, even to hate their forepast happiness. He takes the account of the rich, and proves him a beggar, a naked beggar, which hath interest in nothing but the gravel that fills his mouth. He holds a glass before the eye of the most beautiful, and makes them see therein their deformity and rottenness and they acknowledge it. (*History*, p. 396)

In early December 1623, five years after Ralegh was finally executed, John Donne fell dangerously ill with relapsing fever. He survived, but at the time he believed, with good reason, that he would not. So he wrote about the experience, and did so feverishly – literally – thinking he was recording his own dying. He wrote obsessively about the precariousness of an identity wrecked by change and loss: 'variable and therefore miserable condition of man' (*Selected Prose*, p. 99). Donne used the immediate experience of illness, physical decline and decay as both metaphor for and a real material cause of the radical instability of identity.

If Walton's graphic description of John Donne preaching passionately against the dying life, even as he is literally dying, is revealing, so too is the fact that Donne *commissioned* that portrait of himself wrapped in his winding-sheet. Even more to the point, what he wrote when ill was not random jottings but a book running to many pages. Most remarkably, this meditation on death, disintegration and the futility of desire was ready for publication even before he had left his sickbed; at the time the book was actually published he was still under doctor's orders neither to read nor write. Donne's biographer R. C. Bald tells us that the *Devotions*

were written in less than a month, being first jotted down during a fever which nearly cost the writer his life, and were then put into shape during a convalescence that left the patient so weak that the book was almost in print before he was able to leave his bedroom. (p. 451)

Suffering, mutability and death exhaust, disintegrate and ruin Donne, yet he responds almost indefatigably; to express the experience, to know and articulate the truth about his own and the human condition as one of absence, loss and dissatisfaction, becomes a kind of praxis of death; seemingly, death imparts intellectual energy even as it saps life. Donne was exceptional, but the same paradox lies at the heart of the intense artistic production which characterized this period – which made it, arguably, the time of greatest artistic achievement in Western culture to date.

And Ralegh too: what he writes on death while imprisoned in the Tower is in a long tradition which laments the vanity of human desire and ambition in the face of the most fundamental truth of all: nothing lasts; everything is destroyed in and by time. Decline, ruin and oblivion are the fate of all. What this means is that all human effort is futile, because, as Ralegh puts it elsewhere, under the sway of time 'all is dissolved, our labours come to naught' ('The Ocean to Scinthia', l. 235). Again, Ralegh offers us the familiar idea inviting despair: in the passage quoted above, death holds a mirror before the beautiful, making them see their 'rottenness' not just as an eventual fate, but as something already inherent within them – it is the reflection they see in the mirror *now*. And yet Ralegh too works indefatigably in the face of the ruin of death: this passage comes at the end of his *History of the World.* Under conditions of imprisonment, Ralegh had achieved nothing less than the writing of a monumental world history.[5] The reason he found himself in prison at all was that he had failed in an ambitious commercial venture on a world scale. Death enervates, exhausts and obliterates, and yet it also energizes; from it we learn the futility of all endeavour, yet that truth somehow spurs us on indefatigably.

It would be convenient to conclude that fatalism and despair set in only as a result of the experienced failure of this or that particular human endeavour – becoming, as it were, the rationalization of that failure. That may be true to an extent. But it is also and more interestingly the case that the fatalism seems to have been a condition for the endeavour in the first place. It would also be convenient to explain this paradox by regarding the manic productivity of Ralegh and Donne as attempts to disavow death. But this kind of explanation is itself a disavowal of the significance of death for them, for their culture and, still, for ours. Donne did, after all, write the first published defence of suicide, in which he confessed to the experience of what we might call a self-destructive depression, if not a death-wish, and his writing is steeped in the seductions, the paradoxes and the profundity of death. Again, we are required to revise some of our own assumptions about the history of identity – especially the (so-called) recent 'death of man'.

The death of man?

Modern theories of identity have been preoccupied with the alleged recent disintegration of Western humanism. The argument usually goes like this. Western culture was once underpinned by a confident ideology of subjectivity. The individual experienced himself as unified and (spiritually if not socially) self-determining by virtue of his imagined possession of a pre-social or asocial essence from which spiritual (if not social) value and freedom derive. It was this concept of subjectivity which fed the predominantly masculinist Western ideologies of individualism, and its universal counterpart, 'man'. But these ideologies were relatively short-lived. Often the fully unified subject was said to have emerged in the Renaissance, become ideologically consolidated in the Enlightenment, and experienced its high point in the nineteenth century, before collapsing in our own time (and in a way corresponding to the crisis of the West, of capitalism or empire). This collapse is not usually regarded with regret; in some post-modern versions of this narrative, the modern 'decentred' and mobile subject is also fantasized as the subversion of, or at least the radical alternative to, the ideologies which the individual and man once served.

It is ironic that, far from being the critical act of demystification which it so often aspires to be, the explanatory model at work here – from unity, fullness and freedom to disunity, crisis and fragmentation – echoes, often unawares and in secular form, one of the founding myths of western-European culture, and of Western subjectivity, namely the Fall. We repeat this Fall narrative imagining it as a narrative of the ending of something, whereas in fact it is the narrative of its continuation.

It is apparent from previous chapters that the crisis of subjectivity was present at the inception of individualism in early Christianity, and it has been as enabling as it has been disturbing (enabling because disturbing). The Fall narrative dramatizes this very crisis, indicating as it does that what simultaneously subverted and energized the subject of Western culture was not desire *per se*, but transgressive desire haunted by the death which it brought into being. This of course is what happened in Eden: Adam and Eve, by transgressing God's law, brought death into the world.

Most significant in this tradition has been death's manifestation as a pernicious mutability which always undermines identity. William Drummond writes of how death not only destroys, but in the process (and long before death proper) cruelly transforms everything into its own opposite: 'all Strength by it is enfeebled, Beauty turned in deformity and rottenness, Honour in contempt, Glory into baseness' (pp. 148–9). Working thus through mutability, death inverts, perverts, contradicts and finally destroys. As a result, man is permanently unstable and conflicted: 'His Body is but a Mass of discording humours ... which though agreeing for a trace of time, yet can never be made uniform.' This very discord is at once natural and the agency of death – it is the '*inward cause of a necessary dissolution*'. Man is an entity so inherently and radically unstable, so contradictory, both psychically and physically, that 'we should rather wonder how so fragile a matter should so long endure, than how so soon dissolve, and decay'. This is hardly the fractured, dispersed post-modern subject, but the latter's antecedents are surely here. (And one significant difference between Drummond and some post-modernists is that, intellectually speaking, he at least knew where he was coming from.) Mutability is also experienced as a condition of radical psychic insecurity; Drummond succinctly remarks our perpetual vulnerability even, or especially, at the height of our power, when 'the glance of an Eye is sufficient to undo [us]' (pp. 148, 155, 151–2; my emphasis).

What we might now call the neurosis, anxiety and alienation of the subject in crisis is not so much the consequence of its recent breakdown, but the very stuff of the subject's creation, and of the culture – western-European culture – which it sustains, especially in its most expansionist phases (of which Drummond's own period – what we now call 'the Renaissance' – was undoubtedly one). If man is inhabited by mutability, and in a way which leads him inevitably deathward, it is this same mutability which imparts to him a restless, agonized energy. The crisis of the self is not so much the subjective counterpart of the demise, disintegration or undermining of western-European culture as what energizes both the self and that culture. That is why, for Drummond, the terrible disharmony which is the dynamic of life as death, and which makes for the futility of desire, by the same token generates a kind of negative, forward-directed energy:

[Man] hath no sooner acquired what he did desire, but he beginneth to enter into new Cares, and desire what he shall never be able to acquire . . . He is pressed with Care for what is present, with Grief, for what is past, with Fear of what is to come, nay, for what will never come. (p. 153)[6]

Again, it is in Augustine's *Confessions* (*c.* 397–401) that we find one of the most influential precedents for the way in which 'modern' subjectivity is founded in that same sense of crisis which imparts the restless expansionist energy which is the making of civilization itself. Augustine suggests how individualism was from the beginning energized by an inner dynamic of loss, conflict, doubt, absence and lack, and how this feeds into our culture's obsession with control and expansion – the sense that the identity of everything, from self to nation, is under centrifugal and potentially disintegrative pressures which have to be rigorously controlled. This is a kind of control that is always exceeding and breaking down the very order it restlessly quests for, and is forever re-establishing its own rationale even as it undermines it. The experience of instability is inherited by Augustine and deployed in a religious praxis; the subject in crisis becomes a crucial element in the triumph of Western individualism and all that this has meant. It is this which we have inherited; what we are living through now is not some (post-)modern collapse of Western subjectivity but another development of its enduring dynamic.

The mutable, restless self

In 1739 the philosopher David Hume reconceptualized the self as completely mutable and entirely the prisoner of time. Even the meditation upon the self is pointless, according to Hume, since the kind of self which meditation presupposed is non-existent. Hume makes a crucial point: during introspection one's attention is always caught up in the transient, fleeting impressions of consciousness itself. One can never get behind those impressions to something more substantial and enduring. This leads him to repudiate the idea that 'we are at every moment intimately conscious of what we call our SELF'. Observing that if he tries to concentrate upon his true self he can only settle on this or that fleeting perception, Hume concludes that there is nothing else: we are 'nothing but a bundle or collection of different perceptions, which succeed each other with an inconceivable rapidity, and are *in a perpetual flux and movement*' (pp. 299–301; my emphasis). For Hume, 'There is properly no *simplicity* in [the mind] at one time, nor *identity* in different.' There is absolutely nothing within us which remains unalterably the same through flux and change – certainly not a soul, and not even an unchanging self. Nor does the mind have an unchanging nature or essence; it too is essentially discontinuous. We are nothing more than the movement and flux of consciousness. Beyond these is pure non-being; without movement and flux we should be 'entirely annihilated' (p. 300).

Hume articulates the realization that, desire it as we may, there is no fullness of being in the present moment; ontologically the present is apparently more real – more present – than either the past or the future, and yet it always eludes us. So too does the self which we expect to find in the present moment. In a sense this means that we never ever experience pure existence; consciousness, desire, life itself are a movement towards an ever-elusive fullness of being. As Georges Bataille was to put it, the meaning of being is not so much actually being, but expecting to be – 'as if we never received *being* authentically, but only the anticipation of being, which will be and is not, as if we were not the presence that we are, but the future that we will be and are not' (*Accursed Share*, II.81).

To argue that the so-called 'unified subject' is in part a retrospective projection of modern cultural theory – a convenient fiction which highlights the contrasting, subsequent, drama of the subject's supposed fall from unity – is not to suggest that the optimistic ideologies of Man and the Individual have not made a profound difference. Of course they have, as we shall see in Chapter 15 in relation to Feuerbach and others. But we shall also see that these ideologies were rarely as complacent as contemporary theory implies; they were often wrested from the threat of disintegration and death, or used to defend against them, or to struggle beyond them.

Deifying death

The passage cited earlier from Ralegh's *History of the World* is only the more conventional section of an extraordinary address to death – more an encomium than a meditation. Even as he attributes to it the defeat of all human aspiration, Ralegh deifies and adulates death, and to a blasphemous degree by comparing it with God and finding the latter wanting: death becomes a mocking tyrant even more power-ful than God. Death's awe-full power is revered by Ralegh from a position of abjection; he is imprisoned, perhaps expecting death, and anyway is in a sense already dead, as he wrote to King James after his conviction in 1603:

The life which I had (most mighty prince) the law hath taken from me; and I am now but the same earth and dust out of which I was first framed ... Blood, name, gentry, or estate have I (now) none; no, not so much as a being ... This being the first letter that ever your majesty received from a dead man ... (*Works*, VIII.646–7)

This is what this 'dead man' writes on death at the end of the *History*:

[Death] puts into man all the wisdom of the world, without speaking a word, which God, with all the words of his law, promises, or threats, doth not infuse. *Death*, which hateth and destroyeth man, is believed; God, which hath made him and loves him, is always deferred. *I have considered* (saith Solomon), *all the works that are under the sun, and, behold, all is vanity and vexation of spirit* [Ecclesiastes 1:14], but who believes it till Death tells it us? ... It is therefore Death alone that can suddenly make man to know himself ...

O eloquent, just, and mighty Death! whom none could advise, thou hast persuaded; what none hath dared, thou hast done; and whom all the world hath flattered, thou only hath cast out of the world and despised; thou hast drawn together all the far-fetched greatness, all the pride, cruelty, and ambition of man, and covered it all over with these two narrow words: Hic jacet! (*History*, p. 396)

An adoring identification with a ruthless omnipotence is made from an experience of impotence; precisely because he is powerless, Ralegh becomes beholden to the effortless, stupendous power of a superior force. It is more than significant that death here takes the masculine gender (five times in the full text).

Ralegh both submits to and identifies with death; the submission is masochistic, the identification sadistic or at least vindictive. Death is seen as oblivion and non-being, and as a naked absolute power. And, if there is fear and awe here, Ralegh also derives consolation from death's promise of the obliteration of all differences, including that between human failure and human success. We might also discern here a state of mind which in our own time has been called identification with the oppressor, not least in that interplay of power and desire which recalls Sir Thomas Wyatt's Penitential Psalms.

I find illuminating Stephen Greenblatt's account of how, in these psalms, desire – what Wyatt calls 'hot affect' – is transferred from mistress to God by a characteristically Protestant wish to submit to the domination of a severe divinity which will spur the poet to righteousness:

> I, lo! from mine error
> Am plunged up; as horse out of the mire
> With stroke of spur.

A terror of God leads him to see that, in his flesh,

> Is not one point of firm stability;
> Nor in my bones there is no steadfastness:
> *Such is my dread of mutability* . . .
> (Psalm 38; my emphasis)

Greenblatt finds here an 'ascent through the acceptance of domination', with the corollary that while, for Wyatt, sexuality in its natural state is aggressive and predatory, in its redeemed state it is passive: 'Sexual aggression . . . is transferred entirely to the sphere of transcendent power' (*Renaissance Self-Fashioning*, p. 123). An internalized, dreaded mutability, experienced as desire, leads to abject identification with an omnipotent, vengeful God. To regard this sexualizing of the religious experience as commonplace or conventional is only to say that it probably requires closer attention than that usually given it by those who would describe it thus. For Wyatt it would seem that, if the lack of 'firm stability' and, its corollary, a 'dread of mutability' bind mutability into desire, they are also what provokes the identification with a powerful coherence that is elsewhere and other. Similarly, in his *Holy Sonnets* Donne describes how desire, having intensified the working of death and mutability in himself – 'not one hour I can myself sustain' (I.12) – now requires an abject, adoring, masochistic, erotic prostration before God:

> Batter my heart, three-personed God; for, you
> As yet but knock, breathe, shine, and seek to mend;
> That I may rise and stand, o'erthrow me, and bend

Your force, to break, blow, burn, and make me new.
I like a usurped town, to another due,
Labour to admit you, but oh, to no end . . .

(XIV.1–6)

When Donne preaches his famous last sermon he is literally dying while also (it is not the same thing) speaking from the position of death. As he does so he both submits to and, *as preacher*, identifies with death. And for him too God seems less impressive than death, whose disintegrative effects are dwelt on with awe.

Let us finally recall the precedent of Augustine, for whom death and mutability are punishments for transgression. But these are not externally imposed punishments; they are 'propagated' from within, and so radically that to be living is only to be dying. Sexual orgasm is a kind of death, an extinction of self, and in sexual desire more generally the self contends against itself and control is completely lost – the body's members become anarchic – literally epitomized in the unruly male erection. Again, this leads to abject identification with an omnipotent God: 'incorruptible, and inviolable and immutable' (*Confessions*, 7.1). Identification with and submission to such power substitutes for the stability which is always lacking, and is just one aspect of the restless quest which that lack compels.

Misogyny and the gendering of mutability

And I find more bitter than death the woman, whose heart *is* snares and nets, *and* her hands *as* bands: whoso pleaseth God shall escape from her; but the sinner shall be taken by her. (Ecclesiastes 7:26)

Book IX of Milton's *Paradise Lost* describes Satan persuading Eve to eat of the 'tree of knowledge forbidden'. In doing so she is 'eating death'. Milton's retelling of the Fall narrative indicates some of the erotic and psychic complexity involved in the blaming of woman for bringing death into the world. Realizing what Eve has done, Adam is horrified, but, 'perceiving her lost, resolves through vehemence of love to perish with her'. Adam tells Eve that Satan 'me with thee hath ruined, for with thee / Certain my resolution is to die'. Simply, even in his (as yet) unfallen state, he cannot live without her. But living with her is to admit death into life:

> Should God create another Eve, and I
> Another rib afford, yet loss of thee
> Would never from my heart; no no, I feel
> The link of nature draw me: flesh of flesh,
> Bone of my bone thou art, and from thy state
> Mine never shall be parted, bliss or woe.
>
> . . . .
>
> . . . I with thee have fixed my lot,
> Certain to undergo like doom, if death
> Consort with thee, *death is to me as life*
>
> . . . .
>
> Our state cannot be severed, we are one,
> One flesh; to lose thee were to lose myself.
> (Argument; l. 792; Argument; ll. 906–7,
> 911–16, 952–4, 958–9; my emphasis)

In Shakespeare's sonnets[7] mutability is a recurring theme of the verses supposedly addressed to the young man. But the so-called dark lady sonnets are equally important, because it is here that we again see mutability being internalized as the cause of desire's impossible vicissitudes. In Sonnet 20 the poet seeks to differentiate, in terms of mutability, the (good) beauty of the young man from the (bad) beauty of women:

> A woman's face, with Nature's own hand painted,
> Hast thou, the master-mistress of my passion;
> A woman's gentle heart, but not acquainted
> With shifting change, as is false woman's fashion;
> An eye more bright than theirs, less false in rolling . . .

It is not simply that masculine beauty is good and feminine beauty bad; the young man is as beautiful as he is only because he partakes of feminine beauty. But this makes it even more necessary to 'split' feminine beauty, making its good qualities even better in a masculine context, and its bad qualities definitively bad in the feminine one. In a sense the poet also has to split beauty itself: he has to separate off from 'true' beauty the condition of 'shifting change' which is its precondition. Of course he knows this: 'everything that grows / Holds in perfection but a little moment' (Sonnet 15).

The gendering and displacing of mutability, the way that 'shifting change' is made the condition of the 'false woman', is a familiar misogynist strategy. But these sonnets convey also that such misogyny does not cancel sexual desire for women but remains an inextricable part of it. Also, mutability is identified as an exclusively female attribute precisely because it is in fact the internal dynamic of male desire. The poet knows this too: one minute his desire is being rendered unstably mutable by its own confusions, the next minute it is being decayed by its own excess: '[I] in mine own love's strength seem to decay, / O'ercharged with burden of mine own love's might' (Sonnet 23; cf. Sonnet 80: 'My love was decay').

With Augustine, Wyatt, Ralegh and Donne the experience of mutability and death invites identification with an omnipotent power which is elsewhere and other – in Wyatt's and Augustine's case it is God; in Ralegh's it is death as a surrogate absolute; in Donne's it is probably both. An aside in *All's Well That Ends Well* illustrates yet another kind of identification; it occurs in the form of a reproach to him who would prefer sexual congress to warfare,

> Spending his manly marrow in her arms,
> Which should sustain the bound and high curvet
> Of Mars's fiery steed.
>
> (II.iii.278–80)

To spend sexually: this is another commonplace. But consider what is implied here: 'manly marrow', a self-defining energy and essence constitutive of one's power and one's identity, is being wasted in a way which is debilitating. To avoid both waste and debilitation, manly marrow is identified with a higher power, military and homosocial; it supports that power and in turn is sustained by it.[8] This masculine, military power wreaks waste and debilitation on the world. In other words, mutability is transferred from a sexual to a social domain where it is reproduced on a colossal scale. Here that 'poor benefit of a bewitching minute' (Tourneur, III.v.75), the pathetic, debilitating simulacrum of death, is imagined to be hugely empowered through participation in heroic conquest; the experience of desire as death undergoes a sublimation and a displacement whereby the self is empowered rather than enfeebled through a perpetuation of death on the battlefield. A suffering for, and an identification with, a higher power: this is one response to the internalization of mutability.

At this time the pun on 'die' as both death and orgasm was another commonplace.[9] For us, though not for the Elizabethans, the commonplace forecloses on what it recognizes – it allows us to see partially in order not to see fully. For one thing this idea of propagation as self-death was (ironically indeed, given the dangers of childbirth) mainly a male anxiety: to retain semen was thought to maximize physical strength, whereas to ejaculate was a potentially dangerous squandering of energy. Excessive loss of semen would not only debilitate, but might even result in the individual's death. This was because semen was thought to include some essential, life-sustaining constituents of the brain and of the bone-marrow which, during intercourse, descended down the spine and were expended in ejaculation. As Merry E. Weisner reminds us, such ideas remained powerfully if obscurely influential in early modern witch-hunting: 'Intercourse with female demons (*succubi*) was especially threatening, for such creatures attempted to draw out as much semen as possible, thus drastically debilitating any man' (p. 226). The general idea that the loss of semen is a loss of life-sustaining essences is much older; it is, for example, a topic of debate for classical writers in the fourth century BC. Aristotle believed it was this loss which explained the dejection which followed intercourse.[10] But what begins as a mainly medical idea becomes increasingly also a problem of desire as self-squandering and death.

There are other respects in which the pervasive misogyny of this period connects with the same male fear. This is Donne:

> For that first marriage was our funeral:
> One woman at one blow, then killed us all,
> And singly, one by one, they kill us now.
> We do delightfully ourselves allow
> To that consumption; and profusely blind,
> We kill ourselves to propagate our kind.
>
> (*An Anatomy of the World*, l. 110)

Spenser in *The Faerie Queene* imagines mutability as a violent and hubristic goddess who inverts and perverts the order and stability of nature. This (invented) goddess even precipitates the greatest catastrophe of all, the Fall, and so brings death into the world such that the baby sucks not life from its nurse, but death; she

> . . . death for life exchanged foolishly:
> Since which, all living wights have learn'd to die,
> And all this world is waxen daily worse.
> O piteous worke of *Mutability*!
> By which, we are all subject to that curse,
> And death in stead of life have sucked from our Nurse.
> ('Two Cantos of Mutabilitie', VII.vi.6.4–9;
> cf. 5.4 and 6.3)

After mutability, then, what sustains life is nothing more – or less – than death.

7

'Desire is Death':
Shakespeare

In Shakespeare's sonnets mutability is what threatens to decay the object of desire (the young man), but it is also what erupts inside the restless desire for him, making it an experience of lack and 'torture', a condition in which the poet can 'no quiet find' (Sonnets 27, 28).[1] This is even more marked in the dark lady sonnets. Sonnet 129 is about the self-destructive contradictions which seemingly make desire impossible:

> Th' expense of spirit in a waste of shame
> Is lust in action, and, till action, lust
> Is perjured, murd'rous, bloody, full of blame,
> Savage, extreme, rude, cruel, not to trust,
> Enjoyed no sooner but despisèd straight,
> Past reason hunted, and no sooner had,
> Past reason hated as a swallowed bait
> On purpose laid to make the taker mad . . .

Yet, as has often been remarked, this sonnet has the confident rhythm, poise and pace of high formal control. Desire is consciously sublimated into the performance of form, so that in the very expression of disintegration there is an arrogant excess of control. John Kerrigan has remarked how, in the sonnets, Shakespeare copes with the effects of time through a controlling repetition so that 'even sonnets devoted to a description of Time's violence . . . provisionally recover in their formal discipline something of what Time takes' (Shakespeare, *Sonnets*, ed. Kerrigan, p. 45). Aesthetic order compensates for loss. In those sonnets where mutability has been internalized as desire this process is even more marked; the poet empowers himself through a coherent expression of desire's deeply destructive incoherence.

But given that Sonnet 129 speaks of lust, not love, it might be said that it is only the former which remains imprisoned in a self-destructive obsessive desire for another, and that this is exactly what true love transcends; in marriage, love delivers harmony – albeit of a banal kind:

> Mark how one string, sweet husband to another,
> Strikes each in each by mutual ordering;
> Resembling sire, and child, and happy mother,
> Who, all in one, one pleasing note do sing . . .
>
> (Sonnet 8)

The trouble with this distinction between love and lust is that it makes the latter a dumping-ground for everything unacceptable about the former – especially what it potentially always shares with 'lust', namely infatuation, obsession, fantasy and fetishism. Which perhaps is why Sonnet 147 articulates a similar experience, precisely describing it now as love and not lust – a love wrecked by the desire it would contain. More acutely, desire wrecks its own most perfect conventional expression, and formal discipline remains only to signify the impossibility of the harmony it would impose:

> My love is as a fever, longing still
> For that which longer nurseth the disease,
> Feeding on that which doth preserve the ill,
> Th'uncertain sickly appetite to please.
> My reason, the physician to my love,
> Angry that his prescriptions are not kept,
> Hath left me, and I desperate now approve
> Desire is death, which physic did except.
> Past cure I am, now reason is past care,
> And frantic-mad with evermore unrest;
> My thoughts and my discourse as madmen's are,
> At random from the truth, vainly expressed:
> For I have sworn thee fair, and thought thee bright,
> Who art as black as hell, as dark as night.

Here the desire of the poet is so mutable it becomes completely impossible; his is a longing whose object, far from giving satisfaction, only intensifies that impossibility: 'My love is as a fever, longing still / For that which longer nurseth the disease'. His longing leaves the poet 'frantic-mad with evermore unrest', possessed by thoughts 'At random from the truth, vainly express'd'. Hence: '*I desperate now approve / Desire is death*'. The starkness of the statement should not obscure a lingering ambiguity and ambivalence: it means most obviously 'I experience, I demonstrate – reluctantly, in desperation – that desire is death': less obviously, yet just as literally, it means 'I "approve" that desire is death': 'Racked with an impossible, contradictory, self-annihilating desire, I desire death.'

Time and the young man

For the young man of these sonnets, narcissistic self-regard is not, apparently, a reason for reproducing (that being the rational narrative offered by the poet) but, on the contrary, the basis of an erotic *complicity with* mutability, and even death. The poet declares, 'Nor shall Death brag thou wand'rest in his shade' (Sonnet 18), but that's just what this 'self-willed' youth would risk:

> Unthrifty loveliness, why dost thou spend
> Upon thyself thy beauty's legacy?
> .   .   .   .
> For having traffic with thyself alone,
> Thou of thyself thy sweet self dost deceive.
>
> (Sonnet 4)

Since the poet couches the reproach in onanistic terms, we might infer that what he chides he may also desire; even as he reprimands the youth for having sex with himself, the poet is attracted by the spectacle – or at least the fantasy – of a sexuality which is narcissistic and reckless. He is fascinated by the youth's temporary, fragile beauty ('whose action is no stronger than a flower' – Sonnet 65), by the fact that it becomes momentarily more perfect within the same time that will destroy it (Sonnet 126), and by the youth's narcissistic disregard of precisely this fate.

Perhaps, then, the exhortation to reproduce and to live according to thrift, calculation, contract, profit, audit is a conventional façade for a different kind of interest in the young man. If so, it would help explain why, even as time, death and mutability are deplored in the sonnets, their indifferent power is strangely revered; why an acute sense of physical beauty is inflected by an even more acute fascination with mutability and loss. So much so that there are occasions when the young man is more a foil, even a willing sacrifice, to time and mutability than an object of desire to be rescued from them. Beauty becomes not just the victim of time but its measure – even, in places, its effect. Put another way, although the poet is attracted to the young man, he also identifies with the destructive effects of time; there is a strange and compelling complicity between time and its chronicler such that we might go so far as to say that the author of the sonnets is enamoured more of death than of the boy. Again, as with Donne, Ralegh and the others, inside the submission to death is an identification with it.

It is, after all, a resonant and indicative irony that, despite the poet's alleged wish to immortalize him, and much scholarly detective work since, we do not know who the young man was. 'Your name from hence immortal life shall have,' says the poet, yet the young man is precisely not named or otherwise identified. In fact we are given no vivid individual representation of him at all. The poet says that his verse will distil the 'truth' or essence of the youth, but there is precious little of that either. In some sonnets it is as if the young man is not only a foil to mutability, but someone the poet wants to see destroyed by it. The poet is obviously ambivalent towards the young man: 'civil war is in my love and hate' (Sonnet 35). And, as Sonnet 70 makes clear, to be desired is not necessarily to be liked; beauty incurs resentment as well as desire. From these sonnets we are reminded that desire can itself be a kind of resentment, and a devious one at that. Consider how the poet's confession of his abjection is usually strategic. In Sonnet 66 he cries for 'restful death', and he welcomes its prospect again in Sonnets 71 and 72. Death is imagined as both the cessation and the crowning expression of his abjection, and he masochistically fantasizes his own death as the supreme occasion of achieving attention and sympathy, only to insist that he deserves neither.

The poet scrutinizes the youth for signs of decline, and indirectly makes him the repository of death: 'Thou art the grave where buried love doth live' (Sonnet 31). Of himself the poet declares, 'I, once gone, to all the world must die' (Sonnet 81). Not quite. His investment in his verse is clearly a compensation for disappointment in love – not least because he knows his verse will outlast his desire for, and the beauty of, the love object. In Sonnet 78 he not only acknowledges that the youth's beauty has liberated his verse, but insists on his verse's authenticity and value compared with superficial imitations. So, when he is announcing his concern to immortalize that beauty, he may more plausibly be consciously sublimating his own frustrated desire for it into the kind of cultural capital that beauty can never compete with nor even securely exchange itself for. Even as he is ostensibly writing to urge the boy to guard against loss by reproducing, the poet is compensating through writing for his own loss. He empowers himself by writing unforgettably of the powerlessness of everything under the sway of time. By a miracle, says the poet, 'in black ink my love may still shine bright' (Sonnet 65). 'My love' is surely strategically ambiguous, referring primarily to the beloved, but also to the poet's love for him. Of the two, it's the latter which has lasted.

Desire for the boy manifests itself as ambivalent – both to save him from time and to sacrifice him to it. It issues in some of the most memorable descriptions of mutability and loss ever written:

> Since brass, nor stone, nor earth, nor boundless sea,
> But sad mortality o'ersways their power,
> How with this rage shall beauty hold a plea,
> Whose action is no stronger than a flower?
> O, how shall summer's honey breath hold out
> Against the wrackful siege of batt'ring days,
> When rocks impregnable are not so stout,
> Nor gates of steel so strong but Time decays?
>
> (Sonnet 65)

The most obvious reason why the youth is urged to reproduce is in order to perpetuate himself. There are other reasons given – including for the sake of the world generally, for the sake of the child's mother, for the sake of the poet, even for the sake of the harmony of the family

(Sonnets 3, 10, 8) – but all of these reasons are subordinated to (though by the same token implicated in) the overriding reason: he is urged to reproduce in order to defy, or at least to mitigate, the effects of mutability. All the foregoing – youth, mother, poet – are at once participants in and victims of a life process of which mutability is both the essence and what destroys it:

> For never-resting Time leads summer on
> To hideous winter and confounds him there,
> Sap checked with frost and lusty leaves quite gone,
> Beauty o'ersnowed and bareness everywhere . . .
>
> (Sonnet 5)

Death as fact or event is subsidiary to a mutability which is ever-active, even in death (Sonnet 6), and ever-evocative of the failure of individual life. Simply, 'nothing 'gainst Time's scythe can make defense, / Save breed, to brave him when he takes thee hence' (Sonnet 12). Or rather not 'simply', since the child must also succumb to time.

Mutability enters desire sometimes as a dynamic of change, but more often as an entropic decline or a stultifying contradiction. It also figures as the 'barren rage of death's eternal cold' (Sonnet 13) – at once a silence and a violence, a privation and a force. If one recurring image of mutability is that which shows the actual devastation of time, another, perhaps even more powerful, is that which anticipates the inevitable future devastation which is somehow inside the present moment, the present beauty. Ralegh writes of death holding a mirror before the most beautiful and making them 'see therein their deformity and rottenness'; for Shakespeare

> The wrinkles which thy glass will truly show
> Of mouthèd graves, will give thee memory;
> Thou by thy dial's shady stealth mayst know
> Time's thievish progress to eternity . . .
>
> (Sonnet 77)

Romeo and Juliet

Everything I've described so far about the death/desire dynamic, and the internalization of mutability as desire, suggests the importance of fantasy. The origins of fantasy include the trauma of mutability. A supreme illustration of this is Shakespeare's *Romeo and Juliet*.

That this is a play about the paradoxical binding together of desire and death is clear enough: in the Prologue the passion of the young lovers is described as a 'death-marked love'; Capulet laments that 'Life, living, all is Death's' (IV.iv.67). It has been said that Romeo, when he incites 'love-devouring death' (II.v.7), is desiring and not defying death, and that his belief that Juliet is dead in the tomb is less the cause of his own suicide than the excuse for it. He finds that 'unsubstantial death is amorous' and makes 'A dateless bargain to engrossing death/. . ./ Thus with a kiss I die' (V.iii.103, 115–20). Once again death does not so much defeat desire as emerge from within it, as the dynamic of desire itself – as love, or rather death, at first sight.

The death/desire convergence in this play has been interestingly considered by Denis de Rougemont and Julia Kristeva. We have already looked at de Rougemont's account of how, in the Western tradition, passionate love and death feed off each other in ways epitomized in the *Tristan and Iseult* myth (above, Chapter 4). For him there are two related senses in which desire as conceptualized in the myth can be said to be impossible. One concerns the way in which desire actively seeks the obstacles that prevent its realization and thereby intensify its tendency to self-annihilation. The other suggests an even more fundamental ontological impossibility. Heretical mysticism in the twelfth century, by fatally confusing divine eros with human desire, begins that long obsession which is nothing less than an 'impossible love . . . a truly devouring ardour, a thirst which death alone could quench'. De Rougemont regards *Romeo and Juliet* as 'the most magnificent resuscitation of the myth that the world was to be given' until Wagner's *Tristan and Isolde* (*Love in the Western World*, pp. 145, 178–9, 201, 243).

For Julia Kristeva, too, this play shows how 'erotic expenditure is a race towards death' – but for an entirely different reason. The race towards death occurs not because of the fatal mixing of religion and sexuality, but because of the inherent ambivalence of the lovers' desire for each other, and of desire itself. Because, in short, of the hatred which the lovers feel for each other. Following Freud's famous contention in *Instincts and their Vicissitudes* that, in the relation to the other, hatred is more ancient than love, Kristeva cites Juliet's 'My only love, sprung from my only hate!' (I.v.140). Kristeva declares, 'hatred consumes them in the purest moments of their passion' even as they believe they have overcome the hatred of their times. Their hatred is not to be confused with the social hostility between the two families; this last is the kind of hatred one can look in the eye, and its very existence obscures the other, deeper, kind:

the familial, social curse is more respectable and bearable than the unconscious hatred of the lovers for each other. The fact remains that Juliet's jouissance is often stated through the anticipation – the desire? – of Romeo's death. (p. 221)

Kristeva also rejects the familiar and relatively comforting view that 'love must die ... that eros and the law are incompatible ...' No: 'More deeply, more passionately, we are dealing with the intrinsic presence of hatred in [desire] itself', a hatred 'at the very origin of the amatory surge' (p. 222).

Both accounts are intriguing, but both overlook the extent to which this play is, crucially, a *fantasy representation* of desire overdetermined by the trauma of mutability. More generally, as theatrical event, this play is not just about desire between two people, but about desire itself as a fantasy projection, a wish-fulfilment complete with perverse complications. *Romeo and Juliet* is also an adult fantasy *about* adolescent desire. It's no secret that adolescent sexuality contains a powerful erotic charge for the adult, regardless of sexual orientation. Gay people tend to be explicit about this, but the institutions of heterosexuality are also manifestly invigorated by such eroticism, albeit in more sublimated and displaced forms. And sometimes, of course, in ways not sublimated, e.g. incest; or in ways half sublimated and half sanctioned, as for instance when Capulet, Juliet's father, encourages Paris to seduce his daughter. This was, of course, a commonplace arrangement – a calculated exchange of a daughter within and on behalf of patriarchy. But it may also involve the father identifying with the prospective son-in-law as sexual partner. Initially Capulet tells Paris that Juliet is too young to marry. He nevertheless sympathizes with what 'lusty young men feel' in spring, and so he invites Paris to gaze on Juliet amidst many other beautiful young women at his, Capulet's, house that night:

> ... even such delight
> Among fresh female buds shall you this night
> Inherit at my house ...
>
> (I.ii.26–8)

Later, in the context of mourning the death of one young man, his nephew Tybalt, and seemingly anticipating his own death ('Well, we were born to die', III.iv.4), he abruptly changes his mind and arranges a hasty marriage for Juliet and Paris. Juliet resists, and Capulet coerces her brutally. To modify Freud's insight on narcissism, we might say that the father, confronted with the death of a young kinsman, and in anticipation of his own death, experiences with a new urgency the need to give his daughter to the kind of young man he (and Tybalt?) once was – or the kind of young man he once wanted to be, or, perhaps, who others once wanted him to be. Certainly Capulet's wish to marry Juliet has been an obsessive, long-standing one:

> Day, night; work, play;
> Alone, in company, still my care hath been
> To have her matched ...

Paris fits the predictable patriarchal bill – 'A gentleman of noble parentage, / Of fair demesnes, youthful, and nobly lined'. But that 'youthful' unpacks into something more – something like an erotic homosocial bonding in which an impersonal 'one' is the place where Capulet's erotic identification is projected as Juliet's desire:

> Stuff'd as they say, with honourable parts,
> Proportioned as one's thought would wish a man –
>
> . . . .
>
> An you be mine, I'll give you to my friend ...
>
> (III.v.176–91)

For the adult generally, but perhaps especially for the father, adolescent sexuality is something idealized from the position of loss. (For Capulet, Tybalt's death accentuates that loss.) Which means that adults behold adolescent desire ambivalently, and this is perhaps one reason why, in this play, patriarchal love so often and so quickly turns to hate. This is partly because of a fear of illicit sex and the threat to inheritance which that might entail. Important though this is, it is not sufficient to explain why a father like Capulet, faced with a daughter who resists his marriage arrangement for her, behaves with the vehemence of a spurned lover. Accusing his daughter of 'peevish, self-willed harlotry' (IV.ii.14), he is eager to banish Juliet, consigning her to social death certainly, and even to a literal one: 'hang, beg, starve, die in the streets, / For, by my soul, I'll ne'er acknowledge thee' (III.5.192–3). Adults behold adolescent desire ambivalently because theirs is a gaze invested with hope – a gaze socially sanctioned in the name of hope – yet haunted by loss. The family is supposed to mediate between the two. If death is projected from this ambivalence it may be to pre-empt or avenge the failure and loss which haunt adult desire, and certainly it attests to the failure of the family's mediating role.

Often in plays like this one the death/desire conjunction anticipates that later romantic conjoining of sexuality and death; the resonant early modern pun on orgasm as death becomes the even more resonant romantic fantasy in which the momentary obliteration of self which sexual ecstasy (orgasm) affords is arrested, at once prolonged and dissolved – prolonged by being dissolved – into the stasis of death – not so much to perpetuate ecstasy as, again, to pre-empt the failure and loss which is mutability. At its most romantically intense this manifests as the barely unconscious wish that death – in one respect the cause or at least the condition of mutability – is invoked, embraced, in order to banish mutability: in order to banish one kind of loss (mutability) another kind (death) is embraced. Loss pre-empts loss. In *Romeo and Juliet* there is already a sense of this later tendency, especially in Romeo's description of death as 'unsubstantial'.

But if, as I'm suggesting, in this play at least it is the adult not the adolescent who is identifying ecstasy with death, it raises the question: Who is identifying with Romeo? Who *is* Romeo? I'm reluctant to regard the death desire in *Romeo and Juliet* as intrinsically 'adolescent'.

For one thing the reckless excess of adolescent desire is too endearing and insightful for me to want to deny to it that wisdom which is antithetical to the sensible (the adult's masquerade). More importantly, in this play it's much more the case that adolescent desire becomes itself the object of ambivalent desire, and that the erotics of death – death at first sight – far from being the intrinsic condition of adolescent desire, are another aspect of the adult's ambivalent gaze. Hence that desiring gaze for Juliet dead: 'Death lies on her like an untimely frost / Upon the sweetest flower of all the field' (IV.v.28–9).

This spectacle of death is unbearable yet not undesired, because here death arrests beauty; transience, decay, decline, failure (including parental impotence) are pre-empted in and through 'untimely' death. But then not quite, or rather not at all: at this stage Juliet is drugged and only apparently dead. Here and in the tomb she is brought into the closest possible proximity to decay and decomposition, while being still very much alive. Beauty and death are fantasized as antithetically proximate. And when Juliet finally succumbs to death proper, it's again in a way whereby death momentarily enhances the beauty it has claimed: 'And Juliet, bleeding, warm and newly dead' (V.ii.174). This is a fantasy redolent of that pathos which is synonymous with the tragic vision – a vision which borders on the obscene precisely because and not in spite of its wisdom.[2]

Romeo also kills himself. Not surprisingly perhaps: he's unhappy, having lost his other half. Here we could invoke Aristophanes' founding narrative of desire and death. Romeo might indeed be explained in these terms were it not that he has earlier switched his uncompromising desire from Rosaline to Juliet. Again, it would be evasive to dismiss this as the fickleness of an immature, adolescent love. Let's say rather that Romeo's desire is already rather adult, at once fixated and mobile: on the one hand subject to compulsive repetition, on the other swept along by history. As the Prologue to Act II puts it, the previous love object 'for which love groan'd for and would die' is itself now dead: 'Now old desire doth in his death-bed lie'. But Romeo is by no means free of desire: he 'loves again, / Alike bewitched by the charm of looks' (II.Prologue). Which means that, for him, desire is a serious business, a state of lack which, though in no way indifferent as to its objects, substitutes and replaces them with that inconstancy which 'true' love always disavows but never avoids. There is no distinction here between true and false, mature and adolescent, love: true love also, in its sexual forms, is inherently mutable.

Lacan has said 'there is no such thing as the sexual relationship [*rapport sexuel*]' ((*Feminine Sexuality*, p. 143). If only to avoid incurring the anger of those who are in love, one is tempted to settle for this proposition in its weaker form: there is no such thing as a sexual relationship which lasts. But that's not it; definitely not: for Romeo, Lacan's formulation is to the point. In all this Romeo is the sublime adolescent – which is to say he is already old, already contracted to death, the object and creation of the desiring, ambivalent, adult gaze – as, in a different way, is the young man of the sonnets.

'Be absolute for death'

In Shakespeare's *Measure for Measure* there is a fascinating scene in which a young man, Claudio, imprisoned and awaiting execution for fornication, is visited by a friar who urges that he reconcile himself to death. The audience knows that all is not what it seems: the friar is really Duke Vincentio, the ruler of the city (Vienna). Earlier in the play we saw him strategically retiring from the place of authority and handing the reins of power to others. The city is experiencing political and social disruption; according to the Duke, the people have become virtually ungovernable. He has delegated other, temporary, rulers to restore a strict order, especially in the sexual affairs of the people. Hence Claudio's arrest and impending punishment for having 'got his friend with child' (I.iv.27). Claudio is at the very least a scapegoat, but it is more complicated than that: not for the first time, more fundamental political instabilities are being focused in a witch-hunt against promiscuity. Claudio, who isn't even guilty of promiscuity, is caught up in a crisis which unleashes a potent blend of political paranoia and shrewd machiavellianism.[3]

The Duke never actually intended to depart the scene of power, and now, disguised as a friar, he keeps an eye on political developments.

Nor can he resist testing out his new-found religious power (the play is in part about the relationship between the respective powers of State and Church) – hence his visit to Claudio in prison. There he delivers one of the more famous speeches from Shakespeare, which begins 'Be absolute for death'. What we witness here is the philosophy of death being explicitly put to ideological use: the Duke has already set in motion a programme of overt, draconian political repression; what he is doing now is testing the power of a philosophy of death, here delivered with all the ideological authority of the Church, to encourage voluntary, internalized compliance to complement the overt repression. The Duke wants to get both Claudio and, later, another prisoner called Barnadine to want to die. His speech begins thus:

> Be absolute for death: either death or life
> Shall thereby be the sweeter. Reason thus with life:
> If I do lose thee, I do lose a thing
> That none but fools would keep.

Mutability reaches into, even constitutes, identity:

> Thou art not thyself;
> For thou exists on many a thousand grains
> That issue out of dust . . .

Mutability also reaches into desire, and in a way which renders it difficult –

> Thou are not certain;
> For thy complexion shifts to strange effects
> After the moon . . .

if not impossible –

> Happy thou art not;
> For what thou hast not, still thou striv'st to get,
> And what thou hast, forget'st.

Death is the eternal release from an identity and a desire – identity *as* desire – tormented by mutability and founded on the contradiction that life is a kind of death ('in this life lie hid moe thousand deaths') which, in being avoided, is only hastened: 'For [death] thou labour'st

by thy flight to shun / And yet runn'st towards him still' (III.i.5–40).
For a while at least, Claudio is dutifully convinced:

> I humbly thank you.
> To sue to live I find I seek to die,
> And seeking death, find life. Let it come on.
> (III.i.42–4)

Moments later, speaking to his sister, he eroticizes his very willingness
to die:

> If I must die,
> I will encounter darkness as a bride
> And hug it in mine arms.
> (III.i.82–4)

But, shortly after the Duke leaves, his desire to live returns, stronger
than ever.

What is being dramatized here is the way in which a philosophy of
death appears to work as an ideology of social control, converting
transgressive desire into complete submission to authority, even to
the point of welcoming death – only to fail. Later with Barnadine it
fails completely, without even a semblance of success. But even that
is not the end of the matter. The philosophy of death has a wider
significance in the play, especially the idea that desire is somehow
programmed to self-destruct. Claudio gives it one of its most powerful
metaphorical expressions in Shakespeare,[4] and this even before the
Duke has got to him:

> Our natures do pursue,
> Like rats that ravin down their proper bane,
> A thirsty evil; and when we drink, we die.
> (I.ii.120–22)

In tracing the connections between death and desire in the early
modern period, I've considered the way in which desire experiences
the fatality of *eventual* death in terms of an *ever-present* mutability:
death is not merely the eventual termination of life, but an impossible
mutability within life itself. The for-ever of eventual death becomes

the ever-present process of mutability in life – Shakespeare's 'evermore unrest', Herbert's 'incessant motion', Drummond's 'inward cause of a necessary dissolution'. Of course death reduces us to dust, but to apprehend this process is to experience not only physical dissolution, but also, and more desperately, the hollowing of life from within into desire as loss; a radical mutability lives internally *as* desire. Death is experienced as life's inner impossibility, and, more specifically, mutability is experienced as the inner impossibility of desire. Hence that paradoxical double-despair characteristic of the mutability tradition: first, death and mutability are seen as not only thwarting desire, but rendering it impossible; second, death is welcome as total annihilation, and mutability as at once its truth and what is cancelled by it. Thus is desire enclosed catastrophically, immediately, in that which would otherwise deteriorate it only eventually, yet ineluctably, *in time*. In the process this internalization of death as desire is both gendered and displaced, and generates a fantasy which saturates social as well as psychic life and invests power in complex, fatal and revealing ways. In all such ways the early modern may be said to anticipate the modern.

III

SOCIAL DEATH

8

The Denial of
Death?

'The denial of death': the phrase is Freud's, from his 1915 essay 'Our Attitude towards Death', written when the First World War had been under way for about six months. Before the war, says Freud, the prevailing attitude to mortality had amounted to such a denial, which he further characterizes (twice) as 'cultural and conventional' and which took the form of a forgetting: 'We showed an unmistakable tendency to put death on one side, to eliminate it from life. We tried to hush it up.' The trauma of war, warns Freud, will require a change of attitude, or rather a return to an older attitude, such that now 'If you want to endure life, prepare yourself for death' (pp. 78, 84, 77, 89).

Many writers on death have agreed with Freud about this denial of death, although they have disagreed about when it began. Walter Benjamin, writing in 1936, speaks of it as having been occurring for several centuries, but as getting worse in our own:

Dying was once a public process in the life of the individual and a most exemplary one; think of the medieval pictures in which the deathbed has turned into a throne toward which the people press through the wide-open doors of the death house. In the course of modern times dying has been pushed further and further out of the perceptual world of the living. There used to be no house, hardly a room, in which someone had not once died. (The Middle Ages also felt spatially what makes that inscription on a sun dial of Ibiza, *Ultima multis* [the last day for many], significant as the temper of the times.) Today people live in rooms that have never been touched by death, dry dwellers of eternity, and when their end approaches they are stowed away in sanatoria or hospitals by their heirs. (pp. 93–4)

This attitude of forgetting had, apparently, become so habitual by
the early twentieth century that the First World War did not make
the difference Freud thought it would or should. Nor, according to
later writers, did the Second World War; if anything the extent of the
denial became even greater. In an influential essay of 1955, 'The
Pornography of Death', Geoffrey Gorer spoke of how death had
become not so much forgotten as tabooed, suppressed and unmention-
able – almost obscene. The natural processes of corruption and decay
had become disgusting, and any consideration of them was regarded
as unhealthy and morbid: 'the ugly facts are relentlessly hidden; the
art of the embalmers is the art of complete denial' (p. 172). Twenty-two
years later Philippe Ariès concluded his major study of death with the
claim that in 'the most industrialized, urbanized, and technologically
advanced areas of the Western world . . . society has banished death
. . . Everything in town[s] goes on as if nobody died any more' (*Hour*,
p. 560).

From tame to wild death

Initially in the West, claims Ariès, death was 'tamed' – by which he
means accepted as a familiar part of the order of nature. There was
a harmony between the living and the dead. Whether regarded as an
extension of sleep, or with confidence in an afterlife, death was met
with neither fear nor despair but an attitude halfway between passive
resignation and mystical trust (*Western Attitudes*, pp. 28, 103). Subsequently death became increasingly difficult. Initially this corresponded to a greater emphasis on individuality and on personal, as
distinct from collective, destiny. In the fourteenth century macabre
iconography, showing for instance the partly decomposed corpse,
'betrayed the bitter feeling of failure, mingled with mortality: *a passion
for being, an anxiety at not sufficiently being*' (p. 105). Whereas
Huizinga in *The Waning of the Middle Ages* (1924) had tended to
interpret this obsession with death, decay and transience as evidence
for cultural decadence and enfeeblement, Ariès sees it rather as a
life-affirming resentment of death; if there is an obsession with death
it is not because it is being desired or surrendered to, but just the

opposite. It is in the eighteenth century, during the so-called Enlightenment, that death comes to be denied; an ostensibly rational attitude
to the subject is then in fact motivated by avoidance. For example,
early health reformers wanted graveyards removed from city centres,
and this is seen to reflect a 'removal' of death from the realm of the
living.

In the modern period, death becomes even more traumatic; it is no
longer familiar or tamed: it has become wild (*Western Attitudes*,
p. 14). Modern man cannot come to terms with the fact that he is
going to die. Death, says Ariès, is also regarded as shameful and
forbidden. In part because of such repression, 'the mixture of eroticism
and death so sought after from the sixteenth to the eighteenth century
reappears in our sadistic literature and in violent death in our daily
life' (pp. 85, 92–3). Between the eighteenth century and the present
this association of sex and death did not disappear so much as become
sublimated; death was no longer desirable, but rather 'admirable in
its beauty' (p. 58).

Though richly descriptive and documented, Ariès's thesis is questionable in several respects – not least its underlying argument to the
effect that in the West we have moved from a healthy relationship to
death to a pathological one. As Joachim Whaley remarks, Ariès's
whole work is based on the belief that man's relationship to nature
and death has become increasingly unhealthy and distorted as a result
of progress, with the two worst periods in this respect being the
eighteenth and twentieth centuries (p. 5). The problems with Ariès's
work are accentuated by other writers who, in support of the denial-of-
death argument, reproduce it in an abridged and reductive form, like
Zygmunt Bauman in *Mortality, Immortality and Other Life Strategies*.
Ariès had rightly described different attitudes to death as characteristic
of different epochs, yet also continuous between them. By contrast,
Bauman tends to 'fix' these attitudes to epochs in a way which
misdescribes both. Thus he asserts that in something called the 'pre-
modern era' there was a common assumption about death which
remained 'unchallenged until the dawn of the Age of Reason' and
which entailed a 'resigned yet peaceful cohabitation with "tame"
death' (pp. 94, 96–7). The world was characterized by a monotony
of being, itself experienced as normality. Further, 'Monotony made

existence un-problematic, hence non-visible' (pp. 97, 94). Death was so common that 'everyone had ample opportunity to get used to its presence . . . one had no reason to be puzzled or unduly excited when death, for the umpteenth time, struck in one's close vicinity'. In short,

Death was 'tame' because it was not a challenge in the same sense in which all other elements of the life-process were not challenges in a world in which identities were given, everything was stuck in its place in the great chain of being and things ran their course by themselves. (p. 97)

Bauman's periodization is so overgeneralized and vague that it is unclear when the pre-modern, chain-of-being, everything-stuck-in-its-place existence is supposed to have ended.[1] I doubt that it corresponds to any period. Moreover, such generalizations have been challenged by social historians who rightly insist that class and wealth made a difference to how death was experienced: some people starved to death, others did not; in times of plague the rich could leave the cities, others could not; and so on.

Those who discern in modern culture a denial of death often also claim that the different attitude of earlier cultures was also a more healthy one. Be it through the burying of the dead in the centre of the community rather than at the periphery, or the keeping of the dead alive imaginatively, these earlier cultures are said to have more fully integrated death into life and to have been the better adjusted for it. One of the most reiterated claims is that if only we could properly mourn the dead we would come to terms with their loss, and we might even grow and develop as a result of it. In other words, by dealing sensibly with death we become stronger, perhaps even better, people. In this vein Michael Bronski tells us that the first step to coming to terms with death in the context of AIDS is to bring it out into the open, to talk about it and treat it as a material not a moral reality:

There is no inherent mystery surrounding sex and death – those myths are purely social inventions to control behaviour and make us conform to certain mores and standards.

We as gay people must learn to face the reality of death with the same energy and imagination we have put into claiming and enjoying our sexual desires and experiences. If we do not deal with death it will continue to cause us more stress, more hurt and more self-doubt. (pp. 227–8)

This hope for a healthy attitude to death and loss is on occasions (as here) so trite it could itself be said to be blatantly symptomatic of the denial of death, being apparently incapable of acknowledging on the personal level just how devastating and unendurable death is or can be for those who survive, and on the more general level how profoundly formative the trauma of death has been in the formation of Western culture. It may be, at least for some, that there is no coming to terms with the loss of death. There is only an adjustment, and always at a price: we remain damaged. That, at least, is the implication of writers from Ecclesiastes to Freud – and also of an utterly different kind of text, like this anonymous in memoriam and the countless others it speaks for:

In loving memory of my dear friend 'Dave', who took his life in May 1938 aged 19 years. We kissed in the park and they caught us. / I got nine months – He died. / He used to say 'We'll make it together'. It's been a long time Dave! / And a lonely journey. / I wish I could say 'We'll meet again' / But I have no faith – only memories. – Harry. May I pay tribute to all those who suffered and died with us during the dark years. (*Gay News* 95; cited by Jeffrey Weeks as epigraph to Chapter 11 of *Coming Out*)

Death as social control, and the omniscient analyst

Jean Baudrillard presents the argument for the existence of a denial of death in its most extreme form. For him, this denial is not only deeply symptomatic of contemporary reality, but represents an insidious and pervasive form of ideological control. His account depends heavily upon a familiar critique of the Enlightenment's intellectual, cultural and political legacy. This critique has become influential in recent cultural theory, though Baudrillard's version of it is characteristically uncompromising and sweeping, and more reductive than most.

The main claim is that Enlightenment rationality is an instrument not of freedom and democratic empowerment but, on the contrary, of repression and violence. Likewise with the Enlightenment's secular emphasis upon a common humanity; for Baudrillard this resulted in what he calls 'the cancer of the Human' – far from being an inclusive category of emancipation, the idea of a universal humanity made possible the demonizing of difference and the repressive privileging of the normal:

the 'Human' is from the outset the institution of its structural double, the 'Inhuman'. This is all it is: the progress of Humanity and Culture are simply the chain of discriminations with which to brand 'Others' with inhumanity, and therefore with nullity. (p. 125)

Baudrillard acknowledges here the influence of Michel Foucault, but goes on to identify something more fundamental and determining than anything identified by Foucault:

at the very core of the 'rationality' of our culture, however, is an exclusion that precedes every other, more radical than the exclusion of madmen, children or inferior races, an exclusion preceding all these and serving as their model: the exclusion of the dead and of death. (p. 126)

So total is this exclusion that, 'today, *it is not normal to be dead*, and this is new. To be dead is an unthinkable anomaly; nothing else is as offensive as this. Death is a delinquency, and an incurable deviancy' (p. 126). He insists that the attempt to abolish death (especially through capitalist accumulation), to separate it from life, leads only to a culture permeated by death – 'quite simply, ours is a culture of death' (p. 127). Moreover, it is the repression of death which facilitates 'the repressive socialization of life'; all existing agencies of repression and control take root in the disastrous separation of death from life (p. 130). And, as if that were not enough, our very concept of reality has its origin in the same separation or disjunction (pp. 130–33). Modern culture is contrasted with that of the primitive and the savage, in which, allegedly, life and death were not separated; also with that of the Middle Ages, where, allegedly, there was still a collectivist, 'folkloric and joyous' conception of death. This and many other aspects of the argument are questionable, but perhaps the main objection to Baudrillard's case is his view of culture as a macro-conspiracy conducted by an insidious ideological prime-mover whose agency is always invisibly at work (rather like God). Thus (from just one page), the political economy supposedly '*intends*' to eliminate death through accumulation; and 'our whole culture is just one huge *effort* to dissociate life and death' (p. 147; my emphases).

What those like Baudrillard find interesting about death is not the old conception of it as a pre-cultural constant which diminishes the significance of all cultural achievement, but, on the contrary, its function as a culturally relative – which is to say culturally formative – construct. And, if cultural relativism is on the one hand about relinquishing the comfort of the absolute, for those like Baudrillard it is also about the new strategies of intellectual mastery made possible by the very disappearance of the absolute. Such modern accounts of how death is allegedly denied, of how death is the supreme ideological fix, entail a new intensity and complexity of interpretation and decipherment, a kind of hermeneutics of death. To reinterpret death as a deep effect of ideology, even to the extent of regarding it as the most fundamental ideological adhesive of modern political repression and social control, is simultaneously to denounce it as in some sense a deception or an illusion, and to bring it within the domain of knowledge and analysis as never before.

Death, for so long regarded as the ultimate reality – that which disempowers the human and obliterates all human achievement, including the achievements of knowledge – now becomes the object of a hugely empowering knowledge. Like omniscient seers, intellectuals like Baudrillard and Bauman relentlessly anatomize and diagnose the modern (or post-modern) human condition in relation to an ideology of death which becomes the key with which to unlock the secret workings of Western culture in all its insidiousness. Baudrillard in particular applies his theory relentlessly, steamrollering across the cultural significance of the quotidian and the contingent. His is an imperialist, omniscient analytic, a perpetual act of reductive generalization, a self-empowering intellectual performance which proceeds without qualification and without any sense that something might be mysterious or inexplicable. As such it constitutes a kind of interpretative, theoretical violence, an extreme but still representative instance of how the relentless anatomizing and diagnosis of death in the modern world has become a struggle for empowerment through masterful – i.e. reductive – critique.

Occasionally one wonders if the advocates of the denial-of-death argument are not themselves in denial. They speak about death endlessly yet indirectly, analysing not death so much as our culture's attitude towards it. To that extent it is not the truth of death but the truth of our culture that they seek. But, even as they make death signify in this indirect way, it is still death that is compelling them to speak. And those like Baudrillard and Bauman speak urgently, performing intellectually a desperate mimicry of the omniscience which death denies. One senses that the entire modern enterprise of relativizing death, of understanding it culturally and socially, may be an attempt to disavow it in the very act of analysing and demystifying it.

Ironically then, for all its rejection of the Enlightenment's arrogant belief in the power of rationality, this analysis of death remains indebted to a fundamental Enlightenment aspiration to mastery through knowledge. Nothing could be more 'Enlightenment', in the pejorative sense that Baudrillard describes, than his own almost megalomaniac wish to penetrate the truth of death, and the masterful controlling intellectual subject which that attempt presupposes. And this may be true to an extent for all of us more or less involved in the anthropological or quasi-anthropological accounts of death which assume that, by looking at how a culture handles death, we disclose things about a culture which it does not know about itself. So what has been said of sex in the nineteenth century may also be true of death in the twentieth: it has not been repressed so much as resignified in new, complex and productive ways which then legitimate a never-ending analysis of it.

It is questionable whether the denial of death has ever really figured in our culture in the way that Baudrillard and Bauman suggest. Of course, the ways of dealing with and speaking about death have changed hugely, and have in some respects involved something like denial. But in philosophical and literary terms there has never been a denial of death.[2] Moreover, however understood, the pre-modern period can hardly be said to have been characterized by the 'healthy' attitude that advocates of the denial argument often claim, imply or assume. In fact it could be said that we can begin to understand the *vital* role of death in Western culture only when we accept death as profoundly, compellingly and irreducibly traumatic.

In some more recent cultural theory there has occurred another, rather different, relativizing of death. On the one hand death is (again) said to be a cultural construct, 'the most obvious thing about [which] is that it is always only represented'. On the other hand, death is 'a signifier with an incessantly receding, ungraspable signified, always pointing to other signifiers, other means of representing what is finally just absent'. This makes death the unrepresentable, always absent excess which endlessly destabilizes culture:

it stands as a challenge to all our systems of meaning, order, governance, and civilization. *Any* given cultural construct – from religion and poetry to psychoanalysis and medical technology – may be construed as a response to the disordering force of death. (Goodwin and Bronfen, p. 4)[3]

This is a move characteristic of contemporary theory: what philosophers and others used to call 'the real' is dissolved into representation, but with a strong desire not only for something to remain, and to function as the real once did, but to invest it with an 'excess' which forever destabilizes. So, in a for ever inaccessible space beyond representation, we fantasize an excess which forever disrupts representation. Except that even to speak of a beyond is too metaphysical, so we imagine an outside which is always already inside. In short, contemporary theory evades the classic philosophical problems of ontology and epistemology, and this is because we do not have the conviction of our residual desire for the pre-cultural real; yet we desire it nevertheless, reconstruing it even as we dissolve it. Death, of course, disallows the evasion:

Just in case you thought there was no distinction between representation and reality, there is death. Just in case you thought experience and the representation of experience melted into one another, death provides a structural principle separating the two. See the difference, death asks, see the way language and vision differ from the actual, the irrevocable, the real? (Barreca, 'Writing as Voodoo', p. 174)

9

Degeneration and Dissidence

It is still sometimes assumed that nineteenth-century degeneration theories were little more than pseudo-scientific ranting. They were always, and still remain, much more than that; as William Greenslade has indicated, there is a line of descent from the original degeneration theorists through to the Holocaust of the 1940s.

Nineteenth-century theories of racial and social degeneration indicate how, as older metaphysics of death and mutability decline in relation to various developments of the Enlightenment, including confidence in progress and the possibility of social change, they vacate a cultural and psychic space which is then flooded by new and intense fears of *social* death. While such fears are a direct corollary of social progress, they also incorporate aspects of the older metaphysic which they displace.

Max Nordau's *Degeneration* (1892) was not only one of the most popular of all texts on the subject, but one of the most popular of all texts in Europe in the 1890s. An English translation was published in 1895, just a few months before the Wilde trials, going through seven editions in six months (Greenslade, pp. 255, 120). Degeneration became a theory sufficiently obsessive and persecutory to be able to explain every kind of evil, from individual illness, through national economic decline, to the decay of an empire, and able to demonize any group or individual that was perceived as threatening or just different. Metaphors of disease and plague have always come naturally to believers in degeneration – and not surprisingly, since to them degeneration threatens contagion, the loss of immunity and, ultimately, the threat of social death and species extinction.

There is much about degeneration theory which is specific to the crises and ways of thinking of the late nineteenth century. But it was also a manifestation of Western culture's more enduring fears of disintegration and decline – fears whose most significant precursors included the early modern preoccupation with cosmic decay (above, Chapter 5). In fact degeneration theory has connections with the same metaphysics which animated the cosmic-decay debate. But, whereas in the early modern period social decline was attributed to a more fundamental cosmic decline, now it is rooted in biology. In a sense, the cosmic has become collapsed into the biological, in a way which intensifies anxiety because decline is now radically interior.

Following the pioneering degeneracy theorist Benedict Morel, Nordau defined degeneration as a morbid, genetically transmissible deviation from an original type or normal form. All versions of degeneracy originated in a 'bio-chemical and bio-mechanical derangement of the nerve-cell' (pp. 16, 254), but major causes of degeneration also came from outside the organism. Modern environmental changes were especially dangerous. Cesare Lombroso argued that modernity induced narcotic abuse or nervous illness, which in turn induced debility, which in turn was transmitted through the father's seed. He warned that even otherwise sober parents who at the moment of conception are temporarily drunk beget children who are epileptic, paralytic, idiotic or insane: 'thus a single embrace, given in a moment of drunkenness, may be fatal to an entire generation' (cited from Hurley, p. 67). This fear was powerful for those like Lombroso and Morel: once degeneration had started, its effects could accelerate and magnify in each generation, quickly producing insanity and even extinction. Whereas biological and social evolution had proceeded slowly across millennia, degeneration could disintegrate the highest evolved forms in an instant.

The growing concern that evolution might be halted or even reversed was popularly expressed by H. G. Wells. An essay 'On Extinction' shows very clearly how an older melancholy preoccupation with mutability could be adapted to an evolutionary perspective. Wells here entertains the possibility of the extinction of the human race:

Life, that has schemed and struggled and committed itself, the life that has played and lost, comes at last to the pitiless judgement of time, and is slowly and remorselessly annihilated. (p. 169)

Wells meditates on the creatures of prehistory, now extinct. All that is left of them is the geological traces, in relation to which we speculate uncertainly about what they actually looked like. At issue here is less the extinction of individuals than that of whole species which have left nothing behind – 'no mark, and no tradition . . . Nothing living has any part of them . . .' Fossil fragments are the epitome of the obscure trace, hinting 'merely at shadowy dead sub-kingdoms, of which the form eludes'. They point to that 'unfathomable darkness . . . saying only one thing clearly, the word "extinction" ' (p. 170).

There is no reassurance in existing species domination, since in the case of every predominant species the earth has ever seen 'the hour of its complete ascendancy has been the eve of its entire overthrow' (p. 149). This decline might be due to external causes; for instance, an existing creature, currently in unsuspected obscurity, might develop new capacities which could sweep man away into the darkness from which his universe arose (p. 168). Alternatively or additionally, decline might be due to an inner process – degeneration, or 'degradation' as Wells also calls it – whereby life-forms begin to devolve rather than evolve. Certainly, the idea that life proceeds through a gradual, progressive organic evolution – 'that inevitable tendency to higher and better things' – is now regarded as a myth. The truth is rather that living species have 'varied along divergent lines from intermediate forms, and . . . not necessarily in an upward direction'. Further, 'rapid progress has often been followed by rapid extinction or degeneration' (pp. 149, 159, 167). This idea of evolutionary degeneration, an extreme catastrophic unbinding of civilization, would be powerfully evoked by W. B. Yeats in 'The Second Coming' (1921):

> Turning and turning in the widening gyre
> The falcon cannot hear the falconer;
> Things fall apart; the centre cannot hold;
> Mere anarchy is loosed upon the world,

The blood-dimmed tide is loosed, and everywhere
The ceremony of innocence is drowned;
The best lack all conviction while the worst
Are full of a passionate intensity.

Modernity, decadence and atavism

Nordau at least believed that degeneration could be contained. But, as we'll see, he too was haunted by a fear of degeneration as endemic, chronic and irreversible. He also believed that a major cause of degeneracy was the accelerating pace of modern life and the growth of urban centres – 'the excessive organic wear and tear suffered by the nations through the immense demands of their activity, and through the rank growth of large towns' (p. 43). He attributed to degeneration exactly the character of disease and epidemic: degenerate potentialities, like infectious viruses, are always present in the body (individual and social), but were hitherto only manifested sporadically. They begin to spread alarmingly when 'circumstances arise intensely favourable for their rapid increase'. And that time had come with modernity: 'We stand now in the midst of a severe mental epidemic; of a sort of black death of degeneration' (p. 537).

Degenerates are characterized by numerous kinds of mental and physical ills. Nordau's particular concern is with degeneracy manifested as decadence in artistic culture, deriving from (among many other things) egomania, and 'a madly inordinate eroticism' (p. 129). In degenerates, says Nordau, 'we detect the same ultimate elements, viz., a brain incapable of normal working, thence feebleness of will, inattention, predominance of emotion, lack of knowledge, absence of sympathy or interest in the world and humanity, atrophy of the notion of duty and morality' (p. 536). Nordau lists a bewildering array of pathologies, perversions and aberrations. He admits that, from a clinical point of view, they are 'somewhat unlike each other', but insists nevertheless that they are only 'different manifestations of a single and unique fundamental condition, to wit, exhaustion' (p. 536). And chronic fatigue is indeed the important, underlying condition that preoccupies Nordau – a fatigue which is dangerous not just because it renders the individual ineffectual or apathetic. If that were all, degeneration would be a containable problem. The deeper danger of what Nordau calls this 'vast fatigue' is that it renders both the degenerate and, much more worryingly, society itself terribly susceptible to disintegration.

Sexual perversion became, for Nordau, increasingly significant in the aetiology of degeneracy, and again there is the same concern with enervation and enfeeblement: insofar as it contributes to pornography and the incitement to lasciviousness, sexual excess destroys the bodily and mental health of individuals and ruins society as a whole by rendering it 'too worn out and flaccid to perform great tasks' (p. 557). Likewise, urbanization diminishes the 'vital powers' of the individual (p. 35).

Another characteristic of degeneration is atavism: the re-emergence of a primitive past *within* the civilized present. Degenerates, exhausted and unable to maintain their place in the evolutionary ascent, regress to

the most forgotten, far-away past ... they compose music like that of the yellow natives of East Asia. They confound all the arts, and lead them back to the primitive forms they had *before evolution differentiated them*. Every one of their qualities is atavistic, and we know, moreover, that atavism is one of the most constant marks of degeneracy. (p. 555; my emphasis)

The claim is that there are identifiable diseases in the modern world which are a direct result of a regressive and atavistic 'throw-back' caused in part by harmful environmental factors; hence the re-emergence of earlier and inferior forms of life within the present. But, even as Nordau tirelessly identifies these tendencies, we discern an underlying fear that degeneration is not just a hiccup in evolution, but somehow its logic and destiny. It is as if there is a teleological, 'unconscious' drive in evolution which leads to decline, exhaustion, disintegration and even self-destruction: social death. Instinct and the unconscious, far from being the forces which might guarantee evolutionary progress, are prime carriers of degeneracy.

Degeneration theory was in certain respects a reaction to the perception of something like the death drive understood as an *internal unbinding* of life's highest forms: as an inner, evolutionary process of unbinding which is at work instinctually as the drive to disintegrate and self-destruct. That is why, for Nordau, survival in the face of degeneration requires a vigilant repression of man's 'insensate and self-destructive appetites'. Overt, conscious repression is a necessary condition of progress; survival requires nothing less than 'the expansion of consciousness and the contraction of the unconscious; the strengthening of will and weakening of impulsions; the increase of self-responsibility and the repression of reckless egoism' (p. 554).[1] Nordau had nothing to do with psychoanalysis, yet there are parts of *Degeneration* which anticipate Freud's theory of the death drive – especially the idea that civilization was only ever a detour on the way to death (below, Chapter 14).

Nordau obsessively equates civilization with integration and unity – or, more exactly, with *the integration of the differentiated*. As life-forms evolve they become increasingly differentiated but also increasingly dependent upon harmonious integration with each other. So this unity is not just a natural reflection of man's nature, nor even of his metaphysical essence or *telos*. Even in nature itself the unity of the higher forms of life is an *achieved*, hierarchical and disciplined order. The higher the form of life, the more it involves a complex association of cells and cell systems, each with its own functions and wants, and increasingly vulnerable to internal anarchy:

in order that the collective organism may be able to perform its task, its constituent parts are bound to submit to a severe hierarchical order. Anarchy in its interior is a disease, and leads rapidly to death. (p. 409)

And human consciousness, the highest of all forms of life, is the most 'highly differentiated and "hierarchized" ' of all (p. 247). Following Kant, Nordau affirms that 'to think . . . is to unite and bind' (p. 269). And this is one reason why consciousness is always susceptible to being undermined by instinct and the unconscious, and thereby precipitated into disorder and disintegration. The more sophisticated the integration, the more vulnerable it is to being undone. We might add that, the more evolved a culture regards itself as being, the more it becomes, or at least fears, its own internal dissolution. Nordau quotes Paul Bourget, who, in *Essais de psychologie contemporaine*, described decadence as the process whereby the separate units or cells – of, for instance, language or an organism – break up into anarchic independence:

A society ought to be assimilated to an organism. As an organism, in fact, it resolves itself into a federation of lesser organisms, which again resolve themselves into a federation of cells. In order that the whole organism should function with energy, it is necessary that the component organisms should function with energy, but with a subordinate energy. If the energy of the cells becomes independent, the organisms composing the total organism cease likewise to subordinate their energy to the total energy, and the anarchy which takes place constitutes the decadence of the whole. (Bourget, cited by Nordau, p. 301; cf. Nalbantian, p. 12)

In this respect too, believers in degeneration share something with psychoanalysis. Nordau clearly shared Freud's sense of social and psychic organization as precarious and dependent upon a sustained effort which can never be guaranteed, partly because it is threatened by the return of what is repressed, partly (and relatedly) because it is something for which we never have enough energy – not least because the repressions required by civilization consume so much. And when the effort of maintaining civilization is too great, we are threatened with psychic and cultural collapse. Only a finite quantity of energy is available, and it is never ever quite enough. In both Nordau's positivist biology and Freudian psychoanalysis there is the same sense of energy as a scarce resource, and of social and psychic organization becoming vulnerable when energy falters or fails. For Nordau, even the normal person will at some time succumb to fatigue and fall into that state which, for the degenerate, is chronic (p. 283). Life is a fragile energy, susceptible from the start to the exhaustion which is its destiny. Again, to discern here pre-echoes of Freud's death drive is hardly fanciful, given Nordau's own definition of life as 'a definite measure of force, which makes it possible for us to resist for a given time the influence upon us of Nature's forces of dissolution'. Nordau defends his own scientific world-view against all others because it helps us fend off death for that bit longer, but always in the knowledge that it cannot overcome it (pp. 150, 10).

Nature is the ultimate force of dissolution, and about that we can do nothing. But the degenerates have, as it were, internalized and perversely intensify this characteristic of nature, and about them we can do a lot. They, even more than nature, have an endless capacity for destruction, anarchy and social ruin. It is in Nordau's tireless rage against what he supposes to be the specific maladies of degenerates that his theory is most clearly an expression of, and an attempt to contain, fears about regression, exhaustion and disintegration.

Thus decadent poets pursue linguistic disconnection – itself symptomatic of a 'disorder and permanent chaos' which is already deeply rooted in their sensibilities and their brains. Baudelaire, says Nordau, is drawn to 'death and corruption', while composers like Wagner express 'anarchism, a craving for revolt and contradiction'. Degenerates generally possess a 'mania for destruction'; Ibsen, for example, is a 'theoretic criminal' – i.e. one who translates his destructive impulses into drama rather than actual criminality. He is also a sexual masochist (pp. 270–71, 290, 264, 399, 413).

'Connecting links abound': degeneration and perversion

The agency of the most pernicious and rapid mode of inner disintegration is perversion. In fact it is perversion which drives the degenerate organism to its death: 'in such cases the [separate] organs are suffering from perversions; they exact satisfactions, not only pernicious in their remote consequences to the whole organism, but immediately so to the organs themselves'. Thus sexual perversions run 'directly contrary to the purpose of the instinct, i.e., the preservation of the species' (Nordau, pp. 411, 260). Here and elsewhere in Nordau, sexual perversion is not yet the definitive perversion it would subsequently become, but is clearly anticipating it.

Perversion is pernicious because it is paradoxically made possible by the evolutionary process of organization which morality has undergone:

Morality ... has become, in the course of thousands of generations, an organized instinct. For this reason, like all other organized instincts, it is exposed to 'perversion', to aberration. The effect of this is that the organ, or the whole organism, works in opposition to its normal task and its natural laws, and cannot work otherwise. (p. 259)

Here too is the reason why it is perversion which also focuses most acutely the fundamental tension between, on the one hand, wanting to identify degeneration as manageable and containable, and, on the other, seeing it as chronic, potentially catastrophic and perhaps irreversible. Whereas the manageable view sees in degeneracy something like a natural internal decline, or a containable external threat, the view of it as chronic identifies degeneracy as irrupting from within what should be most removed from it – e.g. progress – and with an intensity which threatens nothing less than social death.

Daniel Pick, in a persuasive account of European degeneration theory, and with due regard to his own caution against underestimating the diverse and incompatible forms which it took, finds a repeated tension between these two views. To regard degeneration as manageable meant that its agents could be effectively isolated through, for example, segregation, transportation or castration. To regard it as chronic meant that it was uncontrollably everywhere, a problem of and for whole populations. Thus, says Pick,

the shared problematic of degeneration across the period could perhaps be summarized as follows: was degeneration separable from the history of progress (to be coded as 'regression', 'atavism', or 'primitivism'), or did it reveal that the city, progress, civilization and modernity were paradoxically, the very agents of decline? (p. 106)

If the manageable view sees degeneration as a problem of containing the 'other', the chronic view sees it as a problem of the 'other' having infiltrated and even become the 'same': civilization is threatened from without, but also, and even more acutely, from within. Hence the fears which Pick elucidates – 'fears of inundation, the subject over-whelmed at every level of mind and body by internal disorder and external attack' (p. 44; cf. pp. 43, 235–6). The old problematic returns in a socio-biological/pathological form: death not as the antithesis of life, but as its inner dynamic. Hence the tendency for degeneracy to shift disconcertingly from being a manageable problem of the individual (for example the cretin and the criminal) to a chronic one of modern society as a (disintegrating) whole; from individual pathology to a sense of social death (p. 4).

It was the chronic view which incited the imagination and which became increasingly obsessed with the pervert. Mapped socially and psychically, the pervert was both outside and inside; mapped teleologically (in relation to the past, present and future of civilization), just everywhere. And increasingly that perversion was sexual. Asserting that the real source of Nietzsche's philosophy was his sadism, Nordau further declares that degenerate art and philosophy is above all rooted in the 'sexual psychopathology' of those who produce it and who consume it: 'All persons of unbalanced minds . . . have the keenest scent for perversions of a sexual kind.' And artistic works of a sexually psychopathic nature excite in abnormal subjects the corresponding perversion. This is because aesthetic and sexual feelings are 'contiguous . . . even coincident' (pp. 451–2; cf. p. 167).

The sexual pervert was also identified with the primitive, and vice versa. Thus the sexuality of primitives was represented as quintessentially excessive, flooding over indiscriminately into the perverse, while, as George Mosse indicates in his study of nationalism and sexuality, the decadent sexual pervert was said to be marked by an excess of libido which linked him or her with the primitive.[2] The seductiveness of this association between the perverse and the primitive is again something which degenerationists shared with Freud:

I am beginning to grasp an idea: it is as though in the perversions, of which hysteria is the negative, we have before us a remnant of a primeval sexual cult, which once was – perhaps still is – a religion in the Semitic East (Moloch, Astarte). Imagine, I obtained a scene about the circumcision of a girl. The cutting off of a piece of the labium minor (which is even shorter today), sucking up the blood, after which the child was given a piece of the skin to eat . . .

Perverse actions, moreover, are always the same – meaningful and fashioned according to some pattern that someday will be understood.

I dream, therefore, of a primeval devil religion with rites that are carried on secretly . . . Connecting links abound. (Freud to Fliess, 24 January 1897, in *Complete Letters*, p. 227; see also Pick, p. 228)

Freud eventually rejected degeneracy as an explanation of perversion, and with important consequences.[3] But Freud's idea of normality as a sequential, evolutionary development, and of perversion as a fixation at, or regression to, an earlier stage, nevertheless warrants comparison with the basic principle of degeneracy – if only to indicate how otherwise divergent theories retain revealing connections, not so much through direct influence, but through shared cultural contexts and interconnecting intellectual histories. Thus Max Nordau: 'The disease of degeneracy consists precisely in the fact that the degenerate organism has not the power to mount to the height of evolution already attained by the species, but stops on the way at an earlier or later point' (p. 556). Like psychoanalysis, though very differently, degeneration theory might challenge Darwinism, but it often did so in evolutionary terms.[4]

This 'regressive' aspect of degeneration was a factor in the way in which degeneration theorists connected sexual perversion with race.[5] Richard Plant, identifying the way anti-Semitism associated Jews with sexual perversion, cites the following passage from Hitler's official newspaper in August 1930:

Among the many evil instincts that characterize the Jewish race, one that is especially pernicious has to do with sexual relationships. The Jews are forever trying to propagandize sexual relations between siblings, men and animals, and men and men. We National Socialists will soon unmask and condemn them by law. These efforts are nothing but vulgar, perverted crimes and we will punish them by banishment or hanging. (p. 49)

Michel Foucault regards 'the medicine of perversions and the programmes of eugenics' as the two great innovations in the technology of sex in the second half of the nineteenth century, with the theory of 'degenerescence' making it possible for them to refer across to one another. This theory

explained how a heredity that was burdened with various maladies . . . ended by producing a sexual pervert (look into the genealogy of an exhibitionist or a homosexual: you will find a hemiplegic ancestor, a phthistic parent, or an uncle afflicted with senile dementia); but it went on to explain how a sexual perversion resulted in the depletion of one's line of descent – rickets in the children, the sterility of future generations. The series composed of perversion–heredity–degenerescence formed the solid nucleus of the new technologies of sex. (*History*, I.118)

Foucault's account stressed the way in which such theories gave scientific credibility to new forms of social control, specifically creating new types of deviant whose study and containment would legitimate new technologies of power. Most subsequent accounts of the history of sexuality follow him in this. However, such connections between sexual perversion and degeneration are only part of the story, and a relatively recent one at that. Degeneracy theory is also deeply indebted to older pre-sexological notions of perversion, and to understand the power of the theory in the late nineteenth century we must recognize its origins in these earlier beliefs, especially the idea of the pervert as an agent of internal deviation.

Morel defined degeneration as a deviation, and deviation is the essence of perversion, from Augustine and before, to Freud and beyond. What made perversion even more important was its becoming increasing sexualized as a concept, in sexology and (later) in psychoanalysis. What this meant was that in the late nineteenth century perversion was being transformed from a mainly theological to a mainly psychosexual category. This was indeed a momentous shift – arguably the single most significant development in the creation of 'modern' sexuality. But the earlier theological category remained disturbingly active within the latter, and – strange as it may seem – subversively so, not least with regard to the connection between perversion and death.

The deviation which characterizes perversion is essentially a paradoxical one. Why is the prima facie innocent activity of separating or departing from something felt to be such a threat to it? Why does deviation become a subversion, corruption or contradiction of that which is departed from (which we will call the normal)? Why, for theology, was *perversion* the supreme evil – the antithesis of *conversion* – and, correspondingly, for the degenerationists, the cause of organic and social death? The answer lies partly in the fact that deviation originates from within that which it perverts. Literally so: to deviate from something presupposes an antecedent point of congruence with it, either as the identical or (more worrying) the indistinguishable.

Typically, this means that perverse deviation discloses something within or about (in proximity to) the normal which the latter must disavow in order to remain itself – a split, a contradiction, a difference; this is one reason why perversion is regarded as dangerous. However, the original proximity (or identity) of the perverse with the normal also enables the normal to displace its own contradictions on to the perverse; proximity is a condition of displacement, which in turn marks the same or the similar as radically other. Mythologically and historically, politically and medically, perversion is a category which incurs the violence of this displacement. But it is also what carries the potentially subversive knowledge both of what is disavowed and of what is displaced. And it always has the potential to return along the very route of the deviation/displacement. Armed with that knowledge, and taking that route, it has the potential to effect the most disturbing of subversions.[6]

One of our culture's founding narratives, the Fall, is rife with this perverse dynamic. It is pertinent to consider how, not least because those like Benedict Morel connected the theory of degeneration to his reading of Genesis, recasting the Fall narrative in pseudo-medical terms. In that narrative, evil (and thereby death) not only erupts from within a divine order which should (in virtue of God's omnipotence) precisely have precluded it, but originates with those beings closest to God – Satan and then 'man'. These allegedly pervert their most divine attribute, free will, becoming in the process the source of *all* evil and bringing death into the world. So original sin might more aptly be regarded as original perversity – the means whereby responsibility for evil is displaced via Satan on to man and then on to woman. At the same time evil remains so subversively implicated in divinity that a whole branch of theology (theodicy) has grown up to explain the fact. But never successfully, and the problem of evil and death has remained intrinsic to divinity: either God is omnipotent, in which case he created evil, or evil is not God's fault (i.e. it is independent of and opposed to him), which means he is not omnipotent.

Returning to Nordau, it is interesting that he insists, or perhaps has to concede, that disease and health are much more closely connected than is usually imagined. The difference between them is not one of kind but one of quantity, in that they share the same 'vital activity'.

Sometimes this activity is accelerated, sometimes retarded, 'and when this deviation from the rule is detrimental to the ends of the whole organism, we call it disease' (pp. 552–3). In short, disease is not 'a state differing essentially from that of health' (p. 555). So, what would now count as a diseased state might once have been healthy. A return to what was, at the primitive stage of the organism's development, a perfectly appropriate and therefore healthy state of things is now a disease. There must be no going back.

Given Nordau's ethical and political project, this is a compromising admission. What separates the healthy from the sick, the normal from the diseased, the natural from the unnatural, is a difference not of kind but of quantity – merely the intensification or retardation of a 'vital' process that they all share in common. And the criteria for determining whether someone or something is diseased or healthy are remarkably relativist: simply 'the circumstances and purposes of the organism'. Thus, 'according to the time of its appearance, *one and the same state may very well be at one time disease and at another health*' (p. 555; my emphasis).

Because it is a question 'of more or less', says Nordau, it is impossible to define the limits of the degenerate: 'extreme cases are naturally easily recognized. But who shall determine with accuracy the exact point at which deviation from the normal, i.e. from health, begins?' (p. 553). Who indeed? One group called upon by Nordau to decide the boundary between the healthy and the degenerate (and to do so with a certainty impossible by his own account) is psychiatrists. He urges them to identify and publicly denounce the degenerates, to unmask their followers as enemies to society, and to caution the public against their lies (pp. 559–60).

The witch-hunting paranoia of some advocates of degeneracy derives from these two facts conceded by Nordau: not only do those who now carry the seeds of social death within them embody a condition which was once normal and healthy, but even now they remain barely distinguishable from the normal.[7] Furthermore, progress is itself responsible, in that degeneracy is produced not only by a falling away from the higher, *but by the very effort of reaching towards it*. For all its 560-odd pages of unflaggingly confident denunciation of the degenerate, and its equally confident affirmation of the truly, self-evidently, civilized, Nordau's book is written in the knowledge that the two are in a terrifying proximity and are often indistinguishable.

In one respect Nordau was only complying with a newer medical model emerging in the nineteenth century, according to which pathological phenomena are identical to corresponding normal phenomena save for quantitative variations. This newer, positivist, conception of disease is to be contrasted with the older, ontological, view, which insisted on a qualitative difference between disease and health. Whereas the positivist view regards disease as a deficiency or an excess of the normal, and thereby posits a relationship of homogeneity or continuity between the two, the ontological view sees it as a fundamentally different condition, obeying laws completely different from those governing the normal state (Canguilhem, pp. 35, 275, 49, 56). The positivist conception of disease rejects what Canguilhem calls 'medical Manichaeanism', whereby 'Health and Disease fought over man the way Good and Evil fought over the World' (p. 103), health being associated with salvation and goodness, and disease with sickness, evil and sin. The medical refusal of the ontological conception of disease is effectively a refusal of disease as evil. Canguilhem cites Claude Bernard, who wrote in 1876, 'These ideas of a struggle between two opposing agents, of an antagonism between life and death, between health and sickness, inanimate and living nature have had their day. The continuity of phenomena, their imperceptible gradation and harmony, must be recognized everywhere' (p. 72).[8]

In *Degeneration* Nordau seeks to advance a socio-political vision based on the old Manichaean dualism, by recourse to the positivist medical model which is in conflict with the most basic tenet of that dualism. It is hardly surprising that he is pressed into contradiction, believing on the one hand that degenerates will perish on their own accord, on the other that they must be ruthlessly exposed and crushed. Thus exhaustion renders degenerates incapable of adaptation, and, lacking the reality principle, they will perish of their own accord: 'that which inexorably destroys them is that they do not know how to come to terms with reality' (p. 540). Yet – and here the inconsistency is glaring – they are also regarded as possessing a terrible energy and being hell-bent on disintegrating and perverting the social, psychic and sexual orders (pp. 6, 22–4, 260, 317ff.). So, for example, the newly identified urban degenerates are on the one hand regarded as enfeebled and unhealthy, on the other as capable of great powers of adaptability and survival. Ironically, it is the non-degenerates who, in the context of urban decay, now become most vulnerable to decline and extinction, being overwhelmed by the disgusting vigour and fecundity of inferior – degenerate – classes and races: what William Greenslade has called 'that threatening degenerative coupling of the fertile and the low' (p. 257).[9]

Another inconsistency concerns the binary opposition between order and disintegration which structures Nordau's entire book. Ideally for Nordau there is a deeper unity-in-differentiation which is the opposite of disintegration. It is, for instance, a mark of evolutionary sophistication, a 'perfection attained very late in organic evolution', that enables humans to differentiate between the various sense perceptions. But deep down in us all he discerns a regressive tendency to undifferentiate the sense perceptions in order to get back to a primal unity which is both a confusion and a perfection: 'a vague intuition of the fundamental unity of essence in all perceptions'. But to approach this primal unity is dangerous, involving 'a retrogression to the very beginning of organic development'. This kind of degeneration entails a disintegration of civilized unity through a movement back to primal unity: 'It is a descent from the height of human perfection to the low level of the mollusc' (pp. 141–2). Again, the resemblance of this to the idea of a death drive is clear.

We can if we like dismiss these inconsistencies as the result of confused, ludicrous thinking. But they were also symptomatic of deeper cultural contradictions emerging and intensifying around fears of social death. At one level the very idea of social death assumes the existence of discrete, identifiable and containable sources of corruption and degeneration. Yet, as we've seen, degeneration theory carries within it an older metaphysic which sees death and disintegration as interior to all life. Thus the normal keeps slipping back into the pervert, the healthy into the sick, the same into the other. This echoes the old problem of evil: it was always intrinsic to, or at least parasitic upon, the good.

It is partly the indeterminacy in Nordau's theory between the normal and the degenerate that makes the latter so terrifying, and leads him to declaim, in the closing pages of *Degeneration*, that 'whoever looks upon civilization as a good, having value and deserving to be defended, must mercilessly crush under his thumb the anti-social vermin', i.e. degenerates (p. 557). Others would call for the same thing – including Friedrich Nietzsche, who advocated 'the remorseless destruction of all degenerate and parasitic elements' in the name of 'a tremendous purification . . . of mankind' (*Ecce Homo*, pp. 51, 53, 67). The threat of degeneration was being conceptualized as never before, and remains central to all those 'secular' programmes of radical social change which have recourse to the idea of social death. Eventually it would license indiscriminate mass-killing, including genocide.

10

Between Degeneration and the Death Drive: Joseph Conrad's *Heart of Darkness*

Kurtz, in Joseph Conrad's *Heart of Darkness*, is one of the more enigmatic and chilling protagonists of modern fiction. He is possessed of a supremely civilized intelligence. We are told, for example (and not without irony), that 'all Europe' contributed to his making, and that his achievements range from being a great musician to being entrusted to report to 'the International Society for the Suppression of Savage Customs' (pp. 71, 103). Yet when Kurtz deviates into the barbaric it is because, not in spite, of being so civilized. In *Heart of Darkness* the overcivilized is seen to have an affinity with the excesses of the primitive. Kurtz embodies the paradox which degeneration theory tries to explain but only exacerbates, namely that civilization and progress seem to engender their own regression and ruin. The very logic of progress evolves civilization into what it had supposedly left behind – into what it is the essence of civilization not to be.

Kurtz resembles what Max Nordau and others called a 'higher degenerate' – someone who is excessively, dangerously, brilliant because endowed with an intelligence which has evolved *too far*, and at the expense of the other faculties, especially the ethical ones, which have become correspondingly atrophied. According to Nordau, the higher degenerate is a genius who is inclined to scepticism, brooding, 'a rage for contradiction' and, of course, atavism; he 'renews intellectually the type of the primitive man of the most remote Stone Age' (pp. 166, 556; cf. pp. 23, 36, 161). Like other degenerates, the higher degenerate becomes the focus for fears that evolution itself cannot guarantee progress. But he especially seems to focus the more intense anxiety that evolution is going into reverse; worse still, that evolution is simultaneously accelerating and regressing, and equally out of control in both respects – a terrifying backward *and* forward unbinding of the arduously achieved higher forms of civilization and biology.

In this respect Kurtz is also a pervert, doing what the pervert does best, accelerating civilization into decadence (the overcivilized), but also, in the same moment – almost as the same process – regressing it back to the primitive (the pre-civilized). The desire of the pervert is characterized by aberrant movement which both progresses and regresses towards death. Put another way, Kurtz (anticipating Aschenbach in Thomas Mann's *Death in Venice*) makes a fatal, perverse deviation from the normative trajectory of an 'advanced' culture whose essence is within him, embracing in the process what that culture defines itself over and against. Crucially, this deviation is not an accident, nor entirely a consequence of the inherent instability of the solitary genius/pervert; he has deviated because and not in spite of following one of his culture's most advanced trajectories. As we saw earlier, perverts are agents of degeneration, but they embody the paradoxes which render unstable the very theory which creates and deploys them. The theory cannot contain the paradoxical dynamic which perversion attests to – that contradictory double movement, a regression into primitive origins and a progression, even an acceleration, into decadent decline such that civilization is doubly beleaguered: behind it is the scandal of its origins, while ahead is the scandal of its destiny, to become everything which it is not yet, yet always was. Nordau castigates the artists of his time because they try to disintegrate the arduously achieved and precarious unities of civilization. My argument here (and subsequently in relation to *Death in Venice*) is that in a certain sense Nordau is right, albeit for the wrong reasons. What we find in writers like Joseph Conrad and Thomas Mann is what Nordau knew and fights fiercely against, including the seductiveness of dissolution.

Cedric Watts has remarked on Kurtz's 'unforgettably perverse individuality', oriented towards what the novel describes as monstrous appetites and passions – 'sexual, sadistic, avaricious, megalomanic' (*Conrad's* Heart of Darkness, pp. 151, 114). Conrad does not make sexuality the key to Kurtz's perversity; his 'unspeakable rites' (*Heart of Darkness*, p. 71) include the sexual, but they cannot be explained exclusively, or even primarily, by it. There is a more inclusive dimension to his deviation, as befits a text which, though chronologically only just prior to Freud's first and major work on the sexual perversions (*Three Essays on the Theory of Sexuality*, 1905), might be described as pre- or even non-Freudian in conception, at least with regard to the issue of sexual perversity.[1]

Both Kurtz and the narrator of the tale, Marlow, are described as wanderers (pp. 8, 80). But it is Kurtz who wanders perversely, deviating from his assigned task; Marlow only follows, seeing and understanding a great deal more than most, but never as much as Kurtz, whose deviation becomes the focus for a radically paradoxical narrative full of dangerous knowledge.[2] In the process, there emerges a desolate affinity between the primitive and the civilized, suggesting that the survival of civilization depends upon the rest of us not wandering (deviating) even as far as Marlow, let alone Kurtz.

That rioting invasion of soundless life

'Going up that river', says Marlow, 'was like travelling back to the earliest beginnings of the world . . . we penetrated deeper and deeper into the heart of darkness.' Discovered there are not so much the distant, obscure origins of civilization as its identity now: 'all of the past is still in the mind of man'. Culture and civilization are merely a 'surface-truth', involving a necessary disavowal of the other always-present truth of distant origins still present (*Heart of Darkness*, pp. 48–52, 55). But this other truth, though compelling, is deeply obscure. Marlow discovers a deserted hut, inexplicably vacated and (equally inexplicably) containing a remnant of its one-time civilized inhabitant, a tattered book called *An Inquiry into Some Points of Seamanship*. The surface of things, including this hut and this book, does not confirm by contrast a deeper truth but on the contrary becomes itself increasingly undecipherable and disorienting. This is the truth – a kind of desublimation which eludes meaning.

An Inquiry into Some Points of Seamanship, as its all too apt title proclaims, is necessarily blinkered in its purposefulness. It reminds us of the chief accountant Marlow has met earlier, who, elegantly dressed and even slightly scented, works industriously at his desk: 'in the great demoralization of the land he kept up his appearance'. His books are in apple-pie order; Marlow encounters him in the middle of the colossal and dark jungle 'making correct entries of perfectly correct transactions' while 'fifty feet below the doorstep I could see the grove of death' (pp. 26, 28). Like this accountant, the book expresses 'a singleness of intention, an honest concern for the right way of going to work' (p. 54), the obsessively narrow, undeviating civilized quest as it was supposed to cut through the jungle. Marlow half-subscribes to the same; to be preoccupied with the mundane tasks, to keep the ship going, is the wise person's blinkered choice; attending to 'the mere incidents of the surface' keeps the 'reality', the 'truth' of the 'mysterious stillness' almost hidden: 'There was surface-truth enough in these things to save a wiser man' (p. 52). Thus the preoccupation with getting hold of some rivets to repair Marlow's ship – 'to stop the hole' (p. 40). Civilization itself is only an intensity of concentration, a blinkered adherence to the straight and narrow. This is an inevitable and not an accidental narrowness, epitomized by the 'civilized' quest itself, the collecting of ivory: a brutal, industrious, determined operation executed by agents necessarily oblivious to all else.

But there occurs the fatal swerve into knowledge, the more terrifying for being a knowledge only of the falsity both of what 'counts' as knowledge and of the assumed difference between the civilized and the primitive upon which the effort of discrimination depends. This is the sense in which the land 'demoralizes': it saps the motivating energy of those civilized subjects entering it. What they thought was the self-sustaining core of their being dissolves away, leaving an emptiness that fills up with otherness. Similarly, civilization's frenzied, blind expression of its own acquisitive dynamic (the quest for ivory) is halted, and civilization becomes dis-organized, unravelled, confused; in the very process of defining itself over and against the primitive, the civilized is invaded by the other whose history and proximity it requires yet disavows. The civilized invasion is doomed once it allows itself to hear that 'rioting invasion of soundless life' (p. 43).

Kurtz deviates from the 'singleness of intention' into the obliterating silence which that singleness also disavows, into a wilderness which whispers to him things he did not know, which 'echoed within him because he was hollow at the core' (p. 83). Yet it is from within this hollowness that 'forgotten and brutal instincts' are also awakened, 'the memory of gratified and monstrous passions. This alone, I was convinced, had driven him out to the edge of the forest ... had beguiled his unlawful soul beyond the bounds of permitted aspirations' (pp. 94–5). What is glimpsed here is the most terrifying paradox: the perverse frenzy of the 'primitive' is both the energetic antithesis of death and its intimate familiar, its prime mover. The 'rioting invasion of soundless life' is also, to echo an earlier and very different writer, George Herbert, 'the blast of death's incessant motion' (above, Chapter 5). A Western obsession is displaced to, rediscovered within, Africa.

After Kurtz's death Marlow returns to London. He visits Kurtz's 'intended', to return to her some letters and a photograph (of her) which Kurtz had given him. He lies to her about Kurtz ('The last word he pronounced was – your name'), and he does so in order to protect her. What Marlow was unable or unwilling to speak to her is hardly revealed, or revealed only as that which confuses what we thought we knew. In the foreground is a mindless contemporary civilization scarcely removed from its origins in a frenzied primeval anarchy. And behind both the contemporary moment and the primeval past is something into which they fade indistinguishably – from it, and from each other: the oblivion, the sea of inexorable time, the great solitude which dissolves all into an entropic oblivion, the darkness which Marlow senses even there, in the London drawing-room of this woman, and which the Romans encountered when they journeyed up the Thames but 'yesterday'. What preoccupies Marlow is perhaps less these primitive forces resurfacing within the blind plundering energies of the civilized than the forces of oblivion inside both: the sea of inexorable time and the great solitude are not only what we eventually dissolve into, but also what pervade the present, flooding it with a past which can be neither known nor escaped in the future – that *is* the heart of darkness:

Nobody moved for a time. 'We have lost the first of the ebb,' said the Director, suddenly. I raised my head. The offing was barred by a black bank of clouds, and the tranquil waterway leading to the uttermost ends of the earth flowed sombre under an overcast sky – seemed to lead into the heart of an immense darkness. (pp. 105, 97, 83, 8, 110)

Kurtz is the quintessentially 'civilized' subject who discovers not only the 'savage within' but a deeper hollowness, the subjective counterpart of a universal emptiness which surrounds and informs all. Kurtz's existential angst cannot plausibly be read as an affirmation of authentic selfhood; it is much more like the appalled recognition of a subjectivity at once informed and rendered utterly insignificant by what has preceded, surrounds, and will survive it.[3] But nor is this merely regression, since the historical narrative which regression presupposes is also obliterated. Which means that this is not yet, not quite, Freud's death drive. A profoundly regressive encounter with the oblivion which is before time and before memory – that *is* reminiscent of the death drive:

We were cut off from the comprehension of our surroundings; we glided past like phantoms . . . We could not understand because we were too far and could not remember, because we were travelling in the night of first ages, of those ages that are gone, leaving hardly a sign – and no memories. (p. 51)

It is not yet the death drive because it occurs in the shadow of 'the incomprehensible frenzy' of the primitive. It is not that the primitive signifies or affirms the life-force; it too is ultimately as insignificant as the civilized in relation to 'the interminable miles of silence' (p. 53). It is rather that Marlow remains fascinated by it all, 'wondering and secretly appalled' (p. 51). As for Kurtz's sense of the horror of it all, there can be no horror, only relief, in the silence which the death drive delivers us to. For Marlow and Kurtz, caught somewhere between degeneration and the death drive, there is residual terror in the seductive encounter with non-being.

IV

MODERNITY AND PHILOSOPHY: THE AUTHENTICITY OF NOTHINGNESS

I I

The Philosophical Embrace
of Death: Hegel

When Schopenhauer declared that 'without death there would hardly have been any philosophizing' (*World*, II.463) he was repeating what was by then a familiar idea, but one which would, if anything, become even truer of certain influential modern philosophers – especially those who make the relationship of consciousness to death of paramount significance. Two such (utterly different) philosophers are Schopenhauer himself and Hegel. Schopenhauer regarded his own philosophy as antithetical to Hegel's, which (and whom) he hated, considering him to be (among other things) an obscurantist. Readers coming anew to Hegel may sympathize with this charge, finding themselves perplexed and alienated by his style and complexity. But it is a complexity which must be tackled, since there is no philosopher more influential in modern thought.

The dialectic of death

Hegel tries to get beyond the dualism, so influential in Western metaphysics, whereby opposition is construed as an absolute difference and distinction between separate identities. So confident is he that the contradictions of consciousness and existence can be ultimately reconciled, he incorporates them within identity, rather than trying to exclude them from it. His dialectic thinking about death constitutes a new and radical phase of death's incorporation into being.

For Hegel, all opposites are eventually 'sublated' into a superior unity; the self-consciousness of absolute spirit finally incorporates all division and contradiction into itself. Experientially we lack ultimate reconciliation in the Absolute; we live stretched across a fierce dialectic in which identity is dependent upon otherness or difference – dependent, that is, upon what it is not. But, crucially, this otherness can never be kept other: to be dependent for my identity upon the other (part of what I *am* is that I am *not that*) means that this otherness is a part of my identity. That which I am *not* is not something alongside and independent of what I am, but, in a contradictory and divisive way, it is also interior to what I am. The other is within the same; difference is integral to identity.

More generally for Hegel, *being* presupposes *not being*, and vice versa. Further, in order to be, everything must undergo a dialectic sublation or negation (*Aufhebung*) by, in or as its opposite. Hegel neatly exploits the contradictory meanings of the German *aufheben*: both 'to annul' and 'to preserve'. As with otherness or difference, negation is not exterior to what it negates, but becomes intrinsic to it. What that means is that everything which negates the Absolute is also a constitutive part of the Absolute by virtue of that negation. This is a crucial aspect of dialectical analysis: what is transcended is also in some sense preserved; the process of overcoming is also a taking into, an incorporation.

So, as we shall see, infinitude takes finitude into itself, and self-consciousness must risk itself in otherness, difference and even non-being, in order to be and to know itself. Submitting God and eternity to the same dialectic philosophy, Hegel infiltrates them too with death.

Hegel describes finitude as 'immediate being', which, in general, 'means nothing more than a process of self-distinguishing'. Further,

Consciousness is precisely the mode of finitude of spirit: distinction is present here . . . something has its limit or end in something else, and in this way they are limited. Finitude is this distinguishing, which in spirit takes the form of consciousness.

But finitude is also 'eternally self-sublating'; its inner nature is 'contradiction – i.e., not to be, but rather to destroy itself – it is self-sublation . . . finite things have the form of perishing – their being is the sort that directly sublates itself' (*Lectures*, III.263; I.422). In other words, death is not merely the escape from finite existence, but its essence and truth:

Our sentient consciousness, too, insofar as it has to do with singular [things], belongs to natural finitude. The finite is defined as the negative ... The universal manifestation [of it] is death – the finite perishes. This is the renunciation of finitude. The finite will not last; it is not what abides – instead there is posited here really and in actuality what it intrinsically is. The sentient vitality of the single being has its terminus in death ... *The whole realm of the senses posits itself as what it really is, in its demise. This is where finitude ceases and is escaped from.* (I.290; my emphasis)

In general, declares Hegel, 'death is both the extreme limit of finitude and ... the dissolution of limitation. [Death is] the moment of spirit' (III.126).

Hegel drives death not only into the centre of life, but, more specifically and most significantly, into thought. Here, death becomes not so much the opposite of thought, but what impels it into activity. Thinking, like desire, begins with death. Both death and thought offer an escape from a 'renunciation of finitude':

The escape from ... finitude in consciousness, however, is not just what is called death; the escape from this finitude is *thought* generally – it is already present in representation so far as thinking is active in that. (III.126)

In the preface to *Phenomenology of Spirit* the association of thought and death becomes dialectical:

The activity of dissolution is the power and work of the *Understanding*, the most astonishing and mightiest of powers, or rather the absolute power ... The tremendous power of the negative ... is the energy of thought, of the pure 'I'.

Equally important, the life of spirit must maintain itself in death, finding itself in its own dismemberment:

Death, if that is what we want to call this non-actuality, is of all things the most dreadful, and to hold fast to what is dead requires the greatest strength ... The life of Spirit is not the life that shrinks from death and keeps itself untouched by devastation, but rather the life that endures it and maintains itself in it. It wins its truth only when, in utter dismemberment, it finds itself. (pp. 18–19)

The bad infinite

Hegel identifies the error whereby, instead of dialectically incorporating the finite into the infinite, we try to escape the former by simply embracing the latter (a move typical of religion and metaphysics). This results only in what Hegel calls the 'bad' or 'spurious' infinite. The main point is this: to try to keep the concepts of the finite and the infinite distinct is to remain in the realm of finite thinking; the binary opposition finite/infinite still presupposes the finite: 'in the very act of keeping the infinite pure and aloof from the finite, the infinite is only made finite' (*Logic*, p. 137). According to this account, Western metaphysics, including all its Christian manifestations, has remained in the realm of finite thinking – that is, remained inside exactly that which it was its *raison d'être* to transcend.

As Hegel puts it in the *Science of Logic*, the bad infinite can be regarded as a straight line going on for ever instead of returning to itself, as in a circle.[1] As such the bad infinite is merely the repetition of the finite, an 'infinite progress' which is akin to an infinite regress in that it defines itself against the finite only to always re-encounter it – a progress which is therefore tediously, fruitlessly, for ever *ad infinitum*. It was because he remained trapped in the spurious 'linear' progress of bad infinitude that Hereclitus believed everything was governed by the change and flux of mutability (*Lectures*, I.422–3). This notion of bad infinity resembles what we have been calling the impossibility or futility of desire.

In his *Aesthetics* Hegel describes the mythical overthrow of the Titans, whose punishments then include an insatiable eagle which for ever devours the self-renewing liver of Prometheus, and the unquenchable thirst of Tantalus. These punishments signify 'the inherently measureless, the bad infinite, the longing of the "ought", the unsatiated craving of subjective natural desire which in its continual recurrence never attains the final peace of satisfaction' (*Aesthetics*, I.466). If Hegel is right, and Western metaphysics remains trapped within a bad infinity which includes this 'unsatiated craving of subjective natural desire', this would suggest why, as we've seen, within that tradition transcendence is so often envisaged as not an alternative reality so much as a self-annihilating freedom from desire.

Hegel's dialectic alternative to bad infinity is radical: in a very real sense it commits us to taking death into life. What this means is that the affirmation of true infinity is contained within the finite in the sense that true infinity is inextricably a part of this process of ceasing to be:

> The finite changes itself; it appears as an other, [and so] other comes to other. What is the case here is that both are the same. The other coincides with itself and in the other comes to itself . . . This is the affirmation, this is being . . . *the genuine other of the finite is the infinite. (Lectures*, I.422–3)

This entails the contentious proposition that the infinite itself is at first something finite or negative – a proposition which seems to require that the finite is the foundation for the being of God (I.424). Hegel accepts this, and the blasphemy it seemingly entails. Spirit, he says,

> must have this character of finitude within itself – that may seem blasphemous. But if it did not have it within itself, and thus it confronted finitude from the other side, then its infinitude would be a spurious infinitude.

Just as the infinitude which is set *over and against* the finite is spurious, so, if God is set over and against the finite, he becomes himself finite and limited. This sounds still more blasphemous, but Hegel is unequivocal: 'Finitude must be posited in God himself' (III.263–4).[2] More severely still, the Absolute must '*tread the path of extinction and death*'. In death is the birth of the spiritual realm, in the sense that spirit has to partake of death; it has the 'element of death in itself as belonging to its essence' (*Aesthetics*, I.348–9; my emphasis).

Hegel's detailed account of what he regards as the 'true' relation of the infinite to the finite, of the Absolute to death, is a crucial determining instance of dialectical negation and a powerful reminder of the radical implications of dialectic reasoning: the finite and the infinite '*are inseparable and at the same time mutually related as sheer others; each has in its own self the other of itself*' (*Logic*, p. 141; my emphasis).

Inspired by the Christian Crucifixion, Hegel also inscribes death into love: 'Death is love itself.' This is interesting not least for the way in which it suggests an elusive yet significant masochistic strain in his dialectic. Declaring that 'the pinnacle of finitude is . . . death, the anguish of death', Hegel adds, 'The temporal and complete existence of the divine idea in the present is envisaged only in [Christ's] death.' Here death becomes the highest love, the identity of the divine and the human at its absolute fearful peak, 'For [love] consists in giving up one's personality, all that is one's own etc.':

[Love] is the supreme surrender [of oneself] in the other, even in this most extrinsic other being of death, the death of the absolute representative of the limits of life. The death of Christ is the vision of this love itself – not [love merely] for or on behalf of others, but precisely *divinity* in this universal identity with other-being, death. The monstrous unification of these absolute extremes is love itself . . . (*Lectures*, III.124–5)

Christ's death, he adds, 'may be represented as a sacrificial death, as the act of absolute satisfaction' (III.126).

The dialectic manifestation of human love promises that profound sense of completion in the other, the sublime transcendence of 'bad infinity' which also entails a loss of the self:

Love is a distinguishing of the two, who nevertheless are absolutely not distinguished for each other. The consciousness or feeling of the identity of the two – to be outside of myself and in the other – this is love. I have my self-consciousness not in myself but in the other. I am satisfied and have peace with myself only in this other – and I *am* only because I have peace with myself; if I did not have it then I would be a contradiction that falls to pieces. This other, because it likewise exists outside itself, has its self-consciousness only in me; and both the other and I are only this consciousness of being-outside-ourselves and of our identity; we are only this intuition, feeling, and knowledge of our unity. This is love, and without knowing that love is both a distinguishing and the sublation of the distinction, one speaks emptily of it. (III.276)

This affirmation of unity is eloquent yet completely vulnerable to being unbound by the death that Hegel has so enthusiastically, radically, embraced in its making.

'No going back'

Was Hegel an atheist? Alexandre Kojève, in the most influential modern interpretation of his work, believes so. He concedes that, in a general sense, Hegel's philosophy is a secularized Christian theology, and insists that Hegel knew this too. But for Kojève the crucial difference is that Hegel embraces a concept of death that denies immortality, which means also that his is a '*philosophy of death* (or, what is the same thing: of atheism)'. ('The Idea of Death', pp. 154, 124). Robert Solomon also believes that Hegel was essentially an atheist, since his Absolute 'is in no interesting sense, God' (p. 630). In contrast, Stephen Houlgate interprets Hegel's philosophy as profoundly Christian (p. 227).

The dispute revolves round issues of interpretation which are unlikely ever to be settled.[3] For our purposes it hardly matters, since the significant point is that Hegel does not rationalize death in the Enlightenment sense of trying to demystify it; rather, he reworks Christianity's paradoxical and even disturbing idealization of death. Further, through the dialectic, he takes death not only into finitude through Christ – that being acceptable and even required by an orthodox Christianity – but also into what supposedly redeems death (God, Eternity, the Infinite), thus pre-empting the Christian quest for a spiritual transcendence of death in that absolutely different order of reality. He is so confident that spirit is able to affirm an *ultimate* unity that he willingly takes division and death into the heart of what traditionally was thought, of its very metaphysical nature, to exclude them.

Arguably, at least for us, now, the Hegelian Absolute can never contain let alone reconcile contradiction and division. We – and that mostly includes even those who would repudiate psychoanalysis – are closer to Freud than to Hegel in believing that reality is recalcitrant, forever disrupting our attempts to replace division with unity. Jacques Lacan says, alluding to Hegel:

A brief aside – when one is made into two, there is no going back on it. It can never revert to making one again, not even a new one. The *Aufhebung* [sublation] is one of those sweet dreams of philosophy. (*Feminine Sexuality*, p. 156)

This is nowhere more true than with death. It is as if, to borrow Ariès's terms, Hegel's idealizing rationality seeks to 'tame' death through incorporation, only to discover that this containing of death (for others, later) renders it 'wilder' than ever, because now more 'inside' thought than ever before. And, if we cannot share Hegel's rationalism or his confidence, the fact remains that philosophically speaking there is no going back; thus embraced, thus internalized, the contradictions may at last be irrevocable.

And yet in another sense Hegel has taken us back: once again death has been discovered to be the essence of life, or rather thought. And if the supreme rationalism of his system could follow only from a hubristic privileging of human reason and consciousness, it is also true that in this same system consciousness ends up being dialectically sublated into Spirit or Absolute Being; in a sense it disappears. And when later thinkers turn away from the idea that Spirit or Absolute Being exists at all, let alone has the capacity for ultimate synthesis, consciousness does not resume its former autonomy; in the most important philosophical writing after Hegel, consciousness will never be able to divest itself of the death and otherness which he inscribed within it.

12

Heidegger, Kojève and Sartre

We know we are going to die; we know everyone dies. Yet, argues Martin Heidegger (1889–1976), we tend to know this truth only inauthentically; we acknowledge it, but in a way which forecloses on its full significance for how we live. Our social existence conspires with this evasion; we exist within the confines of 'average everydayness', gradually wasting our life in the self-deceptions of the collective 'they'. Such an existence 'provides [*besorgt*] a *constant tranquillization about death*' (*Being and Time*, p. 298).[1] To live authentically we must realize that death is not the eventual end of life but the inner possibility of Being or *Dasein*. Death 'is a phenomenon of life' in the sense that, just as Dasein is already and constantly the not-yet of death, so 'it *is* already its end too . . . Death is a way to be, which Dasein takes over as soon as it is. "As soon as man comes to life, he is at once old enough to die" ' (pp. 289–90).

For Heidegger we are fully free only when we have understood what death means. Then and only then do we fully comprehend our possibilities and potential. This profound, disturbing comprehension of the truth of death allows us to grasp, as never before, 'the possibility of understanding one's *ownmost* and uttermost potentiality-for-Being – that is to say, the possibility of *authentic existence*' (pp. 298, 307). All this inevitably occurs in a way which leaves us essentially and ineluctably anxious. Thus Heidegger speaks of '*an impassioned* free-dom towards death *– a freedom which has been released from the Illusions of the "they", and which is factical, certain of itself, and anxious*' (p. 311). Heidegger takes up the old idea that death is not the event which ends life but a profound reality which in-forms it, and he seeks to take this truth so fully into our being that we are compelled to embrace authentic existence and leave the world of false sociableness. Death is what bestows meaning upon life, and, far from being the ultimate negation of human freedom, it actually makes such freedom possible.[2]

Existentialists will find in Heidegger a crucial inspiration (albeit one from which he dissociated himself): becoming aware of our death, which is to say of our finitude, we also become aware that we are not predestined to be anything, and that we do not have an abiding essence which dictates what we should be and do in the world. As Jean-Paul Sartre was to put it in *Being and Nothingness* (thus reversing a priority hitherto fundamental in Western metaphysics), existence precedes essence, not vice versa: 'Freedom is existence, and in it existence precedes essence' (pp. 567–8). Authentic existence is possible only through and after this realization, which for Sartre would also become the philosophical foundation for a radical ethical and political commitment to praxis.

Kojève and nothingness

Heidegger's philosophy is built around a single central concept, Da-sein. Yet it is not possible to say clearly what he meant by Dasein,[3] except that it has an agonizing relation of proximity and distance to nothingness or non-being. Hegel has argued that Being presupposed non-being, and now Heidegger tightens the paradox: 'Da-sein means: being held out into the nothing,' while 'nothing is the negation of the totality of beings; it is nonbeing pure and simple'. Nothing is not the indeterminate opposite of beings, but belongs to the Beings of beings. Hegel is right: 'Pure Being and pure Nothing are therefore the same (*Science of Logic* vol. 1)'. So there is a radical affinity between Being and nothingness.[4] So fundamental is nothingness that for Heidegger the most profound question becomes 'Why are there beings at all, and why not rather nothing?' ('What is Metaphysics?' pp. 105, 99, 110, 112). This has struck many as strange, but, as we shall see, this concept of nothingness comes to play a crucial role for subsequent thinkers like Sartre and, before him, Alexandre Kojève. In the 1930s, in Paris, Kojève gave a course on Hegel, the text of which was published in 1947. Though partial and, in the view of some, erroneous, the influence of Kojève's interpretation of Hegel was extensive, and can be discerned in most of the significant developments in French philosophy in the postwar period, including existentialism, the diverse forms of post-structuralism, and through to post-modernism.[5]

The Heideggerian conviction that man is truly free only when he embraces his own finitude is not only about confronting one's finite existence; it is also about humankind's nothingness – our no-thingness. In developing this second aspect of finitude, Kojève took further Heidegger's view of the relation of being to death. Man is distinguished from the rest of nature in virtue of his self-consciousness. This is of enormous consequence, not least because to be self-aware is already a kind of disturbance and alienation; what one is aware of is not so much one's self, but one's separateness from the rest of the world, and what one introspects is not a self-evident essence or identity, but an emptiness or no-thingness which is the basis of desire – the desire to become, to possess, to be recognized. Kojève defines 'the I of desire' as 'an *emptiness* greedy for content'; 'Man', he says, 'must be an emptiness, a nothingness' (*Introduction*, p. 38). This emptiness is inseparable from a capacity for negation and negativity which includes the negating of that which is given, in order to create what does not yet exist:

the I of Desire is an emptiness that receives a real positive content only by negating action that satisfies Desire in destroying, transforming and 'assimilating' the desired non-I. (p. 4)

Man, says Kojève, is '*Negativity* incarnate, or, as Hegel says, "negative-or-negate-ive-entity" (das Negative). It is only by comprehending Man as Negativity that we [can] comprehend him in his "miraculous" human specificity' ('The Idea of Death', p. 131).[6] Moreover, this negativity is nothing less than the essence of a human freedom which 'manifests itself in its pure or "absolute" state as death' (p. 140). In Kojève's insistence on this point the influence of Heidegger is apparent:

If, therefore, on the one hand, freedom is Negativity, and if on the other hand, Negativity is Nothingness and death, there is no freedom without death, and only a mortal being can be free. We can even say that death is the final and authentic 'manifestation' of freedom. (p. 139)

Kojève finds that death plays a 'primordial role' in Hegel's philosophy: 'acceptance without reserve of the fact of death, or of human finitude conscious of itself, is the ultimate source of all of Hegel's thought'. For Hegel, the search for absolute Knowledge or Wisdom is inseparable from the conscious acceptance of death as complete annihilation. Kojève finds in Hegel a new philosophical articulation of old paradoxes: 'the human being itself is no other thing than . . . [a] death that lives a human life'; 'Man is not only *mortal*; he is *death* incarnate; he *is* his own death'; Man not only knows that he will die, 'he *is* the consciousness of his death' (pp. 114, 124, 134, 151, 153).

Materialist philosophers radically reconceptualize the principle of change (below, Chapter 15). As mutability, it was the agent of death; now, as praxis, it is the route to a different and better existence via revolution. With Kojève, something even closer to death than change becomes the basis of man's true nature: nothingness. In Western theology nothing was associated with evil; we saw how for John Donne man as mortal being is riven with mutability and loss precisely because he is made of nothing (above, Chapter 5). Traditional metaphysics sought for the ultimate, unchanging reality behind appearances, for the substance which was beyond finitude, change and death, which was both essentially and absolutely the metaphysical opposite of nothing. And yet such entities – for instance the human soul – were always hovering on the edge of non-being even as they were said to be the most intense form of being. That is one reason why materialists deny their existence, embracing instead the profound, liberating reality of change. Here, with Kojève, it is non-being as well as change which is being reconceptualized; once the place of death, absence and unfreedom, nothingness is now the place of death, absence and freedom. And, to an extent to which has not yet been fully realized, at least in Anglo-American contexts, this has become an animating principle of all the various anti-humanisms of the last half-century.

The accuracy of Kojève's reading of Hegel has been questioned,[7] but its influence is indisputable; Hegel's own reworking of the paradoxes of severe theology were here given a new existential intensity, most significantly in the idea that man's knowledge of his death – his essential finitude – pervades his whole being, the basis of both his individuality and his freedom. And, crucially, in this line of thinking, the philosophy of praxis is not what substitutes for, or transcends, the philosophy of death, but what embraces it. Praxis, or at least human freedom and potentiality, springs from a nothingness and negativity which include death. Humanism, even in its grimmer phases, never ceases that double movement of expansion and incorporation; perhaps in Kojève there is even a reconceptualization of mortality, with limit taking on the attributes of the limitless.

Kojève has a most revealing footnote where he compares Heidegger and Marx in relation to Hegel:

Heidegger has taken up again the Hegelian themes concerning death: but he neglects the complementary themes concerning Struggle and Labour; thus his philosophy does not succeed in rendering an account of History.[8]

Marx, on the other hand,

retains the themes of Struggle and Labour, and his philosophy is thus essentially 'historicist'; but he neglects the theme of death (even while admitting that man is mortal); that is why he does not see (and even less [do] certain 'Marxists') that the Revolution is not only in fact but also essentially – and necessarily – bloody (the Hegelian theme of the Terror). (p. 156)

For Kojève, taking death back into praxis entails an embrace of literal death.

Sartre

We assert . . . that art is a meditation on life and not on death. (Sartre, *What is* Literature?, p. 232)

Sartre was influenced by Hegel's account of dialectic and Heidegger's account of nothingness, and in *Being and Nothingness* he weaves them together. He takes the Hegelian dialectic into consciousness through an important distinction between being-for-itself and being-in-itself. Provisionally we can say that being-for-itself characterizes consciousness – especially human consciousness – whereas being-in-itself refers to that kind of being which is devoid of consciousness – simply *that which is*, that which is self-identical.

Being-for-itself is defined in terms of lack, always requiring, and always in search of, something to complete it. At one level this is a lack of, and hence a desire for, being in the second sense (the self-identical). But consciousness can never become being-in-itself 'without losing itself as for-itself'. For that reason alone, human existence will always entail suffering (*Being and Nothingness*, p. 90). Following previous philosophers like Descartes and Hegel, Sartre argues that consciousness is always consciousness of something, and this in a radical sense: there is not *first* consciousness and, second, consciousness *of* something; rather, consciousness just is this consciousness of. And to be conscious *of* is always to be conscious *somewhere* – to be positioned within, and in relation to, the world. Likewise with desire, itself inseparable from consciousness: there is not first desire and then a thousand particular desires; desire *is* these desires (p. 565). And consciousness is always of what it is not: what I ceaselessly aim towards, says Sartre, is that which I am not, or not yet; I aim towards my own possibilities.

This confers on consciousness two further attributes: negation and nothingness. Negation refers to the fact that to discern that *this* is the case is necessarily to realize that something else is *not* the case; to discern a particular presence is simultaneously to discern the possibility of its absence; to make this choice is not to make others. And this means, for Sartre, that 'the necessary condition for our saying *not* is that non-being be a perpetual presence in us and outside of us, that nothingness haunt being' (p. 11). As he graphically puts it shortly after, 'Nothingness lies coiled in the heart of being – like a worm' (p. 21). Man is the being who is his own nothingness, and through whom nothingness comes into the world; man's freedom is strangely dependent upon being 'paralysed with nothingness' (p. 45).

'Fundamentally,' says Sartre, 'man is *the desire to be*.' This desire is nothing more and nothing less than a lack: 'desire . . . is identical with lack of being'. This idea of lack is crucial, embodying as it does two barely compatible ideas: on the one hand emptiness, vacancy and permanent incompletion; on the other freedom, agency and responsibility:

The for-itself is defined ontologically as a lack of being ... The for-itself chooses because it is lack; freedom is really synonymous with lack ... the for-itself is the being which is to itself its own lack of being. (pp. 565, 567)

Being-for-itself desires completion in this other kind of being: 'human reality is the desire of being-in-itself ... It is as consciousness that it wishes to have the impermeability and infinite density of the in-itself' (p. 566). At the same time, it ceaselessly desires to 'nihilate' this other kind of being, since to actually become it would entail the demise of itself.

Consciousness is haunted by an impossible contradictory desire which is nevertheless its fundamental project: to attain the 'pure consciousness' which would come of a union of the for-itself and the in-itself – that is, a consciousness devoid of lack and nothingness because now founded on and identical with itself, complete and self-sufficient *as consciousness*: an in-itself which is still a for-itself. In other words, 'To be man is to reach toward being God. Or, if you prefer, man fundamentally is the desire to be God' (p. 566). The euphoric humanism of Feuerbach sought to take God back into man on the grounds that God was only ever a projection of man's best self (see below, Chapter 15). Now the existential humanist is characterized by an impossible desire to be the God who does not exist. That this later humanism is full of anguish does not make it less hubristic than its earlier counterpart: hitherto humanism had taken God back into itself; now it takes the absence of God into self, construing a philosophy of freedom or agency out of lack, absence and nothingness.

Similarly, although Sartre's claim that human reality 'is by nature an unhappy consciousness with no possibility of surpassing its unhappy state' (p. 90) is the pessimistic opposite of Feuerbach, it is no less self-affirming for that. At the end of the main text of *Being and Nothingness* Sartre apparently alludes to Feuerbach when he says, 'man loses himself as man in order that God may be born', and adds, 'but God is contradictory and we lose ourselves in vain. Man is a useless passion' (p. 615). Freer and more heroic in his uselessness than in pseudo-divinity, Sartrean man now takes into himself the contradiction which was the fiction of God and grounds his freedom in it. Being-for-itself is characterized by nothingness. And yet out of nothingness – no-thingness – true freedom is born; not to be essentially anything is to be free to choose. In a sense we are always what we are not yet; we can always conceive of being other than that we are.

But freedom cannot embrace death. Despite taking so much from modern philosophers of death like Heidegger and Kojève, Sartre finally has to eliminate death from the finitude of being. He takes Heideggerian nothingness into self, making it the basis of freedom, but he also privileges selfhood in a way which Heidegger emphatically did not, and resists Heidegger's embrace of death. Sartre knows that to take death so profoundly into being, as did Heidegger and Kojève, threatens the entire project of human freedom as praxis, which is the most important aspect of Sartre's existentialism.

Certainly, for Heidegger, authenticity did not entail praxis, and in his 'Letter on Humanism' he actually repudiated Sartre's attempt to derive from his work a philosophical rationale for existential engagement; so far as Heidegger was concerned, such engagement was only another version of inauthentic 'social' existence, a social evasion of the truth of Being. But was Heidegger's own truth of Being ever more than a state of authenticity whose main objective is obsessively to know or insist on itself as authentic? For all his talk of freedom, there remains in Heidegger a sense in which authenticity remains a petrified sense of self, paralysed by the very effort of concentrating on the profundity of Being, which always seems to be also a condition of mystical impossibility: 'Death is the possibility of the absolute impossibility of Dasein' (*Being and Time*, p. 294).

Not so for Sartre. He recognizes the modern project whereby death is 'interiorized . . . humanized [and] individualized', and that Heidegger gave philosophical form to this process. On the face of it, this is an attractive development, since death as apparent limit on our freedom is reconceptualized as a support of freedom (*Being and Nothingness*, pp. 532–3). But, against Heidegger, Sartre argues that death, far from being the profound source of being and existential authenticity, is just a contingent fact like birth, and this, far from being a limit, is what guarantees one's freedom. Heidegger's entire account of death rests on an erroneous conflation of death and finitude; finitude is essentially internal to life and the grounds of our freedom – 'the very act of freedom is therefore the assumption and creation of finitude. If I make myself, I make myself finite and hence my life is unique' – whereas death is simply an external and factual limit of my subjectivity (pp. 546–7). Quite simply, 'It is absurd that we are born; it is absurd that we die' (p. 547). This perhaps entails a fear of death, since 'to be dead is to be a prey for the living': one is no longer in charge of one's own life; it is now in the hands of others, of the living (p. 543). It is true that death haunts me at the very heart of each of my human projects, as their inevitable reverse side. But this reverse side of death is just the end of my possibilities and, as such, 'it does not penetrate me. The freedom which is *my freedom* remains total and infinite . . . Since death is always beyond my subjectivity, there is no place for it in my subjectivity' (pp. 547–8).

Sartre's significance lies in his uncompromising emphasis on human freedom and responsibility. For a while, in the postwar period, his influence was considerable and worldwide. Yet he was eclipsed surprisingly quickly, even by the standards of intellectual fashion. And one of the main reasons was the anti-humanism of subsequent thinkers like Michel Foucault – in particular their wish to radically decentre man and the individual (a move which was more indebted to Heidegger than is sometimes realized). In order to affirm human freedom and responsibility, Sartre knew he had to break with that line of thought which tried to drive death so relentlessly into the heart of being and consciousness; he knew how inimical was the philosophy of death to the philosophy of praxis. But did he succeed in making that break? Not according to those who argue that his philosophy relentlessly incorporates nothingness, lack and impossibility within the self and makes desire always an unceasing – impossible? – quest for a kind of being that it cannot have. The result, says James Carse, is that Sartre's philosophy posits human consciousness as '*an unrelieved lust after death*' (p. 372; my emphasis).

I believe rather that the very contradiction which Sartre inscribes into conscious being involves a simultaneous embrace and exclusion of death. Existential freedom is stretched across this contradiction, whose tension became more enabling than not. As Cohen-Solal's engaging biography of Sartre demonstrates, his was a life of unceasing commitment to intellectual and political praxis, especially at the time when he became an existential Marxist. Heidegger was certainly for a while, and perhaps for longer, a Nazi. Much has been written about the latter's political identifications. As we shall see, Herbert Marcuse once suggested there was a link between Heidegger's philosophical preoccupation with death and the Nazi death camps. Others are more cautious, asking whether in Heidegger's anti-humanism there is an in-humanism, and in his embrace of nothingness and death a nihilism, which connects with, if not prepares for, Nazism. George Steiner, reminding us that we still disagree over the politics and the impact on politics of writers like Machievelli and Rousseau, is surely right in saying that there are no easy answers to these questions (p. xxv).[9] But one thing seems certain: the radically different political trajectories of Sartre and Heidegger are inseparable from their different philo-sophies of death; Sartre could not have so radically embraced praxis had he not deviated from Heidegger's privileging of death. Social praxis entails a repudiation of a Western metaphysics of death of which Heidegger's work is a powerful mutation. Two years before he died, Sartre reiterated biographically this repudiation of the phil-osophy of death:

Death? I don't think about it. It has no place in my life, it will always be outside. One day my life will end but I don't want it to be burdened with death. I want that my death never enter my life, nor define it, that I be always a call to life. (cited in Cohen-Solal, p. 524)

V

THE DESIRE NOT TO BE: LATE METAPHYSICS AND PSYCHOANALYSIS

13

Dying as the Real Aim of Life: Schopenhauer

An outcry has been made about the melancholy and disconsolate nature of my philosophy. (Schopenhauer, *World*, II.580–81)

Schopenhauer begins as follows a chapter entitled 'On the Vanity and Suffering of Life':

Awakened to life out of the night of unconsciousness, the will finds itself as an individual in an endless and boundless world, among innumerable individuals, all striving, suffering, and erring; and, as if through a troubled dream, it hurries back to the old unconsciousness. (II.573)

If this anticipates Freud, it is also true that Schopenhauer's philosophy represents a compelling summation of previous writing about mutability, loss and the futility of desire, and the conviction that ultimate freedom lies in death, and, before that, partial freedom in those states of being which abolish selfhood.

For Schopenhauer, the will to life is the metaphysical origin of the universe, the most basic 'blind' force or drive, responsible for everything that lives. But, marked by inner contradiction, it is also the 'original discord' (I.333). Manifested as desire, the will to life is marked by want and lack: 'All *willing* springs from lack, from deficiency, and thus from suffering' (I.196). Desire is a condition of continual, restless, longing – 'a striving that is bound to frustrate itself' (II.574). This is the reason why the will strives to return to 'the night of unconsciousness' wherein is found *'the peace of the all-sufficient nothing'*. Until then its desires are unlimited, its claims inexhaustible, and every satisfied desire gives birth to a new one. No possible satisfaction in the world could suffice to still its craving, set a final goal to its demands, and fill the bottomless pit of its heart. (II.580, 573; my emphasis; cf. I.308–9)

The individual who wills and desires 'is constantly lying on the revolving wheel of Ixion, is always drawing water in the sieve of the Danaids, and is the eternally thirsting Tantalus' (I.196).

Again, the fundamental condition of suffering existence is mutability – '*Time* and the *perishability* of all things existing in time'. We live only in the 'fleeting present' and in a state of 'continual becoming without being'. The form of existence is 'essentially unceasing *motion*, without any possibility of that repose which we continually strive after. It resembles the course of a man running down a mountain who would fall over if he tried to stop and can stay on his feet only by running on.' And mutability reaches into the very heart of desire: 'we begin in the madness of carnal desire and the transport of voluptuousness, we end in the dissolution of all our parts and the musty stench of corpses' (*Essays and Aphorisms*, pp. 51–4; my emphases).

This will-to-live is the source of all suffering, but especially the sufferings of sexual passion, which 'brings into consciousness unrest, uneasiness, and melancholy, and into the course of life misfortunes, cares and misery' (*World*, II.568); this sexual desire is 'the kernel of the will-to-live, and consequently the concentration of all willing . . . therefore I have called the genitals the focus of the will' (II.514). The sexual drive is the manifestation of the species; its force so exceeds and consumes us that we can find no adequate expression for it. While the vehicle of the sexual drive, the individual is racked with painful yearning; after release from it, 'contrary to expectation, he finds himself no happier than before' (II.551, 557). Compare W. B. Yeats:

> Eternity is passion, girl or boy
> Cry at the onset of their sexual joy
> 'For ever and for ever'; then awake
> Ignorant what Dramatis Personae spake
> ('Supernatural Songs', VIII)

Satisfaction, if it is achieved at all, is fleeting, and becomes the ground for new desire; for every wish that is satisfied, there arise ten that are not. But satisfaction is also fleeting and illusory for the further reason that, in achieving the things desired, we discover how little worth desiring they actually were. Satisfaction is also elusive since it always lies in the future or the past, never the present; yet the past is irrevocable, and the future is uncertain (*World*, II.573–4). Dissatisfaction leads to pain and suffering, satisfaction to 'a fearful emptiness and boredom'; indeed 'life swings . . . to and fro between pain and boredom, and these two are in fact its ultimate constituents' (I.312). Further, satisfaction partakes of the negative, dissatisfaction of the positive. What Schopenhauer means by this is that we feel pain, but not painlessness; we feel care, not carefreeness. Similarly we become conscious of time when we are bored, not when we are involved. Further, 'we do not become conscious of the three greatest blessings of life as such, namely health, youth, and freedom, as long as we possess them, but only after we have lost them'. Our real existence 'is only in the present, whose unimpeded flight into the past is a constant transition into death, a constant dying' (I.311).

Schopenhauer concludes: 'our existence is happiest when we perceive it least; from this it follows that it would be better not to have it' (II.575). Existence itself is something which should not be, which it would have been better not to have happened; it is a punishment and an expiation – 'a perversity, a path of error', 'the consequence of a false step and a guilty desire'. In this connection the myth of the Fall is the only point in the Old Testament to which Schopenhauer ascribes metaphysical truth, and even then only in an allegorical form. The guilt of which he speaks arises simply out of existence itself, not from the sin of Adam and Eve (II.574, 580, 604). Suffering is the true destiny of human existence, a purifying experience which leads us back from an erroneous, exhausting will-to-live (II.636). We must learn to renounce the will-to-live and to revere death (though suicide is not condoned).

Renunciation and the negation of the self

It is not the will as such which produces suffering, but awareness of it. In itself the will is blind and without knowledge. It is the inner essence of being, and its striving for existence is always satisfied. More precisely, the will can never be satisfied given that it is endless; yet it also cannot know dissatisfaction. The will finds expression in – in fact actually produces – consciousness and knowledge, but remains in conflict with both (II.466, 498). The more conscious and intelligent the being, the greater the suffering. Which means, of course, that humans suffer the most (I.309–10).

In its lower and most common form the will produces only the fear of death. This is because knowledge is an effect of the will, and remains throughout almost entirely subordinate to it. However, there are crucial exceptions: sometimes, especially in the human genius, knowledge can separate itself from the will, and this produces the perspective of art and/or of resignation. But at a price: for this aesthetic view to emerge, individuality has to be abolished, since individuation (the *principium individuationis*) is itself an effect of the will. More exactly, the person involved in aesthetic perception is no longer an individual, for in such perception the individual has necessarily to become lost to himself; he has become a '*pure* will-less, painless, timeless *subject of knowledge*' (I.179), and only in that state can be experienced that 'peace, always sought but always escaping us on that first path of willing' (I.196).

So the cost of this aesthetic attitude is a form of the death of the self and an erasure of the social: 'It is then all the same whether we see the setting sun from a prison or from a palace . . . all difference of individuality disappears so completely that it is all the same whether the perceiving eye belongs to a mighty monarch or a stricken beggar' (I.196–8). We have become 'the eternal world-eye' that looks out of all creatures (II.371).

Here Schopenhauer comes close to mysticism. In fact he declares that quietism, asceticism and mysticism stand in the closest connection (II.613); in them the desiring self has been abolished in favour of knowledge. When the will has been finally and completely extinguished, the individual is 'then left only as pure knowing being, as the undimmed mirror of the world' (I.390). Knowledge in its exalted form is on the side of death (II.466) and makes the subject want to die. It is also in a mystical sense that for Schopenhauer our true nature remains indestructible and the individual carries in himself a 'complete compensation' for the loss of individuality in death. He identifies our true nature with 'the species in which [the individual's] true being objectifies itself' (II.491; cf. II.510). Grafting Platonism on to biology, Schopenhauer insists that in the animal 'the eternity of its Idea (species) is distinctly marked in the finiteness of the individual'. The imperishable true being, the 'universal human element', is also literally to be found in the dust to which we are reduced and from which new life springs (II.482, 491, 472).

Most importantly, our essential nature is to be found in the will. Hitherto, says Schopenhauer, all philosophers have made the mistake of locating in the intellect what is metaphysical and indestructible in man, whereas in fact it inheres only and absolutely in the will. Intellect, consciousness and ego are transient; only the will endures. But can we ever really know the will, this essence of our true nature? No: its nature finally eludes us – 'what it is absolutely in itself, remains unanswerable' (II.496; cf. II.474). We live in the world of representation, which is 'absolutely incommensurable' with the world of the will. Our true nature, though indestructible, is yet without that continuity which is time-bound; for Schopenhauer (following Kant), true being, like the will from which it derives, is untouched by time (II.484). In fact time has no absolute existence but is merely a category of consciousness necessary for perception. This is why our true nature is founded in a 'concept of an indestructibility that was nevertheless not a continuance' (II.494).

The wonderful release of death

For Schopenhauer, we welcome death only after overcoming a powerful and irrational desire to live. Even before reaching this stage, the desire for death is strong; death is anticipated as a 'wonderful release', a state of zero tension and oblivion which is also the annihilation of selfhood. In this sense death is an extension of exalted knowledge:

death is the great opportunity no longer to be I; to him . . . who embraces it . . . Dying is the moment of that liberation from the one-sidedness of an individuality which does not constitute the innermost kernel of our true being, but is rather to be thought of as a kind of aberration thereof. (II.469, 507–8)

Elsewhere Schopenhauer describes 'the I or ego' as 'the dark point in consciousness', the blind spot of the self (II.491). But the desire for death is born of the rational apprehension of the perishableness of things inside the *a priori* necessary form of time, and of the realization that ascetic renunciation is the only kind of freedom from this: 'to die willingly . . . is the prerogative of the resigned, of him who gives up and denies the will-to-live'. In death there is found 'the true original freedom' consequent upon a '*restitutio in integrum* [restoration to the former state]' (II.508).

The annihilation afforded by death is welcomed not only as a release from life, but because '*Dying is certainly to be regarded as the real aim of life*; at the moment of dying, everything is decided which through the whole course of life was only prepared and introduced.' In this moment is the supreme realization of life's lesson, namely that life is futile and contradictory. The truth of life becomes realized in our perishing individuality. Thereby the will to life is denied, subjected to euthanasia (II.634–39; my emphasis). The death of the self is total, and what we get in exchange is 'absolute annihilation' (II.471) or '*nothing*' – what 'The Buddhist faith calls . . . Nirvana, that is to say, extinction' (II.508).[1]

Philosophically speaking, for Schopenhauer the acceptance of death is a rational, ascetic act of renunciation rather than a deep instinctual regression, as for Freud (see below, Chapter 14). In this, as in other respects, Schopenhauer is the summation of what went before. But the way in which he writes about the death-wish suggests at the very least a strong *desire* for non-being which is also the instinctual ground of being. Perhaps he most closely anticipates Freud in his view of existence as an aberration:

To desire immortality for the individual is really the same as wanting to perpetuate an error for ever; for at bottom every individuality is really only a special error, a false step, something that it would be better should not be, in fact something from which it is the real purpose of life to bring us back. (II.491–2)

Death is ... the painful untying of the knot that generation with sensual pleasure had tied; it is the violent destruction, bursting in from outside, of the fundamental error of our true nature, the great disillusionment. At bottom, we are something that ought not to be; therefore we cease to be. (II.507)

14

Freud: Life as a Detour
to Death

Freud's 'On Transience', written and published during the First World War, describes a summer walk, just before the war, on which Freud was accompanied by 'a taciturn friend and . . . a young but already famous poet'. This poet was afflicted with an 'aching despondency' at life's mutability: everything seemed beyond enjoyment because on the edge of oblivion. That the beauty around him, 'like all human beauty, and all the beauty and splendour that men have created or may create', was fated to extinction meant that it became 'shorn of its worth by the transience which was its doom' (p. 287).

This encounter apparently preceded, and influenced, the writing of Freud's 'Mourning and Melancholia'; of the poet's powerful emotional disturbance Freud remarks, 'I believed later that I had discovered what it was,' and proceeds to outline his thesis on the nature of mourning (pp. 288–9).

It is a theory which marks a yet further, and greatly influential, elaboration of the internalization of mutability. Within psychoanalysis, the narrative of human desire riven by loss is unfolded in a dramatically expanded domain of human interiority. Eventually Freud arrives at his theory of the death drive, which draws extensively on the long tradition we have been examining. In previous chapters I drew attention to ideas which anticipate Freud's. What these also mean, of course, is that Freud borrowed extensively from the past. But, as we shall see shortly, he evolved a new language – almost a new mythology – to express the conviction that death is absolutely interior to life.

Freud counters the poet's despondency with an attitude of *carpe diem*. Transience does not diminish the value of life; on the contrary it enhances it: 'Transience value is scarcity value in time. Limitation in the possibility of an enjoyment raises the values of the enjoyment.' Freud also invokes the old idea of *'eterne in mutabilitie'*: the seasonal cycle means that 'in relation to the length of our lives [the beauty of nature] can in fact be regarded as eternal'. If this is optimistic, in other encouragements to the poet he adopts the facile tones of the sober rationalist, identifying exactly what is agonizing about mutability in Western culture – 'the beauty of the human form and face vanish for ever' – only to add, lamely, 'but their evanescence only lends them a fresh charm'. He continues, 'Nor can I understand any better why the beauty and perfection of a work of art or of an intellectual achievement should lose its worth because of its temporal limitation.' A time may indeed come, he says, when what we admire today will crumble to dust, when our culture will be incomprehensible to succeeding ones, when an epoch arrives in which all animate life on earth ceases, 'but since the value of all this beauty and perfection is determined only by its significance for our own emotional lives, it has no need to survive us' (p. 288).

Freud's trite response to the poet is especially surprising given that he is writing during a war which, on his own admission in this very article, shattered human pride in the achievements of civilization, undermined human faith and human hope, and showed 'how ephemeral were many things that we regarded as changeless' (p. 289). Perhaps his optimism was mischievous; certainly it was not without irony: 'I noticed that I had made no impression either upon the poet or upon my friend' (p. 288). The poet's sense of mutability seems poignantly endorsed by a more lasting irony in that we do not know who he was; although by then already famous, according to Freud, his identity has never been established.

In his account of the walk, Freud concludes that his friend and the poet were in a state of mourning. He touches on a typical attitude in the mutability tradition: 'those who . . . seem ready to make a permanent renunciation because what was precious has proved not to be lasting, are simply in a state of mourning for what is lost' (p. 290). Mourning is here described as the inability or refusal of the libido to detach itself from the lost object in order to attach itself to new ones.[1] Actually it is just as likely that the poet was also experiencing the melancholia

which Freud was later to consider as a more severe and even pathological response to loss – one in which libido is withdrawn into the ego,
where it serves to establish a sometimes suicidal identification with
the lost object,[2] and where a traumatic perception of transience and
loss becomes interwoven with the pain of desire.

There is much in Freud's theory which seems questionable or just
implausible; but what is intriguing is the way in which it connects the
perception of mutability, the pain of melancholic desire rooted in loss,
and the pull of death – a connection which is, as we have seen, endemic
in Western culture. Equally compelling is his belief that in melancholy
there is not just an experience of loss, but a deep identification with
what is lost.

The themes of loss and lack pervade Freud's work; and, if they
figure most dramatically in his theory of the death drive, they are
equally important in his theory of human erotic development. In fact,
as we shall see, loss and lack provide some of the crucial links between
the two.

From polymorphous perversity to the death drive

According to Freud, a child's sexuality originally exhibits a strange
blend of self-sufficiency on the one hand, mobility and dispersion on
the other. In other words a child's sexuality is polymorphously perverse, and, as such, undiscriminating in terms of object (e.g. mother or
father, man or woman) or aim (e.g. incest, homosexuality, coprophilia,
heterosexuality). And this is a condition of mobility, in which desire
itself is definitely not unified, but of distinct and different kinds; it
entails 'a widespread and copious but dissociated sexual life . . . in
which each separate instinct pursues its own acquisition of pleasure
independently of all the rest' (*Five Lectures*, p. 74). Polymorphous
perversity and the dissociation of instincts echo primal or Edenic
innocence, which, retrospectively for the adult, is beyond reach and
even difficult to conceive. But this is a challenging, highly sexual
innocence which henceforth can never be smothered by our sentimental
categories of childhood. And the challenge remains even after a 'Victorian' outrage at the very idea of children having a sexuality has

subsided; indeed, perhaps that outrage was itself a displacement of a more fundamental anxiety which persists: in Freud's account the child confronts adults with their own renunciation of instinct; the child *is* what we have lost.

As is well known, for Freud the evolution, not to say the very survival, of civilization depends upon the containment, restriction, repression, sublimation and channelling of sexual desire. The early efflorescence of infantile sexuality is doomed to extinction as we become constrained, organized (fixed/fixated) as subjects in the social order, always haunted by the loss of that original libidinal freedom. Our original instinctual energies remain for ever alienated in order that civilization may be, but those energies are never entirely eliminated; there remains an unending conflict between the demands of the original instincts and those of civilization. Even when the processes of repression are as successful as they can be, that conflict remains at the heart of the human individual. In certain respects the individual becomes a permanent casualty of that struggle. To a greater or lesser degree, we are all repressed, neurotic and narcissistically scarred (*Beyond the Pleasure Principle*, p. 291).

This unremitting clash between instinctual desire and civilization, between nature and culture, leads Freud back to the old idea that there is something about human desire which makes its fulfilment impossible. Human beings are governed by a pleasure principle which has one major problem, namely that 'all the regulations of the universe run counter to it'. Worse still, we are internally constituted to make the pleasure principle doubly incapable of realization. For example, we derive our most intense enjoyment only from a contrast, like the sudden satisfaction of a need long denied. In this and other ways, our possibilities for happiness are already restricted by our constitution. Indeed, 'the programme of becoming happy, which the pleasure principle imposes on us, cannot be fulfilled'. But Freud adds, 'we must not – indeed, we cannot – give up our efforts to bring it nearer to fulfilment' (*Civilization and its Discontents*, pp. 263–4, 271).

Freud lists eight ways by which we typically try to avoid or minimize the suffering which inevitably results. The seventh is love – potentially the most intense experience of happiness, and so, apparently, the most triumphant repudiation of life's inherent suffering. Except that suffering is no sooner left behind than it re-emerges from within love itself as love's very condition: 'we are never so defenceless against suffering as when we love, never so helplessly unhappy as when we have lost our loved object or its love' (p. 270). And it is in the sphere of sexuality that desire becomes somehow self-defeating.

Eighteen years earlier, in 1912, Freud had declared, 'It is my belief that, however strange it may sound, we must reckon with the possibility that something in the nature of the sexual instinct itself is unfavourable to the realization of complete satisfaction' ('On the Universal Tendency', p. 258). One reason is that sexual libido intensifies in relation to the difficulty and obstacles which resist it: 'the psychical importance of an instinct rises in proportion to its frustrations'. But fully to overcome the resistance which impedes desire is also to defeat the possibility of desire's satisfaction:

This is true both of individuals and of nations. In times in which there were no difficulties standing in the way of sexual satisfaction, such as perhaps during the decline of the ancient civilizations, love became worthless and life empty . . . (p. 257)

There are other reasons why desire remains incapable of satisfaction, to do specifically with the repression of the so-called perversions. Freud considers what this means in practice through a brief account of instinctual drives towards incest and coprophilia.

In the case of the first, all 'normal' sexual relations are only poor surrogates for the primary, incestuous desire of the child for its mother, who, in her capacity *as* mother, becomes the child's first seducer, 'established unalterably for a whole lifetime as the first and strongest love object and as the prototype of all later love-relations – for both sexes' (*Outline*, p. 188). But this primary desire has to be surrendered, and 'normal' desire – that is, socially prescribed desire – is founded on this loss; as desiring subjects in the world, we embark on a restless and repetitive (because always inadequate) search for a substitute:

when the original object of a wishful impulse has been lost as a result of repression [in this instance, the incest taboo], it is frequently represented by an endless series of substitute objects none of which, however, brings full satisfaction. This may explain the inconstancy in object-choice . . . which is so often a feature of the love of adults. ('On the Universal Tendency', p. 258)

Freud is quite specific about this. The breast is the child's first erotic object, from which all too soon it has to separate: 'for however long [a child] is fed at its mother's breast, it will always be left with a conviction after it has been weaned that its feeding was too short and too little' (*Outline*, p. 189). Again the theme of loss is paramount; as Malcolm Bowie comments, according to this view, 'Weaning gave a backward drift, a helpless retrospective tenor, to all passion' (p. 6).

Dissatisfaction arises too from the fact that the coprophilic instinctual components have also proved incompatible with culture, 'probably since, as a result of our adopting an erect gait, we raised our organ of smell from the ground'. But the instincts remain active, which is why, still, 'the excremental is all too intimately and insepar-ably bound up with the sexual'. Equally incompatible with culture are the sadistic instincts. The effect of the repression of such perversions always remains, and 'can be detected in sexual activity in the form of non-satisfaction' ('On the Universal Tendency', pp. 258–9).[3]

The ego too is the effect of restriction, and Freud describes this in terms which take us a step closer to the death drive, in that the primary, pre-social 'unity' of being is also a state of non-being or undifferentiation:

originally the ego includes everything, later it separates off an external world from itself. Our present ego-feeling is, therefore, only a shrunken residue of a much more inclusive – indeed, an all-embracing – feeling . . . of limitlessness and of a bond with the universe . . . (*Civilization and its Discontents*, p. 255)

Death and the instincts: Freud's mythology of life's origins

Undergoing repression, desire tends towards a compulsion to repeat[4] which is a manifestation of the death drive (*Beyond the Pleasure Principle*, pp. 283–4). This drive was also there from the beginning, but now comes to the fore (in Freudian theory the human infant is astonishingly invested at birth). Instinct socialized as loss and lack somehow reconnects with the most fundamental instinct of all, which is to die. As life flickered in inanimate substance, says Freud, it endeavoured to cancel itself out. In this way the first instinct came into being: the instinct to return to the inanimate state. It was still an easy matter at that time for a living substance to die . . . (p. 311)

This is the origin of the death drive – that which seeks to 'dissolve' life back into its 'primaeval, inorganic state' (*Civilization and its Discontents*, p. 310).[5] This is the definition of the death drive – an instinctual reaching towards that state in which there is the complete absence of excitation, a state of zero tension characteristic of the inorganic or the inanimate.

We should be clear about what Freud is claiming here: the most basic instinctual drive for satisfaction is in fact a backward movement to death, to the absence of all tension: ' "*the aim of all life is death*" ' (*Beyond the Pleasure Principle*, p. 311; both the emphasis and the quotation marks are his). As he wrote to Albert Einstein in 1932, the death instinct is 'at work in every living creature and is striving to bring it to ruin and to reduce life to its original condition of inanimate matter' ('Why War?', p. 357).

Originally, says Freud, it was relatively easy for living substance to die. Eventually, however, external influences make death more difficult; the organism has to make 'ever more complicated *détours* before reaching its aim of death. These circuitous paths to death . . . thus present us to-day with the picture of the phenomena of life' (*Beyond the Pleasure Principle*, p. 311). Life itself is only a detour to death.

There are those who believe in a future-oriented, human instinct towards perfection. Freud disagrees, believing that

What appears in a minority of human individuals as an untiring impulsion towards further perfection can easily be understood as a result of the instinctual repression upon which is based all that is most precious in human civilization. (p. 315)

He elaborates as follows: because 'the backward path that leads to complete satisfaction' – ultimately death – is blocked by the repressions which constitute social and psychic life (repressions which, we must never forget, are themselves the basis of civilization), the instinct reluctantly – against its will, so to speak – proceeds forward, because that is the only direction in which it *can* go. But this forward movement has no possibility of completion or of reaching a goal. Which means that what drives the instinct forward is not eros, not even energy as such, but social and psychic repression experienced as lack:

it is the difference in amount between the pleasure of satisfaction which is *demanded* and that which is actually *achieved* that provides the driving factor which will permit of no halting at any position attained, but, in the poet's [Goethe's] words, 'presses ever forward unsubdued'. (p. 315)

Desire's impossibility derives from the fact that socialized desire is a lack which it is impossible to appease because it is the lack of death itself, with life merely an enforced substitute for death, a movement in the only direction available, which is forward, and one always undertaken against the more fundamental desire to regress, to die.

If the instinct towards human perfection is an illusion, so too is the notion of instincts of self-preservation. On the contrary, such instincts are in service to the ultimate death of the organism:

the theoretical importance of the instincts of self-preservation, of self-assertion and of mastery greatly diminishes. They are component instincts whose function it is to assure that the organism shall follow its own path to death ... the organism wishes to die only in its own fashion. Thus these guardians of life, too, were originally the myrmidons of death. (pp. 311–12)

Eros

But there is a crucial exception: 'instinctual life as a whole serves to bring about death ... *apart from the sexual instincts*' (*Beyond the Pleasure Principle*, pp. 311, 314). The emphasis here is Freud's own, but, significantly, was added to the text only from 1921 onwards. In his later work this distinction comes to form the basis of the eros/ death opposition upon which he then sought to base everything else. Given this opposition,

The emergence of life would thus be the cause of the continuance of life *and also at the same time of the striving towards death*; and life itself would be a conflict and compromise between these two trends. (*The Ego and the Id*, p. 381; my emphasis)

Or, as he put it in *Civilization and its Discontents*, 'The phenomena of life could be explained from the concurrent or mutually opposing action of these two instincts' (p. 310). The meaning of the evolution of civilization is nothing less than the struggle between eros and death, which, between them, share 'world-dominion' (p. 314).[6] Here, more clearly than in *Beyond the Pleasure Principle*, civilization is regarded as in the service of an eros 'whose purpose is to combine single human individuals, and after that families, then races, peoples and nations, into one great unity, the unity of mankind' (p. 313). Whereas the aim of eros is to establish these ever greater unities, to bind them together, to prolong them and to bring life to a 'higher development', the aim of the death instinct is, 'on the contrary, to undo connections and so to destroy things' ('The Libido Theory', p. 258; *Outline*, p. 148).

One of several difficulties with this account is the way that, on closer scrutiny, the two drives, allegedly in perpetual antagonism, also unite or at least partake of each other. While being convinced that the two instincts do unite, Freud is unsure as to exactly how. On his own admission, the dualistic hypothesis 'throws no light whatever upon the manner in which the two classes of instincts are fused, blended, and alloyed with each other'. But he insists on retaining the assumption that a very extensive fusion and amalgamation does occur, and regularly (*The Ego and the Id*, p. 381). Thus, says Freud, the death drive, or '*instinct of destruction*', is habitually brought into the service of eros (p. 382), sadism and masochism being obvious and important examples (*Civilization and its Discontents*, p. 310). Turned inwards, as masochism, the instinct destroys the organism; turned outwards, as sadism, it constitutes the violence of human history, which is the greatest impediment to civilization, and directly responsible for what, in his 1932 letter to Einstein, Freud calls 'all the ugly and dangerous impulses against which we are struggling' ('Why War?', p. 358).

When a portion of the destructive instinct is sexualized, 'this is sadism proper'. Another portion remains inside the organism and, with the help of sexual excitation, remains libidinally bound there; this is 'the original, erotogenic masochism'. Freud also calls this portion of the death instinct 'primal sadism', and regards it as identical with masochism ('The Economic Problem of Masochism', pp. 418–19).

This primal sadism or erotogenic masochism is a component of the libido, with the self as its object. A 'secondary masochism' may be added to it: in this case an originally projected instinct of destruction – sadism – is introjected, turned back upon the subject; this occurs regularly where a *'cultural suppression of the instincts'* frustrates the subject's need for destructive instinctual expression (pp. 419, 425). Both normal and pathological phenomena can be traced to the internalization of the destructive instinct. Thirdly, there is 'moral masochism', which also originates from the death drive, and also has an erotic component; and this leads to the remarkable proposition that 'even the subject's destruction of himself cannot take place without libidinal satisfaction' (p. 426).

If the life and death drives can become fused, they can also become defused.[7] Even more significantly, they are inherently mutable, each being capable of actually turning into its opposite, as with love turning into hate and hate into love. Freud is not asserting the obvious point that an experience of hate can be succeeded by love, or vice versa, or that a change in the loved object can provoke such a shift of regard; rather, he is claiming that there can occur a direct transformation of hate into love which is purely internal and not dependent upon other meditations. And if this does indeed occur – as it most plausibly does for Freud in paranoia, where homosexual love is transformed into persecutory hate – then, on Freud's own admission, 'the ground is cut away from under a distinction so fundamental as that between erotic instincts and death instincts, one which presupposes physiological processes running in opposite directions' (*The Ego and the Id*, p. 383).

To preserve his dualistic theory Freud obviously wants to resist this conclusion, and he does so by invoking yet another hypothesis.[8] But he cannot get away from the fact that the life and death drives remain intimately, inextricably related. He reiterated this in the letter to Einstein. Declaring that 'human instincts are of only two kinds: those which seek to preserve and unite – which we call erotic . . . and those which seek to destroy and kill', Freud continues:

Neither of these instincts is any less essential than the other; the phenomena of life arise from the concurrent or mutually opposing action of both. Now it seems as though an instinct of the one sort can scarcely ever operate in isolation; it is always accompanied – or, as we say, alloyed – with a certain quota from the other side, which modifies its aim or is, in some cases, what enables it to achieve that aim . . . The difficulty of isolating the two classes of instinct in their actual manifestations is indeed what has so long prevented us from recognizing them. ('Why War?', p. 356)

In short, Freud resorts to this most fundamental of all dualisms only to find that it is unsustainable or, to the extent that it is sustainable, is lacking in explanatory power: the two most elementary and opposed forces in the universe are also so closely bound together as to be indistinguishable. Conceptually the life and death drives are separate; in practice they are not.[9]

Freud's dualism is unpersuasive in other respects too. When speaking of the death drive, he equates its activity of destroying with that of unbinding. But these two activities are not necessarily the same. It is just not plausible that the most fundamental cosmic binary is the opposition between binding/life and unbinding/death. For one thing, in Freud's earlier account of human development it was precisely sexuality itself which had the power to unbind; it was conceived as a force with enormous potential for profound psychic disruption – 'forever threatening the equilibrium of the psychic apparatus from within'.[10] The sexual perversions, for example, had a power of unbinding which, in an important sense, was on the side of life (or at least instinct) against civilization; not only could they inhibit the development of psychic and social unity, they could also re-emerge inside and against that unity, often disarticulating it. But in his dualistic theory (eros *vs.* thanatos) this very capacity to unbind shifts the perversions across on to the side of death. And, whereas desire had once threatened civilization, now Freud implausibly aligns the two: 'civilization is a process in the service of Eros' (*Civilization and its Discontents*, p. 313).[11]

These weaknesses and inconsistencies result, I believe, because Freud resorted to the dualistic theory in order to contain some of the more shocking implications of his theory of the death drive. Footnotes and paragraphs added to later editions of *Beyond the Pleasure Principle* support this. For example, a footnote added in 1925 warns that the death-drive theory 'is the development of an extreme line of thought. Later on, when account is taken of the sexual instincts, it will be found that the necessary limitations and corrections are applied to it' (p. 310). And whereas in *Beyond the Pleasure Principle* Freud acknowledges his closeness to Schopenhauer without reservation, in his *New Introductory Lectures* he distances himself from the philosopher precisely on account of his own emphasis on eros: 'we are not asserting that death is the only aim of life' (p. 141).

Perhaps this is why it was a short step for some to rewrite the death drive as primarily an instinct of aggression. But, as Laplanche remarks, such a rewriting is in error, since for Freud 'the death drive is in the first instance turned, not toward the outside (as aggressivity), but toward the subject . . . it is radically not a drive *to murder*, but a drive *to suicide*, or *to kill oneself*'. It emerges, says Laplanche, from Freud's attempt to 'shatter life in its very foundations', from his 'compulsion to abolish life' (p. 123; cited in Boothby, p. 11). And yet: does not Laplanche here echo the terms of Satanic transgression; and does not Freud's own account of the death drive – the drive to unbind, to undo – do the same? Or, as John Donne put it in 1611, three hundred years earlier, paraphrasing the Augustinian theory of evil:

> We seem ambitious, God's whole work to undo;
> Of nothing he made us, and we strive too,
> To bring ourselves to nothing back . . .
> (*An Anatomie of the World*, ll. 155–7)

Unbinding is an idea with a theological history, and one which included Satan's power to undo (pervert) the created universe, to subvert it from within, to turn it against itself, and bring it back to chaos or nothingness. And this was a mythology which always knew that the power of unbinding was an expression of death working through human desire.

Freud's account of the death drive is a mythology of civilization, indeed of the world, even of the universe: it does, after all, purport to describe nothing less than the origin of life and of death. As such it draws on, or finds confirmation in, earlier philosophers. Keen to co-opt the authority of the ancients against his own contemporary critics, Freud half-acknowledged precedents as close as Schopenhauer and as distant as Empedocles.[12] Virtually without qualification, he embraces the latter's theory of an elemental, everlasting conflict in the universe between *philia* and *neikos*, love and strife, as parallel to his own theory of the 'two primal instincts, *Eros* and *destructiveness*', remarking 'I am very ready to give up the prestige of originality for the sake of such a confirmation' ('Analysis', p. 245). In his letter to Einstein, Freud even conceded the mythological basis of his own 'scientific' theory – albeit somewhat defensively:

It may perhaps seem to you as though our theories are a kind of mythology and, in the present case, not even an agreeable one. But does not every science come in the end to a kind of mythology like this? Cannot the same be said of your own physics? ('Why War', p. 358)[13]

Some four years later Freud seems still unsure about this; in acknowledging again the striking coincidence between his theory and that of Empedocles, he nevertheless distinguishes between the 'cosmic phantasy' of the latter and his own theory, which is 'content to claim biological validity' – only to add, 'at the same time, the fact that Empedocles ascribes to the universe the same animate nature as to individual organisms robs this difference of much of its importance' ('Analysis', pp. 245–6). As for Schopenhauer, the similarities are apparent from what has already been said. Richard Boothby has remarked that

in both the metaphysics of Schopenhauer and the concept of the psychoanalytic death drive, what is at stake is the dissolution of the individual ego that poses an obstacle to the further unfolding of the very forces that constituted it. (p. 196)[14]

I think it is much more than that: Freud was never more provocative, insightful or profound than when, as here, he was being perversely speculative and evasively derivative,[15] when he was rediscovering, yet at the same time trying to circumvent, even to avoid, an ancient, shocking vision – at different times a metaphysic, a theology and a mythology – whereby death is not simply the termination of life (that being the mystifying banality by which we live) but life's driving force, its animating, dynamic principle: simply, in Freud's own words in 1920, ' "*the aim of all life is death*" '; or, as Schopenhauer put it earlier, 'Dying is certainly to be regarded as the real aim of life.' As I suggested earlier, these propositions recall William Drummond's vision of death being to life 'an inward cause of a necessary dissolution', or Montaigne's contention that 'the goal of our career is death. It is the necessary object of our aim' (above, Part II). And out of context they even resemble Old Testament wisdom literature. Freud's persuasiveness derives in part from his brilliant refashioning and incorporation – one might almost say 'implantation' – of these older ideas into the 'new' world of interiority created by psychoanalysis. And, if something of their persuasiveness is thereby reactivated, it is in a form even more internal to the human psyche.

One thing that Freud adds is the theory of all instincts as essentially regressive: *'an instinct is an urge inherent in organic life to restore an earlier state of things'* (*Beyond the Pleasure Principle*, p. 308; his emphasis). All organic instincts are, in this sense, conservative. The earlier mutability tradition is shot through with world-weariness, nostalgia, loss, resignation and regressive desire, but in a way which remains reluctantly forward-looking and forward-driven: desire, savaged internally by death as a living mutability, is nevertheless driven forward by death to its own destruction, and death as future event is awaited as the end or transcendence of desire. Freud describes a similar situation, only now it is a consequence of the lack and dissatisfaction deriving from repression. But deeper than repression, and continually exerting its pull, is an instinctual harmony between death and desire; in the deepest source of life itself is a regressive desire to die.

Death beyond Freud

The death-drive theory has not found wide acceptance among Freud's followers. With significant exceptions like Melanie Klein, it has been explicitly denounced as misconceived biology, unsubstantiated speculation, logically incoherent and/or without evidence. It has also been attributed to Freud's own painful personal circumstances: the death of his daughter, the death of a grandson, his own illness (cancer), and his lifelong preoccupation with death. Of those who have been sympathetic to the idea, most have tended to tame it – as indeed did

Freud himself. One move was to rewrite the instinct as largely an instinct of aggression. But for Freud the aggressive aspect of the death drive had been secondary; the instinct was primarily self-destructive. Sadism derives from a more primordial masochism, which means in effect that human aggression is, originally, self-destructiveness.

Of all subsequent theorists of psychoanalysis, Jacques Lacan takes the death drive most seriously, and most contemporary psychoanalytic attention to it comes via him. To his credit, Lacan does not underplay or tame the death drive, and he locates Freud firmly within the Western tradition when he remarks that Freud questioned life as to its meaning and his answer was not that it had none – 'which is a convenient way of washing one's hands of the whole business' – but that life has 'only one meaning, that in which desire is borne by death' (*Écrits*, p. 277).

According to Lacan, the Freudian world is one not of things, nor even of being, but rather of desire. More so even than Freud, Lacan finds in desire 'the paradoxical, deviant, erratic, eccentric, even scandalous character by which it is distinguished from need'. Although this distinction has been 'always obvious to moralists worthy of the name', psychoanalysis nevertheless misses the point by pursuing an obscurantist reduction of desire to need (p. 286). And that, for Lacan, is a cardinal error. This distinction between desire and need leads him to dwell on something else in both Freud and earlier writers, moralists and otherwise: the relation between desire and lack. In modern psychoanalysis we find a secularized, intensified version of an existential perception that goes back a long way, even though the immediate influences here are Heidegger and Kojève:

Desire is a relation of being to lack. This lack is the lack of being properly speaking. It isn't the lack of this or that, but lack of being whereby the being exists. (Lacan, *Seminar*, II.222–3)

For Lacan, death is the name for a primordial absence intrinsic to presence; as John Forrester puts it, 'presence includes as its very condition the limit beyond which is its absence' (p. 176).[16] To bind desire so resolutely into lack and absence means that it inevitably becomes a kind of essential negativity (Lacan, *Seminar*, I.146)[17] – something premised on an initial failure of satisfaction and which, as such, comes to exist only by virtue of its own alienation; as Juliet

Mitchell puts it, 'Desire persists as an effect of a primordial absence and it therefore indicates that, in this area, there is something fundamentally impossible about satisfaction itself' (Lacan, *Feminine Sexuality*, p. 6). One consequence of this is a radical fragmentation of the human subject.[18]

In one respect Lacan recasts the familiar metaphysical idea that life is rooted in death: 'it is death that sustains existence' (*Écrits*, p. 300). In his development of this idea he combines diverse elements of the Western tradition of desire's impossibility: a theology of desire as death, crossed with something more romantic if no less severe – desire as annihilating excess, a primordial discord. The two elements are fused in those places where, for example, he speaks of 'that desperate affirmation of life that is the purest form in which we recognize the death instinct' (p. 104). These ideas then get reworked according to structuralist and linguistic preoccupations, as when he speaks of the 'frenzy' of desire 'mocking the abyss of the infinite', and of how this amounts to 'no other derangement of instinct than that of being caught in the rails – eternally stretching forth towards the *desire for something else* – of metonymy. Hence its "perverse" fixation at the very suspension-point of the signifying chain where the memory-screen is immobilized and the fascinating image of the fetish is petrified' (p. 167).

In the same vein Lacan suggests that it is from death that existence takes on all the *meaning* it has; the lack which is at the heart of desire is also the price that human beings pay for their admission to language and culture. Death makes life possible in that it makes meaning and representation possible; it is not only before speech but 'primordial to the birth of symbols' (pp. 104–5, 300). Hence Lacan's most well-known formulation, that the unconscious is structured like a language, and his claim to have demonstrated 'the profound relationship uniting the notion of the death instinct to the problems of speech' (*Four Fundamental Concepts*, p. 20; *Écrits*, p. 101). Richard Boothby regards this as the most radical and innovative aspect of Lacan. I remain unconvinced.[19]

Lacan's invocations of death's centrality to life are more derivative than their complex, often obscure, formulations suggest.[20] When he declares that

All that life is concerned with is seeking repose as much as possible while awaiting death. This is what devours the time of the suckling baby at the beginning of its existence . . . Life is concerned solely with dying (*Seminar*, II.233)

we can hear Freud and Schopenhauer most closely, but also Montaigne (especially in that last assertion – 'Life is concerned solely with dying'), who also, incidentally, consolidated his own perception of this truth with extensive citation of classical sources. In the giving over of the newborn child to death we might hear too the early Christian Fathers. Lacan does not exactly disguise his precedents; the passage just cited continues with a reference to Hamlet's 'to die, to sleep, perchance to dream' and to the idea developed by philosophers in antiquity that it would have been better not to have been born. But (and this recalls Freud's own evasive acknowledgment of his influences) in Lacan these allusions to the past are fleeting, in passing, almost secretive; the implication is that these past writers anticipate something which can only properly, and only now, be understood through the lens of Lacanian psychoanalysis, whose complexity is, at the same time, almost guaranteed to defeat the attempt. Some at least of that complexity is obscurantist.

In the wake of contemporary cultural developments, including the perceived failure of sexual radicalism and the trauma of AIDS, there are those who have turned to Lacan for a more honest view of desire, and, via him, are reconsidering a severe account of human desire. I should not speak for them; what I find in Lacan is an overtheorized expression of something more significantly and relevantly expressed elsewhere (in Freud and before). It this respect I believe he is symptomatic of a much wider tendency in (post-)modern theory. But in terms of his influence alone Lacan remains significant for this study. By crossing Freud's death drive with the philosophy of lack and nothingness derived from Kojève's version of Hegel (itself influenced by Heidegger), he continues to drive death ever further into being; now, perhaps more inexorably than ever before, death is the lack which drives desire. In doing that he also exemplifies another significant tendency in modern thought which I have already remarked, namely the anti-humanist wish to decentre 'man' in the name of a philosophy

which is truly adequate to the complexity of being, yet which seeks
to retain a residual human mastery in the very effort of articulating
this complexity. As we have seen, the philosophical bid to comprehend
the truth of being was always a form of intellectual empowerment –
even, or rather especially, when issuing in the declaration that life,
desire and the world have to be renounced. But modern theory, having
lost faith in older philosophical notions of truth, now half-settles for
the mastery of a new kind of complexity which it partly produces
in order to enable this performance of mastery. Phoenix-like, the
omniscient, masterful and above all complex analytic of the modern
theorist rises above his sacrifice of 'man' to death.

VI

RENOUNCING
DEATH

15

The Philosophy of Praxis
and Emancipation:
Feuerbach, Marx, Marcuse

Renunciation to emancipation

Schopenhauer believed that to obtain a full understanding of the human condition was necessarily to achieve a state of profound resignation, and to relinquish the will-to-live. He found such resignation realized most compellingly in the vision of tragedy, where (according to him) heroes die purified by suffering, when the will-to-live has already expired in them (*World*, I.235). This, as we shall see, is what Nietzsche would so influentially react against – not just in Schopenhauer but in the entire Western philosophical tradition, which, he believed, has always tended to pessimism: 'In every age the wisest have passed the identical judgement on life: *it is worthless* . . .' Everywhere and always the wisest express a world-view 'full of doubt, full of melancholy, full of weariness with life, full of opposition to life' (*Twilight*, p. 29). It is in this sense that, for Nietzsche, Western philosophy is decadent – and not just recently, but from its inception. For him, as we have already seen, Socrates and Plato were founding decadents, agents of the decline and degeneration of Greek culture and of a death-wish – 'Socrates *wanted* to die' – and a related eroticism: 'Socrates was also a great *erotic*' (pp. 34, 32; cf. *Birth*, p. 85). As for Plato, he was 'so morally infected, so much an antecedent Christian . . . a coward in the face of reality [who] flees into the ideal'. The Christian God comes to stand only for 'declining, debilitated, wary, condemned life' (*Twilight*, pp. 106–7, 45–6).

For the most part Schopenhauer led a secluded life. He assiduously avoided, and if necessary actually fled, the wars, political struggles and other social disruptions of his own time. His metaphysical view of the world made him conservative in politics. He regarded the State as a necessary evil, there to protect men from each other. He did not believe in progress. History repeats itself; nothing changes and no one really learns anything (*World*, I.183). He was adamantly opposed to revolutionary praxis. In September 1848 political turmoil caught up with him and he became embroiled in revolutionary fervour in Frankfurt. A mob attempted to storm Parliament. Schopenhauer observed the event from his window – in particular the activity of some snipers with rifles. Suddenly some soldiers entered his room, intent upon using his window to fire upon the mob. They changed their mind, deciding that next door afforded an even better opportunity. Schopenhauer, despising all revolutionary activity, offered his opera-glasses to enable them to take better aim (Safranski, pp. 324–5).

Marx will say that hitherto philosophers had only interpreted the world; henceforth the philosophical task is to change it; thinking will become a form of praxis. It was not only that philosophers previously had preferred thought to action; the understanding of the world that many of them had arrived at included the belief that it was impossible, or at least pointless, to try to change it. If philosophical reflection had led them to renounce the very idea of praxis, this seems to have been especially so for those who meditated the truth of death and the nature of human desire. But Marx would also argue that, with many of these philosophers, their thinking about the ultimate truths was conditioned by their own social positioning, and to an extent which they could never know. Certainly their philosophy was not as disinterested as they thought or pretended, either to themselves or to others or both. And yet it hardly requires a Marxist critique to see that Schopenhauer (for instance) hated revolutionary activity partly because he feared for his own security, especially his property, and that this undoubtedly affected his scepticism about the social progress and democratic transformation which others at that time yearned for. It is a resonant image: the cultured philosopher who has renounced praxis finds himself, against his will, embroiled in violent social struggle and responds by offering the forces of law and order the use of his opera-glasses as a makeshift rifle-sight.

What is striking is how many of the other philosophers we have so far encountered also are said or can be seen to have renounced the idea of progress or belief in the possibility of social improvement. Heraclitus, who conceived the universe in terms of process, change and a radical mutability, reputedly refused to engage in politics or take sides in political arguments, and had little sympathy for democracy in the Greek sense. He seems to have had no disciples, and one anecdote depicts him fleeing human society and living as a hermit in the mountains (Kahn, pp. 1–3). Karl Popper finds in Heraclitus the origins of modern anti-democratic tendencies, and speculates that his philosophy of change was prompted by traumatic experiences of revolutionary social and political turmoil. Popper remarks, perceptively if not entirely accurately, that philosophers who conceptualize the world as *essentially* unstable are overcompensating for the fact that they find change disturbing: change itself is elevated into the status of the unchanging law, and so becomes a kind of surrogate for the permanence they yearn for (I.11–17).

Between Heraclitus and Schopenhauer there are many others, and frequently it is social and historical turmoil that not only leads to their renunciation of society, but also proves to be the context, if not the cause, of their meditations upon death and its relation to desire. In other words, it is as much social and political turmoil as the fact of death itself which provokes the philosophy of death. Plato, argues Popper, even more than Heraclitus, suffered desperately under the political instability and insecurity of the time in which he lived (pp. 18–19). Epicurus withdrew from the political chaos of his time, offering the famous injunction 'Live unknown' and describing the world of public affairs and politics as a 'prison' from which we must release ourselves (Epicurus, pp. 139, 115). Lucretius gave up politics and war for philosophy. Seneca and Marcus Aurelius were literally world leaders who, in their philosophy at least, became despairing of the world. We should never forget that, in the context of Stoicism, it is the experienced failures of something like praxis itself which leads directly to a philosophy of renunciation. Schopenhauer is the heir of these philosophers, as indeed are many more recent writers whose modernist credentials sometimes obscure their connection with this longer history. As for the modern theorists of social death, Daniel Pick reminds us that 'the social-biological theory of degeneration emerged in the 1880s most powerfully as a counter-theory to mass-democracy and socialism' (p. 218).

And yet it is worth repeating: the philosophy of renunciation often redoubles the secular effort, but in the form of *reaction*. And we might remark again the irony that Stoicism originates, or is powerfully endorsed by, some of those at the centre of world power.

The darkness which obliterates difference

Consider again Conrad's *Heart of Darkness* in the light of the political question which has been asked of it with increasing urgency in recent times: is it a racist text?[1] In Conrad's defence it can be said that he exposes, either directly or ironically, the brutality of imperialist exploitation in Africa. Also that he relentlessly undercuts the superiority and difference of the civilized to the primitive, even to the point of collapsing the one into the other. And that is important, especially because at the time of the novel's appearance such assumptions of superiority were powerfully active in the ideological justification of exploitation. This merging or collapsing of the assumed differences between Africa and Europe, the civilized and the primitive, is, as we saw, intrinsic to the paradoxical nature of Kurtz: the *most* civilized becomes the one who most 'degenerates', who becomes the focus, even the force, which unbinds the civilized and who epitomizes the fears which degeneration theory tries to contain, namely that civilization is somehow moving forward and regressing to its own ruin.

At the end of the novel, when Marlow returns to London, his lies to Kurtz's intended are to protect her from the darkness which he has perceived just behind the veneer of civilization – a darkness which, as dusk fell, seemed to be gathering even in her own drawing-room (pp. 105–6). He has, of course, prepared us for this at the beginning of his story; moored on the Thames at Gravesend, east of London, he remarks 'this also . . . has been one of the dark places of the earth' (p. 7). He reflects that when the invading Romans struggled up the Thames their encounter with death, disease and the alien closely resembled the Europeans' later experience of Africa, and indeed his own journey up the Congo: 'I was thinking of very old times, when the Romans first came here, nineteen hundred years ago – the other day . . . Darkness was here yesterday' (p. 8). In short, where the primeval darkness is concerned, there is not much to distinguish Africa now from London then. And it is exactly this radical erasure of difference which on the one side makes possible the novel's critique of imperial exploitation *and* on the other renders it vulnerable to the charge of dehumanizing Africa, of making the Congo the blank space on to which Europe maps its own 'spiritual' neurosis even as it materially plunders it.

Edward Said observes that Conrad's 'tragic limitation' was that, while being aware that imperialism involved brutal exploitation, he was so much a creature of his time that he 'could not then conclude that imperialism had to end . . . Conrad could not grant the natives their freedom, despite his severe critique of the imperialism that enslaved them.' Similarly, his characters could not recognize 'that what they disablingly and disparagingly saw as a non-European "darkness" was in fact a non-European world *resisting* imperialism so as one day to regain sovereignty and independence' (pp. 33–4).

Said wants to exonerate Conrad to a degree by making him a creature of his time. But the fact is – and this may make him more, not less, culpable – Conrad claimed to see more than Said allows. As with many writers before him, the metaphysics of oblivion render questions of resistance virtually irrelevant; in the face of what at the end of the novel he calls 'that oblivion which is the last word of our common fate' (p. 105), such things fall into insignificance despite or rather because of our all being reconciled to this 'common fate'. Conrad himself put it like this, in a letter written in January 1898, the year before *Heart of Darkness* was published:

The fate of a humanity condemned ultimately to perish from cold is not worth thinking about. If you take it to heart it becomes an unendurable tragedy. If you believe in improvement you must weep, for *the attained perfection must end in cold, darkness, and silence.* In a dispassionate view the ardour for reform, improvement for virtue, for knowledge, and even for beauty is only a vain sticking up for appearances as though one were anxious about the cut of one's clothes in a community of blind men. Life knows us not and we do not know life – we don't even know our own thoughts . . . Faith is a myth and beliefs shift like mists on the shore; thoughts vanish; words, once pronounced, die; and the memory of yesterday is as shadowy as the hope of to-morrow. (*Collected Letters*, II.17; my emphasis)

In such a world the aspirations of a radical, reforming praxis would be the most radical deception of all. Africa dissolves the rationale not just for the exploitative quest for ivory, but for all other manifestations of praxis in the 'First' World along with any aspiration for change in the Third. Not for the first time, the 'spiritual' obliteration of all difference leaves existing material differences intact. And, if this is offensive to our modern commitment to an emancipatory politics, it is also true that this is a politics which cannot afford even to consider the metaphysics of oblivion.

Earlier I explored *Heart of Darkness* in relation to ideas contemporary with it or which it could be said to anticipate – particularly ideas of degeneration. There are other respects in which it is significantly of its time, or can be said to anticipate modernist aesthetic developments. But this underlying preoccupation with a metaphysics of oblivion which threatens or promises a radical erasure of difference was not new. And nor had it yet found its most extreme modern form, which arguably was Freud's theory of the death drive, itself drawing on sources as recent as Schopenhauer and as old as Empedocles. And Freud, of course, like Conrad, was deeply sceptical of 'the ardour for reform', believing that Marxism fatally ignored 'the untameable character of human nature' (*New Introductory Lectures*, p. 219). And in *Beyond the Pleasure Principle* he even suggested that the 'untiring impulsion towards further perfection' is at heart a frustrated displacement of the death drive itself (p. 315). In certain respects, as we shall see, Freud may have been right.

Reclaiming God

In the preface to the first volume of his collected works (1846), Feuerbach gave this succinct account of what it means to be a radical humanist:

he who says no more of me than that I am an atheist, says and knows *nothing* of me. The question as to the existence or non-existence of God, the opposition between theism and atheism belongs to the sixteenth and seventeenth centuries but not to the nineteenth. I deny [*negiere*] God. But that means for me that

I deny the negation of man. In place of the illusory, fantastic, heavenly position of man which in actual life necessarily leads to the degradation of man, I substitute the tangible, actual and consequently also the political and social position of mankind. The question concerning the existence or non-existence of God is for me nothing but the question concerning the existence or non-existence of man. (cited in Hook, pp. 222–3)

Feuerbach, indebted to Hegel but pushing beyond him, laid the ground for the materialist philosophy of praxis whose influence on the modern world has been inestimable. In that philosophy, God is displaced by man. Or rather, God, having been discovered to be made in man's image, is taken back into man. This is the exhilarating argument of Feuerbach's *The Essence of Christianity* (1841): 'All the attributes of the divine nature are, therefore, attributes of the human nature.' Religion arises when man 'projects his being into objectivity, and then again makes himself an object to this projected image of himself thus converted into a subject' (pp. 33–4).

Feuerbach denies the fundamental dualism which regards God as infinite, perfect, eternal, holy, and man as finite, imperfect, mortal, sinful. Not only is man *not* defined by the inferior terms of this binary opposition, but, at his most exalted, he is worthy of being described by its superior terms. The pure, perfect divine nature is really only the consciousness which the understanding has of its own perfection; intelligence in and for itself is the highest form of understanding and reasoning – it is free of desire, want and passion, and for that reason it has no weakness or deficiency (pp. 33–4). In short – and this is the crucial point – 'God is the highest subjectivity of man abstracted from himself . . . God is, *per se*, his relinquished self' (pp. 14, 29–31).

The Essence of Christianity was a controversial but highly successful book, going through three editions in seven years and contributing to Feuerbach's reputation: he was perhaps the most well-known and widely read philosopher in Germany in the 1840s. He became an important influence for many – most famously Karl Marx, but also (among others) Nietzsche, Kierkegaard, a generation of existentialist philosophers, and possibly Freud. We might expect that, read now, this book would strike us as an uncontroversial precursor of a philosophy that has become familiar and even, from the point of view of the anti-humanism of our own times, somewhat complacent – certainly not scandalous. In fact Feuerbach's humanism was more complicated and significant than this allows, not least in what might paradoxically be called its anti-humanism, or at least its anti-individualism. Feuerbach remains relevant, and nowhere more so than in his account of death, which is often omitted from the philosophical narrative. To think of humanism only as the philosophy that tames, demystifies and rationalizes death for the modern world, and which delivers to secularism the ideology of an integrated, self-sufficient individual, is wrong.

Feuerbach's Thoughts on Death

In 1830, eleven years before *The Essence of Christianity*, Feuerbach had published anonymously another, even more controversial, book: *Thoughts on Death and Immortality*. It was seized from bookshops by censors, and when it became known that Feuerbach was its author his academic career was effectively ruined. Today it is often ignored by those who write about him. In this book Feuerbach does with death what he was later to do with God: he incorporates it into man. Death is not an external law of nature, and nor is it the end of human freedom. Rather, it is the condition and ground of that freedom: 'you die because you are a free, thinking, conscious being . . . Death comes only from Spirit, from freedom. The ground of your life is that consciousness and division is also the true ground and origin of your death' (p. 111).

Feuerbach inaugurates a radical humanism that does not just accept death in the sense of trying to tame it, but, under the influence of Hegel, reincorporates it into being. It echoes the early Christian idea that death is the inherent condition of life, rather than that which defeats it from without, while obliterating the Christian distinction between the finite, fallen condition of man (the breeding-ground for death) and the spirit which escapes death; now spirit becomes the ground of death (p. 113). Death is the seductive, intrinsic condition of being; as Feuerbach puts it elsewhere, in poetic form, death is 'in your very marrow':

Death does disclose the ground of being
. . . .
Being is but in death revealed,
And is, therefore, in death fulfilled.
(cited in Choron, *Death and*
Western Thought, pp. 194, 196)

Death is also eroticized:

Oh death! I cannot wrench myself free from the sweet consideration of your soft essence, so inwardly fused with my own! Gentle mirror of the Spirit, reflected splendour of my own essence! (*Thoughts*, p. 112)

As he puts it in the poem *Reimverse auf den Tod* (1830), 'I am drawn away from this life / So that I surrender to Nothingness' (Choron, p. 194). Love, which is the supreme expression of one's humanity, also requires death: 'Love would not be complete if death did not exist ... death is thus the ultimate sacrifice of reconciliation, the ultimate verification of love' (*Thoughts*, p. 125). In fact death and love are inextricably bound together; there is inside us a death that is 'trapped and bound (*for the binding, bound, and constrained death of the self is love*)', and this inner death 'is only freed, isolated, and unbound in external, sensible death ... What is the source of death if it is not your inmost reality?' (p. 127; my emphasis).

The disappearance of the individual

Feuerbach's philosophy is characteristically humanist in his concern to restore unity where he discerns division. He once conceded that, 'down to the smallest detail, even my senses agree with this inner feeling for the undivided, for that which is at one with itself' (cited in Hook, p. 251). Again, the influence of Hegel is apparent. (It has been said that Feuerbach was Hegel's fate.) But, in this drive to make man the focus for this new unity, Feuerbach incorporates so much into 'him' that he stores up an even greater potential for instability.

In *Thoughts on Death* he also deploys the Hegelian notions of totality in a way which entails subjective death. Thus humanity is a totality whose 'essential unity is the inner essential negation of individuals'; and, anticipating Nietzsche, Feuerbach declares that mortality, decay, change, mutability and even time itself – the detritus of death – are nothing but the expression of the unity of spirit, that is, 'nothing but . . . the *furor divinus*, the Spirit that sweeps away and inspires the world in the stream of its own inspiration'. History is only the manifestation of the same (p. 130). Even love requires the negation and 'continuous ratification of the nothingness of [the] self', which is itself an acceptance of death – 'the total and complete surrender of the self' (pp. 125–6). This is a humanism which embraces death as its own nature, its own truth, and even goes some way to abolishing the individualism on which it founds itself. At its most adventurous, humanism is a philosophy of egoistic appropriation whereby the individual consciousness is expanded to include what was hitherto by definition excluded from it – a process of psychic identification with and incorporation of the excluded, the origins of which were in Renaissance humanism, and which grants radical new potentialities to the human and thereby necessarily destabilizes the more conservative humanist project for a subjectivity grounded in a stable, unchanging essence.

Feuerbach finds in Hegel a justification for his own preoccupation with death, and for dissolving God back into man in a way which, as we shall shortly see, profoundly enables the emerging philosophy of praxis. But death and praxis pull in different directions, to say the least. In the philosophy of praxis there is an inevitable amnesia with regard to death. Maybe this is why *The Essence of Christianity* hardly mentions that preoccupation with death which is so central to *Thoughts on Death*. Feuerbach, the founder of the modern philosophy of praxis, prefigures its subsequent history in being steeped in an attitude to death which that philosophy would disown yet never get free of; the death which praxis transcends remains immanent within it. Thus Marcuse, more than a century later, severely condemns the death-obsessiveness of Western philosophy – and does so in the name of a praxis more radical than Feuerbach's – and yet remains fascinated by what he repudiates, and one of his most well-known works, *Eros and Civilization* (1955), displays a fascination with death not dissimilar to Feuerbach's. But first, Marx.

Marx: praxis and revolution

'Marx ... neglects the theme of death ... (Kojève, 'The Idea of Death', p. 156, n. 9)

For Feuerbach, all the limitless qualities attributed to God are in fact those of the species man. In the individual these qualities are limited, and the experience of that limitation is painful. So we compensate for the lack we feel by imagining its fulfilment in God, who is the idea or essence of the species conceived in individual, but omnipotent, form. To understand the human psychology which has created God is to be ready to re-identify with humanity rather than God:

My life is bound to a limited time; not so the life of humanity. The history of mankind consists in nothing else than a continuous and progressive conquest of limits, which at a given time pass for the limits of humanity, and therefore for absolute insurmountable limits. But the future always unveils the fact that the alleged limits of the species were only limits of individuals. (*Essence*, pp. 152–3)

Thus Feuerbach's transformation of religious pessimism into optimism, quietism into purpose, limit into potential. His identification of activity and productivity as the expression of man's true nature gets very close to praxis, and probably closer than Marx was subsequently to allow; here is Feuerbach again:

The idea of activity, of making, of creation, is in itself a divine idea; it is therefore unhesitatingly applied to God. In activity, man feels himself free, unlimited, happy; in passivity, limited, oppressed, unhappy ... the happiest, the most blissful activity is that which is productive. (p. 217)

It is worth trying to recapture the exhilaration of an idea which promised to dissolve so much of the pain of being, to overcome alienation and contradiction, to restore agency and redeem loss in the prospect of a better future. The old philosophical dream of integrating identity and activity, being and doing, seemed at last possible in a radically demystified form, given the new conviction that the inadequacy of the present is a contingent and changeable state of affairs and not an eternally or naturally unalterable one. And, just as Feuerbach takes God back into man and radically revises our understanding of both, so the process of change ceases to be the negative, defeating and corrosive action of mutability, over which man has no power, and which means to him only loss and decline; it becomes instead an empowering potential for liberation and renewal. Desire realizes itself through transformation rather than possession, and man is now conceived in terms of his capacity for socially transformative activity; his very essence now lies in praxis.

Earlier we saw Shakespeare and John Donne using the word 'revolution' to signify human powerlessness and insignificance in a world governed by mutability (Chapter 5). In *Henry IV* it refers to the obliterating effects of time and change on an almost cosmic scale:

> . . . see the revolution of the times
> Make mountains level, and the continent,
> Weary of solid firmness, melt itself
> Into the sea . . .

Donne also uses the word 'revolution' to refer to the motion of dissolution and dispersal, but now the focus is the rotting of the individual body in the grave. But the process does not stop there; first the body is reduced to dust; then, as the grave itself disintegrates, that dust is blown abroad, now mingling with the dust of the highway, the dunghill, the puddle and the pond, 'such are the *revolution* of the graves'. Hamlet also uses the word in relation to the grave, while regarding a skull recently dug from it (V.i.89). And in *Antony and Cleopatra* the word refers to the uncontrollable mutability of desire itself. Antony has just been told that his wife is dead:

> The present pleasure,
> By revolution low'ring, does become
> The opposite of itself . . .
>
> (I.ii.117–19)

Such uses could not be further from the modern sense of revolution as the focusing of a collective human agency in the calculated overthrow of an existing social order and the replacing of it with a new one.

Behind this linguistic change is a revolutionary shift in the understanding of change itself. Now change is regarded as the dynamic principle of humankind; we change the world, and in that self-same process we change ourselves, because to change the world is to change ourselves:

The coincidence of the changing of circumstances and of human activity or self-changing can only be grasped and rationally understood as revolutionary practice. (Marx, *Theses on Feuerbach* 3; Bottomore and Rubel, p. 83)

The old notion of the individual has to go: whereas, according to Marx, Feuerbach had postulated 'an abstract – *isolated* – human individual', and conceived of the nature of man 'as an inner and mute universal quality', the reality is that 'the essence of man is not an abstraction inherent in each particular individual. The real nature of man is the totality of social relations' (Thesis 6; Bottomore and Rubel, pp. 83–4).

The philosophical reflection which finds death, desire and mutability to be inherently alienating is abolished as an error; indeed, says Marx, such 'philosophy is nothing more than religion brought into thought . . . equally to be condemned as another form and mode of existence of human alienation' (Bottomore and Rubel, pp. 84–5). Without death there would be no philosophy – so said one philosopher after another in the Western tradition. Now, with praxis, there is no need of their kind of philosophy, or the meditation on death which produced it:

All social life is essentially *practical*. All the mysteries which lead theory towards mysticisms find their rational solution in human practice and in the comprehension of this practice. (Thesis 8; Bottomore and Rubel, p. 84)

Feuerbach declares that the species has no limits – which means, among other things, that it does not know death. This is another reason why, in the move from theology to anthropology which *The Essence of Christianity* inaugurates, the philosophical significance of death recedes almost to the point of disappearing. Politically speaking, death has become socialized, almost redundant, since a kind of immortality is available through active identification with the species.

But desire and identity are now not only tied to time but virtually coextensive with it. Feuerbach said that

The more empty life is, the fuller, more concrete is God. The impoverishing of the real world, and the enriching of God, is one act. Only the poor man has a rich God. *God springs out of the feeling of a want.* (*Essence*, p, 73; my emphasis)

In the materialist tradition, to demystify God and the social order which religion typically mystified (for instance, by regarding it as divinely sanctioned and therefore unalterable) was to make the want of which Feuerbach here speaks humanely realizable *in time*. But, as Marx well knew, the very process of meeting needs generates new ones. To commit desire so completely to time intensifies, even as it relieves, the dissatisfaction which hitherto had seemed its inalienable, unalterable condition.

Social death

In *The Eighteenth Brumaire of Louis Bonaparte* Marx famously declares that man makes history but not in conditions of his own choosing. One reason why those conditions prove difficult to negotiate is because they include the 'dead' inheritance of the past: 'the tradition of all the dead generations weighs like a nightmare on the brain of the living'. And just at that moment when men seem most capable of 'revolutionizing themselves and things' they fall back on these past traditions and express themselves through them. In past revolutionary situations this was not necessarily bad:

the awakening of the dead in those revolutions served the purpose of glorifying the new struggles ... of magnifying the given task in imagination, not of fleeing from its solution in reality; of finding once more the spirit of revolution, not of making its ghost walk about again. (*Selected Works*, pp. 97–8)

But, continues Marx, in France in 1848 something like the reverse happened: revolutionary fervour was defeated by this relapsing back into the past. 'An entire people, which had imagined that by means of a revolution it had imparted to itself an accelerated power of motion, suddenly finds itself set back in a defunct epoch.' What had seemed 'long decayed' came back to life. Modern revolution must no longer look to the past but to the future:

It cannot begin with itself before it has stripped off all superstition in regard to the past . . . In order to arrive at its own content, the revolution of the nineteenth century must let the dead bury their dead. (pp. 98–9)

Death is here shifted from the future to the past – to the still active traditions of the dead which may yet defeat revolution and praxis. Death is socialized – as something still existing within the domain of the social which pulls us back to a dead past and kills off our potential for revolutionary change. What is dead is still alive, and perniciously so. It becomes necessary for praxis to kill off this past.

This is even more marked in the Marxist account of the lumpenproletariat. Shakespeare's Coriolanus was fairly representative of past and future ways of thinking when he approached the 'mutable, rank scented' plebians as a threat to the State (*Coriolanus*, III.i.65). Marx and Engels regard the lumpenproletariat similarly, except that they are now a threat to the revolutionary overthrow of the State and as such even more dangerously mutable. In the Marxist theory of revolution, all existing classes, with the exception of the proletariat, are said to undergo 'a process of dissolution' whereby they 'decay and finally disappear in the face of Modern Industry' (*Selected Works*, p. 44). Not so the lumpenproletariat, who are not a class so much as a motley, uprooted and, in many instances, itinerant mass of people who, during this anticipated process of dissolution, become unattached and susceptible to the forces of reaction. Marx's description of this group clearly expresses the idea of degeneration; this is how he described the lumpenproletariat in the *Communist Manifesto* (1848):

The 'dangerous class', the social scum, that passively rotting mass thrown off by the lowest layers of old society, may, here and there, be swept into the movement by a proletarian revolution; its conditions in life, however, prepare it far more for the part of a bribed tool of reactionary intrigue. (*Selected Works*, p. 44)

In *The Eighteenth Brumaire* Marx tells us that this group includes decayed roués, vagabonds, discharged soldiers and jailbirds, escaped galley slaves, swindlers, mountebanks, pickpockets, tricksters,

gamblers, beggars – 'in short, the whole indefinite, disintegrated mass
. . . [the] scum, offal, refuse of all classes' (p. 138). Engels, in the
preface to *The Peasant War in Germany*, also describes this 'scum of
depraved elements from all classes' as especially dangerous – so
much so that any leader of the workers who uses the services of the
lumpenproletariat proves himself by that action alone a traitor to
the movement (p. 243). As we have seen, the revolutionary vision
reconceptualizes the very idea of change. Here is another development
whereby the earlier negative ideas attaching to change (the transient,
the protean, the shifting, the decaying and declining – in a word, the
mutable) are, via the rhetoric of degeneration, also socialized and,
ironically, now attributed to those forces preventing change.

Engels speaks of Germany in the late eighteenth and early nineteenth
centuries in language even more resonant of degeneration:

it was all one living mass of putrefaction and repulsive decay . . . Everything
worn out, crumbling down, going fast to ruin, and not even the slightest
hope of a beneficial change, *not even so much strength in the nation as might
have sufficed for carrying away the putrid corpses of dead institutions.* (from
The State of Germany, cited in Zhdanov, p. 95; my emphasis)[2]

I've remarked already how ambitious programmes of social change
or social control seemingly need the rhetoric of social death in order
to identify and eliminate those elements within the social which prove
recalcitrant. The ways in which this process occurs have never been
simple. Those like Freud attribute the failure of revolutionary creeds
like communism to the recalcitrance of human nature; in particular,
such creeds ignore an ineradicable human impulse to aggression and
hatred:

It is always possible to bind together a considerable number of people in
love, so long as there are other people left over to receive the manifestations
of their aggressiveness . . . When once the Apostle Paul had posited universal
love between men as the foundation of his Christian community, extreme
intolerance on the part of Christendom towards those who remained outside
it became the inevitable consequence. (*Civilization and its Discontents*, p. 305)

Likewise, adds Freud – and he is writing this in 1929 – anti-Semitism
was the complement of the dream of a Germanic world-dominion,

and the persecution of the bourgoisie in Russia was the complement of the communist ideal. But there is something else contributing to the violence which he describes, and another reason why 'bound' human groupings need outsiders, dissidents, degenerates, racial others and the rest – Freud's 'other people'. It is not simply that human beings have a certain quantity of aggressiveness which, because they are forbidden to express it internally, they have to vent on someone, or some group, beyond the boundaries of their own society. It is also manifestly (and, arguably, in modern times increasingly) the case that responsibility for the problems and failures within a particular culture are displaced on to groups and individuals outside, or marginal, or even internal to it. And the stronger the belief that the direction of history can be controlled, and society radically altered to comply with a preconceived ideal, the more necessary become the ideological strategies which enable the displacement of failure. It would be absurd to suggest that a more humane politics resulted from the earlier ways of thinking which regarded the most fundamental historical changes – 'the revolution of the times' – as mostly if not entirely beyond human control. It is rather that some of the diverse later convictions that history can and should be controlled result in strategies for the displacement of failure which involve unprecedented violence.

Zhdanov and artistic degeneracy

Of the numerous instances of this in recent history, my example comes from Stalinism, and a series of speeches given by A. A. Zhdanov (1896–1948) between 1934 and 1948. Zhdanov was a member of the Political Bureau of the Central Committee of the Bolshevik Party, and a significant propagandist for the communist theory of culture. His speeches, translated in 1950 as *On Literature, Music and Philosophy*, contested what he and other leading party members regarded as reactionary tendencies in Russian art and culture. In some respects the terms of his argument have become commonplaces of the history of Soviet realism: socialist realism is advocated over and above Western bourgeois aesthetic practice, which is said to be steeped in formalism, art for art's sake, individualism, decadence and death.

In the unfolding of history, the capitalist order – especially its bourgeois culture – is 'rotten and decaying' (p. 48). That is as it should be, and was predicted. But in its degenerate, exhausted state it still exerts a pull; in fact – and this again borrows from the degenerationists – in this decaying phase of bourgeois order somehow becomes more pernicious than ever. Though chronically enervated and historically doomed to extinction, it still possesses the power to corrupt and defeat the new order which, according to the theory, is inevitably and necessarily replacing it. Zhdanov speaks repeatedly of a capitalist system and a bourgeois culture which are – and these are all words he actually uses – dying, decaying, declining, decadent, depraved, pathological and degenerating. The deplorable state of the bourgeois order is epitomized by the fact that its artistic celebrities include elements of the lumpenproletariat – thieves, prostitutes, pimps and gangsters who preach an art of pessimism. The French writer Jean Genet is singled out for special mention as the 'last word' of bourgeois culture:

Pimps and depraved criminals as philosophers – this is indeed the limit of decay and ruin. *Nevertheless, these forces still have life, are still capable of poisoning the consciousness of the masses.* (pp. 12–13, 26, 109; my emphasis)

Against them are pitted the new revolutionary writers on the side of life, the proletariat and revolution – writers who, in Stalin's profoundly significant words, were to be 'the engineers of the human soul' (pp. 15, 39).

Speaking in 1934, Zhdanov fears, however, that these new writers are not living up to that task. 'On the ideological front, serious . . . failings' have become apparent, compelling the Central Committee, of which Zhdanov was a member, to 'interfere and firmly . . . set matters right' (pp. 39–40). In the realm of aesthetic production 'disorder and anarchy' prevail, requiring a purge. The new engineers of the human soul are in danger of lapsing back into the decadent aesthetic that was dominant in pre-revolutionary times and epitomized in the work of Anna Akhmatova, a member of the Acmeist literary group, who clung to the 'disintegrating bourgeois-aristocratic ideology'. Akhmatova is castigated for her obsession with 'erotic love themes interwoven with notes of sadness, longing, death, mysticism, fatality'. Zhdanov finds in her work 'a sense of fatality (quite comprehensible in a dying group), the dismal tones of a deathbed hopelessness, mystical experiences shot [*sic*] with eroticism' and declares that she is 'a left-over from the world of the old aristocracy now irrevocably past and gone', that class and the intellectuals who supported it having been 'pitched into the dustbin of history' in 1917 (pp. 26, 29). Here, then, the death-wish and the interanimation of death and desire are 'explained' as the product of a dying class. What angers Zhdanov is that now, twenty-nine years later, new interest is being shown in the writing of Akhmatova. On the one hand, she has nothing in common with the people; on the other, she is 'poisoning' their minds, especially those of the young, seducing them away from 'the broad highway of social life and activity into a narrow little world of personal experiences' characterized by despondency. Such artists, and those who publish them, are 'helping our enemies to corrupt our young people' (p. 31).

In a speech given the following year Zhdanov declares that in music too something similar is happening – a deviation from 'natural and healthy standards' towards formalist, individualist, pathological, élitist music which is threatening 'spiritual sterility and a dead end'. Degenerationist thinking is again precisely evident when he speaks of a music which 'ignores the normal human emotions and jars the mind and nervous system', and of the fashionable theories behind it which teach that 'a pathological condition is a higher state, and that schizophrenics and paranoiacs can attain spiritual heights in their ravings unattainable by an ordinary person in a normal state'. Such theories are characteristic of the 'decay and corruption of bourgeois culture' and disturb 'the balance of mental and physiological functions'. He follows Lenin in calling for 'a cleansing of the native language of foreign-bred impurities', of 'alien bourgeois influences from abroad' which sap the strength of the people (pp. 59, 66–8, 70–74). The struggle between vital aesthetic forms on the side of life and degenerate ones on the side of decay, ruin and death, is so fundamental that it characterizes even philosophy itself and the historical reality it describes. The year before his own death, in a speech to Soviet Philosophical Workers, Zhdanov asserts that Russian philosophy too is in danger of stagnation, of becoming 'a dead and barren dogma'.

He interprets the law of dialectics as itself a struggle 'between the old and the new, between the dying and the rising, between the decaying and the developing' (p. 107).

Zhdanov, initially a powerful deputy to Stalin, was involved in the violent purges of the 1930s. He aspired to re-establish the primacy of ideology in party life and the wider culture. Werner Hahn claims that, despite his reputation for being militantly orthodox, he was relatively speaking a moderate, this being a factor in his speedy downfall in 1948: he became the victim of the extremism which he apparently cynically exploited while not actually supporting. Stalin turned against and destroyed Zhdanov's faction. Officially dying of heart failure suddenly in 1948, there is evidence to suggest he was 'eradicated'.[3]

Herbert Marcuse and the ideology of death

Other writers in the materialist tradition will go much further than Zhdanov, arguing that the entire capitalist order thrives on an ideology of death. On this view, death (not unlike God) is regarded as a radical deception in which the biological fact of death is mystified and misconstrued so as to sustain and perpetuate a repressive social order. Herbert Marcuse offers a succinct version of this argument in an article published in 1959 called 'The Ideology of Death'. It is a repudiation of much of the writing and philosophy we have so far been considering.

Marcuse contends that Western thought is steeped in what he calls 'the ontological affirmation of death'; this makes death the *telos* of life, and idealizes it as the source of ultimate meaning, freedom and existential fulfilment. Death is elevated from 'a brute biological fact, permeated with pain, horror, and despair', to an ontological essence, and in a way which requires that life be redeemed by something other than itself.[4] Conversely, the materialist demystification of death – the insistence that it is *only* a biological necessity – embraces a radically different concept of freedom, rooted in praxis and the knowledge that 'life is not and cannot be redeemed by anything other than life'. The imperative point is that *praxis requires the demystification of death* – especially of death as metaphysical necessity:

Necessity indicates lack of power: inability to change what is – the term is meaningful only as coterminus of freedom: the limit of freedom. Freedom implies knowledge, cognition. Insight into necessity is the first step toward the dissolution of necessity, but comprehended necessity is not yet freedom. The latter requires progress from theory to practice: actual conquest of those necessities which prevent or restrain the satisfaction of needs. (pp. 64–5, 66–7)

The ideology of death is the corollary of the ideology of God, in that it is invoked to justify not only unfreedom (renunciation, quietism, defeatism), but also, and inseparably, domination: the 'masochistic' exaltation of one's own death, says Marcuse, entails also the death of others. Moreover, the ideology of death implies acceptance of an existing repressive political order, and marks the birth of a philosophical morality which rationalizes it. In this respect, although Marcuse implausibly imagines that the ontological affirmation of death comes to a close in the philosophy of Heidegger, he anticipates a prolonged later debate when he discerns in Heidegger's work an 'ideological exhortation to death' appearing 'at the very time when the political ground was prepared for the corresponding reality of death – the gas chambers and concentration camps of Auschwitz, Buchenwald, Dachau, and Bergen-Belsen' (p. 69).[5]

What, then, does the materialist demystification of the ideology of death entail? For Marcuse it means that death must be confronted as primarily 'a technical limit' on human freedom, the surpassing of which limit would become the recognized goal of the individual and of social endeavour. To an increasing extent, death would partake of freedom, and individuals would be empowered to determine their own deaths. As in the case of incurable suffering, the means for painless death would be made available. Death would be deprived of its horror, its incalculable power, as well as its transcendental sanctity; reducing death to its biological reality would become the stimulus for incessant efforts to extend the limits of life and to eliminate decrepitude and suffering: 'Man is not free as long as death has not become "his own", that is, as long as it has not been brought under his autonomy' (p. 74). However, says Marcuse, such a sensible alternative to the ideology of death will continue to be repressed, because it would

entail the collapse of the established institutions and values of civilization, and the current forms of social domination, which that ideology
has helped to create and support. The effective destruction of the
ideology of death would entail 'an explosive transvaluation of social
concepts', a process of 'deheroization and desublimation' and 'a new
"reality principle" which would liberate rather than suppress the
"pleasure principle" ' (pp. 69–74).

What is remarkable in this account is the importance attributed to
the ideology of death: it becomes the cornerstone of the entire (and
mainly objectionable) ideological edifice of Western civilization generally, and Western capitalism especially, and via Heidegger it is associated with the Nazi Holocaust.

Eros and Civilization

In passing, and somewhat evasively, Marcuse remarks that the ideology of death is so powerful that it seems hard to reject Freud's
hypothesis that it is the manifestation of an insufficiently repressed
death-wish. This is a revealing remark, and one which takes us back
to Marcuse's most well-known work, *Eros and Civilization*, published
just a few years earlier and subtitled 'A Philosophical Inquiry into
Freud'. Because it was so influential in the 1960s, it is often misre-
membered as being a product of that decade.[6] First published in 1955,
it began as a series of lectures in 1950–51. Its continuing relevance lies
in Marcuse's willingness to cross between disciplines and perspectives
traditionally hostile to each other – especially Marxism and psychoanalysis – and his attempt to forge a positive cultural and philosophical
politics from the traumatic experience of political failure and exile.
(Marcuse fled Nazi Germany in 1933, first to Geneva, and then to
America a year later.)

As in the later article, Marcuse is adamant that the ideology of
death serves an existing repressive culture:

In a repressive civilization, death itself becomes an instrument of repression.
Whether death is feared as a constant threat, or glorified as a supreme
sacrifice, or accepted as fate, the education for consent to death introduces

... surrender and submission ... The powers that be have a deep affinity to death ... (p. 236)

In utter contrast, a philosophy of praxis, which holds out the prospect of 'final liberation', can render death rational and painless (p. 236).

In the ideology of death, memory is the enemy of praxis – the vehicle of a crippling sense of loss and mutability, and of what time has destroyed. As such, memory instils fatalism:

the flux of time is society's most natural ally in maintaining law and order ... the flux of time helps men forget what was and what can be: it makes them oblivious to the better past and the better future. (p. 231)

But memory does not have to be like this. Marcuse wants to transvalue memory, making it the aid of praxis and inspiring of hope. Psychoanalysis stresses the positive value of memory, but mainly towards a therapeutic end. Marcuse recognizes memory as a product of civilization, 'perhaps its oldest and most fundamental psychological achievement', one which has a *truth value* – that is, the ability 'to preserve promises and potentialities which are betrayed and even outlawed by the mature, civilized individual, but which had once been fulfilled in his dim past and which are never entirely forgotten'. In this connection 'regression assumes a progressive function': the recovered past is not reconciled with the present but challenges it, and 'the *recherche du temps perdu* becomes the vehicle of future liberation'. Marcuse mixes nostalgia and optimism: things were better in the past, and can be better again, in the future – especially if we hold on to the truth of that past: 'the memory of gratification is at the origin of all thinking, and the impulse to recapture past gratification is the hidden driving power behind the process of thought'. Even 'time loses its power when remembrance redeems the past' (pp. 19, 31, 232–3).[7]

Marcuse declined the comfortable appropriations of Freud that were current at that time, especially in America, insisting instead on confronting what was most disturbing in Freud's work (and especially so for a progressive politics), namely the death drive. He aimed for an optimistic reworking of Freud's ideas not by playing down the death drive but by trying to historicize it. In fact he believed that this apparently universal or ahistorical idea was, like others in Freud's work, already potentially historical:

The 'unhistorical' character of the Freudian concepts . . . contains the elements of its opposite: their historical substance must be recaptured, not by adding some sociological factors . . . but by unfolding their own content. (p. 35)

For Marcuse the death drive has the function of protesting against the injustice and deprivations of history:

The descent toward death is an unconscious flight from pain and want. It is an expression of the eternal struggle against suffering and repression. And the death instinct itself seems to be affected by the historical changes which affect this struggle. (p. 29)

The death drive and its derivatives, along with the sexual perversions,[8] are an unconscious protest against the insufficiency of civilization; they testify to the destructiveness of what they attempt to destroy – that is, repression. There is therefore an implicit idealism in them: 'they aim not only against the reality principle, at non-being, but also beyond the reality principle – at another mode of being' (p. 109).

Prometheus vs. Orpheus

In its modern 'rational' form the ego is essentially aggressive, anxiously and restlessly committed to the mastery of 'lower' faculties and of the environment; as such it strives to be productive, and is wholly in the service of what Marcuse calls the 'performance principle'. It is antagonistic to those faculties which are receptive rather than productive, and which tend towards gratification rather than control (*Eros and Civilization*, pp. 109–10, 121). Marcuse finds this conception of the ego epitomized in the mythological figure of Prometheus, the archetype-hero of the performance principle, governed by 'toil, productivity, and progress through repression' (p. 161).

Western philosophy consolidates the repressive concept of reason (productivity etc.) but also contains within itself a vision of a higher form of being – one involving 'receptivity, contemplation, enjoyment', the reconciliation of the individual with the whole, fulfilment without repression, freedom to live without anxiety, painless gratification of needs, the integral fulfilment of man and nature, and freedom from guilt and fear (pp. 131, 143–46, 150–53, 160). All this is to be achieved through a non-repressive sublimation of eros, and is mythologically embodied in terms not of Prometheus, but of Orpheus and Narcissus – figures who promise to reconcile eros and thanatos in 'the redemption of pleasure, the halt of time, the absorption of death; silence, sleep, night, paradise – the Nirvana principle not as death but as life' (p. 164). They also promise to overcome the opposition between man and nature, subject and object – and to a fairy-tale degree: 'Orpheus pacifies the animal world, reconciles the lion with the lamb and the lion with man' (p. 166).

The first thing to strike one about this beatific vision is that it glosses over the darker elements of the very mythological figures who are supposed to express it: Orpheus, who gave his love to boys (Ovid), was torn to pieces by the Thracian women. Before that he searched hopelessly in the underworld for his lost lover. As for Narcissus, Marcuse recognizes that he mythologically connects desire and death, and all he can do is lamely accept it: 'If his erotic attitude is akin to death and brings death, then rest and sleep and death are not painfully separated and distinguished' (p. 167). Marcuse is clearly attracted to that mode of transcendence which haunts Western metaphysics and in which all potentiality becomes actuality, in which 'the restless labour of the transcending subject terminates in the ultimate unity of subject and object: the idea of "being-in-and-for-itself", existing in its own fulfillment' which is immanent in this world. Thus Aristotle's *nous theos*, that sublime mode of being in which existence is no longer confined or defined by anything else and is entirely itself in all states and conditions (*Eros and Civilization*, p. 112) – the eternity of God, and the zero-tension of non-being.

This is the remarkable thing about Marcuse's radicalism: even while castigating the ideology of death, it incorporates a benign, idealistic death-wish. Despite, or perhaps because of, the severe repudiation of the ideology of death, Marcuse's Utopian vision is steeped in a desire for that radical freedom from tension which the death drive expresses. This most passionate advocate of the philosophy of praxis echoes the same fascination with death as had Feuerbach, who did so much to develop that philosophy more than a century earlier. Marcuse was most preoccupied, even seduced, by those aspects of the death drive which could not be incorporated within a philosophy of praxis. He described Freud's account of that drive as 'one of the great intellectual ventures in the science of man'. Why? Because of 'the terrifying convergence of pleasure and death' which it proposes, and because 'never before has death been so consistently taken into the essence of life . . . never before also has death come so close to Eros' (pp. 25, 28–9).[9]

In 1966 Marcuse added a 'Political Preface' to *Eros and Civilization*, criticizing the 1955 text for its unjustified optimism. The tone is now severer and confrontational. Marcuse admits to having under-estimated the emergence of new, more insidious and effective, forms of social control. He voices the frustrated sense that freedom is at once possible and impossible: 'liberation is the most realistic, the most concrete of all historical possibilities and at the same time the most rationally and effectively repressed – the most abstract and remote possibility' (p. xv). The reason for this is 'the democratic introjection of the masters into their subjects'. No philosophy or theory can undo this.

At first sight this preface takes even further the socializing of the death drive. We are told that the new political struggle is no longer between eros and thanatos, because the powers that be have eros on their side, even to the extent of protecting, perpetuating and enlarging life – at least for those who comply with repression (p. xx). Yet the preface ends by evoking one of Freud's most provocative remarks about the death drive:

'By nature' the young are in the forefront of those who live and fight for Eros against Death, and against a civilization which strives to shorten the 'detour to death' while controlling the means for lengthening the detour . . . Today the fight for life, the fight for Eros, is the *political* fight. (p. xxv)

In the passage Marcuse here alludes to, Freud declares not only that ' *"the aim of all life is death"* ', but that an organism's apparent resistance of death is not so much an affirmation of the desire to live but a desire to find its own way back to death. This resistance is due only to the frustration of external circumstances; rather like a river compelled to wind its way to the sea, life is a series of 'complicated *détours*' or 'circuitous paths to death' (*Beyond the Pleasure Principle*, p. 311). Marcuse seems to be saying that an oppositional politics cannot eliminate but can only extenuate the death drive – prolonging rather than shortening the detour – and in doing even this it must of necessity become violent.

This becomes especially significant in the context of the Third World; arguably the optimism of the original text with regard to the elimination of scarcity, the erotics of passivity as the basis of a new reality principle, and the elimination of the need for alienated labour, was tenable only if the Third World's relationship with the First was ignored. In the new grim tone is a residue of tragedy; the political struggle has necessarily partaken of the violence of the dominant order ('aggression can be turned against the aggressor'), and those struggling for freedom, including the philosophers of praxis, have now themselves become 'purveyors of Death' (pp. xx, xi).

VII

THE AESTHETICS
OF ENERGY

16

Fighting *Décadence*: Nietzsche against Schopenhauer and Wagner

Friedrich Nietzsche (1844–1900) believed that something like the death-wish had been debilitating Western culture at least since Socrates and was manifested as *décadence*. Compared with, say, Max Nordau, Nietzsche is immeasurably more insightful into the condition he condemns, and so much more perceptive about its prevalence in Western thought, even or especially in those who repudiate it – including himself:

It is a self-deception on the part of philosophers and moralists to imagine that by making war on *décadence* they therewith elude *décadence* themselves. This is beyond their powers: what they select as an expedient, as a deliverance, is itself only another expression of *décadence* – they *alter* its expression, they do not abolish the thing itself. (*Twilight*, p. 34; cf. *Will to Power*, p. 239)

Nietzsche certainly experienced what he repudiates; it could even be said that he willingly took it even further into his being, in order to know it better. This existential struggle against *décadence* is at the heart of a philosophy of life highly influential in some of the main strands of modernism and post-modernism. Nietzsche's heroic battle against what he saw as the anti-life decadence of Western culture quite possibly cost him his sanity and eventually his life.

Nietzsche regarded the modern condition as steeped in a cowardly religion of pity and nihilism beneath which were only weariness and life-exhaustion, an instinctive fear of reality, a loss of manly drives and virtues, and an incapacity for struggle and resistance. All of this entailed a 'contradiction of life' and an abdication of the will to power (*Anti-Christ*, pp. 122, 127–8, 129, 142). 'Instead of saying simply "I am no longer worth anything", the moral lie in the mouth of the *décadent* says: "Nothing is worth anything – life is not worth anything." ' For Nietzsche such a judgement represents a contagious danger, capable of poisoning life for thousands of years ahead. He believed its origins were in Western religion – Christianity above all – and philosophy (*Twilight*, p. 87).[1] All this the modern decadent inherits as world-weariness, the wish to die, to perish, to deny the will to life – conditions expressed supremely by Schopenhauer (*Twilight*, pp. 45–6). And yet, elsewhere, Nietzsche endorses a conception of the human condition which had led many of the writers he opposes to this attitude of world-weariness. Like them Nietzsche is troubled by our intrinsically precarious identity – sick, unstable, competitive, driven by a mutable, questing, restless desire. This is how he put it in *The Genealogy of Morals*:

certainly man is sicker, less secure, less stable, less firmly anchored than any other animal; he is the *sick* animal . . . eternally unsatisfied, vying with the gods, the beasts, and with nature for final supremacy; man, unconquered to this day, still unrealized, so agitated by his own teeming energy that his future digs like spurs into the flesh of every present moment. How could such a brave and resourceful animal but be the most precarious, the most profoundly sick of all the sick beasts of the earth? (p. 257)

It is hardly surprising, then, to discover that Schopenhauer and Wagner were two of Nietzsche's most important early influences, although he subsequently reacted vehemently against what he came to regard as their death-embracing vision of desire. If his greatest work is energized by his vehement repudiation of decadence, it is also never free of its seduction, and he acknowledges precisely this. This means that the energy and brilliance of his work also come from the tension, the conflict, between the repudiation and the seduction. As the above quotation from *The Genealogy of Morals* makes clear, for Nietzsche the heroic repudiation of death and mutability energizes desire because they are already inside it as a sickness which includes the experience of being 'eternally unsatisfied' and forever destabilized by a 'teeming energy' which is in essence sick. And, because he knows this, to either psychoanalyse or deconstruct him is hardly the point.[2] In that Nietzsche subscribed to a wisdom learned through suffering, he remained within a Western spiritual tradition. But no one was more distrustful of what constituted the wisdom of that tradition than he. Further, with him the suffering that led to wisdom was also, and necessarily, physical; actual physical illness produced insight, renunciation and a heroic wilfulness whose imaginative strength was in direct proportion to his actual physical frailty. This is what he called a self-overcoming. Therein lies the history of his religious – specifically Protestant – resolve. Self-overcoming: selfhood for Nietzsche was an imaginative speculative projection, a desire to be, to create and become what he was not.

History as loss

In an early work, *On the Uses and Disadvantages of History for Life* (1874), Nietzsche shows an acute awareness of how overwhelming the experience of transience and loss can be, and argues that extreme measures are necessary to resist it. A repudiation of the past, even to the point of being unhistorical or even anti-historical, was necessary for '*the health of an individual, of a people, and of a culture*' (pp. 63–4). By being 'unhistorical' Nietzsche means exercising 'the art and power of *forgetting*, and of enclosing oneself within a bounded *horizon*' (p. 120). This is not primarily an argument with historians about ways of doing history. And while influential contemporary philosophies of history are castigated, especially those endorsing a Hegelian teleological view, what is threatening in historical awareness proves to be something quite different and much older: it is that regressive pull of the past which passes as wisdom. Thus his larger concern with the incompatibility of 'life and wisdom' (p. 66).

Wisdom threatens because of its complicity with a history which is overdetermined by loss, memory, time, failure and mutability, all of which haunt the present: 'we ourselves bear visibly the traces of those sufferings which afflict contemporary mankind as a result of an excess of history' (p. 116). Man envies the beast, happy because ignorant of time and memory, knowledge of which brings consciousness and, with that, melancholy, satiety and pain:

a moment, now here and then gone, nothing before it came, again nothing after it has gone, nonetheless returns as a ghost and disturbs the peace of a later moment. A leaf flutters from the scroll of time, floats away – and suddenly floats back again and falls into the man's lap. Then the man says 'I remember' and envies the animal, who at once forgets and for whom every moment really dies . . . (p. 61)

This is the peril of the past – that 'dark, invisible burden' (p. 61) with which consciousness travels. As he was to put it later, 'memory is a festering wound' (*Ecce Homo*, p. 15). In contrast, the beast lives unhistorically, as does the unselfconscious child who 'plays in blissful blindness between the hedges of past and future', and whose very existence affects the adult 'like a vision of a lost Paradise' (*Uses and Disadvantages*, p. 61). Too soon will the child be summoned from this unawareness of past and future; it will learn the language of time – that which lets in 'conflict, suffering and satiety' and reminds mankind what existence really is, namely

an imperfect tense that never becomes a perfect one. If death at last brings the desired forgetting, by that act it at the same time extinguishes the present and all being and therewith sets the seal on the knowledge that being is only an uninterrupted has-been, a thing that lives by negating, consuming and contradicting itself. (p. 61)

History is modern man's *memento mori*[3] – in fact, says Nietzsche, our excess of history derives from the medieval *memento mori* – which epitomizes 'a profound sense of hopelessness [which] remains and has assumed that historical colouring with which all higher education and culture is now saddened and darkened' (pp. 101–2). Thus time, or rather the knowledge of time, involves a process of self-destruction and self-contradiction which is *ultimately fatal to the living thing, whether [it] be a man or a people or a culture*' (p. 62).[4] This is why, to become happy or to act, we must learn the power of forgetting: 'it is altogether impossible to *live* at all without forgetting' (p. 61). This in turn facilitates the capacity for feeling unhistorically, which is the foundation of all growth and of what is truly great and human. We must actively create boundaries dividing 'the visible and clear from the vague and shadowy'; life literally depends upon a process of *exclusion* analogous to the process of forgetting: 'This is a universal law; a living thing can be healthy, strong and fruitful only when bounded by a horizon'; if it is incapable of drawing a horizon around itself, it will die (p. 63). The unhistorical sense is the foundation not just of health but of all achievement, be it creative, military or emancipatory.

Being beholden to history becomes comparable to being flooded and confused by cultural difference: the Roman of the imperial era ceased to be Roman 'as he lost himself in the flood of foreigners which came streaming in and degenerated in the midst of the cosmopolitan carnival of gods, arts and customs' (p. 83). And, just as in certain epochs the Greeks were in danger of being 'overwhelmed by what was past and foreign ... a chaos of foreign, Semitic, Babylonian, Lydian, Egyptian forms and ideas', so modern German culture and religion are 'a struggling chaos of all the West and of all the past ages' (p. 122).

More positively, Nietzsche advocates a political and 'critical' history which serves life – exposing, for example, the injustice of something via its past; it is then that 'one takes the knife to its roots, then one cruelly tramples over every kind of piety' (p. 76). But this too is a dangerous process, even for life; again, Nietzsche displays a profound sense of how history (like the decadence it feeds) is deep inside us, and the here and now:

since we are the outcome of earlier generations, we are also the outcome of their aberrations, passions and errors, and indeed of their crimes; it is not possible wholly to free oneself from this chain. If we condemn these aberrations and regard ourselves as free of them, this does not alter the fact that we originate in them. (p. 76)

We have no choice but to live a struggle between an inherited first nature and a new stern discipline, a second nature, which, because often weaker, fights the first without guarantee of success. But a consolation is in the knowledge that the oppressive first nature was once a second, and that the new conquering second nature will eventually become a first.

Schopenhauer and The Birth of Tragedy

I have already remarked Nietzsche's repudiation of his former cultural heroes, Wagner and Schopenhauer. He came to regard Schopenhauer's pessimism as decadent. In the 1886 preface to *The Birth of Tragedy*, entitled 'A Critical Backward Glance', he argues passionately for 'a *strong* pessimism' whose effect would not be Schopenhauerean withdrawal from the pain and tragedy of existence, but a heroic confrontation with them – heroic because risking everything in the name of life's excess. This was what Nietzsche now called the Dionysiac and the tragic.

Nietzsche also develops what might be called a strong masochism, analogous to this strong pessimism; instead of resignation in the face of life's pain, now there is a worship of it. An aspect of this is the fantasy of participating sacrificially in the omnipotent universal life-force whose meaning is 'purely aesthetic'; God the Creator is imagined as

the supreme artist, amoral, recklessly creating and destroying, realizing himself indifferently in whatever he does or undoes, ridding himself by his acts of the embarrassment of his riches and the strain of his internal contradictions. (*Birth*, p. 9)

Thus the aesthetics of energy. The amorality of this Life-God is important for Nietzsche; the aesthetic attitude to life was deeply and necessarily anti-moral, because it is morality (especially Christian morality) which harbours the death drive in its most insidious form. Morality is a symptom of *décadence* – nothing but 'a will to deny life, a secret instinct of destruction' – and Christianity is a degenerated instinct expressing itself as a hatred of life – '*a yearning for extinction, cessation of all effort*' (*Birth*, p. 11, my emphasis; cf. *Ecce Homo*, p. 49).

Earlier he had taken from Schopenhauer the idea that to be in touch with the most profound reality involves a dissolution of individuality, a death of the self. This is an idea which Nietzsche will retain, albeit in modified form. Such dissolution is what happens in Dionysiac rapture: the principle of individuation is shattered in 'mystical self-abrogation' or 'un-selving'; it is shown to be 'a mere figment'. One 'sinks back into' the 'primordial One'. The process involves a 'Lethean element in which everything that has been experienced by the individual is drowned', a 'chasm of oblivion', a 'shattering of the individual', a 'delight felt at the annihilation of the individual' (*Birth*, pp. 22–7, 38–9, 51, 56, 101). There is a resemblance here which will be highly influential for subsequent modernist movements. Schopenhauer advocates withdrawal from desire and from nature and a denial of the will; Nietzsche advocates the opposite, a heroic immersion within the world of change as a way of momentarily realizing the will to power. Yet these otherwise diverging philosophies nevertheless both have as their prerequisite the annihilation of individuality as conventionally known.

The Dionysiac vision is an insight into the will to life:

for a brief moment we become, ourselves, the primal Being, and we experience its *insatiable* hunger for existence. Now we see the struggle, the pain, the destruction of appearances, as necessary, because of the constant proliferation of forms pushing into life, because of the extravagant fecundity of the world-will. We feel the furious prodding of this travail *in the very moment* in which we become one with the immense lust for life and are made aware of the eternity and indestructibility of that lust. (pp. 102–3; my emphasis)

Metaphysical oneness is now an excess – a 'procreative lust' which produces and consumes individuals who cannot survive the sublime amorality of the world-will which 'playfully shatters and rebuilds the teeming world' (p. 143). But the Dionysiac vision is never pure ecstasy; it is also 'traumatically wounded' – not least because it sees, but cannot survive, the 'eternal life continuing beyond all appearance and in spite of destruction', and because, in the Dionysiac state, man becomes 'primal Being', susceptible to an '*insatiable hunger* for existence' (pp. 52, 101–2; my emphasis).

Crucially, the primal oneness Nietzsche envisions is not the conventional metaphysical integration in which pain, division and loss have been dissolved and transcended; on the contrary, this oneness is itself in some sense intolerably conflicted by 'pain and contradiction' (p. 38) – rather like the Schopenhauerean will – and so much so that it requires its misrepresentation:

the original Oneness, the ground of Being, ever-suffering and contradictory, time and again has need of rapt vision and delightful illusion to redeem itself. (p. 32)

The metaphysical solace which all true tragedy provides rests on artistic illusion. The profound Greek, uniquely susceptible to the deep suffering consequent upon penetrating the 'destructive agencies of both nature and history', is saved from the death-wish, the 'Buddhistic denial of the will' which Schopenhauer extolled, only by the illusion of art (pp. 50–51; cf. p. 145). This is partly why Dionysiac ecstasy has to be contained by a principle of Apollonian order. Apollo requires self-control and hence self-knowledge and individuation, and thereby 'tranquillizes the individual by drawing boundary lines'. Apollonian order is more than mere form, control, containment and restraint; it is also, crucially, *illusion*, and the principle of individuation is the basis of the 'redemption in illusion' which Apollo provides (pp. 34, 65, 97).

Nietzsche repudiated the influence of Schopenhauer for one main reason: 'I grasped that my instinct went into the opposite direction from Schopenhauer's: towards a *justification of life*, even at its most terrible, ambiguous and mendacious; for this I had the formula *"Dionysian"* ' (*Will to Power*, p. 521). Nietzsche later believed he had extricated the Dionysian from death; but, by retaining Schopenhauer's emphasis on the need for self-annihilation, the Dionysiac remains an agent of dissolution. And, as we shall see, there were other respects too in which the Dionysiac remained pressured by death.

The seductive dangers of Wagner

Wagner proved if anything even more seductive for Nietzsche than Schopenhauer. And Wagner had himself been profoundly influenced by Schopenhauer, repeatedly remarking that this was a philosopher who had changed his life. What especially attracted him was Schopenhauer's philosophical vindication of death – what, in a letter to Franz Liszt in 1854, Wagner called 'his chief idea, the final negation of the desire of life'. Wagner is unequivocal about what this entails:

the genuine ardent longing for death, for absolute unconsciousness, total non-existence. Freedom from all dreams is our final salvation.

He prefaces this with an important observation: those who have never experienced this longing can never really comprehend its expression:

To me of course that thought was not new, and it can indeed be conceived by no one in whom it did not pre-exist, but this philosopher was the first to place it clearly before me . . . (*Wagner on Music and Drama*, pp. 270–71)[5]

Wagner famously conveys something of this longing in *Tristan and Isolde*, which he also anticipates in this letter:

As I never in life felt the real bliss of love, I must erect a monument to the most beautiful of all my dreams, in which, from beginning to end, that love shall be thoroughly satiated. I have in my head *Tristan and Isolde*, the simplest but most full-blooded musical conception; with the 'black flag' which floats at the end of it I shall cover myself and die. (p. 272)

Death and desire blend, but not quite as, or because of, the impossibility of desire: this is different, and distinctly romantic; if one influence is Schopenhauer, another is Feuerbach.[6] Death, for Wagner, floods desire not because of a contradiction in the latter (the attempt to reach for fulfilment in a way which precisely prevents it); rather, in *Tristan*, desire dies in and as its fulfilment, thus preventing the recurrence of the pain of desire in the moment of its own ecstatic culmination. But this is something the surviving composer cannot participate in; all he can do is let

unslaked longing swell from first avowal of the gentlest tremor of attraction . . . to the mightiest onset, most resolute attempt to find . . . a path into the sea of endless love's delight. In vain! Its power spent, the heart sinks back to pine of its desire . . . (p. 273 (Prelude to *Tristan and Isolde*)).[7]

Perhaps de Rougemont was right: if desire is impossible here, it's because it seeks to be immortal and omnipotent:

one thing alone left living: desire, desire unquenchable, longing forever rebearing itself – a fevered craving; one sole redemption – death, surcease of being, the sleep that knows no waking!
    . . . desire without attainment; for each fruition sows the seeds of fresh

desire, till in its final lassitude the breaking eye beholds a glimmer of the highest bliss: it is the bliss of quitting life, of being no more, of last redemption into that wondrous realm from which we stray the furthest when we strive to enter it by fiercest force. Shall we call it death? Or is it not night's wonder world, whence – as the story says – an ivy and a vine sprang up in locked embrace o'er Tristan and Isolde's grave? (pp. 272–3 (Prelude to *Tristan and Isolde*))

The excess of desire is at once desire for death (release from desire), extinction of self in the ecstasy of desire, and a fantasy of desire's omnipotence which by extension becomes a fantasy of the omnipotence of the self in its very extinction. Wagner's improbable account of Beethoven develops this: because desire entails a yearning which is, of its very nature, 'unfathomed', 'endless', 'boundless and insatiate', 'unallayable', it cannot find contentment in finitude, in any culmination which necessitates its own ending. It is 'a longing which, in its infinity, could only be an "object" to itself'; because this yearning cannot find fulfilment *in* fulfilment it has to perpetuate itself, and it does this in the only way possible, by projecting its own '*endlessness*' as the object of its desire. The infinitude of the yearning becomes its own object, a closed circle of self-perpetuating desire (pp. 156–9). Desire becomes paradoxical in a characteristically romantic way: is it ultimately an experience of life at its most intense, or the desire not to be, the flight *from* life – or are these inseparable if not nearly equivalent?

In 1882 Nietzsche writes, 'My Wagner mania certainly cost me dear. Has not this nerve-shattering music ruined my health?' (*Letters*, ed. Middleton, p. 180). His rejection of the composer becomes fundamentally a question of health, and involves a vehement aesthetic/ethical division between those who embody an overfullness of life and those who negate and hate it – the latter being exemplified by Schopenhauer to a degree, and by Wagner much more so. Wagner exemplifies the 'weariness of the soul' and deals in 'opiates of the senses and the understanding'; he is 'a decaying and despairing decadent, [who] suddenly sank down, helpless and broken, before the Christian cross' (*Nietzsche Contra Wagner*, pp. 663, 669–71, 673, 676). The rejection of Wagner is ultimately a refusal of the desire 'to withdraw from pain into that Nothing, into mute, rigid, deaf resignation, self-forgetting, self-extinction'. Nietzsche urges instead that we embrace pain, because it makes us more profound: a thing is made stronger by whatever does not kill it (pp. 680–81; cf. *Ecce Homo*, p. 11).

But he never entirely escapes the pull of Wagner. Who, Nietzsche had asked in his early work *The Birth of Tragedy* (1872), could hear the third act of *Tristan and Isolde* 'without exhausting himself in the overstretching of his soul's pinions'? He continues:

How is it possible for a man who has listened to the very heartbeat of the world-will and felt the unruly lust for life rush into all the veins of the world, now as a thundering torrent and now as a delicately foaming brook – how is it possible for him to remain unshattered? How can he bear, shut in the paltry glass bell of his individuality, to hear the echoes of innumerable cries of weal and woe sounding out of the 'vast spaces of cosmic night', and not wish, amidst these pipings of metaphysical pastoral, to flee incontinent to his primordial home? (p. 127)

But, adds, Nietzsche, the work does not finally shatter us in this way, because the Apollonian spirit rescues us from the Dionysiac vision. His account of how this occurs is uncertain and ambivalent. (One recalls here Nietzsche's own retrospective description of *The Birth of Tragedy* as 'quite impossible' and 'full of unpalatable ferment' (pp. 5–6).) On the one hand, the Apollonian element, as illusion, succeeds in triumphing over the Dionysiac; on the other hand, at the point that matters most, the Apollonian illusion is broken through and destroyed; the Dionysiac triumphs again (pp. 128–30). An Apollonian illusion seemingly reconstitutes 'the nearly shattered individual'; he is bought back from a point where his hold on life has been rendered 'tenuous' (p. 128). But the pull of Dionysiac ecstasy – which is to say annihilation – remains the stronger. Even here, in his pro-Wagner period, the life-affirming qualities that Nietzsche wanted to find in the composer are tenuous; rather stronger is the pull of extinction.

Years later he had not really changed his mind: in *Ecce Homo*, written in 1888, shortly before his breakdown, Nietzsche declares that he had never encountered a work of such 'dangerous fascination, of a sweet and shuddery infinity equal to that of *Tristan*', adding, 'The world is poor for him *who has never been sick enough* for this "voluptuousness of hell": to employ a mystic's formula is permissible, almost obligatory, here.' But then comes the crucial difference between the earlier and the later response – an existential ethic that transvalues the sick into the vital:

as I am strong enough to turn even the most questionable and most perilous things to my own advantage and thus to become stronger, I call Wagner the great benefactor of my life. (p. 31; my emphasis)

Nietzsche accepts that he is innately conflicted, literally constituted by contradictory tendencies towards life and health on the one hand, death and decadence on the other. These opposed tendencies he inherited, he says, from his mother and father respectively: the first imparted the instinct for 'ascent', the second the instinct to 'decline'. *Ecce Homo* begins with the statement: 'as my father I have already died . . . do I need to say that in questions of *décadence* I am *experienced*?' (pp. 8–9, Nietzsche's emphasis; cf. p. 62).

This incorporation into himself of what he despises is pressured by a Protestant-style self-overcoming; decadence is to be known intimately, the better to be resisted in the name of a more fundamental purity and health in himself: 'every morbid trait is lacking in me'. Overcoming his own decadent tendencies earns him the right to censor them in others (pp. 9–10, 37). In those utterances where Nietzsche seemingly wants to escape from the depth model of the self, as when for example he speaks of 'the entire surface of consciousness – consciousness *is* a surface', it is as if he has to get rid of the deep self in order to escape the decadence he hates.

Illness

Nietzsche's philosophy owes much to a radical, Protestant-inspired resistance to the 'spiritual' sickness of the self. Equally significant was his literal, physical sickness. The ravages of mutability are felt most immediately in physical terms, in the deterioration of the body – something which the severely ill experience in accelerated and intensified ways. An invalid, Nietzsche lived with chronic physical deterioration and disease. At forty-five he went insane, possibly because of syphilitic infection. When he declared that his entire philosophy was made out of his will to health and life (*Ecce Homo*, p. 10), he meant both physical and spiritual health together. At times this will to health had the intensity of self-hatred, but without that desire to belong and conform which self-hatred often produces.

Nietzsche veered between periods of creative ecstasy and jubilation and periods of chronic illness, and the contrast between them was extreme. Inspiration gave

a complete being outside of oneself ... a depth of happiness in which the most painful and gloomy things appear, not as an antithesis, but as conditioned, demanded, as a *necessary* colour within such a superfluity of light ... Everything is in the highest degree involuntary but takes place as in a tempest of a feeling of freedom, of absoluteness, of power, of divinity ... (p. 73)

Illness, by contrast, was a state of intolerable distress, a dying within life (p. 75), the complete loss of energy. In his letters he speaks of terrible suffering, 'scarcely endurable' headaches, and being on the verge of despair, expecting death and many times wanting to die (*Letters*, ed. Levy, pp. 119, 148, 154–7, 275–6). In 1879 he tells his publisher, 'I am on the verge of desperation and have scarcely any hope left. My sufferings have been too great, too persistent.' He signs the letter 'A half-blind man' (p. 121). Later that same year he describes himself as an 'invalid' who is 'encircled by death'. Now illness and depression seem inseparable (as at other times – cf. p. 167), yet it is for that very reason that he wants to keep the enervating effects of both out of his work, and to insist that somehow suffering empowers and enlivens him. And so he asks Peter Gast to scrutinize his latest writing to see if

there are any traces of suffering or depression to be found in it. I *don't believe there are*, and this very belief is a sign that there must be *powers* concealed in these views, and not the proofs of impotence and lassitude after which my enemies will seek. (p. 121)[8]

In *The Gay Science* he declares confidently that he owes to his sickness a *higher* health – one which is made stronger by whatever does not kill it. *I also owe my philosophy to it.* Only great pain is the ultimate liberator of the spirit . . . I doubt that such pain makes us 'better', but I know that it makes us more profound. (*Portable Nietzsche*, pp. 680–81)

In important respects Nietzsche's philosophy, especially its vitalism, is a projected fantasy of health and omnipotence. His repudiation of the decadent contemporary world is in part a projection of his illness, in part an identification, even an empathy, with decadence made possible by illness: 'I am a *décadent*, I am also its antithesis' (*Ecce Homo*, p. 10). Illness generates a fantasy of health which then becomes a vantage point from which to expose the death-wish – 'to look down from the abundance and certainty of *rich life* into the secret labour of the instinct of *décadence*' (pp. 9–10).[9] Here too Nietzsche's critique of *décadence* is a repudiation forged from seduction. In the preface to the second edition of *Human, all too Human*, he speaks of

Long years of convalescence, years full of variegated, painfully magical transformations, ruled and led along by a tenacious *will to health* which often ventures to clothe and disguise itself as health already achieved. (p. 8)

It is under the 'sudden illumination of a still stressful, still changeable health that the free, ever freer spirit begins to unveil the riddle of that great liberation which has until then waited dark, questionable, almost untouchable in his memory' (p. 9). This will to health certainly included erotic identification: the desire for the other that one fantasizes about being but knows one cannot ever be. Sometimes he admires the (phallic?) man who, lacking knowledge, a full range of feeling, judgement and virtually everything else, nevertheless will 'stand there in superlative health and vigour, a joy to all who see him'. It is the same lack of 'culture' which makes possible 'a simple act of will and desire' for which the sexual act is presumably a paradigm. The man of culture and discrimination is sick by comparison (*Uses and Disadvantages*, p. 63; cf. *Twilight*, p. 72).[10]

Embracing mutability

Nietzsche is of course quite right to regard the Western philosophical tradition as profoundly disturbed by mutability – 'change, appearance, mutation, becoming' – and so much so, in fact, that it had to regard it as the source of error and of being led astray, to be contrasted with an unchanging reality behind and beyond the world of change which then became the true criterion of being. As he puts it in *The Will to Power*, philosophers fear 'appearance, change, pain, death, the corporeal, the senses, fate and bondage, the aimless' (p. 220). And this, for Nietzsche, is the underlying problem; we remain 'entangled in error, *necessitated* to error, to precisely the extent that our prejudice in favour of reason compels us to posit unity, identity, duration, substance, cause, materiality, being' (*Twilight*, p. 37). This search for the immutable, the permanent antithesis of mutability, is what eventually produces decadence and exhaustion; the metaphysics which has been so influential in Western culture's energetic centrifugal expansiveness and inclusiveness is also responsible for the exhaustion which haunts it.

Ideally, for Nietzsche, man's very vulnerability to spiritual sickness becomes a source of strength; his restlessness leads him to heroically overreach himself. And even when he gives in to chronic world-weariness – as, allegedly, in medieval times – even then

this tedium, this weariness, this satiety breaks from him with such vehemence that at once it forges a new fetter to existence. As if by magic, his negations produce a wealth of tenderer affirmations. When this master of destruction, of self-destruction, wounds himself, it is that very wound that forces him to live. (*Genealogy*, p. 257)

Here again is the heroic, sacrificial element in Nietzsche – in place of transcendence is an ecstatic, risk-full immersion in mutability, a world which promises joy even as it leads us astray (*Twilight*, p. 37). He insists that mutability is in everything, including thought, thereby contradicting that philosophical tradition which declares that reason can lead us to immutable truth.[11] Nothing remains stable – especially not thought – and one lives this instability precariously and often sacrificially; thus the great human being (and the erotic urgency of this philosophy is once again clear)

expends himself . . . The instinct of self-preservation is as it were suspended; the overwhelming pressure of the energies which emanate from him forbids him any such care and prudence. (*Twilight*, p. 98)

Suffering has to be embraced, and never reluctantly; it has to be refined and worked on so that it becomes energizing rather than debilitating, and ultimately the source of joy – though a joy always under pressure, and inseparable from sacrifice and destructiveness. This life-aesthetic affirms a strenuous engagement with mutability as not the enemy but the essence of life:

Affirmation of life even in its strangest and sternest problems, the will to life rejoicing in its own inexhaustibility through the *sacrifice* of its highest types – *that* is what I call Dionysian . . . *to realize in oneself* the eternal joy of becoming – that joy which also encompasses *joy in destruction* . . . (p. 110)

And yet within fantasies of sacrifice remain even stronger fantasies of mastery, control, repudiation and purification, and an urgent desire to fight the degenerates who are the beleaguering enemies of these 'highest types'. There is, for instance, Nietzsche's insistence on trying to gain strength from what opposes him:

I am strong enough to turn even the most questionable and most perilous things to my own advantage and thus to become stronger. (*Ecce Homo*, p. 31; cf. pp. 11 and 17)

As he says more than once, what doesn't kill him will make him stronger – an idea which assumes a kind of magical, cannibalistic ingestion, the fantasy transmutation of an endangering other into a strengthening same. More generally, the aesthetic view of life is at heart an amoral vitalistic philosophy or fantasy of energy, especially the energy to destroy – the '*joy in destruction*' – which finds expression in war: 'there will be wars such as there have never been yet on earth' (p. 97; cf. p. 52: 'the harshest but most necessary wars').[12]

Nietzsche repudiates the traditional philosophical quest for transcendent being (stasis, duration, identity, perfection), celebrating instead becoming (energy, flux, change, loss, transience, imperfection). But the desire for perfection remains, only now it is played out in this world, and with a vengeance. His willed, intensely moral and sacrificial immersion in mutability and loss produces an aesthetic of energy which is anti-Christian (*Anti-Christ*, p. 186), anti-socialist (p. 179), anti-democratic (pp. 178–9), sometimes recognizably fascist, anti-woman, and prepared to administer rather than submit to death:

Not contentment, but more power; *not* peace at all, but war; *not* virtue, but proficiency . . . The weak and ill-constituted shall perish: first principle of *our* philanthropy. And one shall help them to do so. What is more harmful than any vice? – Active sympathy for the ill-constituted and weak – Christianity . . . (p. 116)

Hence the vitalistic fantasies of punitively cleansing the world of all forms of social death, of engaging in 'the remorseless destruction of all degenerate and parasitic elements' in the name of 'a tremendous purification . . . of mankind' (*Ecce Homo*, pp. 51, 53).

Freud said the will to power is only the death instinct turned outwards. Initially the death instinct dominates the organism, seeking to disintegrate it into a state of inorganic stability. The libido has the task of 'taming . . . the death instinct', of rendering it innocuous with regard to the organism itself, 'by diverting [it] to a great extent outwards . . . towards objects in the external world. The instinct is then called the destructive instinct, the instinct for mastery, or the will to power' ('The Economic Problem of Masochism', p. 418). Nietzsche's aggressive aesthetic certainly derives partly from his struggle against, and turning outwards of, the deathward tendencies of decadence which he believed to be endemic in Western culture, and to which he himself on his own confession was deeply susceptible. He reconceptualized change as the essence and not the enemy of life, and built from it an aesthetics of energy rather than an ethics of transcendence. Now the cultural purveyors of death had themselves to be destroyed, and their destruction was imagined with an intensity which seemingly came of frustration. Nietzsche celebrates sacrificial, heroic immersion in the omnipotent flux of life, but does so from a position of erudition, withdrawal and relative impotence; his is a philosophy which could only be conceived by the modernist man of inaction for whom ecstasy is about the double process of a masochistic submission to change and a sadistic identification with it.

17

Ecstasy and Annihilation:
Georges Bataille

Life is an excess of energy which finally can only be wasted rather than conserved, a force of 'non-productive expenditure', excessive and useless, an effusion fundamentally contrary to equilibrium. This, for Georges Bataille (1897–1962), is the exhilarating but terrible truth of being:

I insist on the fact that there is generally no growth but only a luxurious squandering of energy in every form! The history of life on earth is mainly the effect of a wild exuberance. (*Accursed Share*, I.10–11; cf. I.12, 22, 33–4; II.84–5)

Or, as he puts it in *Erotism*, 'Life is nothing but instability and disequilibrium . . . a swelling tumult continuously on the verge of explosion' (pp. 59–60).

For Bataille, the supreme instance of life as expenditure is the sun. The very source of life, it dispenses its energy without any return, which means of course that ultimately it must expend itself completely and burn out. And, just as the sun will do this violently, so all life is rooted in the destruction of life, of itself: 'the ground we live on is little other than a field of multiple destructions'. The squandering of life is inseparable from a ceaseless destruction of property and bodies; it is this fact which 'ultimately connects life with the senseless luxury and excess of death' (*Accursed Share*, I.28, 23, 34–5).

The fact that life is riven with loss, mutability, death and destruction is, for Bataille, a source of human anguish. But this same fact is also, more fundamentally and remarkably, the cause of exhilaration when we recognize it as the condition of life itself; anguish is overcome when we profoundly – that is, sacrificially, masochistically – identify with, rather than disavow, this truth of being. He is emphatic about this: death and ruin – 'This colossal waste, this squandering annihilation' – are not only necessary for life, they are also its most complete expression. Death is the condition of birth, and life is a product of putrefaction. Death, for Bataille, is nothing less than 'the youth of the world' (*Erotism*, pp. 59–60; *Accursed Share*, II.80, 84).

Bataille's writing is more influential now than ever before. One reason is that it offers the same advocacy of flux and change as in Nietzsche, but in a much more extreme form – extending to a deep fascination with dissolution, annihilation and death which recalls attitudes familiar in the medieval and early modern periods (of which Bataille was a student). With Bataille, the desire for annihilation involves an identification with the energy of the life-force which finally abandons the traditional life/death dualism; the 'incessant motion' of death is now barely distinguishable from the life-force, and the human identification with it is stronger than ever.

Work and prohibition

Bataille observes that the prevailing attitude of humankind to this fundamental truth of life as a squandering annihilation is, predictably, one of disavowal. In fact the whole of culture is built upon that disavowal, and especially those aspects of it which involve the imperatives of labour, prohibition,[1] prodigality, acquisition and utility, all of which have rendered humankind servile, and nowhere more so than under capitalism, which adheres quintessentially to the anti-life principle of producing at the least expense (*Accursed Share*, II.15, 85).[2] In the service of culture, man incessantly negates and transforms both nature and the animal in himself.[3] If one obvious way of doing this is through work and prohibition, another less obvious but equally significant way is through eroticism. Eroticism is the cerebral sexual activity of man, as opposed to animals, and this makes it different from, even opposed to, sexuality (II.52–3).

Yet the underlying natural reality of expenditure unto death exerts a fatal attraction still, even inside capitalism; somewhere deep down we desire to get back to it, to shatter cultural restraint and live again – to squander, expend, destroy:

we are constantly tempted to abandon work, patience and the slow accumulation of resources for a contrary movement, where suddenly we squander the accumulated riches, where we waste and lose as much as we can. (II.107)

More fundamentally, it is through eroticism that we are seduced by the pull of annihilation; we really do want death to 'wreak its havoc at our expense' (*Erotism*, pp. 59–60). Death is experienced most intensely as desire.

However – and this is crucial – the human perception of the truth of life as expenditure can now occur only from *inside* culture; that is, from inside the set of disavowals which constitutes culture. This means that man is a split, divided being. To think that we can simply return to the natural order (or rather natural disorder – the condition of animality which preceded prohibition) is naïve in the extreme, since human nature is now partly constituted by the very prohibitions which separate us from it: '[An] abhorrence of nature [is] built into our essence' (*Accursed Share*, II.23, 70). At the same time, we can never simply comply with the prohibitions of culture. Man initially revolted against the natural world (life as excessive, non-productive expenditure), but now revolts against the very prohibitions he established to protect himself against the natural. But this secondary revolt cannot be conducted from the position of the natural, even though that continues to exert its force:

Since man has uprooted himself from nature, that being who returns to it is still uprooted, he is an uprooted being who suddenly goes back toward that from which he is uprooted, from which he has not ceased to uproot himself. (II.77, 90)

The consequence of this is that desire remains conflicted and potentially alienated from itself; it is the fate of humankind to be constituted by a fundamental ambivalence towards life itself, an alternation between repulsion and transgressive attraction (II.48). But this is also constitutive of human achievement: humanity originates in a 'maze of reactions', and the fact that it never ceases to 'maintain a sum of stubborn and incompatible, *impossibly* rigorous reactions is something worthy of admiration; *indeed nothing merits the same degree of admiration'* (II.82, 18).

One of the most significant conflicts is that between desire and disgust. We experience a profound attraction to the natural world (life as excess, expenditure, dissolution), yet alongside (or rather inside) that attraction is a revulsion, steeped in 'lasting repulsions and insurmountable disgust' (II.23, 52, 70, 28).[4] Freud had found in the individual a similar conflict between desire and disgust which replicates the larger conflict between instinct and civilization. And one reason why this conflict threatens to wreck the human subject is because it entails the hostile, unstable, radical intimacy of each term with the other: at one moment desire finds, in what was once disgusting, a pleasure whose intensity it could never have known without that history of disgust; at another moment desire gives way to a civilizing revulsion the more intense because its history is grounded in the very desire it displaces. This dialectic fascinated George Bataille; it would hardly be an exaggeration to say that he founded an entire anthropology upon it.

Transgression

A recurring point in Bataille is that prohibition, inhibition, horror, disgust – all 'heighten the intensity of erotic pleasure' (*Accursed Share*, II.167). And, despite everything, this is a positive gain which 'can be summed up in a simple statement: the force of a movement, which repression increased tenfold, projected life into a richer world' (II.93). This is why we are sexually attracted towards what is forbidden. Whereas Freud was inclined to regard the attraction of the forbidden as a residue of a primitive sexuality which has escaped repression,[5] Bataille would see it as partly that, but also, and probably more importantly, as eroticism overdetermined and immeasurably intensified by this history of the prohibition it transgresses. Freud sometimes claimed that sexuality in the civilized context is only an inferior version of what it once was, and incapable of giving real satisfaction; for Bataille it is precisely the civilized context which heightens eroticism.

But again there is a deep ambivalence here; desire and aversion are inextricable. Eroticism is inseparable from repugnance – from 'the abhorrence of sexuality, or the sense that it is filthy'. This is not simply danger – that simply frightens one away. Rather it is 'a horror of prohibition that keeps one in the anguish of temptation'. Every horror conceals the possibility of enticement, but with the qualification that excessive horror paralyses desire (II.82, 96; cf. II.149). In one place Bataille speaks of looking down from a great height unprotected by a guard-rail:

the view may cause us to step back, but the image of the possible fall, which is connected with it, may also suggest that we jump, in spite or because of the death we will find there. This depends on the sum of available energy which remains in us, under pressure, but in a certain disequilibrium.

What is certain is that the lure of the void and of ruination does not in any way correspond to a diminished vitality. (II.108; my emphasis)

For Bataille, to be somehow beholden to the self-same order which one desperately desires to transgress is not just bourgeois hypocrisy or existential bad faith but the profound and inescapable condition of being human. Likewise with ambivalence and the conflict between attraction and repulsion: this is no mere individual pathology but, again, the condition of being human. For Bataille we most truly *are* that shudder of revulsion *against*, which is also an intense, ambivalent desire *for*. His understanding of transgression is exceptional, as for instance when he remarks that

To shrink from fundamental stability isn't less cowardly than to hesitate about shattering it. Perpetual *instability* is *more* boring than adhering strictly to a rule. (*Guilty*, pp. 28–9)

What most repulses us is putrefaction; there is no greater human aversion, says Bataille, than that felt towards 'those unstable, fetid and lukewarm substances where life ferments ignobly. Those substances where the eggs, germs and maggots swarm.' One reason why putrefaction revolts is because I know that one day 'this living world will pullulate in my dead mouth'. Death is not just the annihilation of being but this 'shipwreck in the nauseous', the knowledge that in my own decomposition I will once again become 'anonymous, infinite life, which stretches forth like the night, which is death'. Death is never pure non-being, but is ever-present in life as change and decomposition: 'Death is that putrefaction, that stench . . . *which is at once the source and the repulsive condition of life*' (*Accursed Share*, II.80–81; my emphasis). Life in its primal reality is a state of differentiation so excessive that it includes within itself the undifferentiation of death; it is without limit, without boundaries: the viscous movement which is the stuff of life is also 'death gorging life with decomposed substance' (II.95). And it is eroticism which always draws us back to this terrifying prospect:

anguish, which lays us open to annihilation and death, is always linked to eroticism; our sexual activity finally rivets us to the distressing image of death, and the knowledge of death deepens the abyss of eroticism. The curse of decay constantly recoils on sexuality, which it tends to eroticize: in sexual anguish there is a sadness of death, an apprehension of death which . . . we will never be able to shake off. (II.84)

As he puts it elsewhere, it is the fragrance of death which gives sexuality all its power (II.100).[6]

Annihilation of self

In eroticism we also desire to lose ourselves without reservation; we ask of it that it 'uses up our strength and our resources and, if necessary, places our life in danger'; this is one reason why the object we desire most is that most likely to endanger or destroy us. Eroticism 'demands the greatest possible loss', and this is at heart what we want – to lose ourselves and look death in the face (*Accursed Share*, II.101, 113, 141, 104–6). Eroticism fragments the fragile coherence of the self; it violates the ego. When we experience sexual ecstasy we are beside ourselves; our unity is shattered and we wallow in blindness and oblivion; the personality dies: 'desire is only aroused as long as its object causes a chasm no less deep than death to yawn within me' (*Erotism*, pp. 103–5, 59). And obscenity is the name we give to the unease which disrupts 'the possession of a recognized and stable individuality' (pp. 17–18).[7] Anguish arises when we remain trapped in individuation:

Anguish arises when the anxious individual is not himself stretched tight by the feeling of superabundance. This is precisely what evinces the isolated, individual character of anguish. There can be anguish only from a personal, *particular* point of view that is radically opposed to the *general* point of view based on the exuberance of living matter as a whole. Anguish is meaningless for someone who overflows with life, and for life as a whole, which is an overflowing by its very nature. (*Accursed Share*, I.39)[8]

Ultimately we want death: 'A febrile unrest within us asks death to wreak its havoc at our expense' (*Erotism*, pp. 59–60). And we want it because 'the luxury of death is regarded by us in the same way as that of sexuality, first as a negation of ourselves, then – in a sudden reversal – as the profound truth of that movement of which life is the manifestation' (*Accursed Share*, I.34–5).

We yearn for the sexual experience of death because it restores us to the primal continuity of all being. For human beings 'are discontinuous beings, individuals who perish in isolation in the midst of an incomprehensible adventure, but [who] yearn for our lost continuity'. Death offers the possibility of regaining that continuity, which is why we have a profound, nostalgic desire for this 'primal continuity linking us with everything that is' – a continuity at once 'independent of death and . . . *even proved by death*'. In eroticism there is even 'a challenge to death through indifference to death'. Life is only a door to existence: 'life may be doomed but the continuity of existence is not'. Death is also the youth of things; only death guarantees the fresh upsurging without which life would be blind (*Erotism*, pp. 15, 21, 23–4, 59).

Love promises 'a total blending of two beings, a continuity between two discontinuous creatures' (p. 20); 'yet this continuity is chiefly to be felt in the anguish of desire, when it is still inaccessible, still an impotent, quivering yearning' (p. 19). So in the sexual embrace we aspire to mystical dissolution:

the totality of what is (the universe) swallows me . . . nothing remains, except this or that, *which are less meaningful than nothing*. In a sense it is unbearable and I seem to be dying. It is at this cost, no doubt, that I am no longer myself, but an infinity in which I am lost. (*Accursed Share*, II.115–16; my emphasis)

I am embracing the totality without which I was only *outside*: I reach orgasm. (II.118)

Most significantly of all, perhaps, this totality in which the self is lost is not the ethereal transcendent realm of Western metaphysics, but physical decomposition. Indeed, to read Bataille on the erotic, ambivalent urge to annihilation is to realize how different it is to Freud's death drive. Implausible as it may seem, the Freudian death drive resembles the inverted counterpart of religious transcendence. The Freudian instinct towards oblivion, towards a total annihilation of being, where desire is at last dissolved into the zero tension of non-being, is the negative, inverted form of the absolute transcendence of being and desire – the perfect peace before and beyond consciousness that passes all understanding. Pure non-being: zero tension. In Western metaphysics such 'clean' annihilation has always been an aspect of transcendence. For Bataille, by contrast, the death which desire seeks is not this annihilating transcendent, but an immolation in natural process – 'and of the putrefaction that follows it' (II.119). Or maybe it's both: Bataille recovers a medieval obsession with mutability as physical decomposition and crosses it with the romantic desire for a pure annihilation in ecstasy. For him there really is a link between eroticism and death via putrefaction: while the sexual organs in one sense are at the opposite pole to the disintegration of the flesh, 'the look of the exposed inner mucosae makes me think of wounds that suppurate, which manifest the connection between the life of the body and the decomposition of the corpse' (II.130). Bataille also recovers a medieval/early modern view of man as constituted essentially by division, driven forward by the energy which comes from division and incompletion.

It is here that this increasingly influential writer manifests that fundamental conflict between, on the one hand, the erotics of mutability and death and, on the other, the commitment to social praxis. What I have not mentioned so far is that Bataille, especially in *The Accursed Share*, aspired to develop a new political economy from his theory of life as non-productive expenditure. That book runs to three volumes, yet nowhere in it does there emerge a plausible account of what society might be like if reorganized in accord with the truth of life as expenditure. And how could there, if Bataille is even half correct in thinking that 'death, the rupture of the discontinuous individualities to which we cleave in terror, stands there before us more real than life itself' (*Erotism*, p. 19)?

At the opening of *Cultural Materialism: Theory and Practice*, Scott Wilson announces that a 'revitalized, left-wing Marxist project' must engage with the ideas of Bataille – 'one of the most important and most neglected thinkers of the twentieth century' (p. xi). In that Wilson is unable to substantiate this claim, he replicates Bataille's own problem, failing to address let alone resolve the conflict between praxis and (annihilating) desire which recurs through Bataille's writing and is apparent in remarks like the following:

Men committed to political struggle will never be able to yield to the truth of eroticism. Erotic activity always takes place at the expense of the forces committed to their combat. (*Accursed Share*, II.191)

The problem is at least recognized in a remarkable book by Nick Land which really does live up to its title, *The Thirst for Annihilation*. Land derives from Bataille the view that all political opposition to fascism is only ever its timid counter-image:

The thought that there might be a political response to fascism makes me laugh. Shall we set out our little fascism against their big one? Organize ourselves, become disciplined, maybe we could make ourselves some smart uniforms and stomp about in the street? Politics is the last great sentimental indulgence of mankind, and it has never achieved anything except a deeper idiocy, more work, more repression . . . (p. 197)

In a sense Land is right, at least to this extent: the paradoxical nature of a radical, liberating praxis is that it quite probably requires in the achievement of its aims as much if not more repression than does the maintenance of the repressive society it seeks to change. No realistic assessment of the cost and difficulty of large-scale social transformation can avoid this fact. It is just one aspect of the tragedy inherent in revolutionary endeavour. Any aesthetic, political or erotic project which privileges expenditure, and in particular the undoing or the subversion of repression above all else, is a non-starter in terms of radical social change.

18

In Search of Potency:
D. H. Lawrence

Towards the end of D. H. Lawrence's *Aaron's Rod* there occurs a fierce attack on socialism. Published in 1922 and set just after the First World War, this novel is about the relationship and the fortunes of two men, Rawdon Lilly and Aaron Sisson. Both men are aspects of Lawrence himself, and the novel is a thinly fictionalized (though not uncritical) expression of Lawrence's ideas at this time.

For Lilly, formerly a socialist, the idea and the ideal of socialism have 'gone dead – dead as carrion'. But he is reacting against more than socialism; for Lilly/Lawrence in 1922, an optimistic, progressive humanism has already gone terribly wrong:

the ideal of love, the ideal that it is better to give than to receive, the ideal of liberty, the ideal of the brotherhood of man, the ideal of the sanctity of human life, the ideal of what we call goodness, charity, benevolence, public spiritedness, the ideal of sacrifice for a cause, the ideal of unity and unanimity – all the lot – all the whole beehive of ideals – has all . . . gone putrid, stinking. (p. 326)

The conversation is violently interrupted by a terrorist bomb. Fictionally this is a crucial moment, precipitating Aaron into a new phase of his life. For Lawrence it was equally significant in terms of European history: this narrative moment corresponds to his belief at the time that it was the errors of socialism which led to this kind of violence and, eventually, to fascism.[1]

In *Aaron's Rod*, as elsewhere in Lawrence's writing, the modern condition is regarded as one of decline and decadence; degeneration affects everything. There is an acute sense of being beleaguered by social and cultural death, and now socialism is not the answer but part of the problem.[2] Redemption lies elsewhere – in, for instance, a radical individualism and political authoritarianism. Lilly wants to get back to some form of slavery, the inferior ruled by the superior – most especially the superior individual – and he believes that the masses, 'after sufficient extermination', will be brought to agree (p. 327; cf. pp. 112, 128). Lilly/Lawrence wants to replace a humanist philosophy of collective social praxis with an aesthetics of energy in which human desire is revitalized and rescued from a social decadence epitomized in that 'death choice' or 'death courage' characteristic of modern man (p. 146). Bertrand Russell, who for a while had an intense friendship with Lawrence, later wrote, 'I came to feel him a positive force for evil,' and saw him as someone who had developed 'the whole philosophy of fascism before the politicians had thought of it'. Of Lawrence's notion of blood-consciousness, Russell said 'it led straight to Auschwitz'. Russell may have been exaggerating in revenge for Lawrence's own earlier criticism of him. Delivered in a private letter, it so devastated Russell that he contemplated suicide. Even so, Russell had a point (Nehls, I.282–5; Monk, pp. 400–430). Lawrence, like other modernists, was attracted by *potency* in proportion to his conviction that the energies of the modern world were failing.

Returning to the cosmos

In *Apocalypse* (1931) Lawrence, somewhat like Nietzsche before him, imagines a process of social death beginning almost with Western culture itself, but immeasurably worsened by Christianity, which, especially in the Reformation, turned away from the cosmos proper, substituting a vision of 'non-vital . . . forces and mechanistic order'. Thus 'the long slow death of the human being set in'. Lawrence continues:

No doubt this death was necessary. It is the long, slow, death of society which parallels the quick death of Jesus and the other dying Gods. It is death none the less, and will end in the annihilation of the human race . . . unless there is a change, a resurrection, and a return to the cosmos. (p. 31)

The triumph of the intellect and mind over the body and sensuality is another aspect of the same catastrophic history. Lawrence replays and recasts this story of the historical repression of 'blood-consciousness' by intellect.

The most notorious of all advocates of the aesthetics of energy was the Italian Futurist, and fascist, Filippo Marinetti (1876–1944). Under the influence of diverse contemporary philosophies, but especially that of Nietzsche, Marinetti produced his famous *Futurist Manifesto* (1909), in which he urged the young to 'sing the love of danger, the habit of energy and boldness' (*Selected Writings*, p. 41). Art, for Marinetti, 'can be nothing but violence, cruelty, and injustice'. He idealized violence and war, and in 1914 he described the First World War as *'the most beautiful futurist poem which has so far been seen'* (p. 43; R. Griffin, p. 26; emphasis original). Marinetti and the Futurists also idealized mutability. Repudiating the entire previous artistic tradition which lamented transience, the ephemeral and loss, they now celebrate these things; far from being debilitating, ceaseless change is regarded as a dynamic manifestation of everything good, including progress and the excitement of the future itself: 'To the conception of the imperishable, the immortal, we oppose, in art, that of becoming, the perishable, the transitory and the ephemeral.' The aim is to teach people, through art, 'to love the beauty of an emotion or a sensation *to the degree that it is unique and destined to vanish* irreparably'. The oppositions between the eternal and the transient, the absolute and the relative, so fundamental to Western metaphysical traditions of religion and philosophy, are now inverted and reconceptualized: 'We already live in the absolute, because we have created eternal, omnipresent speed' (Marinetti, *Selected Writings*, pp. 67, 41; his emphasis).

This idealization of speed and the machine was where Lawrence disagreed with the Futurists. In a letter written from Italy on 2 June 1914 he approved of the iconoclasm of Futurism: 'This is the revolt against beastly sentiment and slavish adherence to tradition and the dead mind. For that I love it.' But he regarded its vision for change as hopelessly scientific, intellectual and mechanistic:

It's the most self-conscious, intentional, pseudo-scientific stuff on the face of the earth. Marinetti begins: 'Italy is like a great Dreadnought surrounded by torpedo boats.' That is it exactly – a great mechanism. Italy has got to go through the most mechanical and dead stage of all. (*Letters*, II.181–3)

Lawrence's vision of potency was vitalistic, not mechanistic, and for that reason much more vulnerable to those self-same degenerate forces in modern culture to which it was opposed. And yet it is the vitalistic rather than the mechanistic version of the aesthetics of energy which has proved the more enduring.[3]

In the vitalistic version, what is celebrated is not energy *per se*; in fact the unrestricted energy of life's lower forms is itself usually regarded as degenerate and potentially corrupting, and in urgent need of being controlled by their superior and higher forms. Nowhere is this more necessary than with the inferior races, in relation to whom we also encounter a glaring paradox, namely that fertility is a sure sign of degeneracy: as Lilly puts it in *Aaron's Rod*, 'I can't do with folks who teem by the billion, like the Chinese and Japs and Orientals altogether. Only vermin teem by the billion. Higher types breed slower' (p. 119). The highest type of all is the exceptional individual; only 'he' can stand against all the forces of disintegration, degeneration, mediocrity and decline that typify modernity. And he must even fight them in himself, guarding his own vital desires against the forces which would sap and pervert them.

Women are especially pernicious in this respect, sapping men of their will-power, individuality and independence. Women also destroy the bonds between men. Their aim is to dominate men, but, having done that, they are rarely satisfied. Which is why Aaron and Lilly experience life-and-death struggles with women:

What was there in the female will so diabolical, he asked himself, that it could press like a flat sheet of iron against a man all the time?

This is Aaron, speaking of his wife, whom, with great effort, he succeeds in resisting through 'the arrogance of self-unyielding male'. His salvation lies in retreating to 'isolate self-responsibility, aloneness . . . the innermost isolation and singleness of his own soul' (pp. 191, 193, 197).

It is imperative that the male protect from women this core inner self – 'perfected singleness' (p. 156). One is most vulnerable in sex; when Aaron has sex with a woman 'he felt his passion drawn from him as if a long, live nerve were drawn out from his body, a long, live thread of electric fire' (p. 317). In other ways too these characters find that the modern death-wish is inside love – in, for instance, the prevailing notion that the individual should seek in it either self-abandon or the opportunity for complete self-sacrifice. Such aspirations are nothing less than wilful suicide. Ideally, muses Aaron, love should be a process working towards completion: not, as now,

some horror of intensification and extremity wherein the soul and body ultimately perish. The completion of the process of love is the arrival at a state of simple, pure-self-possession, for man and woman. Only that. Which isn't exciting enough for us sensationalists. We prefer abysses and maudlin self-abandon and self-sacrifice, the degeneration into a sort of slime and merge. (pp. 200–201)

This ideal of independence is expressed in natural imagery – a fantasy of *effortless self-sufficiency* here realized through an allusion to the two eagles in Walt Whitman's poem 'Dalliance of Eagles': 'all the time each lifted on its own wings' (p. 202).

The reality, of course, is that this independence involves an unsustainable degree of effort – Lilly's 'soul was against the whole world', while Aaron remains determined to give in 'to no woman, and to no social ideal, and to no social institution' (p. 336). Which is why the obsessive central focus in Lawrence is not the isolated, powerful, effortlessly self-sufficient individual, but all of the forces that threaten him with dissolution and disintegration. It is also why these forces – in a real sense imaginary – are countered with increasingly extreme fantasies of individual omnipotence, along with equally extreme fantasy 'solutions' to what threaten the individual integrity of the 'innermost, integral, unique self' (p. 343).

In the final encounter between the two men, Lilly tells Aaron that there are only two great dynamic urges in life: love and power. And since love has also become degenerate, that leaves power – that 'vast dark source of life and strength in us now . . . Power – the power urge.' This is not conscious power but rather some primal force which urges from within, darkly, for the displacing of the old leaves, the inception of the new. It is powerful and self-central, not seeking its centre outside, in some God or some beloved, but acting indomitably from within itself. (pp. 343–6)

'Of course,' adds Lilly, 'there must be one who urges, and one who is impelled . . .' This means that women must submit to men, and inferior men must submit to greater men – 'the deep fathomless submission to the heroic soul in a greater man' (p. 347).

In that 'of course' is one of the more glaring *non sequiturs* of this creed, itself symptomatic of other obvious inconsistencies. Lilly wants to invoke an asocial, anarchic, undiscriminating, primal energy – 'dark, living, fructifying power' – but in a form which is already socialized and ordered, not to say policed, in accordance with the most familiar hierarchies of class and gender. Similarly, Lawrence's 'return' to the body and its sexual expression was no less rigorously policed by ethical and intellectual considerations. His advocacy of a vital, natural sensuality to combat contemporary decadence derived from a deeply social preoccupation with cultural and psychic health which was at times passionately puritanical. It was this which contributed to his later popularity and influence, especially within the literary/cultural critical movement inspired by F. R. Leavis. At the unsuccessful prosecution of *Lady Chatterley's Lover* in 1960 Lawrence was defended against the charge of obscenity with the claim that he was a deeply moral writer.

Lawrence's fantasy of an absolutely powerful force imagined as primal (the 'power urge'), yet social through and through, is the final solution not just to the mutability and degeneracy of social death, but to the failure of the entire project of a life-affirming individualism which was supposed to transcend social death. As we shall see, the resolve to retreat into 'the central self, the isolate, absolute self' (*Kangaroo*, p. 309) always fails because this place of inner self-sufficiency is already the place of intolerable strain and frustration and the deeper desire for non-being.

Pornography and obscenity

Lawrence is remembered above all for a metaphysic that sought to disentangle sex from death and get it back on the side of life. Freud had declared that 'the excremental is all too intimately bound up with the sexual; the position of the genitals – *inter urinas et faeces* – remains the decisive and unchangeable factor'. This is one reason (of many) why he concluded that it is impossible to reconcile the sexual instincts with the needs of civilization ('On the Universal Tendency', p. 259). In 'Pornography and Obscenity' Lawrence insists on the absolute separation of the excremental and the sexual, and also describes the former in terms which resemble Freud's death drive:

The sex functions and the excrementory functions in the human body work so close together, yet they are, so to speak, utterly different in direction. Sex is a creative flow, the excrementory flow is towards dissolution, de-creation, if we may use such a word. In the really healthy human being the distinction between the two is instant, our profoundest instincts are perhaps our instincts of opposition between the two flows.

But in the degraded human being the deep instincts have gone dead, and the two flows become identical. *This* is the secret of really vulgar and of pornographical people: the sex flow and the excrement flow is the same to them. It happens when the psyche deteriorates, and the profound controlling instincts collapse.

Lawrence goes on to attribute this pornographic personality structure to common and vulgar people, and sees it as never more prevalent than now; it is the sign of the 'diseased condition of the body politic' (pp. 313–14). For him 'there are two great categories of meaning, for ever separate. There is mob-meaning, and there is individual meaning'; and 'the mob is always obscene, because it is always second-hand' (pp. 308–9).

Lawrence also associates masturbation with loss and death, and regards it as the most dangerous sexual vice for society: 'in masturbation there is nothing but loss . . . There is merely the spending away of a certain force, and no return. The body remains, in a sense, a corpse, after the act of self-abuse' (p. 317). Masturbation empties 'the real vitality and the real *being* of men', leaving them dead – 'a nullus, a nothingness'; today 'the sex-flow is dying out of the young, the real energy is dying away' (p. 322). We need to get back to a vision of sex as 'fresh and wholesome', vital and clean (pp. 311, 314).

On the one side, then, is a whole range of ills variously contributing to a contemporary state of social death epitomized in the excremental vision and masturbation; on the other is D. H. Lawrence struggling to reinterpret and redirect Western culture in the direction of a wholesome sexuality resolutely on the side of life. And yet in his fiction Lawrence shows himself to be more than fascinated by the very forces of degeneration he rails against – not least the way in which they conjoin sex and death.

Virtually every significant character in *Women in Love* (1921) is struggling for an intensity of being in proximity to death. Hermione is 'burdened to death with consciousness', while for Birkin she *is* death. Even to be overcome by the beauty of another is to want to die (pp. 45, 344–5, 203). With the more sympathetic characters it is not simply that they are struggling to escape death; rather, the existential authenticity which they seek entails the risk, even the seductions, of death. At one level this is the problem of being beleaguered by various kinds of social death – everything we've seen Lawrence castigate about the modern world, 'the life that belongs to death – our kind of life'. But it is clearly much more; death promises fulfilment:

better die than live mechanically a life that is a repetition of repetitions. To die is to move on with the invisible. To die is also a joy, a joy of submitting to that which is greater than the known; namely, the pure unknown.

This is Ursula, who for a while seems lost in a death-wish: 'the deepest desire . . . to go on into the unknown of death . . . Now was the time to relinquish, not to resist any more.' Death is 'a great consummation . . . a development from life' (pp. 208, 214–16).

The aggressive obverse of this deathward wish is to wish the death of the entire race. Birkin's sense of the mass of mankind as repulsive amounts almost to an illness, so that just to arrive in London 'is real death'. For him, humanity itself is dead – 'a dead letter'. He tells Ursula that he abhors humanity because it is a huge lie, a 'foul . . . universal defilement' which should be completely destroyed. A world completely free of people is 'a beautiful clean thought'. It offers the same attractions as death itself, in that, like 'the pure inhuman otherness of death', it would be 'beyond our sullying' (pp. 65, 67, 120, 141–2, 216–17).

There is a third way of escaping social death, less extreme than either the death-wish or the desire for the annihilation of the race. It involves withdrawing into the authentic being of blood-consciousness (pp. 47–8, 87). And yet this too is profoundly dependent upon death. The false integrity of the social ego has to be destroyed by the blood, but the latter also destroys integrity and identity *per se*. Characters seem caught between the horror of social death and the attraction/ horror of the fantasy of death itself. They are endlessly threatened in body and soul with 'sheer dissolution . . . the horrible sickness of dissolution' (p. 103; cf. pp. 99, 215, 319). And yet the dissolution of 'lapsing out' is a precondition for being rescued from social death back to life. But, yet again, this coming back to life is a kind of surrender of being:

Now he had let go, imperceptibly he was melting into oneness with the whole. It was like pure, perfect sleep, his first great sleep of life . . . here was sleep, and peace, and perfect lapsing out. (p. 199)

Characters are encouraged (by Birkin) to seek out 'the great dark knowledge' of the blood, where 'the mind and the known world are drowned in darkness' and the self dies so as to be reborn: 'It is death to one's self – but it is the coming into being of another.' Pure sensuality depends upon lapsing into unknowingness, giving up volition: 'You've got to learn not-to-be, before you can come into being' (pp. 46–8; cf. p. 193).

But Birkin is more ambivalent towards this philosophy of letting go than this suggests. Later he has fearful intimations of what this involves for world history. He recalls seeing an African 'fetish', a small statuette about two foot high, a figure of a woman who embodies sheer sensuality untainted by spirituality. She represents a race which had 'died, mystically' – that is, a race where sensuality had been separated from thought and become free to follow its own 'mystic knowledge in disintegration and dissolution . . . and corruption'. For the African races the way of complete sensuality is the way of death and dissolution, involving a knowledge far beyond 'phallic know-ledge'. Now 'the white races' are about to repeat the process, but differently; whereas the 'West Africans, controlled by the burning death-abstraction of the Sahara, had been fulfilled in sun-destruction, the putrescent mystery of sun-rays', the white races, with the 'Arctic north behind them, the vast abstraction of ice and snow, would fulfil a mystery of ice-destructive knowledge, snow-abstract annihilation'. Gerald epitomizes these races who are destined to know 'death by perfect cold' (pp. 285–7).

At such moments Birkin reacts violently against dissolution. Redemption is now felt to be in yet another direction, entirely different again: entry into 'pure single being, the individual soul taking pre-cedence' (p. 287). Earlier, Birkin has experienced this same obsessive need to become 'an isolated me, that does *not* meet and mingle', who is free from the 'horrible merging, mingling self-abnegation of love (pp. 162, 225) – only to then veer back towards the attraction of 'degeneration – mystic, universal degeneration' (p. 229).

Characters react to each other with a similar ambivalence, which sometimes verges on the paranoid or the schizoid, and which at its most extreme erupts as a murderous impulse; for Hermione, the desire to kill Birkin is described as sexual – 'unutterable consummation, unutterable satisfaction' (p. 117). At the end of the novel Gudrun and Gerald literally fight it out to the death; he almost kills her before going out into the snow to die himself. During the life-and-death struggle, Gudrun is apparently revealed as an 'African' at heart;[4] inside her apparent sophistication is only darkness, 'the obscene religious mystery of ultimate reduction, the mystic frictional activities of dia-bolic reducing down, disintegrating the vital organic body of life'. It is as if she embodies a death drive somehow harnessed by a fierce wilfulness and directed outwards as sadism, and most intensely at Gerald, whose own will to live dissolves as hers triumphs (p. 508). But this can happen only because Gerald has carried death within him from the beginning. He advances 'the plausible ethics of productivity' (p. 62) because he is dead inside. Even worse, in industry he is the agent of death, substituting the mechanical principle for the organic (pp. 257–60). In love too: when he first has intercourse with Gudrun

Into her he poured all his pent-up darkness and corrosive death . . . And she, subject, received him as a vessel filled with his bitter potion of death . . . The terrible frictional violence of death filled her, and she received it in an ecstasy of subjection, in throes of acute, violent sensation. (p. 388)

Lawrence wants to escape social dissolution by returning to the pulse of authentic being – 'To have one's pulse beating direct from the mystery, this was perfection, unutterable satisfaction. Human or unhuman mattered nothing' (p. 539). But this deeper reality is itself one of dissolution, as Birkin remarks earlier to Ursula: the reality of our being is 'that dark river of dissolution . . . the black river of corruption' which 'ends in universal nothing'. It is from this 'flowering mystery of the death-process' that life springs. Ursula hears in this metaphysic of redemption only the negation of life, and retorts angrily, 'You only want us to know death' (pp. 193–4).

In *The Crown* (1915/1925) Lawrence elaborates the idea. We are, he says, all the time 'balanced between the flux of life and the flux of death'; because both are within us, 'our will-to-live contains a germ of suicide, and our survival-of-the-fittest the germ of degeneracy'. Allowed to run its course, the flux of reduction leads to 'perversity, degradation and death'. And yet death and corruption are not only necessary, but even desirable:

The spirit of destruction is divine, when it breaks the ego and opens the soul to the wider heavens. In corruption there is divinity. Aphrodite is, on the one side, the great goddess of destruction in sex, Dionysus in the spirit. Moloch and some gods of Egypt are gods also of the knowledge of death . . . It is the activity of departure. And departure is the opposite equivalent of coming together; decay, corruption, destruction, breaking down is the opposite equivalent of creation. In infinite going apart there is revealed again the pure absolute . . .

Corruption will at last break down for us the deadened forms, and release us into the infinity. (pp. 287–8, 292–3)

It is astonishing that Lawrence could be celebrated as the prophet of sexual health and a vital individualism; rather, *Women in Love*, his greatest novel (in his own view, and that of most critics), testifies to the extreme crisis of an individualism questing for redemption in erotic intensities driven by every kind of death. The fundamental tension is not between a fear of and a desire for death, but between the desire for death as self-dissolving submission and an identification with death as the ultimate force of control and revenge – an absolute power that will annihilate and eradicate everything Lawrence hates, from social degeneracy to humanity itself. Hence the recurring oscillations between social aggression and metaphysical passivity, between the desire for self-dissolution and the hysterical retreat into the isolated absolute self which aspires to independence yet is obsessed with the forces which beleaguer and threaten it. Hence too the equivocations as to whether dissolution should be restricted to the false social ego or whether it should go further. If the former, it never goes far enough; if the latter, one starts to go the way of 'Africa'. Lawrence's notorious stridency of tone and his tendency to emphatic repetition are an expression less of prophetic conviction than of deep ambivalence and contradiction.

At one level what this means is that the mystery of being is only ever imagined from within the universe of a megalomaniac and paranoid individualism. This is why cultural difference, racial difference and even world history orbit in grotesquely distorted forms around the self-obsessed individual's pursuit of redemption; it is the ultimate stretched-hubris of humanism, the enveloping of everything other into the paltry neuroses of the solitary self. Individuals flail around, questing for difference in the name of authentic being, yet exist in various states of chronic insensibility and ignorance in relation to difference, be it the difference of other individuals or of entire cultures and continents. At crucial points, always heavily invested with the narrative voice, self-obsessed characters perform acts of interpretative violence which reduce otherness to their own vicious egotistical struggles and the diverse crises of the entire individualistic metaphysic. Not surprisingly then, the adoration of power that we find in *Aaron's Rod* is anticipated here: 'it's the last, perhaps highest, love-impulse: resign your will to the higher being' (p. 156).

At the same time, however, this ambivalent and conflicted vision explores, with imagination, honesty and courage, the full extent to which the crises of individualism derive from its internalization – one could say introjection – of the enduring paradoxes of Western death.

And this makes Lawrence a writer of greater not lesser significance. In *Women in Love* he is drawn to pervert his own simplistic binary between life and death, anality and true sex. Birkin apparently has anal sex with Ursula:

He had taken her as he had never been taken himself. He had taken her at the roots of her darkness and shame – like a demon, laughing over the fountain of mystic corruption which was one of the sources of her being . . . As for her, when would she so much go beyond herself as to accept him at the quick of death? (p. 343)

Ursula remains unsure; angrily she denounces Birkin as 'a foul, deathly thing, obscene . . . so *perverse*, so death-eating'. And he inwardly agrees, knowing 'his spirituality was concomitant of a process of depravity, a sort of pleasure in self-destruction' (pp. 346–7). But then they have sex again, and experience 'the most intolerable accession into being' as a result of tapping 'the darkest, deepest, strangest life-force of the human body, at the back and base of the loins . . . deeper, further in mystery than the phallic source'. Later still they experience something similar, and once again it offers a radical release from shame into the truth of being (pp. 354, 464).

A similar but rather more notorious episode occurs in *Lady Chatter-ley's Lover*, where again anal sex seems to be vitally redemptive, but at the risk of just those wholesome virtues the didactic Lawrence put on the side of life – not least the deep, defended self which sodomy apparently annihilates: 'reckless, shameless sensuality shook her to her foundations, stripped her to the very last . . . it was not really love . . . It was sensuality sharp and searing as fire, burning the soul to tinder' (p. 258).

Homoeroticism

And running through it all is the problem, or the promise, of the homoerotic. It is made to carry the burden of *Women in Love*'s deepest tension or contradiction: it is both the agent of death, reduction and degeneration, and the source of the deepest possibility of redemption. The extent of Lawrence's ambivalence towards homosexuality is

striking. His revulsion against the homosexuality of Bloomsbury/
Cambridge figures like Keynes was extreme; he associated it and them
with dissolution – 'the flux of reduction'. Merely to see such people
in their pyjamas threw him into a state of hysteria and deep crisis
(*Letters*, II.319–21; see also Delany, *D. H. Lawrence's Nightmare*).

The influence of degeneration theory is apparent, especially in what
Lawrence wrote about homosexuality in unpublished sections of *The
Crown*. He describes the attraction of a man for a boy, or for 'a lower
type of man', as governed by the

basic desire . . . to get *back* to a state which he has long surpassed. And the
getting back, the reduction, is a sort of progress to infinite nullity, to the
beginnings. He is given up to the flux of reduction, his mouth is upon the
mouth of corruption. *This* is the reason of homosexuality, and of connection
with animals . . . This is David turning to Jonathan, Achilles with Patroclus.
This is always the higher, more developed type seeking to revert to the lower.
(*Reflections on the Death of a Porcupine*, p. 472)

This suggests Loerke in *Women in Love*, 'a Jew – or part Jewish'
(p. 481) and homosexual or bisexual (p. 462), a 'little obscene monster
of the darkness' who lives 'like a rat in the river of corruption . . . [a]
gnawing little negation, gnawing at the roots of life' (p. 481). And yet
it is Loerke who seemingly most fulfils the ideal of individual integrity
– 'He was single and, by abstraction from the rest, absolute in himself'
(p. 509).

Against all this is Birkin's final admission of his own need for
'eternal union with a man . . . another kind of love', and his conviction
that Gerald would not have died if he could have accepted the love
that he, Birkin, had offered him (pp. 540–41). Most remarkable of
all is the suppressed prologue to *Women in Love*, with its explicit
expression of Birkin's intense homoerotic desire:

it was for men that he felt the hot, flushing, roused attraction which a man
is supposed to feel for the other sex . . . The male physique had a fascination
for him, and for the female physique he felt only a fondness . . .

In the street it was the men who roused him by their flesh and their manly,
vigorous movement . . .

He loved his friend, the beauty of whose manly limbs made him tremble with pleasure. He wanted to caress him.

And then in his soul would succeed a sort of despair, because this passion for a man had recurred in him. It was a deep misery to him. And it would seem as if he had always loved men, always and only loved men. And this was the greatest suffering to him.

This was the one and only secret he kept to himself, this secret of his passionate and sudden, spasmodic affinity for men he saw. He kept this secret even from himself. He knew what he felt, but he always kept the knowledge at bay. (*Phoenix II*, pp. 103–4, 107)

At the end of *Apocalypse*, written when he was dying, Lawrence again finds reassurance in dissolution, but the tone becomes different as the most basic premiss of his punitive social philosophy and of his polemic against social death is relinquished. Now the obsession with 'the central self, the isolate, absolute self' (*Kangaroo*, p. 309) dissolves in the perception and the acceptance of transience:

there is nothing of me that is alone and absolute except my mind, and we shall find that the mind has no existence by itself, it is only the glitter of the sun on the surface of the waters.

So that my individualism is really an illusion. I am part of the great whole, and I can never escape. (*Apocalypse*, p. 126)

VIII

DEATH AND THE HOMOEROTIC

19

Wrecked by Desire:
Thomas Mann

Faust rejects as temptation the thought of being saved. (Thomas Mann, *Dr Faustus*, p. 470)

There is a remarkable moment in Thomas Mann's novel *Death in Venice* (1912) when the fifty-three-year-old Gustave von Aschenbach recklessly surrenders to his infatuation with a fourteen-year-old boy called Tadzio – surrenders in the sense not of consummating his desire, but of acknowledging it. For Aschenbach this surrender marks a self-disintegration which is also a temporary, intense self-awakening. Long-repressed energies and desires break into consciousness, momentarily bringing him alive even as they destroy him.

Like Joseph Conrad, Mann was fascinated by what Max Nordau had called the 'higher degenerate', especially the way in which he lived out the paradoxical connections between genius, disease, destruction and death. Throughout his life Mann was drawn back to the romantic idea that the intimate connections between desire and death were mediated and intensified by genius and disease.[1]

The three greatest influences on Mann were Arthur Schopenhauer, Richard Wagner and Friedrich Nietzsche. Arguably, Schopenhauer in *The World as Will and Representation* and Wagner in *Tristan and Isolde* give the most significant explorations in philosophy and music, respectively, of desire's seduction by death.[2] As for Nietzsche, Mann believed (and the evidence is disputable) that this philosopher owed his intellectual creativity to illness and disease, and literally so: he regarded Nietzsche's development as a case history in progressive syphilis, a disease which 'was to destroy his life but also to intensify it enormously. Indeed, that disease in Nietzsche was to exert stimulating effects in part beneficial, in part deadly, upon an entire era' (*Essays*, p. 414; *Last Essays*, pp. 146–7).[3]

For Mann, genius in the grip of disease nurtures an energy at once creative and lethal, and generates the paradox that disease and death are only life manifested in its most vigorous form. Disease – and in this sense love, or at least infatuation, is a disease – effects an unbinding which energizes even as it destroys. Thus Aschenbach. Mann is endlessly fascinated by all this – but it also explains why he cannot entirely dissociate Nietzsche from the fascism that appropriated him. Mann's writing, especially his 1947 novel *Dr Faustus*, remains important not least for the way in which he anatomizes the death/desire dynamic in relation to the political history of the first half of the twentieth century.

Dr Faustus

The composer Adrian Leverkühn, the Faustus figure in this novel, is a brilliant embodiment of Mann's ambivalent attitude not only to Nietzsche, but also to his own creativity, and nowhere more so than in two extraordinary episodes in the novel: the one where Leverkühn enters into a dialogue with the Devil, the other where he deliberately has sex with a prostitute suffering from syphilis.

After having been given a tour of Leipzig, Leverkühn asks his guide to recommend a restaurant. The guide delivers him instead to a brothel. Unawares, Leverkühn enters. A prostitute approaches him and brushes his cheek with her arm. He leaves hurriedly. The encounter affects him obscurely and deeply – on the occasion itself, but even more so subsequently. Fixation grows with recollection. More than a year later he returns to the brothel to look for that same woman, whom he now names Esmeralda. She has left, gone elsewhere for 'hospital treatment'. He follows and finds her. She warns him she is syphilitic, and despite or rather because of this he has intercourse with her.

There is a terrifying kind of daemonic love in the encounter: on her part because she warns him away, on his because he refuses to go. But in Leverkühn there is also another kind of desire – something selfless, defiant, reckless, self-destructive, impossible – in the act of transgression itself, a '*deep, deeply mysterious longing for daemonic conception, for a deathly unchaining of chemical change in his nature*' (p. 151; my emphasis).[4] The encounter manifests the fusion of eros and death, binding and unbinding, disintegrating and decline as the ground of a powerful but agonized and temporary liberation into creativity: 'love and poison here once and for ever became *a frightful unity of experience*; the mythological unity embodied in the arrow' (p. 150; my emphasis). This is desire as compulsion, obsession and fixation, but also desire as a kind of 'choice' within compulsion – which is to say 'a bond of love' (p. 150); a liberation, a temporary creative freedom, a momentary 'frightful unity of experience' that can be realized only in the embrace of death.

Serenus Zeitblom, the humanist narrator of Leverkühn's fate, can never recall this 'brief encounter' but with a shuddering sense of religious awe: in it the one partner found salvation, and the other staked it. For her there was salvation in being *found* in demise, 'loved' by one who could not, and would never, forget her. For Leverkühn it is salvation in the form of its parodic, daemonic inversion: he is liberated into the agony of creativity, and the prostitute's name recurs 'often in its inversion' in the form of six-note series 'of peculiarly nostalgic character', and especially in his late work, 'where audacity and despair mingle in so unique a way' (pp. 151–2).

Leverkühn's encounter with the prostitute is closely based on what Mann believed actually happened to Nietzsche, namely that the philosopher visited a brothel unawares and then fled on realizing where he was. At the time, says Mann, Nietzsche was

unconscious of the impression the incident had made upon him. But it had been nothing more nor less than ... a 'trauma', a shock whose steadily accumulating aftereffects – from which his imagination never recovered – testify to the saint's receptivity to sin. (*Last Essays*, p. 145)

Mann further believes that Nietzsche, like Leverkühn, returned to the brothel a year later and contracted syphilis, perhaps deliberately.

The syphilitic Leverkühn, animated by disease and impending dissolution, becomes creatively potent. The paradox of life animated by death is the focus of his dialogue with the Devil, who tells him that life clutches with joy at that which is brought about 'by the way of death, of sickness', and that life is thereby led 'higher and further' (p. 229). What this means is that

creative, genius-giving disease, disease that rides on high horse over all hindrances, and springs with drunken daring from peak to peak, is a thousand times dearer to life than plodding healthiness. I have never heard anything stupider than that from disease only disease can come. Life . . . takes the reckless product of disease, feeds on and digests it, and as soon as it takes it to itself it is health. Before the fact of fitness for life, my good man, all distinction of disease and health falls away. A whole host and generation of youth, receptive, sound to the core, flings itself on the work of the morbid genius, *made genius by disease*; admires it, praises it, exalts it, carries it away, assimilates it unto itself and makes it over to culture. (p. 236; my emphasis)

This insistence that disease is life-enhancing precisely because it threatens permanent disintegration and impels the individual ineluctably deathward has its counterpart in an epistemology which is radically aesthetic and amoral: 'an untruth of a kind that enhances power holds its own against any ineffectively virtuous truth' (p. 236).

Death in Venice

There is now only one thing left to be done, and that is to try to get well – in Venice! (Nietzsche to Peter Gast, 1 March 1879)

The moment of Aschenbach's surrender to Tadzio in *Death in Venice* occurs when the boy smiles at him. It is the culmination of a development whereby Aschenbach's life-vision of a civilizing integration of the sensual and the spiritual finally collapses. And it is Mann's achievement to make Aschenbach most intensely alive exactly then, at that moment of collapse. I return to this moment via other aspects of this novel, and via Mann's sexuality.

Aschenbach is a compelling incarnation of the tormented Freudian subject, strung out somewhere between desublimation, repression and neurosis. We encounter him at a point when his creativity is haunted by neurotic conflict. His entire life has been an attempt to discipline illicit sexual desire and sublimate it into art. The two main types of sublimated activity described by Freud – artistic creation and intellectual inquiry – both apply to Aschenbach, and in a way which closely follows Freud's further contention that illicit sexuality is sublimated in the service of civilization: we are told that Aschenbach is a hero of the cultural establishment with books like *A Study in Abjection*, which had earned the gratitude of a whole younger generation by suggesting that a man can still be capable of moral resolution even after he has plumbed the depths of knowledge (p. 202).[5] But not knowledge of the depths of repressed desire, which – and again this is a Freudian idea – returns to destroy Aschenbach through the very mechanism which has been used to repress it: Platonism. Aschenbach repeatedly invokes Plato to rationalize his desire – only to desublimate it even further. The irony of this is exquisite, especially if we are even half persuaded by Nietzsche's contention that Plato is one of the founding fathers of Western repression and decadence.

Aschenbach's sublimation is so very fragile; he is the writer who speaks for all those who 'work on the brink of exhaustion, who labour and are heavy-laden, who are worn out but still stand upright'; for him 'art was a war, an exhausting struggle' (pp. 205, 249). The psychic cost of this never-ending struggle is terrible; he is consumed by fatigue in the service of his art. Forever on the edge of this neurotic exhaustion, he bears out Freud's contention that repression is not a one-off event but an interminable, consuming struggle:

the process of repression is not to be regarded as an event which takes place once, the results of which are permanent . . . repression demands a persistent expenditure of force, and if this were to cease the success of the repression would be jeopardized . . . in obsessional neurosis the work of repression is prolonged in a sterile and interminable struggle. ('Repression', pp. 151, 158)

Death in Venice begins at the point where Aschenbach is not only exhausted by but is losing the struggle. As the novel progresses, illicit desire increasingly undergoes desublimation, and the fragile, strained unity which is human identity, especially sexual identity, is disintegrated from within through a return of what has been repressed.

In Aschenbach, Mann explores something which also anticipates aspects of Freud's death drive.[6] Most significantly there is the overwhelming subjective desire to *become unbound*, to undergo a dissolution of consciousness and regress into oblivion, ultimately achieving a state of zero tension before consciousness, before life. Aschenbach gravitates to the (literary) archetype of the degenerate city, Venice, his identity chronically destabilized by the returning repressed and overwhelmed by a desire for release from the strain of being: 'he let his eyes wander in the sea's wide expanse, let his gaze glide away, dissolve and die in the monotonous haze of this desolate emptiness'. There were profound reasons for his attachment to the sea, including the need to 'escape from the demanding complexity of phenomena' and

a forbidden longing deep within him that ran quite contrary to his life's task and was for that very reason seductive, a longing for the inarticulate and immeasurable, for eternity, for nothingness. To rest in the arms of perfection is the desire of any man intent upon creating excellence, and is not nothingness a form of perfection? (p. 224)

Such is the price of maintaining civilization over (which is to say through) the repression and sublimation of the desire which would otherwise threaten it.

Aschenbach exemplifies the desublimation of desire in a way which makes *Death in Venice* much more amenable to a psychoanalytic reading than, say, *Heart of Darkness*.[7] Another justification for such a reading is that, unlike Conrad's novel, where perversity includes sexuality but is not reducible to it, Mann's novel makes perversion essentially sexual, and so contributes towards the sexualizing of perversion. It is because *Death in Venice* is so susceptible to a psychoanalytic reading that I would suspend it, approaching the novel from a different perspective, and with a different question, which is also a question for psychoanalysis: Why should – how can – resurgent homosexual desire become the ground of so very much?

Here it is at the centre of an extraordinary narrative of terrifying acceleration into decline and an equally terrifying regression to a primitive past. It is also the permanent focus for what is so much more than sexual while always remaining at heart 'deeply' sexual. Both Freud and Mann (and to a lesser extent D. H. Lawrence) centre homosexuality in this way. But, rather than use psychoanalysis to

'explain' homosexuality, we should instead regard this very attempt
to explain it as one aspect of a larger historical development whereby
homosexuality is analysed to an obsessive degree and made the focus
of fundamental social, psychic and aesthetic conflicts. In short, *Death
in Venice* emerges from something larger, as does psychoanalysis. To
submit this novel to the psychoanalytic narrative which it undoubtedly
incorporates would be to leave unexamined its other equally significant
representations of deviant desire which link it to a range of Western
culture's recurring preoccupations, ranging from Platonic idealism to
degeneration.

The influence of degeneration theory is surely apparent, not
least in the way in which Mann's novel makes sexual perversion the
vehicle and focus for the same kind of paradox that we encountered in Conrad's novel – the supremely civilized subject is the
one who becomes most susceptible to degeneration. Aschenbach half
recognizes this when he ruefully contemplates how his own life as
an artist 'had deviated from [his ancestors] to the point of degeneracy'
(p. 249). Nor can the question as to why homosexual desire now
becomes the ground of so much be adequately answered without
reference to the modern 'invention' of homosexuality for the purposes
of social control which Michel Foucault and others have explored.
This is indeed important, but too often this history is seen entirely
negatively. Alongside and even inside it there was a more radical
deployment of homosexuality, and it can be discerned in this novel
by Mann.

'The rapture I felt': Mann's homoeroticism

Aschenbach rationalizes his desire for Tadzio by comparing the latter's
physical beauty with his own art. Nature, like the artist, works with
discipline and precision to create perfect form, and the boy's beauty
is the physical counterpart of the spiritual beauty which is the artist's
province. In pursuit of this idea, Aschenbach invokes its Platonic
origins, and in one of its most famous expressions: in the words of
Socrates, as invoked in the novel, 'Beauty is the lover's path to the
spirit – [but] only the path, only a means' (p. 239). Perverse desire is

rationalized into the service of civilization through one of the latter's most influential narratives.

Mann at times inclined towards just such a Platonic rationalization of his own homosexuality.[8] An important letter in 1920 to Carl Maria Weber reveals that he also intended the novel to be a reconciliation of

the difference between the Dionysian spirit of lyricism, whose outpouring is irresponsible and individualistic, and the Apollonian, objectively controlled, morally and socially responsible epic. What I was after was an equilibrium of sensuality and morality such as I found perfected in the *Elective Affinities*, which I read five times, if I remember correctly, while working on *Death in Venice*. (*Letters*, pp. 102–3)

But it is precisely the impossibility of such an equilibrium that the novel discovers. Maybe this is why it is from inside the Platonic/ Apollonian rationalization that the 'truth' of Aschenbach's transgressive desire is suggested; Socrates again, as invoked by Mann: ' "do you believe, dear boy, that the man whose path to the spiritual passes through the senses can ever achieve wisdom and true manly dignity? Or do you think rather (I leave it to you to decide) that this is a path of dangerous charm, very much an errant and sinful path which must of necessity lead us astray?" ' (*Death in Venice*, p. 264).

For sure, in the novel Platonic idealization fails. Illicit desire destroys the idealization invoked to justify it and wrecks the rationalization which would contain it. This is true not only of Aschenbach, but also of the writing of the novel. Which is not to say that Mann is Aschenbach. It might be truer to say that Mann distances and differs himself from Aschenbach because he also identified with him. Mann had trouble finishing the novel. He spoke of being 'tormented' by the work, calling it an 'impossible conception', and on another occasion of being 'terribly strained and worried by it'. Before beginning the novel, he wrote of suffering from fatigue. T. J. Reed, who records these difficulties, also shows how they are related to a change of emphasis in the work. Somewhere in the writing, and under great strain, Mann changes from the Platonic redemption of Aschenbach to the more judgemental ending we have, drawing on Lukács's more pessimistic view of Platonism (Reed, pp. 150–54, 163, 166). In the letter to Weber he indicates why, quoting lines from the prologue to his otherwise unsuccessful poem 'The Lay of the Little Children':

> Amid tears the struggling spirit
> Pressed forward to speak in song. But alas there was no change.
> For a sobering effort began then, a chilling command to control.
> Behold, *the intoxicate song turned into a moral fable* . . .
>
> (*Letters*, p. 103)

Are we to conclude from this that *Death in Venice* also is the intoxicate song turned moral fable? If so, then the moral is as straight-forward as Reed suggests: Aschenbach's disaster stems from his failure to suspect passionate motives in his interest in Tadzio. But Reed overlooks a great deal here, especially when he writes that

Despite the ambiguities which are rooted in the genesis of *Der Tod in Venedig*, at least the direction of development is clear: in what it implies about the Artist, the story constitutes a moral victory which is nothing to do with the morality of homosexual love. (p. 177)

Nothing? Surely not. Reed would see the novel as marking the creation of an ambivalent style, the breakthrough in Mann's long-standing programme to elevate the genre of the novel and to move the novel of ideas beyond allegory; hereafter ambivalence is the central technique of Mann's art: 'Less permanent than the acquisition of this technique was Mann's commitment to critical intellect as the watchdog over human aberration. This had been reaffirmed after a testing experiment' (p. 178). It was never that simple, as the story's difficult genesis and composition make clear – difficulties inseparable from the complex position of homosexuality in Mann's own life, and in modernity more generally. And this complex positioning of homosexuality in turn is the focus for the endless, destructive struggle between, in Freud's terms, desire and civilization, or, in Mann's (via Nietzsche and the Greeks), the Dionysian and the Apollonian.

Explaining in the same letter to Weber his attitude to homosexuality and its part in *Death in Venice*, Mann said that what he originally wanted to deal with was 'not anything homoerotic at all' but 'Passion as confusion and as a stripping of dignity', suggested by the seventy-four-year-old Goethe's infatuation with a seventeen-year-old girl.

However, 'what was added to the amalgam at the time was a personal, lyrical travel experience that determined me to carry things to an extreme by introducing the motif of "forbidden" love . . .' (*Letters*, pp. 103–4). Here, intriguingly, the letter to Weber breaks off. Speculation as to why takes us back to the novel, a 'personal, lyrical travel experience' which Mann also had trouble finishing, in which simply the act of travelling is represented as a kind of deviation: the solitude of the traveller encourages thoughts which are 'wayward, and never without a melancholy tinge', and which give birth to the original, to the beautiful, and to poetry, but also 'to the perverse, the illicit, the absurd' (p. 25).

Resuming the letter – 'I had to put this letter aside for a while' – Mann declares, 'I see nothing unnatural and a good deal of instructive significance, a good deal of high humanity, in the tenderness of mature masculinity for lovelier and frailer masculinity.' He respects this mode of feeling because it is 'almost necessarily infused with mind' – a point reiterated later: 'in spite of its sensuality [it] has very little to do with nature, far more to do with mind'. How simultaneously confident and implausible was this attitude can be glimpsed in a 1934 diary entry where Mann reflects upon, and rationalizes, homoerotic attraction as aesthetic only – that is, requiring 'no fulfilment'. That day he has been 'pleasurably smitten by the sight of a young fellow working . . . very handsome, and bare to the waist':

The rapture I felt at the sight of such common, everyday, and natural 'beauty', the contours of his chest, the swell of his biceps, made me reflect afterward on the unreal, illusionary and aesthetic nature of such an inclination, the goal of which, it would appear, is realized in gazing and 'admiring'. Although erotic, it requires no fulfilment at all, neither intellectually nor physically. This is likely thanks to the influence of the reality principle on the imagination; it allows the rapture, but limits it to just looking. (*Diaries*, p. 207)

Although diary entries indicate a strong homoerotic appreciation of male beauty and acknowledgement of homoerotic desire (e.g. pp. 118, 119, 207), the full extent of Mann's homosexuality has only recently been documented.[9] Some days after writing the letter to Weber, Mann notes in his diary a 'stimulation failure' in relation to his wife, which he attributes to 'the customary confusion and unreliability of my "sex-life" ' and accounts for 'by the presence of desires that are directed the other way. How would it be if a young man were "at my disposal"?' (p. 101). In contrast to such entries, the letter to Weber endorses a sublimated homoeroticism, referring appreciatively to Hans Blüher's *The Role of the Erotic in Male Communities* (1917). In this and another book influential in the formation of the German youth movement (*The German Youth Movement as an Erotic Phenomenon*, 1912) Blüher argued that it was the homosexual who created communities and held them together through male bonding which was libidinally invested – but, crucially, in a sublimated form, and hence spiritual rather than physical. Mann describes Blüher's ideas as 'greatly and profoundly Germanic' (*Letters*, p. 103).[10] The important point for Mann is that this idealized, intellectualized, homoerotic love is not allied to 'effeminacy'. It is further distinguished from what he calls its 'repulsively pathological' forms, as in degeneracy and hermaphroditism. In short, while Mann repudiated the idea of homoeroticism as unnatural, and refused to denounce it, his public defence of it was as sublimated desire – a mixture of Greek idealism, Freudian sublimation and contemporary German advocacy of what is now called male or 'homosocial' bonding. *Death in Venice* is partly about how all these sublimations, along with the 'bourgeois compromise' that sanctions them, are wrecked by that which they would contain.

In the same letter to Weber, Mann also refers to his (Mann's) *Betrachtungen* (*Reflections of a Nonpolitical Man*) as a covert expression of his own homoeroticism. This is far more than a question of sexual preference: covert homoeroticism is here being advanced as the mainspring of Mann's aesthetic and political philosophy. In the last and one of the most interesting chapters in the book, 'Irony and Radicalism', Mann expresses again his preoccupation with the 'extremely delicate, difficult, exciting and painful' tension between 'life' and 'intellect' – one 'charged with irony and eroticism' (*Letters*, p. 105; cf. *Reflections*, p. 419). It is also a relationship marked by yearning, not only of intellect for life, but vice versa, and by a kind of bisexuality which passes back and forth between mind and life '*without clarification of the sexual polarity*' (*Letters*, p. 105; Mann's emphasis). For Mann, the intellectual must be 'either an ironist or a radical; a third choice is not decently possible'. Perhaps there is not even a choice between these two, since the love which intellect has for life is anyway profoundly ironic:

Intellect that loves is not fanatic, it is ingenious, it is political, it woos, and its wooing is erotic irony. One has a political term for this: it is 'conservatism'. What is conservatism? The erotic irony of the intellect. (*Reflections*, pp. 419–20)

That the love Mann has in mind here is homoerotic is apparent from his reference to Friedrich Hölderlin's poem 'Socrates and Alcibiades', which he regards as one of the world's most beautiful love poems, and as encapsulating his own philosophy as just outlined:

'Holy Socrates, why always with deference
   Do you treat this young man? Don't you know greater things?
      Why so lovingly, raptly,
         As on gods, do you gaze on him?'

Who the deepest has thought loves what is most alive,
   Wide experience may well turn to what's best in youth,
      And the wise in the end will
         Often bow to the beautiful.
                              (Hölderlin, *Poems and Fragments*, p. 67)

Behind all the reticence and talk of irony, Mann speculates about founding an aesthetic philosophy from the intense apprehension of, a yearning for, male beauty: 'Who the deepest has thought loves what is most alive.' And yet there remains a kind of impossibility in the yearning of intellect for life. First because the yearning is essentially 'covert', marked by a 'sly longing'. Indeed, says Mann, it is this ' "covert" yearning which perhaps constitutes the truly philosophical and poetical relationship of mind to life' (*Letters*, p. 105).[11] Then there is what Mann calls '*the problem of beauty*', namely that intellect and life each perceive beauty to reside in the other; somehow this means that between life and intellect there can be no union, 'only the short intoxicating illusion of union and understanding, eternal tension without resolution' (*Reflections*, p. 420). Aschenbach in *Death in Venice* dies because he cannot maintain that 'eternal tension'. As we shall see, he also dies in the wake of a powerful mythology connecting desire with psychic and social death.

Twelve years after *Reflections*, Mann published an even more revealing essay, on the homosexual German writer August von Platen (1796–1835), a figure alluded to in *Death in Venice*. Again we see how profoundly the experience of male beauty was influencing not just the themes Mann chose to write about, but his entire aesthetic. Aspects of Aschenbach derive from Platen's life; the latter fled Italy to escape a cholera epidemic, but later died of the disease anyway. He wrote seventeen sonnets about Venice, a city which attracted him deeply though disturbingly.[12] The extent to which Aschenbach derives from Platen can be seen from Mann's remark about the latter's death: 'After a further nine years' stress of emotions and their suppression, he died at Syracuse of a vague typhus attack which was nothing but a pretext for the death to which obviously he was devoted from the first' (*Essays*, p. 269). Mann identified Aschenbach with Platen, and personally identified with both. Which is why his essay about Platen is both reverential and critical, in places callous: as with Aschenbach, Mann needed to distance himself from, as well as express himself through, the writer. Some would call this 'irony'; perhaps it is also nothing less than a strategy of survival.

Mann is especially appreciative of Platen's poem 'Tristan', which affirms the intimate connection between desire and death:

> The man who has once fed his eyes on beauty
> Moves by that very act into death's keeping
>
> .   .   .   .
>
> God! he must sicken like the failing wellspring,
> Wants to suck poison from each breeze, putrid
> Decay from every flower he loves smelling . . .
>
> (ll. 1–2, 11–13)

Beauty evokes a longing, a yearning that cannot be satisfied; for him who has perceived exquisite male beauty 'The ache of love with him is everlasting' (l. 6). Mann commends the poem for its '*endless* psychological riches' (p. 262; my emphasis). Platen was afflicted with 'melancholy, adoring love . . . endless, unquenchable love which issues in death, which *is* death, because it finds no satisfaction on earth'

(p. 261). Mann rightly observes that the fatal connection here is more between *beauty* and death than between *love* and death – 'the arrow of beauty is the arrow of death and eternal pain of yearning' (p. 261). One of Adrian Leverkühn's greatest works is called *Apocalypse*, and it expresses an 'inaccessibly unearthly and alien beauty of sound, filling the heart with longing without hope' (*Dr Faustus*, p. 364). This surely is one of romanticism's most persistent themes: the intense apprehension of beauty whose precondition seems to be suffering, failure, tragedy and death.

And for Platen that love of beauty was gloriously abject; his ideal was, says Mann, 'a naked idol of perfection with a Greek-Oriental eye-formation, before whom he knelt in abasement and agonizing longing'. In the fantasy of fellatio alluded to here there is much emotional complexity – and maybe, for Mann, hints of a certain fascistic adoration which has its roots in self-loathing: before this heavenly image of male beauty, imagines Mann, Platen's own pathetic, hypochondriac self 'dissolved in shame' (p. 263). And then the hint of contempt and again of fellatio: in practice as distinct from fantasy, and again with strains of Aschenbach, Platen 'made sensible moan over the . . . upstandingness [*Nichts-als-Gerade-gewachsenheit*] of a quite ordinary and average youth or two' (p. 265).

This homoerotic worship of male beauty is deeply a question of intellect. That is why it led Platen into 'a radical anti-morality, a deep bond with the beautiful, even contrary to the interests of nature' and an aestheticism which involved the most conscious formal structure, 'a most deathlike rigidity' which teaches that the principle of beauty and form does not spring from life; indeed its only relation to life 'is at most one of stern and melancholy critique: it is the relation of mind to life'. And the more this kind of aestheticism lifts itself out of the sensual, 'the more masculine it becomes'. For Platen, unrequited desire became self-destructive; anger and struggle did not exalt him but dragged him down – 'they were dammed up, they kept stagnating in psychological embitterment, turning into a hatred of mankind, in which, with perfect clarity, he recognized the forerunner of death' (pp. 261, 267–8). So death is latent both in the aspiration of the sensibility and in the consequence of its being thwarted.

The smile which wrecks Aschenbach is, we're told, a speaking, winning, captivating smile; the smile of Narcissus: curious, faintly uneasy, and bewitching. After receiving it, Aschenbach literally collapses before rushing into the dark night, all composure lost. The lifting of repression can only be whispered as a hackneyed phrase – simply, 'I love you.' (Aren't we always least original when in love?) Yet this cliché, this radical *un*originality, marks Aschenbach as momentarily more alive than at any other time in his life:

And leaning back, his arms hanging down, overwhelmed, trembling, shuddering all over, he whispered the standing formulae of the heart's desire – impossible here, absurd, depraved, ludicrous and sacred nevertheless, still worthy of honour even here: 'I love you!' (p. 244)

It's as if de-repressed desire meets with, and momentarily animates, the ego before shattering it.

From this point on homoerotic desire becomes the focus and the medium for yet more, now linking together disease, death and the decadent city. Decadence was always there; Tadzio radiates a beauty which is said to be noble, and austere, yet almost immediately he is observed to have unhealthy teeth, a sign of the anaemic, the delicate and the sickly. Aschenbach reflects that the boy will not live to grow old, but 'made no attempt to explain to himself a certain feeling of satisfaction or relief that accompanied this thought' (pp. 227–8). This is not exactly the heroic, romantic or tragic refusal of age and failure through early death; more the decadent and perhaps vengeful pleasure of realizing that the object of his desire will succumb to an inherent degeneracy.

Homoerotic desire also mediates between the primeval past and the decadent present. The 'progressive' city, just as much as 'timeless' nature, bears the traces of the primeval. Before arriving in Venice – a city built on swamps – Aschenbach imagines 'a landscape, a tropical swampland under a cloud-swollen sky, moist and lush and monstrous, a kind of primeval wilderness' (p. 199). A primeval past is archaeologically just beneath as well as geographically just beyond the degenerate present.[13] Now, this city's own 'guilty secret . . . merged with his own innermost secret', and, just as desire has fatally re-energized Aschenbach, so the 'pestilence had undergone a renewal of its energy, as if the tenacity and fertility of its pathogens had redoubled'. Forbidden desire, like disease, is at first latent, then spreads, then erupts:

Asiatic cholera had been showing an increased tendency to spread and migrate. Originating in the sultry morasses of the Ganges delta, rising with the mephitic exhalations of that wilderness of rank useless luxuriance, that primitive island jungle shunned by man . . . the pestilence had raged. (pp. 246, 256–7)

Disease here works as a metaphor for the resurgence of the primeval in and through the decadent, and homosexual desire is its trigger. It culminates in a 'terrible dream', an orgy of lust in which

the scene of the events was his own soul, and they irrupted into it from the outside, violently defeating his resistance – a profound intellectual resistance – as they passed through him, and leaving his whole being, the culture of a lifetime, devastated and destroyed. (p. 259)

Fear is mixed with desire and (fine touch) 'a horrified curiosity'. The desire is to some extent passive: what is in prospect is a 'shameless . . . uttermost surrender' in which Aschenbach fantasizes fearfully about being annihilated or being fucked senseless, unsure of the difference. The sequence of the dream follows a process of violent desublimation: from fear and resistance through beguilement to naked desire – 'a blindness, a dizzying lust' and a craving with all his soul to join the dance paying homage to the 'obscene symbol, wooden and gigantic' of the godhead. In this 'orgy of limitless coupling . . . his very soul savoured the delirium of annihilation' (p. 260). Aschenbach awakens and, now shameless, follows Tadzio through the Venetian streets, feeling as though the moral law has fallen in ruins and only the monstrous and perverse hold out a hope (p. 261). If the death drive delivers oceanic dissolution, desublimated eros drives towards Dionysiac self-destruction in a way, and to an extent, which binds together eros and thanatos more closely even than Freud imagined.

To be wrecked by a winning smile – from such moments as these can be told the truth, pleasure, arrogance, vulnerability and pathos of love, and the ways in which it is inflected by masochism. But not by Mann; not quite. To have allowed Aschenbach to go this far was necessarily also to regard him, or at least his desire, as unredeemable.

Hence the emergence of that other representation of homosexual desire: the Freudian narrative of desublimated perversion unites with the pathological narrative of the degenerate, the decadent and the primitive; together they shatter the Platonic rationalization which had precariously held that desire in place. Recall that the homoeroticism which Mann wanted to defend had to be distinguished from its 'repulsively pathological' forms. He was, he says, compelled to see Aschenbach '*also* in a pathological light', with the consequence that 'in *Death in Venice* the highest is drawn down into the realm of decadence' (*Letters*, pp. 103, 105).

On desire as the ruin of identity, the shattering of self, *Death in Venice* is insightful, occasionally sublime. Fortunately, if unsurprisingly, its success in this respect wrecked Mann's rather banal original aim of affirming an equilibrium between sensuality and morality. But this made it the more urgent to try to discriminate 'civilized' homoeroticism from its degenerate and decadent forms. Aschenbach deviates from the one to the other, and so succumbs to decadence, disease and death.[14] Aschenbach's 'devolution' is similar to that of Kurtz in Conrad's *Heart of Darkness*, and it too reflects the influence of degeneration theory. But still the novel speaks this other truth of perversion: the challenge is not so much of homosexuality *per se*, the definitive sexual perversion in the discourses of sexology and psychoanalysis, but of the perverse dynamic working in and through homosexuality. *Death in Venice* anticipates what Guy Hocquenghem said some sixty years later in a different context: 'homosexual desire is neither on the side of death nor on the side of life; it is the killer of civilized egos' (p. 136). The return of the perverse wrecks its former disavowal to an extent made possible by the fact that the perverse is now deeply sexual and its disavowal is an organizing repression of an identity, an aesthetic and, increasingly, an entire culture.

That is what the novel explores. So do Mann's *Diaries*, and in ways which still apparently require censorship more than seventy years later. That is because yet again the perverse emerges in just the place it might least be expected – both conventionally and according to Mann himself – that is, inside the bourgeois family. Mann confessed himself divided between 'bourgeois' family life and something else – 'associations of men . . . eroticism, unbourgeois intellectually sensuous adventures' (*Letters*, p. 105). Recall that Aschenbach reflects that passion is like crime, welcoming every challenge to the bourgeois structure because finding in the ensuing chaos circumstances it can turn to its own advantage (*Death in Venice*, p. 246).

Days after outlining his thoughts on homoeroticism in the letter to Weber, Mann records an experience similar to Aschenbach's, only now incestuous as well as homoerotic; it occurs in relation to his son, aged fourteen – the age of Tadzio in the novel:

Am enraptured with Eissi, terribly handsome in his swimming trunks. Find it quite natural that I should fall in love with my son . . . I came back Friday evening on the very fast new train . . . short conversation with the attractive young man in white trousers sitting next to me in third class. Very pleasurable. It seems I am once and for all done with women? . . . Eissi was lying tanned and shirtless on his bed, reading; I was disconcerted. (Sunday July 25 1920)

Then, three months later, seeing his son naked:

Deeply struck by his radiant adolescent body; overwhelming. – [. . .] (*Diaries*, pp. 101, 103)

(The bracketed ellipsis at the end of this quotation indicates a passage censored in the German edition of the *Diaries* on the grounds that it was too private.)

Mann had told Weber that he had felt compelled to write *Death in Venice* from a perspective described as

the altogether non-'Greek' but rather Protestant, Puritan ('bourgeois') basic state of mind not only of the story's protagonists but also of myself; in other words our fundamentally mistrustful, fundamentally pessimistic relationship to passion in general. (*Letters*, p. 103)

Prejudice against the puritan and the bourgeois should not lead us to underestimate the scope of the pessimism invoked here; Mann is speaking of nothing less than the pessimism of the Western tradition itself. In this novel homosexuality inherits the burden of a tradition already embedded in the culture, and immeasurably strengthened in the relatively recent mythologies of romanticism, degeneration theory and psychoanalysis (the last of which Mann partly anticipates), all of which (albeit in incommensurately different ways) find death inside desire. Thus the cholera-ridden Aschenbach, moments before his death, watching Tadzio walk out to sea, sees him seemingly beckoning him into 'the nebulous vastness . . . an immensity rich with unutterable expectation' (p. 267).

It may also be that homoeroticism inherits, via a displacement, the cultural burden of incest: in the diary entries just cited, and others, including one written the day after the letter on homosexuality to Weber, Mann speaks of his erotic attraction towards his son in the context of reflections on his own homosexuality, apparently regarding the first as an aspect of the second. By 'cultural burden' is meant more than individual guilt, which Mann never seemed much susceptible to anyway; it refers to the much longer and more inclusive process I have been describing whereby homosexuality becomes the symbolic focus for cultural preoccupations which far exceed it and yet which are now inextricably involved with it. Perhaps too homosexuality inherits the burden of paedophilia: the story of *Death in Venice* was based closely on an actual trip to Venice in which Mann developed an infatuation with a Polish boy who was later identified as Wladyslaw, subsequently Baron, Moes. At the time, this real-life counterpart of Tadzio was not fourteen but ten.[15]

20

Promiscuity and
Death

At the outset of the AIDS crisis, in the early 1980s, the tabloid press angrily denounced, even as it recorded in salacious detail, the numbers of sexual partners gay men were alleged to have in a day, a month or a year. Orgiastic sexual freedom had become the way of death, and if Christians who believed AIDS to be the wages of sin were a vocal but relatively insignificant minority, those who regarded AIDS as somehow the inevitable if not appropriate fate for sexual deviants were less vocal but more numerous. The gay bathhouses became the focus of intense hostility. Whereas a decade earlier gay writers like Guy Hocquenghem could celebrate them as the scene of a 'primary sexual communism' (p. 97), now, in the popular imagination (and this included the imagination of some gay people), they figured as places of contagion and danger, where the sexually obsessed deviant became at once suicidal and murderous. Which leads back to this book's point of departure: Hugo, the character from Oscar Moore's *A Matter of Life and Sex*, in the Parisian bathhouses; the philosopher Michel Foucault in the Californian ones.

This association of homosexual promiscuity and death had been made before, and by some gay people themselves. James Baldwin writes vividly of the New York homosexual underworld which he knew in his teens:

Sometimes, eventually, inevitably, I would find myself in bed with one of these men, a despairing and dreadful conjunction, since their need was as relentless as quicksand and as impersonal, and sexual rumour concerning blacks had preceded me. As for sexual roles, these were created by the imagination and limited only by one's stamina.

At bottom what I had learned was that the male desire for a male roams everywhere, avid, desperate, unimaginably lonely, culminating often in drugs, piety, madness or death. It was also dreadfully like watching myself at the end of a long, slow-moving line: soon I would be next. All of this was very frightening. It was lonely, and impersonal and demeaning. I could not believe – after all, I was only nineteen – that I could have been driven to the lonesome place where these men and I met each other so soon, to stay. ('Here be Dragons', p. 683)[1]

Before AIDS, homosexual promiscuity was often regarded as epitomizing an impossibility of desire unique to the homosexual by virtue of his or her supposed immaturity and inauthenticity. Hocquenghem, writing in 1972, had remarked the tendency to think of homosexual promiscuity as indicative of 'the fundamental instability of the homosexual condition, the search for a dream partner through a series of brief, unsatisfactory affairs' (pp. 117–18).[2] In the context of AIDS, there were some for whom this specifically gay version of desire's impossibility became intensified into a kind of death-driven futility. Rupert Haselden, self-identified as gay, writing in 1991[3] in the British left/liberal newspaper *The Guardian*, asks why the London cruise bars are filling up again, despite AIDS. He concludes:

There is an inbuilt fatalism to being gay. Biologically maladaptive, unable to reproduce, our futures are limited to individual existence and what the individual makes of it. Without the continuity of children we are self-destructive, living for today because we have no tomorrow.

So, continues Haselden, gay men try to escape from a hostile world by becoming promiscuous. At the same time they exemplify a general futility of existence, reminding others of their own mortality. As regards AIDS, which 'dangles like a flashing neon sign in the bars and clubs', fear has given way to acceptance: 'we are coming to see it as our fate'; AIDS has become an excuse for a fatalistic attitude to life, intensified by the thrill of 'dicing with death, of tempting fate'. And, according to this same writer, the same thing is happening all round the world in the dangerously promiscuous scenarios of gay culture.[4]

Here be dragons

Almost as important as the promiscuous activity itself is its location: Haselden's article was accompanied by a graphic black-and-white shot of a gay bar 'packed with men ... pushing gently past one another in a tide of desire' (p. 14). In fiction especially the gay underworld has often been a place of both death and redemption. The title of the essay from which the Baldwin passage above is cited, 'Here be Dragons', invokes those ancient map markings signifying the dangerous, unknown, mythically remote terrains, extensive and uncharted, which were fearful and fascinating, terrifying and seductive, precisely because they were so far beyond our own horizons. Such places echo in the mythology of the modern city underworld – residually wild, but above all shadowy and transient, full of some magic and rather more loss.

Epitomizing that world is the basement club. Sometimes such clubs are exclusive: more often they are accessible to all who meet the dress code and have the entrance fee; even so, they remain places of adventure – especially for the alienated modern writer out to recapture the thrill of descending into the dark night of the soul's darker desires, just as did Baldwin years ago. He, after all, became a fine novelist more because than in spite of his alienating experience in that underworld. His 1957 novel *Giovanni's Room* describes a tragic homosexual relationship between David and Giovanni which leads to Giovanni's execution for murder. At the end of the novel, David, the survivor, stares at himself, naked, in a mirror:

I look at my sex, my troubling sex, and wonder how it can be redeemed, how I can save it from the knife. The journey to the grave is already begun, the journey to corruption is always, already, half over. Yet the key to my salvation, which cannot save my body, is hidden in my flesh. I must believe that the heavy grace of God, which has brought me to this place, is all that can carry me out of it. (pp. 126–7)

In gay fiction from Radclyffe Hall onwards we encounter the gay underworld as a place where the hero or heroine suffers into truth, and, by dissociating himself or herself from the tormented inhabitants of that place, writes of its tragedy. These heroes and heroines are romantic, fallen figures who suffer, and maybe redeem, or at least atone for, that alienation which they find at the heart of deviant desire. So charged are such scenes they could almost be regarded as a convention of some gay writing – by which I mean not a formalist disregard of reality, but rather a representation of distress, of lack and longing, which makes sense of it by recourse to art, and in ways which elicit understanding and even identification, without having to be trusted. Whatever, such scenes have been one way of trying to struggle free from, of redeeming, the apparent mutual implication of death and desire. Another way was revolution.

Revolution and redemption

Briefly in the 1970s the promiscuous homosexual encounter became the inspiration for revolutionary aspirations, the new spearhead of an already existing sexual radicalism:

Promiscuous homosexuals (outlaws with dual identities . . .) are the shock troops of the sexual revolution. The streets are the battleground, the revolution is the sexhunt, [and] a radical statement is made each time a man has sex with another on a street . . .

This radicalism promised life, or orgasm, instead of death:

Cum instead of blood. Satisfied bodies instead of dead ones. Death versus orgasm. Would they bust everyone? With cum-smeared tanks would they crush all? (Rechy, p. 301)

But, even as John Rechy was writing this, the wild space of the promiscuous encounter was narrowing even further (from underworld to bar to bathhouse), with the sexual practices becoming more transgressive (sado-masochism and fist-fucking) but rather harder to represent as revolutionary; the wilderness of a once vaguely defined illicit sexuality became in a sense even wilder, yet now *precisely* defined and ritualized.

Not inappropriately, Michel Foucault once called the bathhouses laboratories of sexual experimentation. It is this urban confinement of homosexual transgression that is most striking in postwar gay culture. Where once the romantic homosexual exile wandered abroad, sometimes literally across seas and continents, in search of the liberation of the foreign and the exotic, now he tends to haunt the claustrophobic spaces of the bathhouse. Yet even there we hear echoes of those earlier times. After an unsuccessful sexual encounter, the narrator of Michael Rumaker's *A Day and a Night at the Baths*, laments, 'I have always felt myself a person in exile, anonymous in the cities, inconspicuous in the windowless cubicles of baths such as this; banned from the rural places . . .' (p. 27).

In Rumaker's text, contemporary with Rechy's *The Sexual Outlaw* (1977), sexual revolution is already only an ironic half-hope, half-joke: 'If this secret gets out, it'll revolutionize the world,' whispers a boy whom the narrator has just blown (p. 32). Rumaker affirms a view of promiscuous, deviant sex as now benignly redemptive rather than tragically redemptive (Baldwin) or violently revolutionary (Rechy). His narrator is cautious, domesticated and very much on the side of ordinary life, taking with him to the baths not drugs but a packed lunch of health food. While there, he's careful to stub out his cigarettes in the right places to avoid fire hazard, regrets having forgotten his skin moisturizer, and is careful about hygiene.

If revolution is unrealistic, Rumaker is nevertheless optimistic about the democracy of the bathhouse. Here 'without estrangements of class or money or position, or false distinctions of any kind . . . was the possibility to be nourished and enlivened in the blood-heat and heartbeat of others, regardless of who or what we were. Nurturing others we nurture ourselves' (p. 17). Having had sex with an old man, he says afterwards, 'Gay father . . . thank you' (p. 63). Good sex brings 'a surge of renewed aliveness I hadn't known since childhood' with a man who, departing, says, 'I'll see you at the next Gay Pride March' (p. 55, cf. p. 17). From such experiences the narrator envisions, albeit briefly, a Utopian world where sex is free and benign and healing; in great green parks people will engage in 'mutually consenting and courteous erotic play'. The narrator even imagines that every home town in America will one day have a free public bath in which purified mothers and other women teach the girl-children and purified fathers and other men teach the boy-children, in gentle massage, in merry bubble-winking strokes of beginning awareness . . . in encouraging right and clean and courteous ways . . . and then none can ever be unkind to another. (p. 47)

Then gay children will live again, the mental hospitals will empty, and the prison population will be depleted (p. 47).

When the narrator gets fucked in group sex, gender division is effortlessly transcended: 'Now I am a woman, and now I am a man, there's no confusion. The falseselves slide away in my nakedness.' Still being fucked, he is possessed by revelation, as in the mystery rites, 'subsumed in the will and drive of eros . . . taken down and down into the nameless, faceless, anonymous dark of the flesh . . . To know it is all *a beauty of beginning, of the sane and healthy lust that makes us all* . . .' Here, ecstasy is a 'revelation . . . that will keep me sane and whole' (pp. 71–2; my emphasis). Ecstasy becomes the truth of self and of history and of time: 'Let this be my history now to know what has always been' (p. 72).

This allegorical appropriation of primitive sexual ritual provides a significant contrast with that in Thomas Mann's *Death in Venice*, explored in the previous chapter. For Rumaker the connection with a primitive past is all about a therapeutic recovering of a lost wholeness, of being freed from the 'falseselves' of sexual difference, of being put back in touch with the 'sane and healthy lust that makes us all'. For Mann's Aschenbach it's just the opposite; as we saw, the primitive sexual ritual of which he dreams does indeed hold out the possibility of a liberation of the self, but one inseparable from an anarchic annihilation of the self: 'his very soul savoured the lascivious delirium of annihilation'. As with Bataille, the dissolution being dreamed is profoundly spiritual yet also physical; in this, Mann is true to his Greek sources. Aschenbach dreams his own death with an ambivalent mixture of fear, desire, joy and curiosity, in a ritual which is anarchic, violent, bestial and stinks of 'wounds, uncleanness, and disease'. The 'uttermost surrender' that Aschenbach desires when drawn irresistibly to 'the obscene symbol' of the godhead, 'wooden and gigantic', is a masochistic, penetrative ecstasy whose climax is death (pp. 259–61). Little room here, then, for Rumaker's packed lunches and safety-first.[5]

Mann subscribes to a view of sexual desire, especially deviant sexual desire, as offering the prospect of a sexual ecstasy with the potential to wreck the self and even challenge the existing social order. This is a conception of desire which exists residually in Rumaker's text, but which is now overwritten by the historically much more recent view of desire as intrinsically benign, wholesome and redemptive. In Rumaker's world, gay people have arrived at maturity when they feel 'comfortable' with their sexuality. Although he doesn't single out Rumaker's text, it expresses exactly the kind of normalizing, pastoralizing and redemptive version of homosexuality that Leo Bersani criticizes so cogently in a famous article called 'Is the Rectum a Grave?' He is against this vision, first, because it is 'unnecessarily and even dangerously tame'; second, because it is disingenuous about the revulsion which homosexual behaviour inspires, and, third, because it wants to dilute the menace which homosexuality holds for a homophobic society:

The revulsion it turns out is all a big mistake: what we're really up to is pluralism and diversity, and getting buggered is just one moment in the practice of those laudable humanistic virtues. (pp. 218–19)

Reading Rumaker, one wonders how anyone could ever imagine that sexual desire could ever be thought to redeem so much while at the same time occluding even more; in other words, how can desire be so completely and unrealistically colonized by the language of saneness, health, wholeness and optimism? If Rumaker's exiles, prowling 'the litter and stink of this hidden-away bathhouse', are seeking 'the miracle of a barely imagined paradise . . . a tiny glint of the shy and elusive flower that enfolds the secret and the meaning' (p. 46), they are searching for nothing less than the meaning of existence and the redemption of self and the world. Can sex, even deviant sex, carry such a religious responsibility? When it fails to deliver, as it must, then the quest for redemption, just like the religiosity from which it borrows so heavily, so often becomes death-haunted. Such, in fact, is the case with Rumaker's text.

Actually it begins with death: on his way to the baths, the narrator encounters the aftermath of a suicide who had jumped from the Empire State Building. 'Intimate with suicide among us', he wonders if the victim was gay, and so tormented by 'traditional ignorance . . . the hostility around him, and, finally, his own' that he had flung himself 'with unutterable relief' from the eighty-fifth floor (p. 2). A little later we encounter the desperate and pathetic desire of those close to death (pp. 19–20), and the aggressive behaviour of those who remind him of the sexually brutal men he had searched out in the past, 'unconsciously seeking my own internalized need for punishment and death' (p. 59). Then there is the youth, aged maybe fifteen or sixteen, who is already old and trapped for the rest of his days in one of these bathhouse cubicles,

his desire gone meaningless, only the spasms of habit remaining, returning him again and again to this spot; someone damned to haunt these hallways forever, even long after the building collapsed in decay and dust or burned . . . the aborted and beaten spirit of him prowling always. (p. 27)

Such desperation – the old impossibility of desire – is concealed by a flat expression or bored, indifferent eyes (p. 39).

Of course, all this misery can be attributed to social oppression – which is to say that, in the better society which it is in our power to achieve, it will disappear. And, for the narrator, even as we are waiting for that social transformation to occur, the negative sexual scenario can resolve itself into a benignly redemptive one, just as in the midst of clap and syphilis there are always penicillin, free VD examinations, and the Gay Men's Health Project in Greenwich Village (p. 28). Even so, and despite the fact that Rumaker is writing pre-AIDS, there is, throughout his text, a fear of ineradicable disease, and a persistent connection of desire with such disease. This connection is literal, but also works as a metaphor for the helpless self-destructiveness of desire: the narrator imagines a beautiful arse to be 'rampant with hepatitis, the penises that flamed with passion flaming with spirochetes as well'; he also imagines sailors carrying all manner of disease from all parts of the globe to this one place – 'carrying here centuries-old infections of the fathers'. And the 'gay sons' driven by desire to risk these infection, 'driven to this contagious harbor again and again', there being 'no ports free of the contaminating fathers' (p. 28).

So, as the narrator explores this misery, there is the sense that redemption might not be so easy after all. He remarks, poignantly, the 'love-scrawls of KY-sticky fingers' on the cubicle walls, 'graffiti tracks of passion' evoking 'the cries and breaths and urgencies of all who had ever come in secret yearning to this cubicle' (p. 23). On the one hand, those scrawls are the definitive traces of urban transience and anonymity, inside of which the most memorable of all experiences may occur; on the other, they document the endlessly repeated sexual encounter in which nothing changes, least of all the loneliness of desire – a loneliness invulnerable even to redemptive sex: 'So many of us frightened here . . . *so many faces that passed me with the look of urgent and perilous need that seemed to have nothing to do with sex*' (p. 45; my emphasis).

Rumaker's vision of desire as benign remains haunted by death because his vision of homosexual desire in both its alienated and its redeemed forms is through and through religious. Likewise with Rechy. It is not surprising to find this advocate of the revolutionary fuck telling an interviewer, 'after a night of hustling and dark cruising alleys, I think of suicide'. To another interviewer – there is a strong confessional need here too – he says, 'Finally, that's the only freedom you have . . . the freedom to die' (pp. 71, 48). For Rechy, for most of the time, the alienation which precipitated such suicidal lows can mainly be laid at the door of social oppression. But his entire aesthetic/theological take on sexual deviance remains rooted in an older view as expressed by Baldwin, above: 'the male desire for a male roams everywhere, avid, desperate, unimaginably lonely, culminating often in drugs, piety, madness or death'. Likewise with Hugo in Moore's *A Matter of Life and Sex*. What emerges is the sense of desire as somehow impossible; he is 'helpless. Pinioned by lust' (p. 255), yet unable to achieve ecstasy. His sexual life 'was a future whose past was always more exciting . . . a future with loneliness sewn into the seam and death woven into the fabric, unseen until too late, a single sinister thread' (p. 144). Sometimes he strains 'for the relief of an orgasm which, when it came, was only a spasm without the shudder, an anti-climax that offered no feeling of relief. Just a small grey wave of depression' (p. 39).

Hugo's sexual compulsiveness suggests an inner futility to desire obscurely linked to a sense of loss which eventually binds death into desire. Meanwhile, for Rupert Haselden homosexuality is intrinsically

self-destructive, death-desiring *and* death-dealing – qualities epitomized in its allegedly compulsive promiscuity; indeed, qualities that for
him are almost synonymous with promiscuity and his belief that
homosexuals are 'biologically maladaptive, unable to reproduce'.

It might just be arguable that all, rather than just some, of the
foregoing gay writers remain preoccupied with death because of an
internalized homophobia. If Haselden is the most vulnerable to that
charge, it is especially significant that Oscar Moore, the least vulnerable
to it, said shortly before he died from AIDS that in the voices of those
gays who attacked Haselden for saying what he did he detected an
anger 'tinny with self-justification and unease' ('Rites of Fatality',
p. 19). In recent years, Leo Bersani, one of the most innovative gay
intellectuals, has confronted this unease head-on.

Ecstasy and self-annihilation

Bersani considers that phallocentrism is not primarily the denial of
power to women but rather the denial of the value of powerlessness
in both men and women. By 'powerlessness' he means not gentleness,
non-aggressiveness, or even passivity, but rather the positive potential
for a 'radical disintegration and humiliation of the self' (p. 217). This
is masochism in the sense of a sexual pleasure that crosses a threshold,
and which shatters psychic organization; in which 'the self is exuber-
antly discarded' and there occurs 'the terrifying appeal of a loss of
the ego, of a self-abasement' (pp. 218, 220). A kind of death.

This means that the problematic aspects of sexuality cannot be seen
to derive simply from bad social relations. On the contrary, 'the social
structures from which it is often said that the eroticizing of mastery
and subordination derive are perhaps themselves derivations (and
sublimations) of the indissociable nature of sexual pleasure and the
exercise or loss of power' (p. 216). The terrifying appeal of a loss of
the ego is, he continues, why men who engage in 'passive' anal sex
are demonized. He points to the anthropological evidence which
suggests a widespread condemnation of such sex even in cultures that
have not regarded sex between men as unnatural or sinful. Even or
especially for the Athenians, to be penetrated was to abdicate power.

Bersani concludes, in what has become a controversial passage, 'if the rectum is the grave in which the masculine ideal (an ideal shared – differently – by men *and* women) of proud subjectivity is buried, then it should be celebrated for its very potential for death'. He adds, in a passage less frequently cited:

Tragically, AIDS has literalized that potential as the certainty of biological death, and has therefore reinforced the heterosexual association of anal sex with a self-annihilation originally and primarily identified with the fantasmatic mystery of an insatiable, unstoppable female sexuality. It may, finally, be in the gay man's rectum that he demolishes his own perhaps otherwise uncontrollable identification with a murderous judgment against him. (p. 222)

Bersani also wonders whether we should say, not that so-called passive sex is 'demeaning', but rather that *'the value of sexuality itself is to demean the seriousness of efforts to redeem it'* (p. 222). In that sense homoerotic desire especially might produce or enact that which society cannot endure, and it does this because, rather than in spite of, its own intricate connections with its own social condemnation. In short, the homoerotically perverse encounter of the death/desire dynamic produces a knowledge of desire unavailable elsewhere.

More generally, the challenge of desire lies in its potential for acting out an awkward, provocative, ambivalent version of what otherwise remains culturally and psychically disavowed. An interesting instance of this is Bersani's description of (some) gay men's relationship to masculinity. Against the 'easy' political line that gay machismo is straightforwardly a parodic subversion of masculinity, Bersani contends that it includes a worshipful tribute to, a *'yearning* toward' the straight machismo style and behaviour it defiles. And if, in Jeffrey Weeks's phrase, quoted by Bersani, gay men 'gnaw at the roots of a male heterosexual identity' this is because, 'from within their nearly mad identification with it, *they never cease to feel the appeal of its being violated'* (p. 209).

Instead of a straightforward identity politics which resists oppression in the name of what we truly and healthily are or could be, given the social space to breathe, is this other scenario wherein identity is conflicted by desire, fantasy and ambivalent identification; potentially (and strangely) identity is even annihilated in the process of being affirmed. And nowhere more so than in getting fucked, when, says Bersani, there occurs the terrifying appeal of a loss of the ego, of a self-abasement. Perhaps Foucault, in his famous essay 'Preface to Transgression', was saying something similar, though in relation to transgression more generally. In transgression of the limit, he says, the limit is suddenly 'fulfilled by this alien plenitude which invades it to the core of its being' (*Language*, p. 34). What is being explored here is a fundamentally different attitude to loss. No longer is there a struggle to redeem or transcend it; rather, loss is embraced as dynamic and liberating, the condition of ecstatic renewal.

Foucault on death

Foucault was influenced by Georges Bataille (above, Chapter 17), and indeed celebrated him. And, for someone otherwise so reticent about himself, Foucault was strangely open about his own fascination with death. In a 1982 interview he declared, hinting at his own sense of desire's impossibility:

I would like and I hope I'll die of an overdose [*laughter*] of pleasure of any kind. Because I think it's really difficult and I always have this feeling that I do not feel *the* pleasure, the complete, total pleasure and, for me, it's related to death . . . the kind of pleasure I would consider as *the* real pleasure would be so deep, so intense, so overwhelming that I couldn't survive it. I would die.

Once, when high on opium, he was hit by a car. As he lay in the street, for a few seconds, 'I had the impression that I was dying and it was really a very, very intense pleasure . . . It was, it still is now, one of my best memories' (*Michel Foucault*, p. 12).

Having apparently made one or more suicide attempts when younger, Foucault defended the right to kill oneself; in fact he celebrated suicide. No conduct, he said in 1982, 'is more beautiful or, consequently, more worthy of careful thought than suicide. One should work on one's suicide throughout one's life.' It might be said that all this is only psycho-biography based on a few facetious interviews. In fact Foucault's concern with the death/desire dynamic, and its connection with the negation of self, recurs through his writing, and in ways which are both fascinating and disturbing: 'The border is often narrow between a permanent temptation to commit suicide and the birth of a certain form of political consciousness' (J. Miller, pp. 351, 193).

Crucially for Foucault, as for some other gay intellectuals, anti-essentialism or anti-humanism involved much more than showing that Western concepts of 'man' or of the individual are philosophical errors; when he spoke or wrote of the death of the author, the death of man, the death of humanism, the death of the subject, he really wanted to destroy certain normalizing and oppressive ways of thinking and being. Behind all this is a Utopian ideal of release which is both psychic and social: in place of so-called 'man', what must be produced 'is something that absolutely does not exist, about which we know nothing ... the creation of something totally different' (J. Miller, p. 336).[6] Later he came to believe that homosexuality, especially the extreme scenarios of sado-masochism, could provide something like that ideal; in such scenarios it was possible to 'invent oneself' poly-morphously, especially with the help of certain drugs. More generally, his vision for gay culture was that it would invent new ways of living (Macey, pp. 365, 371, 367). Not surprisingly, he was against identity politics and gay essentializing; the following remark, with which many have since identified, is from 1969:

Do not ask who I am, and do not ask me to remain the same: leave it to our bureaucrats and our police to see that our papers are in order. At least spare us their morality when we write. (*Archaeology*, p. 17)

Such self-disidentification also led him eventually to renounce the very idea of desire, speaking instead of pleasure. For Foucault desire is a notion already imbued with oppression; to desire is already to be subjectively policed: ' "Tell me what your desire is and I will tell you who you are, whether you are normal or not, and then I can qualify or disqualify your desire." ' By contrast, 'there is no pathology of pleasure, no "abnormal" pleasure. It is an event "outside the subject" or on the edge of the subject' (Macey, p. 365).

Foucault seemed to have an almost mystical regard for the potential of drugs to effect a dissolution of identity. When high on LSD he reportedly compared the experience with having sex with a stranger: 'Contact with a strange body *affords an experience of the truth* similar to what I am experiencing now' (J. Miller, p. 251). To reiterate: for Foucault the disidentification of the self, which in turn involved a fascination with death itself, was at once personal, political and historical. The experience of all this remains crucial – not experience essentialized, but the experiential dimension of anti-essentialism. It was also an intellectual imperative. In the preface to Volume 2 of *The History of Sexuality* (1984) he said that it was curiosity that motivated him to write. In a passage later read at his funeral by Gilles Deleuze, he went on to say that this is not the curiosity which seeks confirmation of what one wants to hear, but the kind of curiosity which 'enables one to get free of oneself', the curiosity for a knowledge that leads to 'the knower straying afield of himself' (p. 8).[7]

Curiosity finds its way to death – until recently a largely ignored aspect of this philosopher's thought. Foucault (among others) is influential for revealing the complex, paradoxical, unstable nature of binary oppositions in the socio-cultural sphere – oppositions like madness and sanity; normality and deviation; the natural and the unnatural. And yet his interrogation of the life/death binary has until recently been overlooked. Throughout his work there are cryptic, lyrical, paradoxical speculations on how we *live* death – how, that is, death's changing face organizes our identity, language, sexuality and future – speculations which are sometimes disorientating even as they fascinate and engage.

In *The Birth of the Clinic* he argues that, whereas in the Renaissance death was the great leveller, in modern culture (from the nineteenth century) it becomes *constitutive of singularity*; it is in the perception of death that the individual finds himself or herself; death gives to life 'a face that cannot be exchanged. Death left its old tragic heaven and became the lyrical core of man: his invisible truth, his visible secret' (pp. 170–72).[8] At the close of *The Order of Things* (1966) there occurs that famous anti-humanist remark to the effect that 'man' is an invention of recent date, soon to be erased, 'like a face drawn in the sand at the edge of the sea' (p. 387). The imagery here may be traditional; but what prepares for it is a consideration of death which

places Foucault within the modern philosophical tendency to internalize death (above, Parts IV–V). Foucault's own philosophy, and in
particular his ideas about self-disidentification, derive from an engagement with the philosophical internalization of death. Whereas Lacan
would develop this philosophy psychoanalytically, Foucault attempts
it without psychoanalysis.

Foucault suggests that if death – 'the Death that is at work in
[man's] suffering' – is the precondition of knowledge, and if desire –
'the Desire that has lost its object' – is what remains 'always *unthought*
at the heart of thought', then death and desire are already in a paradoxical enabling proximity within us and our culture (p. 376). A few years
later he speculates that language itself is structured by this proximity:

It is quite likely that the approach of death – its sovereign gesture, its
prominence within human memory – hollows out in the present and in
existence the void toward which and from which we speak . . .

Perhaps there exists in speech an essential affinity between death, endless
striving, and the self-representation of language . . . In this sense death is
undoubtedly the most essential of the accidents of language (its limits and
its centre): from the day that men began to speak toward death and against
it, in order to grasp and imprison it, something was born, a murmuring
which repeats, recounts, and redoubles itself endlessly, which has undergone
an uncanny process of amplification and thickening, in which our language
is today lodged and hidden. (*Language*, pp. 53, 55)[9]

Not surprisingly, many were, and still are, disturbed by Foucault's
anti-humanism. He was uncompromising about its implications,
especially here, in the idea of a language animated by death. It is now
commonplace to characterize anti-humanist thought as that which
proposes that we do not speak but are spoken – a way of summarizing
a complex philosophical argument which regards identity as not the
source but the effect of language. But the idea that we are 'spoken by
death' is not commonplace, even though, in saying so, Foucault, like
Lacan but without psychoanalysis, is recasting an earlier idea in
linguistic terms. In the conclusion of *The Archaeology of Knowledge*
he affects sympathy with humanist aspirations and rehearses them,
but only to relish their demise and to reinstate death at the centre
of the timid post-Christian attempt to preserve immortality. The

humanist, says Foucault, wants to discern in discourse 'the gentle, silent, intimate consciousness' of its author, and, through that, the 'murmur . . . of insubstantial immortalities'. But what the humanist must realize is that in speaking or writing 'I am not banishing my death, but actually establishing it; or rather . . . I am abolishing all interiority in that exterior that is so indifferent to my life, and so *neutral*, that it makes no distinction between my life and my death' (p. 210).

In later works Foucault wants to show how death is strangely at work in the power/sexuality dynamic. His argument that sex is constitutive of identity has been immensely influential in the last two decades, but there is more to it than is usually recognized: death as well as power constitutes modern sexuality.[10] In an argument which is still non- and often anti-Freudian, he describes a process whereby modern States administer life through the production and control of sexuality, and in the process wreak death on an unprecedented scale. This occurs after a fundamental change in the historical operations of State power. Whereas earlier in Western culture 'the sovereign' ruled through the limited threat of death; now, situated and exercised 'at the level of life, the species, the race, and the large-scale phenomena of population', power perpetuates world wars on an unprecedented scale, holocausts and massacres (*History*, I.137).

This control of life works crucially through the constitution of sex and sexuality. Sex is an ideological illusion and a lived reality. At the juncture of the 'body' and the 'population', sex became a crucial target of a power organized around the management of life rather than the menace of death (p. 147):

Sex – that agency which appears to dominate us and that secret which seems to underlie all that we are, that point which enthralls us through the power it manifests and the meaning it conceals, and which we ask to reveal what we are and to free us from what defines us – is doubtless but an ideal point made necessary by the deployment of sexuality and its operation.

The result is that now 'it is through sex . . . that each individual has to pass in order to have access to his own intelligibility'; sex has become more important than our soul; it is the secret of the self, minuscule in each of us, yet of a density that makes it inexhaustibly and ultimately sacrificially significant:

The Faustian pact, whose temptation has been instilled in us by the deployment of sexuality, is now as follows: to exchange life in its entirety for sex itself, for the truth and sovereignty of sex. *Sex is worth dying for.* It is in this (strictly historical) sense that sex is indeed imbued with the death instinct. When a long while ago the West discovered love, it bestowed on it a value high enough to make death acceptable; nowadays it is sex that claims this equivalence. (*History*, I.155–6; my emphasis)

Against psychoanalysis Foucault tries to identify the historical ground not only of the death drive, but also of desire's impossibility, which now, at least partly, derives from the fact that 'we expect our intelligibility to come from what was for many centuries thought of as a madness [i.e. sex]' (*History*, I.156).[11] But if the death drive is in this sense an effect of power working through sexuality, death (like desire) thereby also has the potential to elude power, even through suicide:

Death is power's limit, the moment that escapes it; death becomes the most secret aspect of existence, the most 'private'. (I.138)

Foucault cruising

'Sex is worth dying for': this is the belief that those like James Miller attribute to the Foucault who cruised the bathhouses of San Francisco in the early 1980s. The rumour that Foucault deliberately tried to infect others is discounted by Miller; although circulating for almost a decade, he finds no evidence for it. It is true that Foucault was deeply sceptical about AIDS, but so were many others in 1982–3, and, at the time, with some reason; certainly they were right to discredit the idea of a 'gay cancer', as it was then called. As D. A. Miller says, 'it wasn't as if people didn't know about AIDS, but everyone was unwilling to believe it would attack you because you were gay' (J. Miller, p. 349). But Foucault did, apparently, say to D. A. Miller, 'To die for the love of boys: What could be more beautiful?' Such remarks lead James Miller to conclude that

the crux of what is most original and challenging about Foucault's way of thinking. . . is his unrelenting, deeply ambiguous and profoundly problematic preoccupation with death, which he explored not only in . . . his writing, but also, and I believe critically, in . . . sado-masochistic eroticism. (p. 7)

The anonymous sexual encounter, perhaps also in an S and M context, continues Miller, offered the prospect of being liberated into something different – a 'limit experience'. AIDS became another limit experience, and now a fatal one, leading Foucault into

potentially suicidal acts of passion with consenting partners, most of them likely to be infected already; deliberately throwing caution to the wind, Foucault and these men were wagering their lives together . . . (p. 381)

To act out self-annihilating fantasies sexually is hardly unknown. But, in speculating that Foucault actualized such fantasies in life-threatening ways, those like Miller reproduce a tendentious conflation between death, AIDS, promiscuity and sado-masochism which some at least of their audience have been waiting to hear. Ironically, what Foucault had to say on death was largely ignored until it could be revisited as 'evidence' for this supposed erotic, suicidal and/or murderous obsession with the subject. Perhaps what compels this 'biographical' quest are ideas of the anti-humanist Foucault – he who had dared to declare the death of the author, of the human subject, of man and of humanism – fucking others to death, or, better still, being fucked to death himself.

21

The Wonder of
the Pleasure

'Sexual practices', Roland Barthes once wrote, 'are banal, impoverished, doomed to repetition, and [in] this . . . disproportionate to the
wonder of the pleasure they afford.' Barthes wrote this in a preface
to Renaud Camus's *Tricks* (p. viii), a narrative of twenty-five 'promiscuous' homosexual encounters graphic enough to have merited
the charge of obscenity. His remark alludes to the idea of desire's
impossibility: these practices are banal, impoverished, doomed to
repetition. For many of the writers explored so far this would support
the idea of desire as a futile, frenzied and compulsive quest for an
impossible gratification. And yet, insists Barthes, sexual acts are also
the source of pleasure. But in putting it like that I have already
misrepresented him and missed precisely what is significant: if Barthes
invokes the impossibility of desire in order to circumvent it, he does
so not by simply acknowledging the pleasure of sex; rather, he speaks
of *the wonder* of this pleasure. I end this book with that wonder
and a kind of love which is its inspiration – fetishistic, voyeuristic,
onanistic, aroused not just by the desire for another but also by the
desire of another – another's narcissism. Also I want to consider
its importance for a certain homosexual aesthetic which registers a
vulnerable insight into how this most fragile and elusive of experience
negotiates loss.

Hegel once described wonder as prompted by the contradiction
between the world and the spirit. It is, he says, 'a contradiction in
which objects prove themselves to be just as attractive as repulsive,
and the sense of this contradiction along with the urge to remove it
is precisely what generates wonder'. He continues:

The man who does *not yet* wonder at anything still lives in obtuseness and stupidity ... on the other hand whoever wonders *no longer* regards the whole of the external world as something which he has become clear about, whether in the abstract intellectual mode of a universally human Enlightenment, or in the noble and deeper consciousness of absolute spiritual freedom and universality. (*Aesthetics*, I.315)

Hegel wants to transcend wonderment and thereby be free of that strange mix of uncertainty and insight, vulnerability and awe, humility and arousal, which inspires it. While acknowledging wonder as a preliminary stage of true knowledge, he wants to dissolve it in favour of universal enlightenment or, even better, the deeper consciousness of absolute spirit. Only then can we be free of the contradictions of desire (attraction and repulsion).

It is at points like this that one wonders if Hegel's entire philosophical edifice is any more than an arid, rationalist rewriting of the desire for eternity: an absolute freedom bought at the price of a metaphysical nullification of everything that moves. To pit the fragile reed of wonderment against the massive rationalist edifice of the Hegelian system seems ridiculous if not absurd, especially in relation to the promiscuous sexual encounter; it seems like a rather disastrous example of what philosophers call a 'category mistake'. And yet this is what I propose. And if this is partly about reclaiming the tradition of *carpe diem* it is more importantly a wish to consider wonderment itself as a form of meditation or erotic attention which redeems loss.

This is the first stanza of W. H. Auden's popular poem 'Lullaby':

> Lay your sleeping head, my love,
> Human on my faithless arm;
> Time and fever burn away
> Individual beauty from
> Thoughtful children, and the grave
> Proves the child ephemeral:
> But in my arms till break of day
> Let the living creature lie,
> Mortal, guilty, but to me
> The entirely beautiful.

Is this poem, as the title suggests, addressed by an adult to a child, or rather to the youthful partner in a fleeting (homoerotic) casual encounter (trick)? The rest of the poem suggests it is probably the latter, and an occasion for the wonder of which Barthes speaks and which is here pervaded by mutability. Mutability is the precondition not only of beauty, but of the perfection of beauty, that *'entirely'* being predicated on a loss which mutability will also guarantee. And, even as it deprives it of its object, mutability animates desire into a 'faithless', imitative impermanence. Auden's 'faithless arm' warrants comparison with Barthes's 'faithless benevolence' in this, the latter's memorable description of the trick, the wonder of its pleasure:

Trick – the encounter which takes place only once: more than cruising, less than love: an intensity, which passes without regret. Consequently, for me, *Trick* becomes the metaphor for many adventures which are not sexual; the encounter of a glance, a gaze, an idea, an image, ephemeral and forceful association, which consents to dissolve so lightly, a faithless benevolence: a way of not getting stuck in desire, though without evading it; all in all, a kind of wisdom. (*Tricks*, p. x)

The sense of the trick as described by Barthes is obviously different from the self-destructive promiscuity described by Oscar Moore, or John Rechy's revolutionary fuck, or Michael Rumaker's benignly redemptive one, or even Leo Bersani's perspective of desire as self-shattering. 'A way of not getting stuck in desire' – far from being an expression of desire's impossibility, the trick here becomes a way of negotiating it.

Mixing memory and desire

One night in Australia, while wandering through the house of a stranger – it was too hot to sleep, and I was too enamoured to leave – I found a copy of E. M. Forster's collection of essays *Two Cheers for Democracy*. The title-page of the book had a decades-old inscription to its owner from a lover, and also a recent second-hand price. Had the owner discarded the book in a clear-out? Or had he died and someone else cleared it out? Why did I pause to wonder about that? Perhaps only because it was that time of night when concentration seems to come from the stillness of the small hours, rather than from any conscious effort; perhaps too because there is no trace of mutability more quietly telling: the loving inscription and the second-hand price together, on the one page.

In this book Forster writes about the poet C. P. Cavafy. He says that, for Cavafy, the casual homosexual encounter involves

the power to snatch sensation, to triumph over the moment even if remorse ensues. Perhaps that physical snatching is courage; it is certainly the seed of exquisite memories and it is possibly the foundations of art.

He adds that such casual sexual encounters 'create the future' (p. 247). That is a remarkable claim, but one which Cavafy precisely confirms in a poem called 'Understanding':

> In the loose living of my early years
> The impulses of my poetry were shaped
> The boundaries of my art were plotted.[1]

In another poem he recalls having sex urgently, furtively, in a public place:

> Delight of flesh between
> half-opened clothes;
> quick baring of flesh – a vision
> that has crossed twenty-six years
> and now comes to rest in this poetry.
> ('Comes to Rest')

And after another 'illicit' sexual encounter:

> But what profit for the life of the artist:
> tomorrow, the day after, or years later, he'll give voice
> to the strong lines that had their beginning here.
> ('Their Beginning')

Sexual transgression is not only the occasion of creativity, and the stimulus for it; there is a profound affinity between them – not least because both violate conformity. As with the expression of deviant desire, 'to grow in spirit' requires that we 'violate / both law and custom, and go beyond / the established, inadequate norm' ('Growing in Spirit').

For Cavafy, creativity derives from a twofold courage: of acting out illicit desires in the transient encounter, and of refusing the lure of the conventional – 'routine love affairs' ('To Sensual Pleasure').[2] In the transient encounter the beauty of the stranger or the intensity of the pleasure may be heightened by the 'inappropriateness' of the surroundings – a shop, a café, a 'room . . . cheap and sordid' ('One Night'). One poem, dating from September 1907, beautifully indicates how, for Cavafy, homosexual desire is illicit in a way which is both naïve and knowing. Two young men meet on the street:

> Their looks met by chance
> and timidly, haltingly expressed
> the illicit desire of their bodies.
> Then a few uneasy steps along the street
> until they smiled, and nodded slightly.
> ('The Window of the Tobacco Shop')

Something else about this poem: it suggests how the casual anonymous encounter is contained by, yet internally distanced from, its own moment and context; how such meetings have always been at the heart of ordinary society yet have been largely invisible to it. Thus its first lines: 'They stood among many others / close to a lighted tobacco shop window.'

The celebration of illicit desire as the impetus for art does not make that desire secure or safe; on the contrary. And while the poet does not experience homoerotic desire as shameful, nor does he want to naturalize it or even regard it as normal; its intensity and sensuality in part derive from its being shame*less* and audacious, and even from its fatality ('Chandelier', 'Dangerous Thoughts', 'In the Street', 'He Swears'). The creative potential of homoerotic desire derives too from the fact that such desire is fetishistic and perverse. So, to love beauty might also be to love beauty wounded; the poet dresses a youth's wounded shoulder: 'and I liked looking at the blood. / It was a thing of my love, that blood.' After the wounded youth leaves, the poet fetishizes the old dressing, 'the blood of love against my lips' ('The Bandaged Shoulder').

'Things Ended' speaks of how we strive desperately to avoid anticipated dangers – 'the obvious danger that threatens us so terribly' –
only to then be swept away by an unimagined, unexpected disaster.
To *know* that this is so is an inducement to have the courage of desire,
and abandon the deluded struggles for security in everyday life. Nor
does the celebration of illicit desire defend from mutability; if there
is occasionally a retirement from the pain of mutability into the
security of form, that is only because, for the most part, Cavafy's
erotic aesthetic makes him more, not less, vulnerable to the devastating
interactions of time, loss and mutability. Memory mixed with desire
is never safe: now it affirms, vindicates, relives the moments of intensity
which have given meaning to the poet's life; now it haunts and wounds
by intensifying loss, transience and mutability.

Cruising and memory

Sometimes Cavafy writes of memory as erotically gratifying; the
recollection of a lover, and of the room in which they made love, is
so vivid 'that now as I write, after so many years, / in my lonely house,
I'm drunk with passion again' ('One Night'). Wandering through a
neighbourhood, the recollection of making love there renders the
whole place suddenly beautiful – 'my whole being radiated / the
sensual pleasure stored up inside me' ('Outside the House'). And
memory even has the power to circumvent time, avoid loss, as in
'Grey'. To recall a past encounter is to relive transience with the
resonance of what it is to be alive; the encounter becomes the concrete
universal of life – its specific instance and its symbol. In 'On the Stairs'
it's as if life itself depends on the chance encounter, and on the seizing
of the opportunity it offers. But this is also a poem about regret for
something which never happened, the lost opportunity. Two people
meet on the stairs of a brothel, and in the instant they exchange
glances each knows the other can give what can't be found in that
place. 'But we both hid ourselves, flustered.' Illicit love is difficult
enough to find, and, even when found, may be refused for the same
social reasons that made it difficult to find in the first place.

Against all that, memory of the casual sexual encounter may also entail an acute sense of mutability and loss. In some poems the briefness of the encounter is recognized to hold what is best about it; but at the same time one remains for ever beholden to that moment in a way which intensifies later loneliness ('In the Evening', 'Before Time Altered Them'). An old letter echoes a wonderful sensuality soon over and long ago, but 'read over and over till the light faded' brings only sadness ('In the Evening'). Cavafy's poems are pervaded by loss – most immediately in terms of the death of lovers, more generally by the loss of beauty. 'Candles' confesses to the sadness, even the terror, induced by a contemplation of time passing; the past is a kind of death measured by burnt-out candles. And then there is the misery of ageing (in the mouth of a poet in AD 595):

> The ageing of my body and my beauty
> Is a wound from a merciless knife.
> I'm not resigned to it at all.
>
> .   .   .   .   .   .
>
> Bring your drugs, Art of Poetry –
> they do relieve the pain at least for a while.
>
> ('Melancholy . . .')

Here poetry alleviates the distress, and in another poem of the same period poetry compensates for the incompleteness, even the inadequacy, of desire itself:

> I've brought to Art desires and sensations:
> things half-glimpsed,
> faces or lines, certain indistinct memories
> of unfulfilled love affairs.
> Let me submit to Art:
> Art knows how to shape forms of Beauty,
> almost imperceptibly completing life,
> blending impressions, blending day with day.
>
> ('I've Brought to Art')

But aesthetic recompense only goes so far; the risk of desire is always there, and never more so than in the experience of loss. 'In Despair' describes one whose lover has left him, and who desperately 'Through fantasy, through hallucination' seeks in the arms of others to re-experience the lost lover again. Hauntingly it remembers the vulnerability of love, and the limits of fantasy.

The risk of desire is also inside memory, which can turn against the poet, now haunting rather than consoling. In one poem loss is prefigured, and then, years later, recalled, in the stillness of the after-noon sun:

> Beside the window the bed;
> the afternoon sun used to touch half of it.
>
> ... One afternoon at four o'clock we separated
> for a week only ... And then –
> that week became forever.
>
> ('The Afternoon Sun')

The stillness of the sun in the then-present is evoked as an almost-already-past, but in a way which still differentiates it *from* the past. In the now-present the stillness invokes a time-scale in which the past, the then-present and the here and now are all equally on the edge of oblivion, 'like distant music fading away at night', as he puts it in 'Voices'.

It is the very transience of the joyful encounter which returns to haunt; although immediately welcome, and the very condition of the desire that is being affirmed, in memory the transient dimension of the encounter intensifies loss, rather than compensates for it:

> I never found them again – all lost so quickly ...
> the poetic eyes, the pale face ...
> in the darkening street ...
>
> I didn't find them any more – mine entirely by chance,
> and so easily given up,
> then longed for so painfully.
>
> ('Days of 1903')

And then there is loss in the sense of something not done; 'An Old Man' describes one who 'in the miserable banality of old age' bitterly regrets 'impulses bridled, the joy / he sacrificed'. Loss shades into remorse, even guilt; the finality of death makes a retrospective demand for a completeness in the casual encounter which was impossible in the living circumstance.

Memory haunts not only, not even mainly, because the loss is deeply narcissistic; indeed these are poems which show how inadequate are the commonplace assumptions about narcissism. In 'Since Nine o'Clock' the recollection of the poet's own young body reminds not only of 'daring passion' but of

> streets now unrecognizable,
> bustling night clubs now closed,
> theatres and cafés no longer there.
>
> .   .   .   .   .   .
>
> family grief, separations,
> the feelings of my own people,
> of the dead so little recognized.

Time gradually but ineluctably erases even the memories upon which creativity depends – as with the poem about the craftsman who begs memory to help him recreate in art the face of the young man whom he loved, who died as a soldier fifteen years before ('Craftsman of Wine Bowls'). Here the inspiration of memory seems viable, but only just; the craftsman is on the memory-edge of what it is possible to recall and hence create.

Not only beauty and desire, but their memory and the redemptive creativity memory enables (by re-creating lost desire and beauty in verse) are subject to loss. Sometimes memory can only be the memory of loss, and of the impending loss of memory itself. All this means that Cavafy's verse is steeped in mutability. And there are places where mutability seems almost internalized as the impossibility of desire – when, for example, intensity is found in the moment of decline. Sensual pleasure achieved 'morbidly, corruptingly, creates / an erotic intensity which health cannot know', but such pleasure 'rarely finds the body able to feel what it requires' ('Imenos'). 'Tomb of Iasis' suggests more directly the impossibility of desire – 'excess wore me out, killed me'. Here and in other poems desire is self-destructive, a 'sickness' that consumes ('A Young Poet in his Twenty-Fourth Year'). One poem describes how a casual encounter has left one youth obsessed with another and repeatedly searching for him in the place of their first encounter, 'sick with longing' and 'endless desire'. Inevitably desire is reckless:

> . . . he tries not to give himself away.
> But sometimes he almost doesn't care.
> Besides, he knows what he's exposing himself to,
> he's come to accept it: quite possibly this life of his
> will land him in a devastating scandal.
> ('The Twenty-Fifth Year of His Life')

And yet the impossibility of desire – desire as death – never becomes the dominant theme in Cavafy, which means that desire is never conceptualized as impossible. This has much to do with the ways in which creativity and transgression converge with wonderment.

Wonder

Erotic wonderment could never be unique to gay writing, but it finds powerful expression in it. Psychoanalysts sometimes tell us that we desire desire (we desire to be desired, or desire the desire of another); in such situations (they say) the desire to possess, even to annihilate, the other is often urgent, impossible, contradictory. Poets, on the other hand, sometimes tell us that the desire of another becomes the object of an erotic attention whose aim is very different and not necessarily one of possession. Cavafy writes memorably about this.

Youths in his poems are rarely only objects of desire; the youth expressing narcissistic desire is also the urgent agent of desire and, as such, a very different kind of object – that's to say, an object of aesthetic, erotic attention. Hence Cavafy's poem about the young man who intends to read ('He's completely devoted to books'), but succumbs instead to onanistic desire ('He Had Planned To Read'). In another poem a frustrated youth 'goes to bed . . . full of sexual longing': 'all his youth on fire with the body's passion / his lovely youth given over to a fine intensity' ('In the Boring Village'). Here, the boy's own sexual longing is itself first an object of beauty before it is an object of desire. Masturbatory fantasy mediates between the two, and yearning obviously confuses that distinction. Nevertheless, here in Cavafy is a voyeuristic aesthetic, a desiring gaze which includes wonderment. When 'a simple boy' is 'overcome / by forbidden erotic ecstasy' he 'becomes something worth our looking at, for a moment / he too passes through the exalted World of Poetry' ('Passing Through').

Likewise with a passage from Rumaker's *A Day and a Night at the Baths*, in which male sexual narcissism, and the adoring voyeuristic gaze it elicits, are deemed if not entirely innocent then certainly the occasion of the wonderment that innocence evokes. A youth massages himself erect while others watch. The youth is unselfconscious and unembarrassed, and for the narrator there is no craving to possess. While the youth 'looked around him with a level clearness but at nothing or anyone in particular', the narrator 'watched, not furtive, likewise unembarrassed in my looking, content only to watch' and appreciative of how the boy's eyes, 'with their absorbed smile of serious pleasure and play, held the hint of an inward secret of barely contained happiness' (pp. 16–17). Here, as in Cavafy, masturbation is the focus. Obviously important as the activity of the young men who are Cavafy's subject, it also belongs to the poet's creative gaze in which memory becomes a state of onanistic arousal melting past and present together: 'In deep reverie, / all receptiveness . . . / . . . I'll form visions' ('To Call Up the Shades'). At the same time there is something scandalously anti-humanist about this desire, which hardly at all depends on the so-called real person behind the mortal beauty but expresses itself rather as an 'over-riding devotion / to perfectly shaped, corruptible white limbs', incompatible with cultural, ethical and religious sublimation ('Of the Jews (A.D. 50)'). Beauty is anonymous, and the person irrelevant in a certain precise and sensitive way. The poet sees and mentally undresses a twenty-two-year-old, certain that 'about that long ago / I enjoyed the very same body' ('The Next Table'): beauty as generational resemblance is unsocialized, homoerotically disconnected from its most respectable location, the family.

Cavafy suggests how a desire which is fetishistic, voyeuristic, onanistic both is and is not blind, is and is not obliterative of the other. With that twenty-two-year-old the poet is sensitive to the detail of physical beauty, recognizing not just his form, but 'every motion he makes'. The beauty which takes one's breath away is often in the indefinable detail; a question, then, not just of perfectly shaped limbs (though definitely that too) but of the 'particular impression on the brow, the eyes, the lips' ('At the Café Door') – what elsewhere Cavafy calls, perfectly, 'the beauty of anomalous charm' ('In an Old Book'). And the desire can be for the awkwardness of the inexperienced youth, his beauty expressed by the same ('Days of 1901'). To love in this way is to fully know for the first time the contingency of the beloved's being, even in the moment of exalting and adoring him.

There is a facile kind of literary humanism which, for all its obsession with interiority and its talk of wanting to commune with, or express, the authentic self, reproduces a mundane and conformist notion of individuality. In Cavafy, by contrast, it's the anonymous, elusive gesture or expression which most captures cultural difference and individual uniqueness. Related to this is the way he is aware of how beauty and ecstasy are strangely dependent upon their mundane circumstances; the titles of many poems signify exactly that mundaneness – 'In the Street', 'The Afternoon Sun', 'The Window of the Tobacco Shop'. Many of the poems are about experiences or events which are precisely inconsequential; they do not resonate with a symbolic or allegorical significance beyond themselves. These poems have the courage of their own transience; their only life is prior to allegory and symbol; it is as if the written record can register the full intensity of desire only by avoiding allegory and symbol. They endure as representations because of a poignant ordinariness, an arbitrary familiarity recognizable (at least) to those who have noticed.

Mutability destroys everything. It is impossible to be reconciled to it. So to desire is necessarily to suffer. To be there in 'the darkening street', racked with this vagrant desire, may well be about risking danger, even death; certainly it is about desire at its most intense, overwhelming in a way which blinds us to its contingency and brevity, and, just because of that, also the source of creative and sustaining memory.[3] So, for Cavafy, desire is always about risk. Only thus can it carry the potential to bring us back to life, metaphorically and perhaps literally. The memory of such moments, even when it is vulnerably on the edge of its own oblivion, can momentarily slip free of loss:

I'd like to speak of this memory,
but it's so faded now – as though nothing's left –
because it was so long ago, in my adolescent years.

A skin as though of jasmine . . .
that August evening – was it August? –
I can still just recall the eyes: blue, I think they were . . .
Ah yes, blue: a sapphire blue.

('Long Ago')

There is one last reason why desire does not become impossible for Cavafy – one related, albeit strangely, to these qualities of wonderment, erotic attentiveness and onanistic passivity: I'm thinking of his own self-effacement, a reticence devoid of shame and strangely prophetic:

From my most unnoticed actions,
my most veiled writing –
from these alone will I be understood.
But maybe it isn't worth so much concern,
so much effort to discover who I really am.
Later, in a more perfect society,
someone else made just like me
is certain to appear and act freely.

('Hidden Things', 1908)

The erotics of self-disidentification

If in homoerotic writing we find insightful contemporary explorations of the Western preoccupation with the convergence of desire and death, we also find a compelling alternative to it. Barthes speaks of a certain kind of promiscuity, the trick, as a way of not getting stuck in desire; also of the trick as a kind of wisdom. Wisdom, the first great sacrifice to desire in the Western tradition (and certainly that which is said to be thrown to the wind in cruising), is rediscovered within the ephemeral, desiring encounter. But Barthes also makes the trick a metaphor for the eroticizing of non-sexual cultural practices, as in his own cultural and literary theory, wherein *draguer* – to cruise, seduce, loiter, follow, to engage with anonymously/publicly – becomes central not only for a homoerotic aesthetic, but, more generally, for the urban, modernist, literary aesthetic to which Barthes contributed so significantly. Again, self-disidentification is crucial at all levels: the erotic, the aesthetic and the social. In relation to Stendhal he speaks of the 'amorous plural', a pleasure 'analogous to that enjoyed today by someone "cruising" ', and involving an *'irregular discontinuity* . . . simultaneously aesthetic, psychological, and metaphysical'; a plural passion which 'necessitates leaping from one object to another, as chance presents them, without experiencing the slightest sentiment of guilt with regard to the disorder such a procedure involves' (*The Rustle of Language*, pp. 298–9).

For Barthes, as for homosexuals before him – Wilde pre-eminently – the casual sexual encounter has the potential for not so much a discovery of his true self as a liberation *from* self, from a self-oppressive identity – especially the subordinated identity:

What society will not tolerate is that . . . the something I am should be openly expressed as provisional . . . insignificant, inessential, in a word irrelevant. Just say 'I am' and you will be socially saved. (pp. 291–2)

Anti-essentialism as a merely theoretical statement about identity is misleading to the point of being useless. As I remarked before in relation to Foucault, what needs to be recovered is the experiential dimension of anti-essentialism. And that is found most significantly in homoerotic writing. Certainly for Barthes anti-essentialism was felt experientially; again, in this he followed Wilde: in the latter's transgressive aesthetic a marginal decentred sexuality informs a deviant sensibility which is translated into a philosophy of subjectivity wherein the self is disidentified and wherein prescriptive, essentialist sexual norms are provoked into disarray.[4]

There have been some who regard Barthes's version of this as just a precious Parisian aesthetic with nothing much to say to hard-core sexual politicians. But what we learn from Barthes (as from Foucault and Wilde, albeit differently in each case) is that oppression inheres in those subjected to it *as* their or our identity, and must eventually be experienced and contested there, *and never more so than when this subjection involves desire.* Identity for the homosexual is always conflicted: at once ascribed, proscribed and internalized, it is in terms of identity that self-hatred, violence, mutilation and death have been suffered. Conversely, identity is also that in the name of which liberation is fiercely fought for. Not surprisingly, then, this self-realization has always been strangely bound up with a defiant refusal of self.

Historically and aesthetically, the promiscuous encounter focuses this, enacting the possibility of a simultaneous identification and *dis*identification, which, together, may then involve a *re*identification – ceasing to be the fixed, tyrannized subject and becoming . . . becoming what, exactly? One hesitates here only because *what* one becomes is never secure, never as certain as is promised by the euphoria of self-discovery or the securities of identity politics. For sure, one becomes something other, yet, equally surely, never the abstract free-floating subject of the post-modern; and this is because what remains in place is always at risk: psychically, socially, sexually, legally and in other ways, and probably all at once, inseparably. To be socially dislocated means that one can never be entirely unselfconscious, least of all when cruising. But, still, desire enables a self-realization which is also a defiant refusal of self. Still, now: as a gay poet wrote in 1991 about the anonymous encounter,

> You were the emptiness I sought,
> The escape from thought.
>
> . . . .
>
> There was truth & trust wrapped in the swift embrace
> Of strangers who could vanish without trace;
> Their light could only pass
> Through clear glass.
>
> (Alan Brayne, 'Our Shadows')

For this poet, 'truth & trust' derive not from a fullness of subjective being, not from the authentic encounter between self and other, nor even from the completion of the 'I' in another, but from the other as 'the emptiness I sought, / The escape from thought', and from strangers who can vanish 'without trace'. The word 'strangers' equalizes the you and I: fantasy and identification circulate because of anonymity.

Once, while taking drugs, Foucault said, 'Contact with a strange body *affords an experience of the truth* similar to what I am experiencing now' (above, p. 307). 'An experience of the truth': what might such a philosophically reckless remark, uttered by one sceptical of both 'experience' and 'truth', mean in this context? Perhaps that, in the anonymous yet intensely subjective encounter with the absolute uniqueness of the 'anybody', the divide between reality and fantasy momentarily shifts and even dissolves, as do other divisions too, including those between public and private, self and other. And yet this is an encounter which presupposes, which occurs only because of, these divisions, even as it momentarily suspends them, in fantasy and actually – in short, an encounter in which desire is experienced as at once an effect and a refusal of history, a moment of intensity so marked by its history yet at the same time internally distanced from it. And inside this encounter is the longer history we have explored whereby the Western struggle for individual self-realization necessitates a negation of self. But self-disidentification, even as it can become the ground of freedom, also makes us more vulnerable than ever to those apprehensions of loss endemic to our culture and which can render the experience of desire as also an experience of grieving.

Notes

Introduction

1 Death or at least decay is there from the start. Anonymous old men encountered in public toilets are like 'insects crawling out from behind the stained tiles . . . limed with the damp stench of the soggy bogroll world' (p. 44). What is seemingly most disturbing about these old men is not so much their decaying bodies but the fact that, in this decayed state and so close to death, *they still desire*. Almost literally embodying desire as death, they bear silent witness to this dreadful proximity, and in the same moment also bear witness to the intolerable desirability of the young. One old man, allowed to watch Hugo fuck another young man, 'winked and gasped, watched as his dick dribbled white spots onto the carpet and, rubbing them in with his slipper, left the room' (p. 45). Repelled by these old men, Hugo nevertheless cannot or does not avoid them. Sometimes he performs before them: 'straining for the relief of an orgasm which, when it came, was only a spasm without the shudder, an anti-climax that offered no feeling of relief. Just a small grey wave of depression' (p. 39).

2 Or Cyril Collard's autobiographical novel, *Savage Nights*, which became the basis of a controversial film of the same name with Collard as lead and director.

3 Compare, from a decade earlier, Andrew Holleran's *Dancer From the Dance*: '. . . five feet away from the corpse, people lay taking the sun and admiring a man who had just given the kiss of life to a young boy. Death and desire, death and desire' (pp. 30–31).

4 See David M. Halperin, *Saint Foucault*, esp. pp. 126–85.

5 Moore also wrote a widely admired column in the *Guardian* newspaper on living with AIDS. These pieces have been collected in *PWA: Looking AIDS in the Face*.

6 Ellis Hanson reminds us that this association is not new: notions of death have been at the heart of nearly every historical construction of same-sex desire. Recently, in the media, people living with AIDS have been made vampire-like, 'the dead who dare to speak and sin and walk abroad, the undead with AIDS' (Fuss, *Inside/Out*, pp. 324–5). In another article in the same book, Jeff Nunokawa shows that this connection between homosexuality and death is not just something

done to gay culture by a homophobic dominant culture; within gay culture too, homosexuality has been regarded fatalistically, morbidly, and as somehow doomed of its very nature. Nunokawa identifies texts as different as Oscar Wilde's *The Picture of Dorian Gray*, Randy Shilts's *And the Band Played On* and James Merrill's *The Inner Room* as inclined to 'cultivate the confusion of gay identity with a death-driven narrative', and representing 'doom as the specific fate of gay men' (p. 317).

7 In an important essay of 1930, Thomas Mann realized that to comprehend the paradoxical interanimation of love and death one has first to get beyond its commonplace representations – 'piquant, half-playful, half-macabre . . . externally and sentimentally romantic', especially facile in the mouths of 'wits and romantics' (*Essays*, p. 261).

8 Writing perceptively of modernist philosophy, Simon Critchley argues that, because finitude always remains beyond our grasp, we will never be able to comprehend death in a way which renders it life-enabling and life-affirming. The ultimate meaning of human finitude is precisely that we cannot find meaningful fulfilment within it (*Very Little . . . Almost Nothing*, esp. pp. 24−7).

9 Compare Shakespeare's Antony, who, hearing that his wife is dead, reflects on the vicissitudes of desire:

> Thus did I desire it:
> What our contempts doth often hurl from us,
> We wish it ours again. The present pleasure,
> By revolution low'ring, does become
> The opposite of itself: she's good, being gone;
> The hand could pluck her back that shoved her on.
>
> (*Antony and Cleopatra*, I.ii.115−20)

10 Unless indicated to the contrary, all italics in quotations are those of the original source.

11 Paglia takes the view of Sade rather than Rousseau, Hobbes rather than Locke, Nietzsche and Freud rather than Marx (p. 2). Which means she is sceptical of ameliorative politics, progressivism and emancipation movements – especially feminism.

12 It has also recently been argued that the major ideas behind Jean-Paul Sartre's *Being and Nothingness* came from Beauvoir; see Kate and Edward Fullbrook, *Simone de Beauvoir and Jean-Paul Sartre*, esp. p. 3.

13 But such representations are always misrepresentations, inasmuch as 'they repress what they purport to reveal and they articulate what they hope to conceal'. Femininity and death point to a reality or an excess which is beyond, yet disruptive of, all systems of language (Bronfen, pp. xi−xii). So potentially dangerous is this disruption that the conjoining of femininity and death in representation is already a reaffirmation of the stability which they threaten. However, this is an unstable containment; in particular, it harbours and even intensifies a fascination with

precisely what has been repressed. It is also violently voyeuristic, in the sense that all representations of dying are voyeuristic (by virtue of implying the safe position of the spectator), and fetishistic, in that it separates the body from its real materiality and its historical context.

Chapter 1

1 Compare the following, from centuries later:

> For mortals, mortal things. And all things leave us.
> Or if they do not, then we leave them.
> > (Lucian, *c.* AD 115–80; in Jay, p. 279)

> Everything's laughter
> everything dust
> everything nothing.
> > (Glykon, in Jay, p. 319)

2 Unless otherwise stated, the translations are from the edition by Charles H. Kahn.

3 Kahn (pp. 288–9) questions the authenticity of this fragment.

4 Modern commentators go to great lengths to harmonize Heraclitus' thought with our own; some fragments get pages of commentary to this end. But it is salutary to recall again that we come up against beliefs which are not only paradoxical but irreducibly alien: in fragment xlvii he declares that the sun is the size of a human foot, and in xlviiia that it is relit every day. We also encounter a strange (and disputed) way of dying: according to Diogenes Laertius, when Heraclitus was dying he buried himself in manure and was devoured by dogs (Heraclitus, pp. 5–6).

5 Cf. Marcuse, 'The Ideology of Death', pp. 67–8, and below, Chapter 15.

6 See Jennifer Wallace, 'Shelley, Plato and the Political Imagination'.

7 Shelley used a free translation of the following epigram, sometimes attributed to Plato, as the epigraph for *Adonais*:

> You were the morning star among the living:
> But now in death your evening lights the dead.
> > (*Aster*, in Jay, p. 45)

8 These three themes – violence, exhaustion/expenditure and death – can be found in other times, places and creeds; Foucault also remarks, via the work of R. Van Gulik, their presence in ancient Chinese culture (*History*, II.137). Even if Foucault's discussion of this aspect of Greek experience adds little that is new, his devoting of a chapter to the topic is significant of the renewed interest in this aspect of Greek culture.

9 Anne Carson puts it like this:

Eros is an experience that assaults the lover from without and proceeds to take control of his body, his mind, and the quality of his life . . . to enfeeble his mind and distort its thinking, to replace normal conditions of health and sanity with disease and madness . . . [Eros's] action is to melt, break down, bite into, burn, devour, wear away, whirl around, sting, pierce, wound, poison, suffocate, drag off or grind the lover to a powder . . . No one can fight Eros off . . . Very few see him coming. He lights on you from somewhere outside yourself and, as soon as he does, you are taken over, changed radically. You cannot resist the change or control it or come to terms with it. (p. 148; cf. pp. 3–9. See also Winkler, *Constraints of Desire*, esp. Chapter 3.)

10 Cf. Vermeule, pp. 163–4: 'To take Greek myth at face value . . . is to learn that the gods have only two easy ways of communicating with men: by killing them or raping them.'

11 'Limb-relaxing longing': compare Sappho's famous fragments in which the subject of desire is also being dis-organized into a kind of death of the self; speech 'fails' her, her tongue is 'paralysed', her eyes 'blinded' – 'I feel as if I'm not far off dying.' And again: 'Love, the loosener of limbs, shakes me again, an inescapable bittersweet creature' (West, pp. 38–9; Trypanis, p. 150).

12 Vernant also cites Alcman's fragment to make the point: 'By the desire that loosens the limbs she [a woman] has a gaze that is more dissolvent than . . . Thanatos' (p. 101).

13 Of the several hundred volumes Epicurus is said to have written, very little survives; my summary here is indebted to Nussbaum.

14 Lucretius' term *primordia rerum* corresponded to the *atomoi* of Epicurus; it is generally translated as 'atoms', but also as 'elements', 'seeds' and 'generative particles'. The void (*inane*) is also translated as 'illimitable void', 'vacuum' and 'vacuity' (Lucretius, pp. 16–17, 28–9).

15 Stoic philosophy seeks not only to control, but to eradicate the passions (*pathos*). The truly wise person will be completely invulnerable to them. A story is told of Anaxagoras that, greeted with the news of his child's death, he replied, 'I was already aware that I had begotten a mortal' (cited in Nussbaum, p. 363).

By 'passion' the Stoics meant an impulse or drive which is excessive, uncontrolled, and which results in mental disturbance. In that sense passion overlaps with but is not synonymous with what we mean by 'desire' in its broad (i.e. more than sexual) sense: lust (*epithymia* – a yearning after something) was a passion, but so too was fear. The passions were reprehensible because they subverted reason. For the Stoics, reason was of the utmost importance, protecting the individual against the passions and against misfortune. Passion was also regarded as a kind of disease.

16 Only the soul can escape time, loss and misfortune – the soul which is 'a god dwelling as a guest in a human body'. One may, says Seneca, leap to heaven from the very slums, and he quotes Virgil: 'mould thyself to kinship with thy

God' (*Epistulae Morales*, I.229). In places Seneca subscribes to the Stoic idea that the soul temporarily survives the death of the body; in others he regards death as complete extinction.

17 For a brief account of this, see Anna Lydia Motto, *Seneca*, esp. Chapter 2, and Miriam T. Griffin, 'Imago Vitae Suae'.

18 Most severely by those like F. L. Lucas, who, unable to forgive Seneca the fact that the Elizabethans were so fascinated by him, declares that the philosopher was afraid of life and floated on the tide of things like 'a rigid corpse'. He finds the judgement of Bernard Shaw's Hypatia (in *Misalliance*) to be a fit epitaph for Stoicism: 'Old, old, old. Squeamish. Can't stand up to things. Always on the shrink' (pp. 47–8).

Chapter 2

1 The text is sometimes cited in its familiar and most influential form, from the Authorized Version of the Bible, and sometimes from the modern, more literal, translation of R. B. Y. Scott ('AV' and 'Scott' respectively).

2 Cf. Job 14:1–2: 'Man *that is* born of a woman *is* of few days, and full of trouble. He cometh forth like a flower, and is cut down: he fleeth also as a shadow, and continueth not.'

3 For further similarities with Ecclesiastes see also the Babylonian text called 'A Pessimistic Dialogue between Master and Servant', dating from the same period: 'Climb the mounds of ancient ruins and walk about: look at the skulls of late and early (men); who (among them) is an evildoer, who a public benefactor?' (Pritchard, p. 438). Another text, 'A Dialogue concerning Human Misery', contains enough parallels to have been called the Babylonian Ecclesiastes (pp. 438–40)

Chapter 3

1 I owe this realization to Elizabeth A. Clark of Duke University.

2 On the influence of Gnosticism on Christianity, see, most recently, Ranke-Heinemann, *Eunuchs for Heaven,* and Osborne, *The Poisoned Embrace.* On the relationship of Gnosticism to Buddhism, see Welbon, *The Buddhist Nirvana,* pp. 7–10.

Chapter 4

1 Montaigne then immediately quotes from an elegy of Catullus: 'Iucundum cum tas florida ver ageret' ('When my age flourishing / Did spend its pleasant spring' (*Essayes*, p. 30).

2 The idea that death is not the event which terminates life so much as a condition which pervades it was widely repeated. Compare More:

Which measuring of time and diminishing of life, with approaching towards death, is nothing else but from our beginning to our ending, one continual dying: so that wake we, sleep we, eat we, drink we, mourn we, sing we, in what wise soever live we, all the same while die we. So that we never ought to look towards death as a thing far off, considering that although he made no haste towards us, yet we never cease ourselves to make haste towards him. ('Four Last Things', p. 475)

And this is how Thomas Browne puts it in a well-known work: 'If we begin to die when we live, and long life be but a prolongation of death, our life is a sad composition; we live with death, and die not in a moment' ('Urn Burial', p. 161). This recalls Mephostophilis's famous remarks in Marlowe's *Dr Faustus* to the effect that hell is less a place than a state of consciousness:

> Hell hath no limits, nor is circumscrib'd
> In one self place, but where we are is hell,
> And where hell is, there must we ever be.
>
> (V.122–4)

3 Eros retains from its mystical origin, where the two kinds of eros (the divinizing eros and sexual passion) were first and fatally confused, 'an indefinable divine element, falsely transcendent, an illusion of the liberating glory of which suffering remained the sign!' However, this attempt at surpassing becomes 'no more than an exaltation of narcissism' (de Rougemont, *Love in the Western World*, pp. 178–9).

4 Lawrence Osborne revives aspects of de Rougemont's argument, but extends its historical reach, when he claims, though without ever quite showing why, that the sexual optimism of recent times shares the fundamental structure of the Christian sexual pessimism it replaces; there is a continuity between St Augustine and Wilhelm Reich: 'sexual pessimism may have been buried, at least partially, but it continues to nourish the grass that grows on its grave':

Sexual pessimism . . . destroys pleasure, but glorifies it inadvertently. It represses but cultivates passion. It scorns but exacerbates desire. It humiliates love, but then deepens it.

As a consequence sexual love becomes a destructive, dangerous, yet infinitely attractive adventure, a sacred perversion of Christ's Passion (pp. xi, 237).

5 This is elaborated in a consideration of how life is affected by art. Literature bestows its vocabulary on passion; the use of that vocabulary fosters the rise of the latent feelings most apt to be expressed through it. When 'passion goes beyond instinct and becomes truly itself, it tends to self-description, either in order to justify or intensify its being, or else simply in order to keep *going*' (de Rougemont, *Love in the Western World*, p. 183). So, if the language of desire enables specific desires to be avowed, and made conscious, a new rhetoric of desire invariably causes 'neglected potentialities of the heart suddenly to become

profusely actualized'. De Rougement concurs with La Rochefoucauld: few people would fall in love had they never heard of love (p. 183). And to some extent with Wilde: life imitates art.

6 In fact there's more than an echo of degeneration theory in de Rougement's account of cultural transmission, and especially in the idea of the profanation of the Tristan myth. (By 'profanation' he means both 'secularization' and 'sacrilege' – *Love in the Western World*, p. 184.) On degeneration theory, see Chapter 9 below.

7 In his 1973 article on 'Love' for the *Dictionary of the History of Ideas*, de Rougemont elaborates his views of the dialectical relationship between passion and religion. Courtly love or the 'love-passion' was condemned by religious orthodoxy as a heresy. Here a familiar binary dependence obtains: the heresy survives only as long as the orthodoxy; each needs the other. But in this instance there is something else that binds them in antagonism: the heresy finds its inspiration in the orthodoxy; it is a perversion of the very orthodoxy which condemns it. Orthodox religion (and, one should add, morality) animates, combats and is combated by the love heresy. And the real danger to such passion – indeed to all passion – is not religion but 'a culture *indifferent* to religion'. From this same violent dialectic de Rougemont reiterates one theme of *Love in the Western World*: '*passion is deepened and releases its energies only in proportion to the resistance it meets*' (p. 101). This is why courtly passion actively seeks out natural, sacred, social or legal obstacles, and would even invent them if necessary. This in turn means that sexual permissiveness is inimical to passion: 'nothing makes passion suffer more than facile access . . . one recoils in dismay at the idea of Isolde's becoming Mrs. Tristan' (p. 105).

8 Kerrigan argues that 'the invention and dissemination of mechanical time in the renaissance brought about a complete reordering of sensibility'. He regards this as central to if not the major cause of that sixteenth-century 'dislocation in man's sense of himself and the world so massive that arguably nothing like it has been seen again until, in this century, man discovered that he had the power to destroy not only himself but "the great globe itself . . ."' Kerrigan also discusses the importance of Protestantism, clockmaking and the dissemination of mechanical time, conceding that it is impossible to determine which preceded the other: the religion or clock technology (Shakespeare, *Sonnets*, pp. 45, 33–37). He finds Shakespeare fascinated with 'the idea that, appearing to possess time [e.g. the time-piece], man was possessed by it' (p. 38). Time as a principle of order, unity and coherence actually contains the seeds of destruction and oblivion.

With its symmetry, order, precision and absolute predictability, the time-piece seems to possess and tame time. Yet the apparent facts of possession and control of a time-piece are actually the means for time to gain greater possession of us; what we think we have tamed we have actually internalized even more deeply and more destructively.

9 Compare the opening lines of the same sonnet: 'Thy glass will shew thee how thy beauties wear, / Thy dial how thy precious minutes waste'.

The 1609 Quarto edition of the sonnets has 'were', which is amended by modern editors to 'wear'. In his edition Booth comments that 'were' was a reasonably common variant spelling of 'wear', adding: ' "were"[,] meaning "used to be"[,] is not immediately meaningful here, and *wear* is'. He does allow a meaning like 'show thee how thy beauties were' – 'remind you of the beauty you had' (p. 267). I suggest 'were' carries a stronger meaning. 'Wear' externalizes the process (as in 'wear away'), even suggesting that beauties are worn like garments or cosmetics. 'Were' is also necessary not just in the sense of 'reminding you what you've lost', but in reminding you that this decay is *what your beauties always were*.

Chapter 5

1 *Biathanatos* was not published until 1646 – nearly forty years after it had been written, and fifteen years after Donne's death.

2 One MS has 'my affliction'. That Donne was susceptible to a suicidal depression disproportionate to the situation is suggested in a letter of 1608 in which he speaks of experiencing a frequent 'thirst and inhiation [i.e. the act of desiring greedily] after the next life' and, a moment later, of 'a desire of the next life'. He experiences this desire not just when stricken with ill-fortune and weariness of this life (as at the time of writing this letter), but equally strongly in other, more fortunate, times: 'I had the same desires when I went with the tide, and enjoyed fairer hopes than now' (*Selected Prose*, p. 92).

3 *blast*: to wither, shrivel, blight; 'blasting withers up the brightness, freshness, beauty, vitality, and promise of living things' (*OED*).

4 See Victor Harris, *All Coherence Gone*, and George Williamson, 'Mutability, Decay and Seventeeth-Century Melancholy'.

5 The discovery that the earth is not at the centre of the universe is often taken to be the first significant episode in the long and troubling decentring of 'man' – that is, the displacement of man from the centre of creation, along with the repudiation of creation theory itself. Other such episodes include Darwin's evolutionary downgrading of man's privileged place in creation, Marx's theory of man as determined by (rather than being responsible for) his social conditions, and Freud's theory of the unconscious as the real determinant of our actions. Freud declares, citing Georg Groddeck, 'what we call our ego behaves essentially passively in life, and that, as [Groddeck] expresses it, we are "lived" by unknown and uncontrollable forces' (*The Ego and the Id*, p. 362). Though overlooking important distinctions, this account of a long process of decentring beginning in the late sixteenth century does usefully remind us of the extent to which the concern over mutability and change connects with the anxieties about identity discussed in Chapter 6.

6 See Dollimore, *Sexual Dissidence*, esp. pp. 117–21, 148–54.

7 As Edmund Spenser put it, desire is a 'web of will, whose end is never wrought' and the lover who escapes it is left 'Desiring nought but how to kill desire' ('Thou blind man's mark', in Williams, p. 173).

8 As Drummond's editor points out, this title was also intended to place the text in the tradition of midnight meditations on death (p. 199).

Chapter 6

1 All references to Browne are to the edition edited by Symonds, unless otherwise stated.

2 I've explored this at length in *Radical Tragedy*; see esp. Part III, 'Man Decentred'.

3 This recalls Ulysses' speech in Shakespeare's *Troilus and Cressida*, a play of the same date:

> ... no man is the lord of anything,
> Though in and of him there be much consisting,
> Till he communicate his parts to others.
> Nor doth he of himself know them for aught
> Till he behold them formèd in th'applause
> Where they're extended ...
>
> (III.iii.110–15)

Compare Marlowe's *Edward II*: 'But what are kings when regiment is gone, / But perfect shadows in a sunshine day' (V.i.26–7).

4 See Juliana Schiesari, *The Gendering of Melancholia*.

5 The 1829 edition of the work covered almost 3,000 pages and extended to six volumes; see Patrides (ed.) in Ralegh, *History*, p. xi.

6 Compare Machiavelli (1469–1527): 'nature has created men so that they desire everything, but are unable to attain it; desire being thus always greater than the faculty of acquiring, discontent with what they have[,] *and* dissatisfaction with themselves[,] results from it' (cited in Greenblatt, *Sir Walter Ralegh*, p. 40).

7 Unless otherwise stated, all quotations from the *Sonnets* are from the edition edited by John Kerrigan.

8 'Sustain' also means 'to endure, to suffer' (as in 'to sustain an injury'); Shakespeare several times used it in this sense. Thus manly marrow sustains (in the sense of supports) 'the bound and high curvet' of the steed, but also suffers and endures on its behalf. Even (especially?) in the supportive self-empowerment of the steed/war fantasy, masochism figures via sacrifice.

It might be said that I'm reading too much into what is, after all, only an aside in a comedy. But such asides are exactly where we find a great deal of Shakespeare's thoughtful reflection. Another instance, now resonant with ironic implications for the displacement of mutability across gender, is Proteus's remark near the end of *The Two Gentlemen of Verona*:

O heaven, were man
But constant, he were perfect! That one error
Fills him with faults . . .
                    (V.iv.110–12).

9 And not infrequently the occasion for laboured wit, as in the following anonymous poem, 'Stand, Stately Tavie':

Stand, stately Tavie, out of the codpiece rise,
And dig a grave between the Mrs. Thighs;
Swift stand, then stab 'till she replies,
Then gently weep, and after weeping die.
Stand, Tavie, and gain the credit lost;
Or by this hand I'll never draw thee, but against a post.
                    (Cole, p. 175)

10 The classical debate is usefully summarized by Michel Foucault in *The Use of Pleasure*, pp. 130–33. Clement of Alexandria was just one of those who expressed this conviction in terms which were also violently gendered:

Does not lassitude succeed intercourse because of the quantity of seed lost? 'For a man is formed and torn out of a man.' See how much harm is done. A whole man is torn out when the seed is lost in intercourse. (*Christ the Educator*, pp. 172–3)

Chapter 7

1 Unless otherwise stated, all quotations from the *Sonnets* are from the edition edited by John Kerrigan.
2 This representation of Juliet finds confirmation in Elisabeth Bronfen's analysis of later works of literature and art in *Over Her Dead Body: Death, Femininity and the Aesthetic* – see the Introduction above.
3 I have discussed these and other aspects of this play in 'Transgression and Surveillance in *Measure for Measure*' in Dollimore and Sinfield (eds.), *Political Shakespeare*.
4 Compare *Macbeth*: 'Thriftless ambition, that will ravin up / Thine own life's means!' (II.iv.28–9).

Chapter 8

1 Equally simplistic is the idea that 'death blatantly defies the power of reason', that it 'is the scandal, the ultimate humiliation of reason' (Bauman, p. 15).
2 To some extent the disagreement might seem to reduce if we distinguish between, say, an artistic, philosophical and arguably élitist preoccupation with the metaphysics of death and the more general social life of larger populations – the domain of social historians. But the distinction does not really hold, since

the most influential historical arguments for the denial of death have tended to draw significantly on the philosophical and the artistic, especially the literary. Even more important is that social historians like David Cannadine ('War and Death, Grief and Mourning in Modern Britain') have questioned the denial-of-death arguments by exploring both the actuality and the diversity of people's response to death. This kind of social history takes us into into the immensely *varied* experiences of grief, loss and endurance.

3 Goodwin and Bronfen, Introduction to *Death and Representation*, p. 4; cf. Denis Hollier: 'Death ... is the other of everything known; it threatens the meaning of discourses. Death is hence irreducibly heterogeneous to homologies; it is not assimilable' (*Against Architecture*, p. 36).

Chapter 9

1 Compare A. R. Wallace, a more progressive thinker, and contributor to the evolutionary theory of natural selection, who argued that the threat of degeneration teaches 'the absolute necessity of labour and effort, of struggle and difficulty, of discomfort and pain, as the condition of all progress' (cited in Pick, p. 217).

2 Mosse, *Nationalism and Sexuality*, Chapters 2, 7 and 8, esp. pp. 17, 25, 34, 36; see also Gilman, 'Sexology, Psychoanalysis, and Degeneration'.

3 It is interesting to find in Michel Foucault's *The History of Sexuality*, otherwise one of the most influential modern challenges to psychoanalysis, a recognition of how psychoanalysis nevertheless 'rigorously opposed the political and institutional effects of the perversion–heredity–degenerescence system' (I.119).

4 Thus Edwin Lankester, writing in the *Encyclopaedia Britannica* (11th edn, 1910–11), contested the optimistic view that evolution and progress implied each other; on the contrary, evolution could be a return from a complex to a simpler state – what he called 'a progressive simplification of structure' (cited in Pick, p. 218).

5 On the connection between the perverse and the primitive, see further Gilman, 'Sexology, Psychoanalysis, and Degeneration', pp. 73, 87–89. On the racist transfer of the sexual stereotype of the degenerate, see Mosse, *Nationalism and Sexuality*, p. 36. The most informative recent account of ideas of degeneration in relation to race is Robert Young's *Colonial Desire*, esp. Chapter 4.

6 I argue this more fully in *Sexual Dissidence*, esp. Parts 5 and 6; for a summary of the argument, see Dollimore, 'The Cultural Politics of Perversion'.

7 Some advocates of degeneration tried to prove it phrenologically – in, for instance, the shape and weight of the skull. Others, like Morel, also invoked the hidden workings of degeneracy. This tension between its visible and invisible workings paralleled the representation of the degenerate urban classes: 'Perceived as visibly different, anomalous and racially "alien", the problem was simultaneously their apparent invisibility in the flux of the great city' (Pick, pp. 51–2).

8 Compare William Hirsch, another advocate of degeneration theory, writing in 1887: 'Between any form of disease and health there are only differences of

degree. No disease is anything more than an exaggeration, or disproportion, or anharmony [*sic*] of normal phenomena' (p. 73).

9 See also Greenslade pp. 20–46, 253–63 *passim*. And compare D. H. Lawrence (below, Chapter 18).

Chapter 10

1 Watts sees Conrad more as reminiscent of Nordau than as anticipatory of Freud (*Conrad's* Heart of Darkness, pp. 132–4).

2 Watts, *Conrad's* Heart of Darkness, pp. 3–4; also Christopher L. Miller, *Blank Darkness*, esp. p. 172.

3 Cf. the suicide of Decoud in Conrad's *Nostromo*. Adrift in a boat on the ocean, doubting his own individuality, unable to differentiate it from the inanimate world around him, and perceiving the universe as a 'succession of incomprehensible images', he shoots himself. The sea into which he falls remains 'untroubled by the fall of his body'; he disappears 'without a trace, swallowed up by the immense indifference of things' – the proverbial, quantifiably indistinct and indiscernible drop in the ocean (pp. 409, 411–12).

Chapter 11

1 'The image of the progress to infinity [bad infinity] is the *straight line*, at the two limits of which alone the infinite is, and always only is where the line – which is determinate being – is not, and which goes *out beyond* to this negation of its determinate being, that is, to the indeterminate; the image of true infinity, bent back on itself, becomes the *circle*, the line which has reached itself, which is closed and wholly present, without *beginning* or *end*' (Hegel, *Logic*, p. 149).

2 Hegel also makes God coextensive with reason: 'God is essentially rational', and this is a rationality 'that is alive and, as spirit, is in and for itself' (*Lectures*, I.139). Correspondingly, 'as pure knowing or as thinking [spirit] has the universal for its object – this is eternity. Eternity is not mere duration (in the sense that the mountains endure) but *knowing* – the knowing of what is eternal' (III.209). Thus the hubristic reach of Hegel's rationalism: the irreconcilable otherness of God and that of Eternity – other, that is, to man – are abolished not through their demystification but rather through their incorporation.

3 Feuerbach and Marx both regarded Hegelian philosophy as the last rational refuge of theology. But this was not the end of theology; it meant that henceforth it could only proceed irrationally – which was no great sacrifice.

Chapter 12

1 Elsewhere Heidegger refers to our tendency to 'hasten into the public superficies of existence' ('What is Metaphysics?', p. 106). The italics throughout this chapter are Heidegger's unless otherwise stated.

2 For a fuller elucidation of Heidegger on death, see Lingis, *Deathbound Subjectivity*, esp. Chapters 5 and 8.

3 In the 1992 preface to his *Heidegger*, George Steiner remarks, 'Notoriously, Heidegger himself was unable to arrive at a definition of *Sein*, of Being and the being of Being, that is not either a pure tautology or a metaphoric and infinitely regressive chain. He himself admitted this fact, attributing to human speech itself some radical inadequacy in the face of Being.' One problem, as Steiner points out, is Heidegger's attempt to think Being independently of what actually and existentially is (pp. xix–xx). This problem is closely connected with another, namely that Heidegger – one of the greatest influences in Continental thought – is also notoriously difficult to understand. His defenders believe the difficulty is inseparable from his profundity, whereas his critics assert that he is talking non-sense. Some even regard Heidegger's impenetrable style to be connected with his reprehensible politics.

4 One of Heidegger's more intriguing remarks about being concerns its relation to boredom: 'Profound boredom, drifting here and there in the abysses of our existence like a muffling fog, removes all things and men and oneself along with it into a remarkable indifference. This boredom reveals being as a whole' ('What is Metaphysics?', p. 101).

5 On the influence of Kojève's account of Hegel, see Vincent Descombes, *Modern French Philosophy*, and Shadia B. Drury, *Alexandre Kojève*. It should be added that Kojève's reading of Hegel is also influenced by Marx, Feuerbach and Heidegger.

6 This is a subsequent translation of a chapter of Kojève's lectures significantly omitted from the original English translation.

7 See Inwood, 'Hegel on Death', and Drury, *Alexandre Kojève*, esp. note 7, p. 222.

8 On Heidegger's indebtedness to Hegel, see Kojève, 'The Idea of Death', pp. 133, 148, 156, and Inwood, p. 115.

9 This preface of Steiner's is one of the best short accounts of the problems I have read, but see too Chapter 7, 'Settling Accounts: Heidegger, de Man and the ends of Philosophy', in Christopher Norris's *What's Wrong with Postmodernism*.

Chapter 13

1 Cf. *World*, I.356, paraphrasing Buddhism: ' "You shall attain to Nirvana, in other words, to a state or condition in which there are not four things, namely birth, old age, disease, and death." '

Chapter 14

1 The following are elementary glosses on some of the concepts used by Freud. For fuller accounts see Laplanche and Pontalis, *The Language of Psychoanalysis*. *Libido* refers to the energy of the sexual instincts. The *ego* is the organized part

of the mind, the 'I' of the self; the *id* is the uncoordinated instincts ('the dark, inaccessible part of our personality' – *New Introductory Lectures*, p. 105). The ego, which lies between reality and the id, works towards defensive integration, whereas the id often threatens such integration. Whereas everything that happens in the id remains unconscious, processes in the ego may or may not be conscious. The *superego* occupies a special position between the ego and the id and is the critical, moralizing part of the mind; it is the vehicle for what we call conscience. The id, ego and superego are potentially always in conflict with each other.

2 Unlike in mourning, with melancholia the loss is not necessarily conscious; and, even where it is apparent what or whom has been lost, the significance of that loss and what it represents to the subject may not be. From his analysis of melancholia, Freud believes that the ego can kill itself only if, owing to the return of object-cathexis, it comes to treat itself as an object. He also believes that the ego is equally overwhelmed by the object in the otherwise completely opposed situations of being most intensely in love and of suicide. Melancholia does often end in suicide, because in this state the superego becomes 'a kind of gathering-place for the death instincts'; what holds sway in the superego of the melancholic is, as it were, 'a pure culture of the death instinct, and in fact it often enough succeeds in driving the ego into death' ('Mourning and Melancholia', pp. 258, 261; *The Ego and the Id*, pp. 394–5).

3 If the effect of the repression of instinct remains as the experience of non-satisfaction, it is also the case that such pleasure as is obtainable derives from the surviving remnants of primitive instincts. Freud speaks for example of 'crude and primary instinctual impulses [which] convulse our physical being', of 'wild instinctual' impulses 'untamed by the ego', and contrasts these with instinctual satisfaction that has been so tamed, or sublimated. There is just no comparison: the primary type is 'incomparably more intense'. He adds, 'The irresistibility of perverse instincts, and perhaps the attraction in general of forbidden things finds an economic explanation here' (*Civilization and its Discontents*, p. 267).

4 This idea remained troublingly inconsistent if not contradictory; as Laplanche remarks:

From an economic point of view the major contradiction consists in attributing to a single 'drive' the tendency towards the radical elimination of all tension, the supreme form of the pleasure principle, and the masochistic search for unpleasure, which, in all logic, can only be interpreted as an increase of tension. (*Life and Death*, p. 108)

5 Recall Schopenhauer: 'Awakened to life out of the night of unconsciousness, the will finds itself as an individual in an endless and boundless world, among innumerable individuals, all striving, suffering, and erring; and, as if through a troubled dream, it hurries back to the old unconsciousness' (*World*, II.573).

6 '. . . the problem of the origin of life would remain a cosmological one; and the problem of the goal or purpose of life would be answered *dualistically*' (*The Ego and the Id*, p. 381; Freud's emphasis).

7 A prime instance of defusion is sexual sadism functioning independently as a perversion:

Making a swift generalization, we might conjecture that the essence of a regression of libido (e.g. from the genital to the sadistic-anal phase) lies in a defusion of instincts, just as, conversely, the advance from the earlier phase to the definitive genital one would be conditioned by an accession of erotic components. (*The Ego and the Id*, p. 382)

8 Namely that there exists a 'displaceable and indifferent energy', a desexualized libido, which can be added to either an erotic or a destructive impulse, to augment its total cathexis. He concludes that, whereas the death instincts are by their nature mute, 'the clamour of life proceeds for the most part from Eros' (*The Ego and the Id*, pp. 385, 387).

9 Freud also equivocates as to which instinct is primary. Thus he says of the id that it would be possible to imagine it as under the domination of the death drives, only to add 'but perhaps that might be to underplay the part played by Eros' (*The Ego and the Id*, p. 401).

10 Laplanche and Pontalis, p. 418; cf. p. 103, and Laplanche:

Whereas, ever since the beginnings of psychoanalysis, sexuality was in its essence hostile to binding—a principle of 'un-binding' or unfettering (*Entbindung*) which could be bound only through the intervention of the ego – what appears with Eros is the *bound and binding form* of sexuality, brought to light by the discovery of narcissism. It is that form of sexuality, cathecting its object, attached to a form, which henceforth will sustain the ego and life itself, as well as any specific form of sublimation. (*Life and Death*, pp. 123–4)

Freud cannot simply change his theory in this respect without casting real doubt on other aspects of it. For example, erotic binding is inextricable from social and psychic binding more generally, and all such binding involves a simultaneous process of differentiation, not to mention the precarious disjunctions entailed by identification and disavowal – potential undoings of the most radical kind. Leaving aside the terms of psychoanalysis, we need only recall some of the literary and philosophical considerations of desire encountered in earlier chapters to be reminded that its potential to unbind is formidable. To reply that this force of unbinding is actually the work of the death instinct fused with eros is really only to make the theory true by definition and again rob it of any explanatory power.

11 I've argued in *Sexual Dissidence* (pp. 169–204) that, while Freud's theory required the idea of the sexual perversions – most especially homosexuality – they came to take on a troubling centrality in his work, growing in significance (though inexplicably), and often foregrounding inconsistencies. Placing them on the side of the death drive would be one way back to a certain theoretical coherence. The two perversions which he hitherto accorded such high priority, namely sadism and masochism, help in the discovery of the death drive, being manifestations of it strongly alloyed with eros (*Civilization and its Discontents*, pp. 310–11).

12 Freud is, however, notoriously guarded – not to say evasive – in his acknowlege-ment of more recent influences:

The large extent to which psycho-analysis coincides with the philosophy of Schopenhauer – not only did he assert the dominance of the emotions and the supreme importance of sexuality but he was even aware of the mechanism of repression – is not to be traced to my acquaintance with his teaching. I read Schopenhauer very late in my life. Nietzsche, another philosopher whose guesses and intuitions often agree in the most astonishing way with the laborious findings of psycho-analysis, was for a long time avoided by me on that very account; I was less concerned with the question of priority than keeping my mind unembarrassed. ('An Autobiographical Study', p. 244)

13 Cf. *New Introductory Lectures*: 'The theory of the instincts is so to say our mythology. Instincts are mythical entities, magnificent in their indefiniteness' (p. 127).

14 Boothby also shows that Nietzsche's thinking in *The Birth of Tragedy* also bears comparison with Freud, as does the metaphysics of Hegel (*Death and Desire*, pp. 188–91, 196–203). Relatedly, Freud's account of the conflict between the two principles (pleasure and reality) – a conflict which the discovery of the death drive revises – reworks the traditional dichotomy exercising philosophers from Aristotle to Spinoza and beyond, between passion and reason.

Another influence on Freud was contemporary biology. In certain important respects Freud was seeking to reformulate this older vision in biological terms. But Frank Sulloway argues persuasively that Freud's death-drive theory was both implied and rendered necessary by several existing and intractable theoretical problems in his work. In the process he turned to contemporary biological science (*Freud, Biologist of the Mind*, esp. pp. 394–5, 412–13).

15 As Laplanche observes of *Beyond the Pleasure Principle*, 'Never had Freud shown himself to be so profoundly *free* and as audacious as in that vast meta-psychological, metaphysical, and metabiological fresco' (*Life and Death*, p. 106).

16 At that limit, says Henry Staten, human desire becomes the desire to 'contract into the infinite particularity of one's own being as a being of nothingness'; desire is the difficult and demanding place in which authenticity can be found, but the price of such authenticity is 'confrontation with the *absolute* nothingness of the self' (pp. 168, 185).

17 Malcolm Bowie evokes something of Lacan's own tortured version of the idea when he says that desire 'is not a state or a motion but a space, and not a unified space but a split and contorted one' (p. 137). Bowie also remarks that Lacan's style of theorizing is an attempt to write 'transience back into the psychoanalytic account of the human mind' (p. 10). And not only negatively: there are places where Lacan speaks more vitalistically of desire, connecting it with 'an original organic disarray ... a vital dehiscence that is constitutive of man ... a "negative" libido that enables the Heraclitean notion of Discord, which the Ephesian believed to be prior to harmony, to shine once more' (Lacan, *Écrits*, p. 21).

18 Mitchell again, summarizing one of Lacan's basic and most influential principles:

the unconscious reveals a fragmented subject of shifting and uncertain sexual identity. To be human is to be subjected to a law which decentres and divides: sexuality is created in a division, the subject is split; but an ideological world conceals this from the conscious subject who is supposed to feel whole and certain of a sexual identity. (Lacan, *Feminine Sexuality*, p. 26)

19 Boothby has attempted to render the Lacanian account more coherent and thereby render the theory of the death drive more generally acceptable. He does so by arguing that the instinct aims at the death not of the organism but of the self, or ego. Like all Lacanian arguments, this one is intricate and question-begging, but the important point seems to be this: as a radical force of unbinding, the death drive must be interpreted psychologically. This means that what is subject to 'death' is not the biological organism but the unity of the imaginary ego. Thus 'the death drive may . . . be said to be the return of the real against the defensive organization of the ego that excludes it'; the ego is undone by energies foreign to its organization, energies associated specifically with the id: 'the oceanic forces of the id are destined again and again to overtake the ego and threaten to wash away the face of its identity' (pp. 71, 84, 105, 185, 224).

20 For example, 'it is in effect as a desire for death that [the subject] affirms himself for others; if he identifies himself with the other, it is by fixing him solidly in the metamorphosis of his essential image, and no being is ever evoked by him except among the shadows of death' (*Écrits*, pp. 104–5). Henry Staten finds that Lacan 'preserves in a sophisticated new fashion the Christian/Platonic depreciation of the worldly libidinal object as a "*vanitas*", a deceptive appearance that lures the subject away from her ontological destiny'. St Augustine is particularly important for Lacan, who knew where he was coming from 'even if many of his followers do not' (pp. 167, 182).

Chapter 15

1 Chinua Achebe wrote, 'Conrad was a thoroughgoing racist . . . And the question is whether a novel which celebrates this dehumanization, which depersonalizes a portion of the human race, can be called a great work of art. My answer is: No, it cannot' ('An Image of Africa', p. 267). His essay is reprinted in Brooker and Widdowson (eds.), *A Practical Reader in Contemporary Literary Theory*, which has several other essays on this novel. Craig Raine disputes Achebe's view of Conrad as a racist in a review of Achebe's *Hopes and Impediments* in the *London Review of Books*, 22 June 1989, pp. 16–18. This article gave rise to a dispute in the letters column extending to December 1989. See also D. C. R. A. Goonetilleke (ed.), *Heart of Darkness*, esp. pp. 14–29.

2 Zhdanov describes this as a 'clear, sharp, exact, profoundly scientific characterization' (p. 95).

3 See Werner Hahn, *Postwar Soviet Politics*, and Gavriel Ra'anan, *International Policy Formation*.

4 Recalling Nietzsche, Marcuse traces the ideology of death back to Socrates' devaluation of earthly existence, and of the body, and his association of truth with self-denial and self-renunciation ('The Ideology of Death', pp. 67–8).

5 On Heidegger's Nazism see above, Chapter 12.

6 This error is not unconnected with the fact that, by the 1980s, *Eros and Civilization* was being disregarded, often mentioned only in passing as a foil to Foucault's influential anti-essentialist account of power and resistance to it. Foucault presumably had Marcuse in mind when he declared, in *The History of Sexuality*, that 'there is no single locus of great Refusal, no soul of revolt, source of all rebellions, or pure law of the revolutionary. Instead there is a plurality of resistances . . .' (I.95–6). Since this was taken to refer to Marcuse's irredeemable essentialism – at least by those who had not read him – it is instructive to recall how Marcuse endorses the way in which psychoanalysis necessarily dissolves the individual, finding in the 'autonomous personality' merely 'the *frozen* manifestation of the general repression of mankind'. Both rationality and self-consciousness are forms of repression, internal and external; psychoanalysis can undermine 'one of the strongest ideological fortifications of modern culture – namely, the notion of the autonomous individual' (*Eros and Civilization*, p. 57). It is also worth noting that Marcuse's notion of 'repressive desublimation' anticipates Foucault's own account of the relationship between sexuality and power.

7 Similarly, phantasy, by linking the deepest layers of the unconscious with the highest products of consciousness (art), the dream with the reality, 'preserves the archetypes of the genus, the perpetual but repressed ideas of the collective and individual memory, the tabood images of freedom'; phantasy also possesses a truth value of its own (*Eros and Civilization*, pp. 141–3). Compare *One-Dimensional Man*: 'Remembrance of the past may give rise to dangerous insights' (p. 98).

8 Marcuse gives a suggestive if sketchy account of sexual perversions, which clearly interest him greatly. He regards them as both an effect of repression and a challenge to it in the name of a 'fuller Eros'. Because they represent a rebellion against the subjugation of sexuality, they have revolutionary potential – and this, seemingly, because and not in spite of their intimacy with the death instinct (*Eros and Civilization*, pp. 171, 202–3; see also pp. 49–52, 109, 146).

9 This has proved to be one of the most controversial aspects of Marcuse's philosophy. In *The Crisis of Psychoanalysis* Erich Fromm pronounces Marcuse a victim of neurosis and psychosis. Like some avant-garde artists, from de Sade onwards, Marcuse is attracted by 'infantile regression, perversion and . . . destruction and hate'; by 'the refusal to grow up, to separate fully from the

mother and soil, and to experience fully sexual pleasure'. In short, Marcuse 'glorifies the morbidity of the society he wants to change'. In the process, claims Fromm, he constructs a Freudian theory which is the complete opposite of all that is essential in Freud's thinking (pp. 29–30). A more sympathetic and perceptive critic, Morton Schoolman, reproves Marcuse for celebrating the death instinct and proposing a Utopia which entails 'mental death of the individual'; for attempting to reduce the conflict between eros and thanatos in a way which actually brings life 'even more securely within the orbit of death' (*The Imaginary Witness*, pp. 112, 116).

Chapter 16

1 Nietzsche celebrates the Renaissance as 'the last great age' (*Twilight*, pp. 91, 98). But, as we have seen, that period included something like the decadent vision Nietszche despises. Those like Walter Ralegh who would presumably qualify as Nietzsche's ideal type of great man, full of the will to power, were often those who expressed the mutability aesthetic most strongly, and its concomitant deathward vision. Nietzsche's view of the Renaissance is a simplistic reconstruction which eliminates an obvious paradox about it, namely that the mutability aesthetic and even the death-wish may emerge from an energetic encounter with the real; in Nietzsche's terms, the will to power, even as it aspires to transcend and abolish *décadence*, also helps to generate it.

2 Freud, who (implausibly) denied that Nietzsche had in any way influenced him, also (according to Ernest Jones) said several times of Nietzsche that he 'had a more penetrating knowledge of himself than any other man who ever lived or who was likely to live' (Jones, II.385).

3 It is apparent from Nietzsche's letters that he experienced transience and mutability intensely. Sometimes he mocks himself for doing so (*Letters*, ed. Levy, p. 57); he also writes perceptively of ageing, loss and death:

To grow old and to grow solitary seem to be synonymous, and at last a man is all alone and makes others feel lonely by his death.

The curtain falls on our past when our mother dies; it is then for the first time that our childhood and youth become nothing more than a memory. And then the same process extends; the friends of our youth, our teachers, our ideals of those days, all die, and every day we grow more lonely, and ever colder breezes blow about us. (pp. 89–90, 132)

The same thoughts recur – 'everything is *over*, it is the past, forbearance' (*Letters*, ed. Middleton, p. 220). But there is a compensating empowerment in writing; in the same letter, referring to his *Zarathustra*, he inquires whether 'vigour, flexibility and euphony have ever consorted so well in our language' (p. 221).

4 In the section 'Of Redemption' in *Thus Spake Zarathustra*, Zarathustra turns to his disciples and 'with profound ill-humour' declares:

And it is all my art and aim, to compose into one and bring together what is fragment and riddle and dreadful chance . . .

To redeem the past and to transform every 'It was' into an 'I wanted it thus!' – that alone do I call redemption! . . .

Willing liberates: but what is it that fastens in fetters even the liberator?

'It was': that is what the will's teeth-gnashing and most lonely melancholy is called. Powerless against that which has been done, the will is an angry spectator of all things past. *The will cannot will backwards; that it cannot break time and time's desire – that is the will's most lonely melancholy.*

Because of its inability to 'break time's desire', the will takes revenge 'on all that can suffer' (*Zarathustra*, trans. Hollingdale, pp. 161–2; my emphasis).

5 Elliott Zuckerman finds that 'Renunciation in one form or another runs through all Wagner's work from *The Flying Dutchman* to *Parsifal*. The Dutchman gains redemption, according to Wagner's explanation of the plot, "through *a woman* who shall sacrifice herself for the love of him. Thus it is the yearning for death that spurs him on to seek this woman" ' (p. 34).

6 Feuerbach's *Thoughts on Death and Immortality* was a significant influence for Wagner before Schopenhauer – so much so that the composer dedicates his *The Art Work of the Future* to Feuerbach. See Irving Singer, *The Nature of Love*, II.472–6. There are other influences: Wagner regarded Christianity in its pure and unalloyed form – uncontaminated by 'narrow-hearted Judaism' – as nothing but a branch of Buddhism, of which, in early Christianity, we still see distinct traces, including the desire for the extinction of the individual personality. According to Wagner, the early Christians desired extinction (*Wagner on Music and Drama*, pp. 277–8).

7 The first chord of *Tristan* contains two dissonances, one of which is then resolved, the other not. Throughout the piece the longing for the resolution of discord is partially satisfied and partially not – 'the entire work is a sort of musical equivalent of Schopenhauer's doctrine that existence is an inherently unsatisfiable web of longings, willings and strivings from which the only permanent liberation is the cessation of being' (Bryan Magee, *The Philosophy of Schopenhauer*, p. 356). Magee also points out that in *Tristan* the traditional symbolism of night and day is inverted: day is the world of appearance and illusion, night of ultimate truth, timeless reality – i.e. death (p. 361).

8 In 1881, writing to Gast, Nietzsche says of his own works, 'there is something in [them] that always fills me with a sense of shame; they are counterfeits of a suffering imperfect nature'. Elsewhere he speaks of being ashamed to reveal the extent of his pain (*Letters*, ed. Levy, pp. 123, 140, 217). In his letters he also writes frequently of loneliness (though accepting it as a condition of his appointed task), and he increasingly complains of the neglect of, and contempt for, his work by those whose opinion he elsewhere says he despises. In 1883 to Gast:

Out of a *veritable abyss* of the most undeserved and *most enduring* contempt in which the whole of my work and endeavour has lain since the year 1876, I long for a word of wisdom concerning myself. (p. 162)

He confesses in another letter ten days later that he is succumbing to a feeling for which he has contempt: resentment (p. 162; cf. p. 208). For all his renunciation, he still aspires to be the leading philosopher of the age – and more (p. 218). He does his best work and comes most alive on clear days in winter, and complains about the pain of spring, almost as if stimulus to libido, in the widest sense, is dangerous:

spring attacks me unconsciously; I dare not tell you into what abyss of despair I sink under its influence. My body (and my philosophy, too, for that matter), feels the *cold* to be its appointed preservative element – that sounds paradoxical and negative, but it is the most thoroughly demonstrated fact of my life. (p. 199; *Letters*, ed. Middleton, p. 267)

9 Nietzsche's chronic illnesses included exhaustion and depression. In 1883 he tells his sister that he is low-spirited for at least eight months in the year.

Shall I ever attain to inner freedom? It is very doubtful. The goal is too remote, and even if one gets within measurable distance of it, one has by that time consumed all one's strength in a long search and struggle. When freedom is at last attained, one is as lifeless and feeble as a day-fly by night . . . For the moment I am really very very tired of everything – more than tired.
    My health, by-the-bye, is excellent. (*Letters*, ed. Levy, p. 96)

In 1882 he speaks of depression and 'weariness with life' overcome only by his writing (*Letters*, ed. Middleton, p. 146). Some months before his final breakdown in January 1889 he writes of being 'extraordinarily depressed and melancholy' (*Letters*, ed. Levy, p. 236). In the context of remarks about Buddhism, he adds:

The conviction that life is valueless and that all goals are illusory impresses itself on me so strongly, especially when I am sick in bed, that I need to hear more about it, but not mixed with Judaeo-Christian phraseology. (*Letters*, ed. Middleton, p. 139)

In 1884: 'Ah, dear friend, what an absurdly silent life I lead! So much alone, so much alone! So "childless"' (*Letters*, ed. Levy, p. 174).
10 I believe Nietzsche experienced intense homoerotic desire, and that this is partly what he is speaking about in a letter to his sister in 1866 about the loneliness of the intellectual unable to communicate his thoughts; he speaks of

him who is 'different'; who has never met anyone who precisely belonged to him, although he has sought well on all sorts of roads; who in his relationship to his fellows always had to practise a sort of considerate and cheerful dissimulation in the hope of assimilating himself to them, often with success . . .

Sometimes, too, he has given vent to

349

those dangerous, heartrending outbursts of all his concealed misery, of all the longings he has not yet stifled, of all his surging and tumultuous streams of love . . .

Just as painful is

the sudden madness of those moments when the lonely man embraces one that seems to his taste and treats him as a friend, as a Heaven-sent blessing and precious gift, only to thrust him from him with loathing an hour later, and with loathing too for himself . . . A deep man needs friends. (*Letters*, ed. Levy, p. 183)

Compare this letter from the following year:

Who has ever approached me with even a thousandth part of my passion and my suffering! Has anyone even an inkling of the real cause of my prolonged ill-health over which I may even yet prevail? I am now forty-three and am just as much alone now as I was as a child. (p. 205; *Letters*, ed. Middleton, p. 276)

11 And yet he never stopped wanting 'a completely radical institution for *truth*', one necessarily subversive, and in ways that institutionalized university life can never be (*Letters*, ed. Middleton, p. 73). What he approves in Hippolyte Taine, he strongly wants for himself: 'reckless courage . . . absolutely sincere intellectual conscience . . . stirring and modest stoicism amid acute privations and isolation'. The effort was difficult, often unendurable; to Gast again, in 1883: 'For, truth to tell, *I am well nigh crushed to death*' (*Letters*, ed. Levy, pp. 201, 161).

12 Thomas Mann, *Last Essays*, pp. 162–8, writes perceptively and persuasively on Nietzsche's rhetoric of war, and his relationship to fascism and Nazism.

Chapter 17

1 Importantly, Bataille stresses that cultural prohibitions are variable and always arbitrarily defined: 'what disturbs one man leaves another indifferent, and, what is more, the same individual that such an object lacerates one day is indifferent the next'. Human life is regulated by the fact of prohibition, not by this or that particular prohibition (*Accursed Share*, II.54, 69, 151).

2 Cf. *Erotism*: 'The wish to produce at cut-prices is niggardly and human. Humanity keeps to the narrow capitalist principle . . .' (p. 60).

3 Here the influence of Hegel, via Kojève, is decisive; see esp. Bataille's 'Hegel, Death and Sacrifice'.

4 Bataille contends that the recent history of a progressive but slow lifting of sexual prohibitions changes nothing in this regard. For example, 'the shame connected with the excremental orifices or functions would still testify to the divorce between man and nature', and this 'indelible shame' will always transfer across to the adjacent domain of the reproductive organs. He cites Augustine – 'inter faeces et urinam nascimur': 'we are born between faeces and urine' (*Accursed Share*, II.62).

5 It is also true to say that Freud elsewhere provides the terms of Bataille's own account of the dialectic between desire and repression.

6 Bataille cites de Sade approvingly, though with hesitation: 'There is no better way to know death than to link it with some licentious image' (*Erotism*, p. 11).

7 Eroticism destroys the self-contained character of its practitioners, and so radically that 'in essence, the domain of eroticism is the domain of violence, of violation ... What does physical eroticism signify if not a violation of the very beings of its practitioners? – a violation bordering on death, bordering on murder'. And 'death opens the way to the denial of our individual lives. Without doing violence to our inner selves, are we able to bear a negation that carries us to the furthest bounds of possibility?' (*Erotism*, pp. 16–17, 24).

8 'Primary anguish bound up with sexual disturbance signifies death' (*Erotism*, p. 104).

Chapter 18

1 See Lawrence's *Movements in European History*, p. 262.

2 Cf. *Women in Love*: 'The last impulses of the last religious passion left on earth, the passion for equality, inspired them' (p. 253).

3 In another letter, written three days later, Lawrence admits to having found in Marinetti 'something of what I am after', namely that the 'non-human, in humanity, is more interesting to me than the old-fashioned human element – which causes one to conceive a character in a certain moral scheme and make him consistent'. A remark from later in the same letter – 'You mustn't look in my novel for the old stable *ego* – of the character' – is often cited by those who, wanting to assimilate Lawrence to a (now) respectable modernist anti-essentialism of character, leave out the accompanying remarks about Marinetti. Lawrence continues, 'There is another *ego*, according to whose action the individual is unrecognisable, and passes through, as it were, allotropic states which it needs a deeper sense than any we've been used to exercise, to discover are states of the same single radically unchanged element' (*Letters*, II.181–3). What disrupt the old stable ego are fundamental, unchanging, non-human forces. For Birkin, in *Women in Love*, such forces render humanity insignificant: 'Let mankind pass away – time it did ... Humanity is a dead letter' (p. 65).

4 In *The Rainbow* Skrebensky is described as having returned from, and perhaps having been corrupted by, an Africa of darkness, where every life-form seeks its own annihilation in the very excessiveness of its 'urgent ... fecund desire'. This is what he brings to Ursula: 'Gradually he transferred to her the hot, fecund darkness that possessed his own blood. He was strangely secret. The whole world must be abolished.' Skrebensky kisses Ursula 'and she quivered as as if she were being destroyed, shattered'. She responds completely, 'her mind, her soul gone out' (pp. 446–7).

Chapter 19

1 This is a renewed preoccupation in the 1990s; see for example *High Risk 2: Writings on Sex, Death and Subversion*, whose editors, Amy Scholder and I. Silverberg, remark that many of their contributors 'are preoccupied with death, mortality, suicide, and the disintegration of the body . . . But what is central here is sex's relationship to death: in some cases morbid, in some cases, elegiac' (Introduction).

2 Not surprisingly, Schopenhauer's work was the single most important intellectual influence on Wagner, while Schopenhauer and Wagner were also two of Nietzsche's most important early influences, although he subsequently reacted vehemently against what he regarded as the 'decadence' of their deathward vision of desire – see above, Chapter 16.

3 In his essay on Freud, Mann remarks that the morbid mental state associated with disease is the instrument of profound knowledge not only for the artist and the philosopher, but also for the psychoanalyst, who discovers the truth of human nature through abnormality and neurosis (*Essays*, p. 414).

4 Most of the following references to *Dr Faustus* are from the translation by Lowe-Porter. This is the only currently available English translation of the novel, but is not entirely reliable – on this and other shortcomings of Lowe-Porter's translations of Mann, see David Luke's introduction to Mann's *Selected Stories*, pp. xlvii–lii, and Timothy Buck, 'Neither the Letter nor the Spirit', *Times Literary Supplement*, 13 October 1995, p. 17.

5 All citations of *Death in Venice* are of the translation by David Luke.

6 *Beyond the Pleasure Principle*, where Freud developed the idea of the death drive, appeared in 1920 – some eight years after *Death in Venice*.

7 For a single-minded psychoanalytic interpretation of this type, see Heinz Kohut, 'Death in Venice: A Story About the Disintegration of Artistic Sublimation'.

8 It seems he planned and possibly part-wrote a more lyrical, affirmative treatment of Aschenbach's homoerotic desire – one explicitly sanctioned by even more extensive and precise Platonic allusion. It enabled Mann to describe the project in 1911 as 'serious and pure in tone, treating the case of an elderly artist's passion for a boy. "Hm, hm!", you say. But it is all very proper' (cited in Reed, p. 150).

9 Most enthusiastically by Anthony Heilbut in *Thomas Mann: Eros and Literature*.

10 But, characteristically, in the same letter Mann cites Blüher's definition of eros as the 'affirmation of a human being, irrespective of his worth', adding that, although this definition 'comprehends all the irony of eros', the moralist replies 'no thanks!' Compare the distrustful remark in *Death in Venice*: 'in almost every artistic nature is inborn a wanton and treacherous proneness to side with the beauty that breaks hearts, to single out aristocratic pretensions and pay them homage' (pp. 27–8). On Blüher, see George Mosse, *Nationalism and Sexuality*, pp. 56–8, and Richard Plant, *The Pink Triangle*, pp. 42–3.

11 Mann is perceptive on the way that the disavowal of intellect is itself inescapably intellectual (*Reflections*, pp. 419–20).

12 'Venice attracts me, indeed, it has made me forget my whole earlier life and deeds so that I find myself in a present without past . . . I find, on the other hand, how little Italy can be home to a German, as it were, how his whole nature changes and how thoughtless my life seems at this time' (cited in Aldrich, *The Seduction of the Mediterranean*, p. 66).

13 Cf. Tony Tanner: 'From the Aschenbach–Munich point of view, Venice is an oriental city where the East more than meets the West – rather, penetrates, suffuses, contaminates and undermines it . . . Venice is notoriously a site where opposites begin to blur and distinctions fade' (pp. 354, 356).

14 Compared with one of his sources, Euripides' *The Bacchae*, Mann might be said to have tried to demonize some of his best insights. *The Bacchae* is a terse and brilliant dramatization of the perverse dynamic, the authoritarian Pentheus being destroyed from within by the self-same forces he seeks to define and suppress as other. On this, see Cedric Watts's brief, illuminating reading of Mann's indebtedness to Euripides in *The Deceptive Text*, pp. 167–75.

15 See Heilbut, *Thomas Mann*, pp. 246–9, and David Luke's introduction to Mann's *Selected Stories*, pp. xxxiv–xxxvi.

Chapter 20

1 In 1954, writing about Gide, Baldwin had declared that 'the really horrible thing about the phenomenon of present-day homosexuality . . . is that today's unlucky deviate can only save himself by the most tremendous exertion of all his forces from falling into an underworld in which he never meets either men or women, where it is impossible to have either a lover or a friend, where the possibility of genuine human involvement has altogether ceased' (*Nobody Knows My Name*, p. 131).

2 Hocquenghem responds with a sexual radicalism which is equally of its time: 'We could say that on the contrary homosexual love is immensely superior, precisely because anything is possible at any moment'; this is a promiscuous love 'unaware of the law of exclusive disjunction', a 'mechanical scattering [which] corresponds to the mode of existence of desire itself' (p. 97).

3 In an interview conducted some months before his own death from AIDS, Haselden reflected on the controversy this article caused – see Garfield, pp. 12–25.

4 David Revill is also worried by gay promiscuity, but opts too easily for a social-constructionist rationalization of it: he speaks of the extent to which promiscuity in gay culture – 'that casual, faceless voraciousness' – 'stems not from sexual orientation, but has more to do with how male desire in general is constructed and construed in exploitative ways' (*Times Higher Education Supplement*, 5 May 1989, p. 21). Douglas Crimp gives a contrary account of gay promiscuity: 'Our promiscuity taught us many things, not only about the pleasures

of sex, but about the great multiplicity of those pleasures. It is that psychic preparation, that experimentation, that conscious work on our own sexualities that has allowed many of us to change our sexual behaviors . . .' So, against the claim that promiscuity will destroy the gay community, Crimp insists 'in fact *it is our promiscuity that will save us*'. Further, 'all those who contend that gay male promiscuity is merely sexual *compulsion* resulting from fear of intimacy are now faced with very strong evidence against their prejudices. For if compulsion were so easily overcome or redirected, it would hardly deserve the name' ('How to Have Promiscuity in an Epidemic', p. 253). Cf. Andrew Lumsden: 'as I've known it, men are never so peaceful, so unviolent (physically and emotionally), so graceful with each other (no matter how "crude" the act) as they are – as we are – when content to take each other without the addition of names, or beds, or flats, or even of any clear impression of one another's looks' (*Gay News*, no. 235, 4–17 March 1982, p. 17).

5 Compare Guy Hocquenghem: 'Homosexual desire is neither on the side of death nor on the side of life; it is the killer of civilized egos' (p. 136). Actually, the fire-consciousness of Rumaker's narrator turns out to be justified, the book concluding with a dedication to the victims of an actual fire in the very bathhouse which is its subject:

> And, out of the ashes and ruin of all despair,
> and in spite of it,
> to the spirit of the rainbow gay and lesbian phoenix, rising.

Fundamentalists could hardly resist seeing the fire as providential intervention, a divine punishment for sexual evil, the secular equivalent of burning in hell. Even a gay-identified perspective, while obviously and vigorously dissenting from *that* view, might see the fire as having more resonant implications, be they symbolic, ironic or socio-political. But not Rumaker: even that actual fire can be collected into a banal narrative of redemption.

6 And yet one of Foucault's most notorious metaphors for the death of man is so traditional as to suggest that beyond 'him' is only the silence of inanimate nature: 'Man is an invention of recent date' soon to be 'erased, like a face drawn in sand at the edge of the sea' (*The Order of Things*, p. 387).

7 Cf. 'One must give rise to thought as intensive irregularity – disintegration of the subject' (Foucault, *Language*, p. 183).

8 Cf. 'the experience of individuality in modern culture is bound up with that of death: from Hölderlin's Empedocles to Nietzsche's Zarathustra, and on to Freudian man, an obstinate relation to death prescribes the universal its singular face, and lends to each individual the power of being heard for ever; the individual owes to death a meaning which does not cease with him. The division that it traces and the finitude whose mark it imposes link, paradoxically, the universality of language and the precarious, irreplaceable form of the individual' (Foucault, *Birth of the Clinic*, p. 197).

9 Cf. 'Headed toward death, language turns back upon itself; it encounters something like a mirror; and to stop this death which would stop it, it possesses but a single power: that of giving birth to its own image in a play of mirrors that has no limits. From the depths of the mirror where it sets out to arrive anew at the point where it started (at death), but so as finally to escape death, another language can be heard – the image of actual language, but as a minuscule, interior, and virtual model; it is the song of the bard who has already sung of Ulysses before the *Odyssey* and before Ulysses himself (since Ulysses hears the song), but who will also sing of him endlessly after his death (since, for the bard, Ulysses is already as good as dead); and Ulysses, who is alive, receives this song as a wife receives her slain husband' (Foucault, *Language*, pp. 54–5).

10 Foucault apparently lamented the fact that critics of *The History of Sexuality* were unwilling to discuss its arguments about death – see J. Miller, p. 294. In Vol. 2 of the *History* (pp. 125–39) Foucault addresses the connections in Greek culture between sexuality and death (see above, Chapter 1).

11 Earlier, in a speculative, influential and difficult essay on transgression, Foucault had written of a modern form of sexuality which 'offers itself in the superficial discourse of a solid and natural animality, while obscurely addressing itself to Absence'. He speculates that this sexuality

is tied to the death of God and to the ontological void which his death fixed at the limit of our thought; it is also tied to the still silent and groping apparition of a form of thought in which the interrogation of the limit replaces the search for totality and the act of transgression replaces the movement of contradictions. (*Language*, pp. 31, 50)

Chapter 21

1 The Cavafy extracts are taken from the translation by Edmund Keeley and Philip Sherrard.

2 Cf. 'And I Lounged . . .'

3 As most recently in the writing of David Wojnarowicz; see esp. his *Close to the Knives* and *Memories that Smell Like Gasoline*.

4 I explore this more fully in *Sexual Dissidence*, Part 3.

Bibliography

Note: irrespective of the practice in the source volume, spelling has been modernized when sixteenth- and seventeenth-century authors have been quoted in the text.

Achebe, Chinua, 'An Image of Africa: Racism in Conrad's *Heart of Darkness*', in Brooker and Widdowson (eds.), *A Practical Reader in Contemporary Literary Theory*.

Agamben, Giorgio, *Language and Death: The Place of Negativity*, trans. Karen E. Pinkus with Michael Hardt. Minneapolis: University of Minnesota Press, 1991.

Aldrich, Robert, *The Seduction of the Mediterranean: Writing, Art and Homosexual Fantasy*. London: Routledge, 1993.

Alexiou, Margaret, *The Ritual Lament in Greek Tradition*. Cambridge: Cambridge University Press, 1974.

Alvarez, A., *The Savage God: A Study of Suicide* [1971]. Harmondsworth: Penguin, 1974.

Apter, T. E., *Thomas Mann: The Devil's Advocate*. London: Macmillan, 1978.

Aquinas, Sir Thomas, *An Aquinas Reader*, ed. Mary T. Clark. London: Hodder & Stoughton, 1974.

Ariès, Philippe, *The Hour of Our Death*, trans. H. Weaver. New York: Alfred A. Knopf, 1981.

—— *Images of Man and Death*, trans. Janet Lloyd. Cambridge, Mass., and London: Harvard University Press, 1985.

—— *Western Attitudes Toward Death: From the Middle Ages to the Present*, trans. Patricia M. Ranum. Baltimore and London: Johns Hopkins University Press, 1974.

Aschheim, Steven, *The Nietzsche Legacy in Germany 1890–1990*. Berkeley: University of California Press, 1993.

Auden, W. H., *Collected Shorter Poems 1927–1957*. London: Faber, 1966.

—— *Forewords and Afterwords*, selected by Edward Mendelson. New York: Random House, 1973.

Augustine, Saint, *The City of God*, trans. Henry Bettenson, intro. David Knowles. Harmondsworth: Penguin, 1972.

—— *The City of God*, trans. John Healey, intro. Sir Ernest Barker. London: Dent, 1945.

—— *Confessions*, trans. and intro. R. S. Pine-Coffin. Harmondsworth: Penguin, 1961.

Bacon, Francis, *Essays*, ed. and intro. Henry Morley. London: Routledge, 1887.

Bal, Mieke, *Death and Dissymmetry: The Politics of Coherence in the Book of Judges*. Chicago: University of Chicago Press, 1988.

—— *Lethal Love: Feminist Literary Readings of Biblical Love Stories*. Bloomington and Indianapolis: Indiana University Press, 1987.

Bald, R. C., *John Donne: A Life*. Oxford: Clarendon, 1970.

Baldick, Chris, *The Social Mission of English Criticism: 1848–1932*. Oxford: Clarendon, 1983.

Baldwin, James, *Giovanni's Room* [1956]. London: Corgi, 1977.

—— 'Here be Dragons', in *The Price of the Ticket: Collected Non-Fiction 1948–1985*. London: Michael Joseph, 1985.

—— *Nobody Knows My Name*. New York: Dell, 1961.

Barreca, Regina (ed.), *Sex and Death in Victorian Literature*. London: Macmillan, 1990.

—— 'Writing as Voodoo', in Goodwin and Bronfen (eds.), *Death and Representation*.

Barthes, Roland, *Camera Lucida: Reflections on Photography*, trans. Richard Howard. New York: Noonday Press, 1981.

—— Preface to Renaud Camus, *Tricks: 25 Encounters* [1979], trans. Richard Howard. New York: St Martin's Press, 1981. Reprinted in Barthes, *The Rustle of Language*, trans. Richard Howard. Oxford: Blackwell, 1986.

Bataille, Georges, *The Accursed Share*, trans. Robert Hurley, 3 vols. New York: Zone Books, 1988 (vol. 1), 1991 (vols. 2–3).

—— *Erotism: Death and Sensuality* [1957], trans. Mary Dalwood. San Francisco: City Light Books, 1986.

—— *Guilty*, trans. Bruce Boone, intro. Denis Hollier. Venice, Calif.: Lapsis Press, 1988.

—— 'Hegel, Death and Sacrifice', trans. Jonathan Strauss, in Allan Stoekl (ed.), *On Bataille*, Yale French Studies Vol. 78. New Haven: Yale University Press, 1990.

—— *On Nietzsche*, trans. Bruce Boone. London: Athlone, 1992.

—— *The Tears of Eros*, trans. Peter Connor. San Francisco: City Light Books, 1989.

Baudrillard, Jean, *Symbolic Exchange and Death* [1976], trans. Iain Hamilton Grant, intro. Mike Gain. London: Sage Publications, 1993.

Bauman, Zygmunt, *Mortality, Immortality and Other Life Strategies*. Cambridge: Polity Press, 1992.

Beauvoir, Simone de, *The Prime of Life*, trans. Peter Green. London: Weidenfeld & Nicolson, 1962.

Becker, Ernest, *The Denial of Death*. New York: Free Press 1973.

Benjamin, Walter, *Illuminations*, ed. and intro. Hannah Arendt, trans. Harry Zohn. New York: Schocken Books, 1969.

Bersani, Leo, 'Is the Rectum a Grave?', in D. Crimp (ed.), *AIDS: Cultural Analysis, Cultural Activism*. Cambridge, Mass.: MIT Press, 1988.

Bing, Peter, and Cohen, Rip (eds.), *Games of Venus: An Anthology of Greek and Roman Erotic Verse from Sappho to Ovid*. London: Routledge, 1991.

Boothby, Richard, *Death and Desire: Psychoanalytic Theory in Lacan's Return to Freud*. New York and London: Routledge, 1991.

Borges, Jorge Luis, *Other Inquisitions: 1937–1952*, trans. Ruth Simms, intro. James Irby. London: Souvenir Press, 1973.

Bottomore, T. B., and Rubel, M. (eds.), *Karl Marx: Selected Writings in Sociology and Social Philosophy*. Harmondsworth: Penguin, 1963.

Bowie, Malcolm, *Lacan*. London: Fontana, 1991.

Brantlinger, Patrick, *Rule of Darkness: British Literature and Imperialism, 1830–1914*. Ithaca and London: Cornell University Press, 1988.

Brayne, Alan, 'Our Shadows', in Daniels (ed.), *Take Any Train*.

Bredbeck, Gregory W., *Sodomy and Interpretation: Marlowe to Milton*. Ithaca and London: Cornell University Press, 1991.

Brenan, Gerald, *St John of the Cross: His Life and Poetry*, with a translation of the poetry by Lynda Nicholson. Cambridge: Cambridge University Press, 1973.

Bronfen, Elisabeth, *Over Her Dead Body: Death, Femininity and the Aesthetic*. Manchester: Manchester University Press, 1992.

Bronski, Michael, 'Death and the Erotic Imagination', in Erica Carter and Simon Watney (eds.), *Taking Liberties*. London: Serpent's Tail, 1989.

Brooker, Peter, and Widdowson, Peter (eds.), *A Practical Reader in Contemporary Literary Theory*. Hemel Hempstead: Harvester Wheatsheaf, 1996.

Brown, Peter, *The Body and Society: Men, Women and Sexual Renunciation in Early Christianity*. New York: Columbia University Press, 1988.

Browne, Thomas, *Religio Medici, Urn Burial, Christian Morals and Other Essays*, ed. and intro. John Addington Symonds. London: Walter Scott, n.d.

Burnet, John, *Early Greek Philosophy*, 4th edn. London: Adam & Charles Black, 1930.

Burtt, E. A. (ed., intro. and notes), *The Teachings of the Compassionate Buddha: Early Discourses, the* Dhammapapda *and Later Basic Writings*. Ontario: New American Library, 1955.

Bynum, Caroline Walker, *Fragmentation and Redemption: Essays on Gender and the Human Body in Medieval Religion*. New York: Zone Books, 1991.

—— *Holy Feast and Holy Fast: The Religious Significance of Food to Medieval Women*. Berkeley and Los Angeles: University of California Press, 1987.

Calvin, John, *Institutes*, trans. Henry Beveridge, 2 vols. London: Clarke, 1949.

Camus, Renaud, *Tricks: 33 Recits*. Editions Mazarine, 1979; trans. as: *Tricks: 25 Encounters*, preface by Roland Barthes, trans. with a note by Richard Howard. New York: St Martin's Press, 1981.

Canguilhem, Georges, *The Normal and the Pathological* [1966], intro. Michel Foucault, trans. Carolyn R. Fawcett with Robert S. Cohen. New York: Zone Books, 1989.

Cannadine, David, 'War and Death, Grief and Mourning in Modern Britain', in Whaley, *Mirrors of Mortality*, pp. 187–242.

Canneti, Elias, *The Human Province*, trans. Joachim Neugroschel. New York: Seabury Press, 1978.

Carey, John, *John Donne: Life, Mind and Art*. London: Faber, 1981.

Carse, James P., *Death and Existence: A Conceptual History of Human Mortality*. New York: John Wiley & Sons, 1980.

Carson, Anne, *Eros: The Bittersweet*. Princeton: Princeton University Press, 1986.

Castiglione, Baldassare, *The Book of the Courtier* [1528], trans. Sir Thomas Hoby [1561], intro. J. H. Whitfield. London: Dent, 1975.

Cavafy, C. P., *Collected Poems*, trans. Edmund Keeley and Philip Sherrard, ed. George Savidis. London: Chatto & Windus, 1990.

—— *Complete Poems*, trans. R. Dalven, intro. W. H. Auden. London: Hogarth, 1961.

Choron, Jacques, *Death and Western Thought*. New York: Macmillan, 1963.

—— *Modern Man and Mortality*. New York: Macmillan, 1964.

Chrysostom, John, *On Virginity – Against Remarriage*, trans. Sally Rieger Shore, intro. Elizabeth A. Clark. New York and Toronto: Edwin Mellen Press, 1989.

Claridge, Laura, *Romantic Potency: The Paradox of Desire*. Ithaca: Cornell University Press, 1992.

Clement of Alexandria, *Christ the Educator*, trans. Simon P. Ward. New York: Fathers of the Church, 1954.

Cohen-Solal, Annie, *Sartre: A Life*. London: Heinemann, 1987.

Cole, William (ed.), *Erotic Poetry*. London: Weidenfeld & Nicolson, 1964.

Collard, Cyril, *Savage Nights* [1989], trans. William Rodarmor. London: Quartet, 1993.

Conrad, Joseph, *Collected Letters*: Vol. 2: *1898–1902*, ed. F. R. Karl and L. Davies. Cambridge: Cambridge University Press, 1986.

—— *Heart of Darkness* [1899]. Harmondsworth: Penguin, 1973.

—— *Nostromo* [1904]. Harmondsworth: Penguin, 1963.

Conrad, Peter, *A Song of Love and Death: The Meaning of Opera*. London: Hogarth, 1989.

Conze, Edward (ed.), *Buddhist Texts through the Ages*. Oxford: Bruno Cassirer, 1954.

Cornford, F. M., *From Religion to Philosophy: A Study in the Origins of Western Speculation*. London: Edward Arnold, 1912.

Craik, H. (ed.), *English Prose Selections*: Vol. 2: *Sixteenth Century to the Restoration*. London: Macmillan, 1894.

Crimp, Douglas, 'How to Have Promiscuity in an Epidemic', *October*, no. 43 (1987), pp. 237–271.

Critchley, Simon, *Very Little . . . Almost Nothing: Death, Philosophy, Literature*. London: Routledge, 1997.

Daniels, Peter (ed.), *Take Any Train: A Book of Gay Men's Poetry*. London: The Oscars Press, 1991.

Dean, Tim, 'The Psychoanalysis of AIDS', *October*, no. 63 (1993), pp. 83–117.

Delany, Paul, *D. H. Lawrence's Nightmare: The Writer and his Circle in the Years of the Great War*. Brighton: Harvester, 1979.

Deleuze, Gilles, and Guattari, Felix, *A Thousand Plateaus: Capitalism and Schizophrenia*, trans. and foreword Brian Massumi. Minneapolis: University of Minnesota Press, 1987.

Descombes, Vincent, *Modern French Philosophy*, trans. L. Scott-Fox and J. M. Harding. Cambridge: Cambridge University Press, 1980.

Dews, Peter, *Logics of Disintegration: Post-structuralist Thought and the Claims of Critical Theory*. London: Verso, 1987.

Dollimore, Jonathan, 'The Cultural Politics of Perversion: Augustine, Shakespeare, Freud, Foucault', in Joseph Bristow (ed.), *Sexual Sameness: Textual Differences in Lesbian and Gay Writing*. London: Routledge, 1992.

—— *Radical Tragedy: Religion, Ideology and Power in the Drama of Shakespeare and His Contemporaries*, 2nd edn. Hemel Hempstead: Harvester Wheatsheaf, 1989.

—— *Sexual Dissidence: Augustine to Wilde, Freud to Foucault*. Oxford: Clarendon, 1991.

Dollimore, Jonathan, and Sinfield, Alan (eds.), *Political Shakespeare: New Essays in Cultural Materialism*, 2nd edn. Manchester: Manchester University Press, 1994.

Donne, John, *Biathanatos* [c. 1608], ed., intro. and commentary Michael Rudick and M. Pabst Battin. New York and London: Garland 1982.

—— *The Complete English Poems*, ed. A. J. Smith. Harmondsworth: Penguin, 1971.

—— *The Epithalamions, Anniversaries and Epicedes*, ed., intro. and commentary W. Milgate. Oxford: Clarendon, 1978.

—— *Paradoxes and Problems*, ed., intro. and commentary Helen Peters. Oxford: Clarendon, 1980.

—— *Selected Prose*, ed. and intro. Neil Rhodes. Harmondsworth: Penguin, 1987.

Drummond, William, of Hawthornden, *Poems and Prose*, ed. R. H. MacDonald. Edinburgh: Scottish Academic Press, 1976.

Drury, Shadia B., *Alexandre Kojève: The Roots of Postmodern Politics*. London: Macmillan, 1994.

Eagleton, Terry, *The Ideology of the Aesthetic*. Oxford: Blackwell, 1990.

Eijk, Ton H. C. Van, 'Marriage and Virginity, Death and Immortality', in J. Fontaine and C. Kannengiesser, *Epektasis*. Paris: Beauchesne, 1972, pp. 209–235.

Eliot, T. S., *Four Quartets* [1944]. London: Faber, 1954.

Epicurus, *Epicurus: The Extant Remains*, trans. and notes by Cyril Bailey. Oxford: Clarendon, 1926.

Faulkner, William, *The Unvanquished* [1934]. Harmondsworth: Penguin, 1955.

Feher, Michel, Naddaff, Ramona, and Tazi, Nadia (eds.), *Fragments for a History of the Human Body*, 3 vols. New York: Zone Books, 1989.

Feuerbach, Ludwig, *The Essence of Christianity* [1841], trans. George Eliot [1854], intro. Karl Barth, foreword H. Richard Niebuhr. New York: Harper, 1957.

—— *Thoughts on Death and Immortality* [1830], trans., intro. and notes by James A. Massey. Berkeley: University of California Press, 1980.

Flacelière, Robert, *Love in Ancient Greece* [1960], trans. James Cleugh. London: Frederick Muller, 1962.

Forrester, John, *The Seductions of Psychoanalysis: Freud, Lacan and Derrida*. Cambridge: Cambridge University Press, 1990.

Forster, E. M., *Two Cheers for Democracy*. London: Edward Arnold, 1951.

Foucault, Michel, *The Archaeology of Knowledge* [1969], trans. A. M. Sheridan Smith. London: Tavistock, 1972.

—— *The Birth of the Clinic* [1963], trans. A. M. Sheridan. London: Tavistock, 1973.

—— *The History of Sexuality*: Vol. 1: *An Introduction* [1978], trans. Robert Hurley. New York: Vintage Books, 1980. Vol. 2: *The Use of Pleasure* [1984], trans. Robert Hurley. London: Penguin Books, 1985.

—— *Language, Counter-Memory, Practice: Selected Essays and Interviews*, ed. and intro. D. F. Bouchard, trans. D. F. Bouchard and Sherry Simon. Oxford: Blackwell, 1977.

—— *Michel Foucault: Politics, Philosophy, Culture: Interviews and Other Writings 1977–84*, trans. Alan Sheridan et al., ed. and intro. Lawrence D. Kritzman. London and New York: Routledge, 1988.

—— *The Order of Things: An Archaeology of the Human Sciences* [1966]. London: Tavistock, 1974.

Fraunce, Abraham, *The Lamentations of Amyntas* [1587], ed. F. M. Dickey: a translation of Thomas Watson's Latin *Amyntas* [1585], ed. W. F. Staton Jr, (parallel texts). Chicago: University of Chicago Press for The Newberry Library, 1967.

Freud, Sigmund, 'Analysis Terminable and Interminable' [1937], in *The Standard Edition*, Vol. 23, pp. 209–54, ed. and trans. James Strachey. London: Hogarth, 1964.

—— 'An Autobiographical Study' [1924/1925/1935], in *Psychoanalysis: Its History and Development*, The Pelican Freud Library Vol. 15. Harmondsworth: Penguin, 1986.

—— *Beyond the Pleasure Principle* [1920], in *On Metapsychology: The Theory of Psychoanalysis*, The Pelican Freud Library Vol. 11. Harmondsworth: Penguin, 1984.

—— *Civilization and its Discontents* [1929/1930], in *Civilization, Society and Religion*, The Pelican Freud Library Vol. 12. Harmondsworth: Penguin, 1985.

—— *The Complete Letters of Sigmund Freud to Wilhelm Fliess 1887–1904*, trans. and ed. Jeffrey Moussaieff Masson. Cambridge, Mass.: Harvard University Press, 1985.

—— 'The Economic Problem of Masochism' [1924], in *On Metapsychology: The Theory of Psychoanalysis*, The Pelican Freud Library Vol. 11. Harmondsworth: Penguin, 1984.

—— *The Ego and the Id* [1923], in *On Metapsychology: The Theory of Psychoanalysis*, The Pelican Freud Library Vol. 11. Harmondsworth: Penguin, 1984.

—— *Five Lectures on Psychoanalysis* [1910], in *Two Short Accounts of Psychoanalysis*, trans. and ed. James Strachey. Harmondsworth: Penguin, 1962.

—— 'The Libido Theory' [1922/1923], in *The Standard Edition*, Vol. 18, pp. 255–9, ed. and trans. James Strachey. London: Hogarth, 1955.

—— 'Mourning and Melancholia' [1915/1917], in *On Metapsychology: The Theory of Psychoanalysis*, The Pelican Freud Library Vol. 11. Harmondsworth: Penguin, 1984.

—— *New Introductory Lectures on Psycho-Analysis* [1932/1933], The Pelican Freud Library Vol. 2. Harmondsworth: Penguin, 1973.

—— 'Our Attitude towards Death' in *Thoughts for the Times on War and Death* [1915], in *Civilization, Society and Religion*, The Pelican Freud Library Vol. 12. Harmondsworth: Penguin, 1985.

—— *An Outline of Psycho-Analysis* [1940 (1938)], in *The Standard Edition*, Vol. 23, pp. 141–209, ed. and trans. James Strachey. London: Hogarth, 1964.

—— 'Repression' [1915], in *On Metapsychology: The Theory of Psychoanalysis*, The Pelican Freud Library Vol. 11. Harmondsworth: Penguin, 1984.

—— 'On Transience' [1915/1916], in *Art and Literature*, The Pelican Freud Library Vol. 14. Harmondsworth: Penguin, 1985.

—— 'On the Universal Tendency to Debasement in the Sphere of Love' [1912], in *On Sexuality*, The Pelican Freud Library Vol. 7. Harmondsworth: Penguin, 1977.

—— 'Why War?' [1932/33], in *Civilization, Society and Religion*, The Pelican Freud Library Vol. 12. Harmondsworth: Penguin, 1985.

Fromm, Erich, *The Crisis of Psychoanalyis*. London: Jonathan Cape, 1971.

Fullbrook, Kate, and Fullbrook, Edward, *Simone de Beauvoir and Jean-Paul Sartre*. Hemel Hempstead: Harvester Wheatsheaf, 1993.

Fuss, Diana (ed.), *Inside/Out: Lesbian Theories, Gay Theories*. New York and London: Routledge, 1991.

Garfield, Simon, *The End of Innocence: Britain in the Time of AIDS*. London: Faber 1994.

Garland, Robert, *The Greek Way of Death*. London: Duckworth, 1985.

Gilman, Sander L., 'Sexology, Psychoanalysis, and Degeneration: From a Theory of Race to a Race to Theory', in J. Edward Chamberlain and Sander L. Gilman (eds.), *Degeneration: The Dark Side of Progress*. New York: Columbia University Press, 1985.

Goodwin, Sarah Webster, and Bronfen, Elisabeth (eds.), *Death and Representation*. Baltimore and London: Johns Hopkins University Press, 1993.

Goonetilleke, D. C. R. A. (ed.), *Heart of Darkness*. Ontario: Broadview Press, 1995.

Gorer, Geoffrey, *Death, Grief and Mourning in Contemporary Britain*. London: Cresset Press, 1965.

Grant, Robert M., *Gnosticism: A Sourcebook of Heretical Writings from the Early Christian Period*. New York: Harper, 1961.

Greenblatt, Stephen J., *Renaissance Self-Fashioning: From More to Shakespeare*. Chicago: University of Chicago Press, 1980.

—— *Sir Walter Ralegh: The Renaissance Man and his Roles*. New Haven and London: Yale University Press, 1973.

Greenslade, William, *Degeneration, Culture and the Novel 1880–1940*. Cambridge: Cambridge University Press, 1994.

Gregory, Saint, of Nyssa, 'On Virginity' in *Ascetical Works*, trans. Virginia Woods Callahan. Washington: Catholic University of America Press, 1952.

Griffin, Miriam T., 'Imago Vitae Suae', in C. D. N. Costa (ed.), *Seneca*. London: Routledge and Kegan Paul, 1974.

Griffin, Roger (ed.), *Fascism*. Oxford: Oxford University Press, 1995.

Gunn, Thom, *The Man with Night Sweats*. London: Faber, 1992.

Hahn, Werner G., *Postwar Soviet Politics: The Fall of Zhdanov and the Defeat of Moderation, 1946–53*. Ithaca and London: Cornell University Press, 1982.

Halperin, David M., *One Hundred Years of Homosexuality: And Other Essays on Greek Love*. New York: Routledge, 1990.

—— *Saint Foucault: Towards a Gay Hagiography*. New York and Oxford: Oxford University Press, 1995.

Hangstrum, Jean H., *Eros and Vision: The Restoration to Romanticism*. Evanston: Northwestern University Press, 1989.

—— *The Romantic Body: Love and Sexuality in Keats, Wordsworth, and Blake*. Knoxville: University of Tennessee Press, 1985.

Hanson, Ellis, 'Undead', in Fuss (ed.), *Inside/Out*.

Hardy, Thomas, *Collected Poems*. London: Macmillan, 1930.

Harris, H. S., *Hegel's Development: Night Thoughts (Jena 1801–1806)*. Oxford: Clarendon, 1983.

Harris, Victor, *All Coherence Gone: A Study in the Seventeenth Century Controversy over Disorder and Decay in the Universe*. London: Cass, 1966.

Hartsock, Nancy M., *Money, Sex and Power: Toward a Feminist Materialism*. New York and London: Longman, 1983.

Haselden, Rupert, 'Gay's Inn', *Impact*, autumn 1991, pp. 14–15; reprinted in *Weekend Guardian*, 7–8 September 1991, pp. 20–21.

Hegel, Georg Wilhelm Friedrich, *Aesthetics: Lectures on Fine Art*, trans. T. M. Knox, 2 vols. Oxford: Clarendon, 1975.

—— *Lectures on the Philosophy of Religion*, ed. Peter C. Hodgson, trans. R. F. Brown, P. C. Hodgson and J. M. Stewart, 3 vols. Berkeley: University of California Press, 1984–7.

—— *Phenomenology of Spirit* [1807], trans. A. V. Miller, with analysis of the text and foreword by J. N. Findlay. Oxford: Clarendon, 1977.

—— *Science of Logic* [1812, 1816], trans. A. V. Miller, foreword J. N. Findlay. Atlantic Highlands, NJ: Humanities Press, 1969.

Heidegger, Martin, *Being and Time* [1927], trans. John Macquarrie and Edward Robinson. London: Blackwell, 1962.

—— *An Introduction to Metaphysics* [1935], trans. Ralph Manheim. New Haven and London: Yale University Press, 1959.

—— 'Letter on Humanism' [1947], in *Basic Writings*, ed. David Farrell Krell. New York: Harper Row, 1977.

—— 'What is Metaphysics?' [1929], in *Basic Writings*, ed. David Farrell Krell. New York: Harper & Row, 1977.

Heilbut, Anthony, *Thomas Mann: Eros and Literature*. New York: Alfred A. Knopf, 1996.

Heraclitus, *Heraclitus: The Cosmic Fragments*, ed., intro. and commentary by G. S. Kirk. Cambridge: Cambridge University Press, 1954.

Herbert, George, *The English Poems*, ed. C. A. Patrides. London: Dent, 1974.

Hirsch, David A. Hedrich, 'Donne's Atomies and Anatomies: Deconstructed Bodies and the Resurrection of Atomic Theory', *Studies in English Literature*, vol. 31 (1991), pp. 69–74.

Hirsch, William, *Genius and Degeneration: A Psychological Study*, trans. from 2nd German edn. London: Heinemann, 1887.

Hirschman, A. O., *The Rhetoric of Reaction: Perversity, Futility, Jeopardy*. Cambridge, Mass.: Harvard University Press, 1991.

Hocquenghem, Guy, *Homosexual Desire* [1972], trans. Daniella Dangoor, preface Jeffrey Weeks. London: Allison & Busby, 1978.

Holck, F. R. (ed.), *Death and Eastern Thought: Understanding Death in Eastern Religions and Philosophies*. Nashville and New York: Abingdon Press, 1974.

Hölderlin, Friedrich, *Poems and Fragments*, trans. Michael Hamburger. London: Routledge & Kegan Paul, 1966.

Holleran, Andrew, *Dancer from the Dance*. London: Jonathan Cape, 1979.

Hollier, Denis, *Against Architecture: The Writings of Georges Bataille*, trans. Betsy Wing. Cambridge, Mass.: MIT Press, 1989.

Holmes, Richard, *Shelley: The Pursuit*. London: Weidenfeld & Nicolson, 1974.

Homer, *The Iliad*, trans. E. V. Rieu. Harmondsworth: Penguin, 1966.

—— *The Odyssey*, trans. Robert Fitzgerald. London: Panther, 1965.

—— *The Odyssey of Homer*, trans. T. E. Shaw. London: Oxford University Press, 1935.

Hook, Sidney, *From Hegel to Marx: Studies in the Intellectual Development of Karl Marx* [1936]. Ann Arbor: University of Michigan Press, 1962.

Houlgate, Stephen, *Freedom, Truth and History: An Introduction to Hegel's Philosophy*. London: Routledge, 1991.

Huizinga, J., *The Waning of the Middle Ages* [1924], trans. F. Hopman. Harmondsworth: Penguin, 1965.

Hume, David, *A Treatise of Human Nature* [1739–40], ed. and intro. Ernest C. Mossner. London: Penguin, 1969.

Hurley, Kelly, *The Gothic Body: Sexuality, Materialism, and Degeneration at the* Fin de Siècle. Cambridge: Cambridge University Press, 1996.

Inwood, M. J., 'Hegel on Death', *International Journal of Moral and Social Studies*, vol. 1 (1986), summer, pp. 109–22.

Jay, Peter (ed.), *The Greek Anthology and Other Ancient Epigrams*. Harmondsworth: Penguin, 1981.

Jonas, Hans, *The Gnostic Religion: The Message of the Alien God and the Beginnings of Christianity* [1958], 2nd edn [1963]. London: Routledge, 1992.

Jones, Ernest, *Sigmund Freud: Life and Work*, 3 vols. London: Hogarth, 1953–7.

Jusdanis, Gregory, *The Poetics of Cavafy: Textuality, Eroticism, History*. Princeton: Princeton University Press, 1987.

Kahn, Charles H., *The Art and Thought of Heraclitus: An Edition of the Fragments with Translation and Commentary*. Cambridge: Cambridge University Press, 1979.

Keats, John, *Letters of John Keats*, ed. Robert Gittings. Oxford: Oxford University Press, 1970.

—— *Selected Poems*, ed. N. Roe. London: Dent, 1995.

Keeley, Edmund, *Cavafy's Alexandria: Study of a Myth in Progress*. London: Hogarth, 1977.

Killilea, Alfred G., *The Politics of Being Mortal*. Lexington: University Press of Kentucky, 1988.

Kohut, Heinz, 'Death in Venice: A Story About the Disintegration of Artistic Sublimation', in H. M. Ruitenbeek (ed.), *Psychoanalysis and Literature*. New York: Dutton, 1964.

Kojève, Alexandre, 'The Idea of Death in the Philosophy of Hegel', trans. Joseph J. Carpino, *Interpretation*, vol. 3 (1973), pp. 114–56; originally published as Appendix II in Kojève's *Introduction à la lecture de Hegel* (Paris: Gallimard, 5th edn, 1947, pp. 527–73).

—— *Introduction to the Reading of Hegel*, assembled by Raymond Queneau, ed. Allan Bloom, trans. James H. Nichols Jr. Ithaca and London: Cornell University Press, 1980.

Kopelson, Kevin, *Love's Litany: The Writing of Modern Homoerotics*. Stanford: Stanford University Press, 1994.

Kristeva, Julia, *Tales of Love*, trans. Leon S. Roudiez. New York: Columbia University Press, 1987.

Kurtz, Benjamin J., *The Pursuit of Death: A Study of Shelley's Poetry* [1933]. New York: Octagon, 1970.

Lacan, Jacques, *Écrits: A Selection*, trans. Alan Sheridan. London: Tavistock, 1977.

—— *The Ethics of Psychoanalysis 1959–1960: The Seminar of Jacques Lacan*, Book VII, ed. Jacques-Alain Miller, trans. Dennis Porter. London: Routledge, 1992.

—— *Feminine Sexuality: Jacques Lacan and the École Freudienne*, ed. J. Rose and J. Mitchell. London: Macmillan, 1982.

—— *The Four Fundamental Concepts of Psycho-Analysis*, ed. Jacques-Alain Miller, trans. Alan Sheridan. London: Hogarth, 1977.

—— *The Seminar of Jacques Lacan*: Book I: *Freud's Papers on Technique 1953–54*, ed. Jacques-Alain Miller, trans. and notes John Forrester; Book II: *The Ego in Freud's Theory of Psychoanalysis 1954–1955*, ed. Jacques-Alain Miller, trans. Sylvana Tomaselli, with notes by John Forrester. Cambridge: Cambridge University Press, 1988.

Land, Nick, *The Thirst for Annihilation*. London: Routledge, 1992.

Lankester, Edwin Ray, *Degeneration. A Chapter in Darwinism*. London: Macmillan, 1880.

Laplanche, Jean, *Life and Death in Psychoanalysis*, trans. and intro. Jeffrey Mehlman. Baltimore and London: Johns Hopkins University Press, 1976.

Laplanche, J., and Pontalis, J.-B., *The Language of Psychoanalysis*, trans. D. Nicholson-Smith. London: Hogarth, 1983.

Lavrin, Janko, *Nietzsche: A Biographical Introduction*. London: Studio Vista, 1971.

Lawrence, D. H., *Aaron's Rod* [1922]. Harmondsworth: Penguin, 1950.

—— *Apocalypse* [1931]. Harmondsworth: Penguin, 1974.

—— *Collected Letters*, ed. and intro. Harry T. Moore, 2 vols. London: Heinemann, 1962.

—— *The Crown*, in *Reflections on the Death of a Porcupine and Other Essays*.

—— *Kangaroo* [1923]. Harmondsworth: Penguin, 1950.

—— *Lady Chatterley's Lover* [1928]. Harmondsworth: Penguin, 1960.

—— *The Letters of D. H. Lawrence*, vol. 2, ed. G. J. Zytaruk and J. T. Boulton. Cambridge: Cambridge University Press, 1981.

—— *Movements in European History* [1921], ed. Philip Crumpton. Cambridge: Cambridge University Press, 1989.

—— *Phoenix II: Uncollected, Unpublished and Other Prose Works*, collected and ed. with intro. and notes by Warren Roberts and Harry T. Moore. London: Heinemann, 1988.

—— 'Pornography and Obscenity', in *A Selection from Phoenix*, ed. A. A. H. Inglis. Harmondsworth: Penguin, 1971.

—— *The Rainbow* [1915]. Harmondsworth: Penguin, 1949.

—— *Reflections on the Death of a Porcupine and Other Essays*, ed. Michael Herbert. Cambridge: Cambridge University Press, 1988.

—— *Women in Love* [1921]. Harmondsworth: Penguin, 1961.

Leavis, F. R., *Revaluation: Tradition and Development in English Poetry*. London: Chatto & Windus, 1962.

—— (ed.), *A Selection from Scrutiny*, 2 vols. Cambridge: Cambridge University Press, 1968.

Lesy, Michael, *The Forbidden Zone*. London: André Deutsch, 1988.

Levi, Peter, *The Pelican History of Greek Literature*. Harmondsworth: Penguin, 1985.

Lilla, Mark, 'A Taste for Pain', a review of James Miller, *The Passion of Michel Foucault*, and Didier Eribon, *Michel Foucault*, in *Times Literary Supplement*, 26 March 1993.

Lingis, Alphonso, *Deathbound Subjectivity*. Bloomington and Indianapolis: Indiana University Press, 1989.

Llewellyn, Nigel, *The Art of Death: Visual Culture in the English Death Ritual, c. 1500 – c. 1800*. London: Reaktion, 1991.

Long, A. A., and Sedley, D. N. (eds.), *The Hellenistic Philosophers*: Vol. 1: *Translations of the Principal Sources with Philosophical Commentary*. Cambridge: Cambridge University Press, 1987.

Lucas, F. L., *Seneca and Elizabethan Tragedy*. Cambridge: Cambridge University Press, 1922.

Lucretius, *On the Nature of the Universe*, trans. and intro. R. E. Latham. Harmondsworth: Penguin, 1951.

MacDonald, M., and Murphy, T. R., *Sleepless Souls: Suicide in Early Modern England*. Oxford: Clarendon, 1990.

Macey, David, *The Lives of Michel Foucault*. London: Hutchinson, 1993.

MacKillop, Ian, *F. R. Leavis: A Life in Criticism*. London: Allen Lane, 1995.

Magee, Bryan, *The Philosophy of Schopenhauer*. Oxford: Clarendon, 1983.

Mahood, M. M., *Shakespeare's Wordplay*. London: Methuen, 1957.

Mann, Thomas, *Death in Venice* [1912], trans. H. T. Lowe-Porter. Harmondsworth: Penguin, 1971.

—— *Death in Venice* [1912], in *Selected Stories*, trans. and intro. David Luke. London: Penguin, 1988.

—— *Diaries 1918–1939*, trans. Richard and Clara Winston, London: André Deutsch, 1983.

—— *Dr Faustus: The Life of the German Composer Adrian Leverkühn as told by a Friend* [1947], trans. H. T. Lowe-Porter. Harmondsworth: Penguin, 1968.

—— *Essays of Three Decades*, trans. H. T. Lowe-Porter. New York: Alfred A. Knopf, 1976.

—— *Last Essays*, trans. Richard and Clara Winston and Tania and James Stern. London: Secker & Warburg, 1959.

—— *Letters 1889–1955*, selected and trans. Richard and Clara Winston, 2 vols. New York: Alfred A. Knopf, 1970.

—— *Reflections of a Nonpolitical Man* [1918], trans. and intro. Walter D. Morris. New York: Frederick Ungar, 1983.

Marcus Aurelius, *Meditations*, trans. Jeremy Collier, rev. and intro. by Alice Zimmern. London: Walter Scott, 1893(?).

—— *Meditations*, trans. C. R. Haines. London: William Heinemann, 1961.

Marcuse, Herbert, *Eros and Civilization: A Philosophical Inquiry into Freud* [1955], with new preface by author. Boston: Beacon Press, 1966.

—— 'The Ideology of Death', in H. Feifel (ed.), *The Meaning of Death*. New York: McGraw-Hill, 1959, pp. 64–76.

—— *One-Dimensional Man*. Boston: Beacon Press, 1964.

Marinetti, Filippo, *Marinetti: Selected Writings*, ed. and intro. R. W. Flint, trans. R. W. Flint and A. A. Coppotelli. London: Secker & Warburg, 1972.

Marks, Elaine, *Simone de Beauvoir: Encounters with Death*. New Brunswick: Rutgers University Press, 1973.

Marlowe, Christopher, *Dr Faustus*, ed. John Jump. London: Methuen 1962.

—— *Dr Faustus and Other Plays*, ed. David Bevington and Eric Rasmussen. Oxford: Oxford University Press, 1995.

Marston, John, *What You Will*, ed. M. R. Woodhead (Nottingham Drama Texts). Nottingham: Nottingham University Press, 1980.

Marvell, Andrew, *Complete Poems*, ed. Elizabeth Story Donno. Harmondsworth: Penguin, 1985.

Marx, Karl, and Engels, Frederick. *Selected Works*. London: Lawrence & Wishart, 1968.

Meyers, Jeffrey, *Homosexuality and Literature 1890–1930*. London: Athlone, 1977.

Miller, Christopher L., *Blank Darkness: Africanist Discourse in French*. Chicago: University of Chicago Press, 1985.

Miller, James, *The Passion of Michel Foucault*. New York: Simon & Schuster, 1993.

Milton, John, *Paradise Lost*, ed. Alastair Fowler. London: Longman, 1976.

Moi, Toril, *Simone de Beauvoir: The Making of an Intellectual Woman*. Oxford: Blackwell, 1994.

Monk, Ray, *Bertrand Russell: The Spirit of Solitude 1872–1921*. London: Jonathan Cape, 1996.

Montaigne, Michel, *Complete Essays*, trans. Donald M. Frame. Stanford: Stanford University Press, 1965.

—— *Essayes*, trans. John Florio [1603], intro. Sir John Lubbock. London: George Routledge & Sons, 1891.

Moore, Oscar, *A Matter of Life and Sex*. London: Penguin, 1992. First published in 1991 under the pseudonym Alec F. Moran by Paper Drum, London.

—— *PWA: Looking AIDS in the Face*. London: Picador, 1996.

—— 'Rites of Fatality', in *Weekend Guardian*, 21 September 1966, pp. 16–21; reprinted as 'Fatality Rites' in Sarah Dunant and Roy Porter (eds.), *The Age of Anxiety*. London: Virago, 1996, pp. 63–84.

More, Thomas, 'The Four Last Things', in *The English Works of Sir Thomas More*, vol. 1, ed. W. E. Campbell. London: Eyre & Spottiswoode, 1931, pp. 459–99.

Mosse, George L., *Nationalism and Sexuality: Respectable and Abnormal Sexuality in Modern Europe*. New York: Howard Fertig, 1985.

Motto, Anna Lydia, *Seneca*. New York: Twayne, 1973.

Mulhern, Francis, *The Moment of Scrutiny*. London: Verso, 1979.

Nalbantian, Suzanne, *Seeds of Decadence in the Late Nineteenth Century Novel: A Crisis in Values*. London: Macmillan, 1983.

Nehamas, Alexander, 'Memory, Pleasure and Poetry: The Grammar of the Self in the Writing of Cavafy', *Journal of Modern Greek Studies*, vol. 2 (1984), pp. 295–319.

Nehls, Edward (ed.), *D. H. Lawrence: A Composite Biography*, 3 vols. Madison: University of Wisconsin Press, 1957.

Nicholls, Peter, *Modernisms: A Literary Guide*. London: Macmillan, 1975.

Nietzsche, Friedrich, *The Birth of Tragedy* [1872] and *The Genealogy of Morals* [1887], trans. Francis Golffing. New York: Doubleday, 1956.

—— *Ecce Homo: How One Becomes What One Is* [1888], trans. and intro. R. J. Hollingdale. Harmondsworth: Penguin, 1979.

—— *Human, All too Human: A Book for Free Spirits* [1878], trans. R. J. Hollingdale, intro. Erich Heller. Cambridge: Cambridge University Press, 1986.

—— *Nietzsche Contra Wagner*, in *The Portable Nietzsche*, ed. and trans. Walter Kaufmann. Harmondsworth: Penguin, 1976.

—— *Selected Letters*, trans. A. N. Ludovici, ed. O. Levy. London: Soho Book Co., 1985.

—— *Selected Letters of Friedrich Nietzsche*, ed. and trans. Christopher Middleton. Chicago and London: University of Chicago Press, 1969.

—— *Thus Spoke Zarathustra: A Book for All and None* [1883–5], trans. Thomas Common; vol. 11 of *The Complete Works of Friedrich Nietzsche*, ed. Oscar Levy. London: Allen & Unwin, 1909–11.

—— *Thus Spoke Zarathustra: A Book for All and None* [1883–5], trans. R. J. Hollingdale. Harmondsworth: Penguin, 1969.

—— *Twilight of the Idols* [1889] and *The Anti-Christ* [1895], trans. and intro. R. J. Hollingdale. Harmondsworth: Penguin, 1968.

—— *On the Uses and Disadvantages of History for Life* [1874], in *Untimely Meditations*, trans. R. J. Hollingdale, intro. J. P. Stern. Cambridge: Cambridge University Press, 1983.

—— *The Will to Power*, trans. Walter Kaufmann and R. J. Hollingdale, ed. and commentary Walter Kaufmann. New York: Vintage Books, 1968.

Nordau, Max, *Degeneration* [1892], trans. from 2nd edn. New York: Appleton and Co., 1895; reprinted 1993, Lincoln, Nebr., and London: University of Nebraska Press, with intro. by George L. Mosse and index from 1900 reprint.

Norris, Christopher, *What's Wrong with Postmodernism: Critical Theory and the Ends of Philosophy*. Hemel Hempstead: Harvester Wheatsheaf, 1990.

Norse, Harold, 'Breathing the Strong Smell', in Stephen Coote (ed.), *The Penguin Book of Homosexual Verse*. Harmondsworth: Penguin, 1983.

Nunokawa, Jeff, 'All the Sad Young Men: AIDS and the Work of Mourning', in Fuss (ed.), *Inside/Out*.

Nussbaum, Martha C., *The Therapy of Desire: Theory and Practice in Hellenistic Ethics*. Princeton: Princeton University Press, 1994.

Osborne, Lawrence, *The Poisoned Embrace: A Brief History of Sexual Pessimism*. London: Bloomsbury, 1993.

Pagels, Elaine, *Adam, Eve and the Serpent*. London: Weidenfeld & Nicolson, 1988.

Paglia, Camille, *Sexual Personae: Art and Decadence from Nefertiti to Emily Dickinson*. Harmondsworth: Penguin, 1992.

Pascal, Blaise, *Pensées and other Writing*, trans. H. Levi, intro. and notes A. Levi. Oxford: Oxford University Press, 1995.

Pater, Walter, *The Renaissance* [1873]. London: Macmillan, 1910.

Pick, Daniel, *Faces of Degeneration: A European Disorder, c. 1848 – c. 1918*. Cambridge: Cambridge University Press, 1989.

Pinchin, Jane Lagoudis, *Alexandria Still: Forster, Durrell, and Cavafy*. Princeton: Princeton University Press, 1977.

Plant, Richard, *The Pink Triangle: The Nazi War Against Homosexuals*. Edinburgh: Mainstream Publishing, 1987.

Plato, *Apology*, in *The Last Days of Socrates*, trans. and intro. Hugh Tredennick. Harmondsworth: Penguin, 1969.

—— *Cratylus*, trans. Benjamin Jowett, in *The Collected Dialogues of Plato*, ed. and intro. Edith Hamilton and Huntington Cairns, Princeton: Princeton University Press, 1961.

—— *Phaedo*, in *The Last Days of Socrates*, trans. and intro. Hugh Tredennick. Harmondsworth: Penguin, 1969.

—— *The Symposium*, trans. W. Hamilton. Harmondsworth: Penguin, 1951.

Popper, Karl, *The Open Society and its Enemies*: Vol. 1: *The Spell of Plato* [1945]. London: Routledge, 1995.

Powell, Enoch, *Joseph Chamberlain*. London: Thames and Hudson, 1977.

Preston, John (ed.), *Flesh and the Word: An Anthology of Erotic Writing*. New York: Penguin, 1992.

Pritchard, James B., *Ancient Near East Texts Relating to the Old Testament*, 3rd edn with supplement. Princeton: Princeton University Press, 1969.

Ra'anan, Gavriel D., *International Policy Formation in the USSR: Factional*

'Debates' during the Zhdanovschina, with a foreword by Robert Conquest. Hamden, Conn.: Archon Books, 1983.

Ralegh, Sir Walter, The History of the World [1614], ed. C. A. Patrides. London: Macmillan, 1971.

—— Poems, ed. Agnes M. C. Latham. London: Constable, 1929.

—— Works [1829], 8 vols. New York: Burt Franklin: Research and Source Works no. 73, 1964.

Ranke-Heinemann, Uta, Eunuchs for Heaven: The Catholic Church and Sexuality, trans. John Brownjohn. London: André Deutsch, 1990.

Rechy, John, The Sexual Outlaw: A Documentary [1977]. London: W. H. Allen, 1978.

Reed, T. J., Thomas Mann: The Uses of Tradition. Oxford: Clarendon, 1974.

Richards, I. A., Poetries and Sciences, a reissue of Science and Poetry [1926, 1935], with commentary. New York: Norton, 1970.

Richards, J., Sex, Dissidence and Damnation. London: Routledge, 1990.

Rilke, Rainer Maria, The Notebooks of Malte Laurids Brigge, trans. Stephen Mitchell. New York: Vintage Books, 1985.

Rist, J. M., Stoic Philosophy. Cambridge: Cambridge University Press, 1969.

Rougemont, Denis de, 'Love', in Philip P. Wiener (ed.), Dictionary of the History of Ideas: Studies of Selected Pivotal Ideas, vol. 3. New York: Charles Scribner and Sons, 1973, pp. 94–108.

—— Love in the Western World [1940], trans. Montgomery Belgion, rev. and augmented edition [1956]. New York: Fawcett, 1966.

Rumaker, Michael, A Day and a Night at the Baths [1977]. San Francisco: Grey Fox Press, 1979.

Safranski, R., Schopenhauer and the Wild Years of Philosophy, trans. Ewald Osers. London: Weidenfeld & Nicolson, 1989.

Said, Edward, Culture and Imperialism. London: Chatto & Windus, 1993.

Sandbach, F. H., The Stoics. London: Chatto & Windus, 1975.

Sartre, Jean-Paul. Being and Nothingness [1943], trans. H. Barnes, intro. Mary Warnock. London: Routledge, 1989.

—— What is Literature? [1948], trans. B. Frechtman, intro. David Caute. London: Routledge, 1993.

Schiesari, Juliana, The Gendering of Melancholia: Feminism, Psychoanalysis, and the Symbolics of Loss in Renaissance Literature. Ithaca: Cornell University Press, 1992.

Schleifer, Ronald, Rhetoric and Death: The Language of Modernism and Postmodern Discourse Theory. Urbana and Chicago: University of Illinois Press, 1990.

Scholder, A., and Silverberg, I., High Risk 2: Writings on Sex, Death and Subversion. London: Serpent's Tail, 1994.

Schoolman, Morton, The Imaginary Witness: The Critical Theory of Herbert Marcuse. New York and London: Free Press, 1980.

Schopenhauer, Arthur, *Essays and Aphorisms*, selected, trans. and intro. R. J. Hollingdale. Harmondsworth: Penguin, 1970.

—— *The World as Will and Representation* [1819/1844], trans. E. F. J. Payne, 2 vols. New York: Dover, 1966.

Scott, R. B. Y., *The Anchor Bible: Proverbs/Ecclesiastes*, intro., trans. and notes by R. B. Y. Scott. New York: Doubleday, 1965.

Seneca, Lucius Annaeus, *Epistulae Morales*, trans. Richard M. Gummere, 3 vols. London: Heinemann, 1917.

—— *The Morals of Seneca: A Selection of his Prose*, ed. Walter Clode, trans. Sir Roger L'Estrange and Thomas Lodge. London: Walter Scott, 1888.

—— 'On the Shortness of Life' and 'On Tranquility', in *The Stoic Philosophy of Seneca: Essays and Letters*, trans. and intro. Moses Hadas. New York: Doubleday, 1958.

Shakespeare, William, *The Complete Works* (Compact Edition), ed. Stanley Wells and Gary Taylor. Oxford: Clarendon, 1988.

—— *King Henry IV Part II*, ed. A. R. Humphreys. London: Methuen, 1966.

—— *Shakespeare's Sonnets*, ed. and analytic commentary by Stephen Booth. New Haven and London: Yale University Press, 1977.

—— *The Sonnets and A Lover's Complaint*, ed. and intro. John Kerrigan. Harmondsworth: Penguin, 1986.

Shelley, Percy Bysshe, 'On Love' [1818], in Duncan Wu (ed.), *Romanticism: An Anthology*. Oxford: Blackwell, 1994, pp. 860–61.

—— *Shelley*, selected by Kathleen Raine. Harmondsworth: Penguin, 1974.

Sinfield, Alan, *Literature, Politics and Culture in Post-War Britain*. Oxford: Blackwell, 1989.

Singer, Irving, *The Nature of Love*: Vol. 1: *Plato to Luther*, 1984; Vol. 2: *Courtly and Romantic*, 1984; Vol. 3: *The Modern World*, 1987. Chicago and London: University of Chicago Press.

Skelton, Robin, *Two Hundred Poems from the Greek Anthology*, selected and trans. Robin Skelton. London: Methuen, 1973.

Smart, Ninian, 'Attitudes Towards Death in Eastern Religions', in Toynbee et al., *Man's Concern with Death*.

Solomon, Robert C., *In the Spirit of Hegel: A Study of G. W. F. Hegel's* Phenomenology of Spirit. New York and Oxford: Oxford University Press, 1983.

Soper, Kate, *Humanism and Anti-Humanism*. London: Hutchinson, 1986.

Sourvinou-Inwood, Christiane, *'Reading' Greek Death to the End of the Classical Period*. Oxford: Clarendon, 1996.

Spenser, Edmund, *The Faerie Queene*, ed. Thomas P. Roche Jr. Harmondsworth: Penguin, 1978.

Staten, H., *Eros in Mourning: Homer to Lacan*. Baltimore and London: Johns Hopkins University Press, 1995.

Steiner, George, *Heidegger*, 2nd edn. London: Fontana, 1992.

Sulloway, Frank J., *Freud, Biologist of the Mind*. London: André Deutsch, 1979.

Tacitus, Publius Cornelius, *Historical Works*, trans. Arthur Murphy, 2 vols. London: Dent, 1907.

Tanner, Tony, *Venice Desired*. Oxford: Blackwell, 1992.

Thomas, Edward, *Collected Poems*, with foreword by Walter de la Mare. London: Faber, 1969.

Tourneur, Cyril (attrib.), *The Revenger's Tragedy*, ed. R. A. Foakes. London: Methuen, 1966.

Toynbee, Arnold, et al., *Man's Concern with Death*. London: Hodder & Stoughton, 1968.

—— 'Traditional Attitudes Towards Death', in Toynbee et al., *Man's Concern with Death*.

Trypanis, Constantine A. (ed. and trans.), *The Penguin Book of Greek Verse*. Harmondsworth: Penguin Books, 1971.

Tyler, Carole-Anne, 'Boys Will be Girls: The Politics of Gay Drag', in Fuss (ed.), *Inside/Out*.

Vermeule, Emily, *Aspects of Death in Early Greek Art and Poetry*. Berkeley: University of California Press, 1979.

Vernant, Jean-Pierre, *Mortals and Immortals: Collected Essays*, ed. Froma I. Zeitlin. Princeton: Princeton University Press, 1991.

Wagner, Wilhelm Richard, *Prelude and Transfiguration from Tristan and Isolde*, ed. Robert Bailey. New York and London: Norton, 1985.

—— *Wagner on Music and Drama: A Compendium of Richard Wagner's Prose Works*, ed. Albert Goldman and Evert Sprinchorn, trans. H. Ashton Ellis. New York: Dutton, 1964.

Wallace, Jennifer, 'Shelley, Plato and the Political Imagination', in Anna Baldwin and Sarah Hutton (eds.), *Platonism and the English Imagination*. Cambridge: Cambridge University Press, 1994.

Walton, Izaak, *Lives*, intro. George Saintsbury. London: Oxford University Press, 1927.

Watts, Cedric, 'A Bloody Racist: About Achebe's View of Conrad', *Yearbook of English Studies*, vol. 13 (1983), pp. 196–209.

—— *Conrad's* Heart of Darkness: *A Critical and Contextual Discussion*. Milan: Mursia, 1977.

—— *The Deceptive Text: An Introduction to Covert Plots*. Brighton: Harvester, 1984.

Weeks, Jeffrey, *Coming Out*. London: Quartet, 1977.

Weisner, Merry E., *Women and Gender in Early Modern Europe*. Cambridge: Cambridge University Press, 1993.

Welbon, Guy Richard, *The Buddhist Nirvana and its Western Interpreters*. Chicago and London: University of Chicago Press, 1968.

Wells, H. G., *Early Writings in Science and Science Fiction*, ed., critical commentary and notes by R. M. Philmus and D. Y. Hughes. Berkeley: University of California Press, 1975.

West, M. L. (ed. and trans.), *Greek Lyric Poetry*. Oxford: Oxford University Press, 1993.

Whaley, Joachim, *Mirrors of Mortality: Studies in the Social History of Death*. London: Europa, 1981.

Wilde, Oscar, *The Picture of Dorian Gray* [1890/91]. Harmondsworth: Penguin, 1949.

Williams, J. (ed.), *English Renaissance Poetry: A Collection of Shorter Poems*. New York: Anchor Books, 1963.

Williamson, George, 'Mutability, Decay and Seventeeth-Century Melancholy', *English Literary History*, vol. 2 (1935), pp. 121–50.

Wilson, Scott, *Cultural Materialism: Theory and Practice*. London: Blackwell, 1995.

Winkler, John J., *The Constraints of Desire: The Anthropology of Sex and Gender in Ancient Greece*. New York and London: Routledge, 1990.

Winston, Richard, *Thomas Mann: The Making of an Artist 1875–1911*, with afterword by Clara Winston. New York: Alfred A. Knopf, 1981.

Wojnarowicz, David, *Close to the Knives: A Memoir of Disintegration*. London: Serpent's Tail, 1991.

—— *Memories that Smell Like Gasoline*. San Francisco: Artspace Books, 1992.

Woodward, Kathleen, *Aging and its Discontents: Freud and Other Fictions*. Bloomington: Indiana University Press, 1991.

Woolf, Virginia, *To the Lighthouse* [1927], ed. Stella McNichol, intro. and notes by Hermione Lee. London: Penguin, 1992.

Wyatt, Sir Thomas, *Poetical Works*. London: Bell & Daldy, 1866.

Yeats, W. B., *Collected Poems*. London: Macmillan, 1971.

Young, Robert, *Colonial Desire: Hybridity in Theory, Culture and Race*. London and New York: Routledge, 1995.

Zhdanov, A. A., *On Literature, Music and Philosophy* [1934–48], trans. E. Fox, S. Jackson and H. C. Feldt. London: Lawrence & Wishart, 1950.

Zuckerman, Elliott, *The First Hundred Years of Wagner's Tristan*. New York and London: Columbia University Press, 1964.

Index